"Washington at Valley Forge" by N.C. Wyeth. (The Hill School Collection, Pottstown, PA, photographed by C.C.F. Gachet.)

Valley Forge

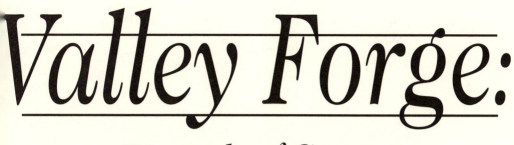

Valley Forge:

Pinnacle of Courage

by
John W. Jackson

THOMAS PUBLICATIONS
Gettysburg PA 17325

Front cover illustration: "March to Valley Forge" by William B.T. Trego, 1883, courtesy of the Valley Forge Historical Society.

Cover design by Ryan C. Stouch.

To

Dr. John D.R. Platt

For his friendship and guidance over the years

and

Mrs. Joan Marshall Dutcher

For her encouragement in writing the story of

Valley Forge

Preface

VALLEY FORGE HAS been aptly described as the symbol of endured hardship and fortitude by the Continental soldier. The tatterdemalion force that straggled into Valley Forge on December 19, 1777, represented the hopes and strength of the new nation. It was an undisciplined hungry rabble with most of the men lacking various articles of clothing or shoes. Blankets were an unheard of luxury, with those fortunate to possess one sharing it with their comrades.

In July 1775, when Washington assumed command of the militia surrounding Boston, his sense of orderliness was appalled by the chaotic conditions in camp. He candidly acknowledged that his lack of experience and ability made him illsuited to mold the rabble into a disciplined army. Late one night while alone in the quiet of his headquarters, Washington reflected on the uncertainties of his situation asking what do the American people expect of me. In his dilemma he pondered what can I do "without men, without arms, without ammunition, without anything for the accommodation of a soldier?"

Washington became defiant as Congress, through indifference and inexperience, ignored repeated requests for food, clothing, shoes and other necessities for the soldiers, a condition that regrettably persisted throughout the war. His problems worsened as Congress adamantly refused to recruit a regular army to serve for three years or the duration of the Revolution. It became implicit that Congress's shortsighted policy endangered the Continental cause, compelling Washington to recruit a new army each year while confronting a powerful enemy. Later Congress recognized the futility of its position and authorized three year enlistments.

At Valley Forge Washington subtly but firmly pointed the finger of responsibility at Congress for the hardships existing at the encampment. He warned that the troops were mutinous and had only been held in

Washington in meditation pondering "what do the American people expect of me and and the ragged Continentals." From a nineteenth-century drawing by C.S. Reinhart. (Dover Publications, Inc.)

restraint by the courage of loyal officers. With rising indignation he charged that armchair generals, who were comfortably ensconced before a warm fire, had been negligent in their duty to the hungry and cold soldiers.

Washington's concern for their welfare had not gone unnoticed by the soldiers. They exhibited their loyalty and dedication to him as they became aware of his futile attempts to better their lot. Conversely, their resentment and anger would be directed at Congress, who was blamed for their plight.

Washington stubbornly refused to accept the setback at Germantown on October 4, 1777, as a defeat. He declared it was a much needed training experience that all young soldiers needed. Previously, he had "marveled" at the "fortitude" of "his soldiers." His confidence and respect for the bravery of his undisciplined Continentals were manifest when he wrote they were the equal of any similar body of British or Hessian troops.

After the selection of Valley Forge, Washington first considered the comforts of the troops. When the erection of huts and fortifications were underway, he turned his attention to building a well-drilled army. The awkward militia had fought valiantly but their lack of discipline was obvious on the battlefield. Unfortunately, the Continental Army did not have an officer qualified to fill the post of Inspector General to drill and train the troops. Congress and Washington agreed to search among the foreign officers in the army to locate one to fulfill the post. A move by Congress naming General Thomas Conway proved to be abortive. Fortuitously for the Continental Army, in February, 1778, "Baron" von Steuben arrived at Valley Forge. Washington quickly discerned the Prussian's qualifications and asked him to serve as volunteer Inspector General until Congress would officially appoint him.

As the narrative unfolds it will disclose the growth of Washington's leadership and the effectiveness of Steuben's disciplinary exercise. From the proving ground of Valley Forge, a Continental Army would emerge that was instilled with pride and confidence.

Wherever possible I have permitted the participants involved in the narrative at the Valley Forge encampment to tell their own story, in their own way. No effort has been made to modernize the orthography or punctuation except where necessary to clarify the meaning of a letter or document. Eighteenth-century writers tended to write involved, and often detailed, flowery sentences; however, to cut up or change their sentiments would lose the life and color of their thoughts.

Many individuals have contributed time and materials to the preparation of this study.

I can never adequately express my appreciation to my friend and colleague Dr. John D.R. Platt for his critical and meticulous reading of the entire manuscript. His indispensable comments helped to clarify the final draft.

Warren D. Beach, Superintendent of Valley Forge National Historical Park, graciously granted me permission to use the facilities of the Park's Library and Archives.

I am especially grateful to another friend and Park Historian, Joan Marshall-Dutcher, who read the manuscript and offered many suggestions that contributed to its improvement. She also gave unstintingly of her time to place at my disposal numerous copies of letters, diaries, orderly books and journals to ease my excursions through the labyrinth of research.

Phyllis Ewing, Museum Technician, offered invaluable assistance and information. Her untiring efforts in the selection of illustrations and maps are greatly appreciated.

Others at the Park to whom I am indebted for support and encouragement are Robert Dodson, Frances McDevitt and Barbara Fox. Also, my thanks are extended to John Tyler (now Superintendent of Fort McHenry National Monument and Historic Shrine) and Betty Browning, formerly at Valley Forge.

Another friend and colleague, Dr. David J. Fowler, Director of the David Library of the American Revolution, graciously made their marvelous microfilm and print collections available for my inspection.

My appreciation is tendered to Linda Stanley, Chief of Manuscripts, at the Historical Society of Pennsylvania and Roy Goodman of the American Philosophical Society for their many courtesies.

To my friend and authority on the American Revolution Dr. Kemble Widmer, I am indebted for clarifying a few gray areas of army routine.

I value the wholehearted support of another friend David Dutcher, Chief Historian at Independence National Historical Park, ably assisted by Anna Coxe Toogood, Shirley Mays and Theresa Hyatt. They generously made the Park's Library and Archives available for my examination.

Early in my research on the British Army in Philadelphia, I gathered materials on Valley Forge. For this assistance I am indebted to Dr. Isabel Kenrick who researched in England and Scotland. Also to Dr. John Dann, Director of the Clements Library, University of Michigan, for his permission to examine their extraordinary collection of British Headquarters Papers.

For those individuals whose names have been inadvertently omitted, please accept my apologies and sincere gratitude for your valued cooperation.

I wish to express my appreciation to all the sources that facilitated my research; most can be found in the bibliography and notes.

As is customary, I have reserved mention of my wife Kathryn until the end. Her encouragement, patience and dedication made completion of the book possible. The volume is due to her perseverance in typing and retyping the manuscript, plus reading and offering suggestions that added to its clarity.

John W. Jackson
Philadelphia, Pa.
1992

Contents

Maps and Illustrations

Valley Forge

Prologue

THE YEAR PRECEDING the encampment of the Continental Army at Valley Forge was characterized by intermittent periods of victory and defeat. Before Christmas 1776, hysteria had spread throughout the three states abutting the Delaware River. When Sir William Howe, commander in chief of the British Army in America, with a large force of British and Hessian troops approached the river they posed a threat to Philadelphia, the young nation's provisional capital. With his customary deliberative generalship, Howe had permitted General George Washington and a daily dwindling Continental Army to make a leisurely withdrawal through New Jersey and cross the Delaware to take posts on its western bank. The panic-stricken members of the Continental Congress in Philadelphia, hearing of Howe's presence near Trenton, hastily packed their legislative body's official papers and personal belongings and hightailed it to Baltimore. Not to be left behind, their peers in the Pennsylvania Assembly and large numbers of the citizenry were preparing to seek refuge in the interior towns of the state.

Ever circumspect, Howe surveyed the broad expanse of the river and visualized the disastrous losses that would be suffered by a direct assault on the American position on the opposite river bank. He further reflected that the lateness of the season made winter campaigning unnecessarily hazardous. Unquestionably, Howe buttressed his indecisiveness with the comforting thought of the conviviality of a winter in New York.

Without an undue twinge of conscience, Howe consoled himself with the belief that the ragtag and bobtail rebels would disintegrate and disperse during the cold winter months, making a conquest easy in the spring. Before retiring to New York he resolved to quarter units of Hessian troops at Trenton and other key towns along the Delaware River.

In succumbing to his cautiousness and the anticipation of a pleasurable winter, Howe underestimated the resourcefulness of his adversary.

VALLEY FORGE

Washington was fully cognizant that the American cause had reached a critical phase, and that he was faced with a grievous shortage of clothing, provisions, and accoutrements, articles needed to hold the army together. With the enlistments of several regiments expiring at the end of the year, the fate of the country rested in his hands. With time running out it was mandatory that an immediate stroke be made against the Hessian garrisons. Complying with the urgency, Washington adopted an ambitious plan to simultaneously attack the various Hessian positions. Under his command most of the Continental Army units would cross the river at McKonkey's Ferry and move south in two columns to attack Trenton. Another column composed principally of Pennsylvania militia was assembled opposite Trenton to cross and deliver a coordinated attack. Further down the Delaware, at Bristol, a fourth column of militia was to pass over the river and assault the Hessians at Burlington.

Washington was aware that many residents on both sides of the river remained loyal to the King; therefore, the deployment of the various columns must be cloaked in utmost secrecy. On Christmas night Washington and the Continentals passed over the ice-clogged river and reaching the outskirts of Trenton surprised and inflicted a devastating defeat on the festive Hessians who had been celebrating the holy season. Washington's victory was so complete his only casualties were four wounded, while the Hessian losses of killed, wounded and prisoners were over 1,000. Unfortunately, a greater victory was lost when the two militia columns found it impossible to cross the icebound river.

The triumph at Trenton was followed on January 3, 1777, with another success at Princeton; this time the opponents were British troops. These victories had an electrifying effect on the morale of the Continental Army and the American people, disproportionate to the small number of troops engaged.

Except for an occasional skirmish, both armies passed the winter in relative quiet with the Continentals at Morristown, New Jersey, and the British in New York. During the late spring of 1777, bewildering maneuvers by Howe left a perplexed Washington uncertain as to the British objective for the forthcoming campaign—would Howe sail up the Hudson River to unite with General "Johnny" Burgoyne's invasion army from Canada, or move against Philadelphia? The mystery was solved in late July when a large British fleet was observed sailing south along the New Jersey coast. Washington was not completely reassured as Howe could bypass the roadstead at the mouth of the Delaware Bay and sail south to land in Virginia or South Carolina. Confusion still persisted as the British fleet halted momentarily off the Delaware Capes, then again sailed south to the Chesapeake Bay and proceeded up that inlet, landing at Head of Elk on August 23. The fleet's progress up the Bay had been marred by a dangerous shortage of fresh water and the resultant loss of virtually every horse belonging to the army.

At Head of Elk Howe divided the army into two columns and, at his characteristically slow pace, marched across northern Maryland into Delaware. Frequent halts were made to dispatch foraging parties throughout the countryside to seize provisions, other supplies, and commandeer horses to mount the dragoons.

Shortly after entering Delaware the British Army was opposed by an American light infantry detachment commanded by General William Maxwell. A lively fire fight ensued at Cooch's Bridge. This engagement occasioned only a momentary pause before the British could resume their march up the south bank of the Brandywine Creek to Kennett Square, Pennsylvania. Meanwhile, Washington had concentrated the Continental Army near Newport, Delaware, a position that would permit him to oppose a British march toward Philadelphia, or take a parallel line of march with their advance. Advised of Howe's apparent destination, he moved up the north bank of the Brandywine and placed his troops astride Nottingham Road (Baltimore Pike, Route 1) at Chadd's Ford. In this position he would be able to defend the city as demanded by Congress.

In the interim, Howe, ever hesitant to make a direct assault conceived a plan to use two columns in an enveloping movement against the American position at the Brandywine. One column, commanded by General Wilhelm von Knyphausen was to advance east on Nottingham Road and initially act as a feint to give time for a larger column under Lieutenant General Lord Charles Cornwallis, accompanied by Howe, to move obliquely left, using back roads to outflank Washington's army and come up in their rear. At dawn on September 11, the two columns moved out of Kennett Square. Cornwallis's column succeeded in reaching its objective, making contact with a hastily deployed Continental right wing. The Americans offered a valiant defense but eventually withdrew. Knyphausen, as soon as he heard the sound of Cornwallis being engaged, attacked across the Brandywine.

Washington had suffered a severe setback due, in part, to faulty intelligence and the mistaken belief that Knyphausen's force comprised the main elements of the British Army. Washington's biographer, Douglas Southall Freeman, considered the Brandywine Washington's most confused battle, stating that he "conducted the Brandywine operation as if he had been in a daze."[1]

During the two weeks following the battle, both armies nursed their respective wounds while jockeying for a position that would give them command of the inner lines that blocked access to Philadelphia. The clamorous outbursts of Continental Congress and citizens of Philadelphia continued to din into Washington's ear with a demand to defend the city.

However, he knew it was manifestly impossible for the exhausted troops, weakened in numbers by the debacle at Brandywine, to take the offensive against a superior enemy. As he reviewed the army Washington observed, in tearful compassion, that hundreds of soldiers were shoeless, while others had only tattered excuses for uniforms to protect them against inclement weather. In addition, most units had a significant shortage of arms and ammunition. The only hope was to regroup and refurbish the troops by withdrawing to a less exposed position. Washington selected the area around Pottsgrove. He was cognizant that further outcries would accompany this decision, but it allowed the time needed to save the army though opening the region north of Philadelphia to British domination.

Before the advent of the opposing armies into the Great Valley, the peaceful calm of Valley Forge had rarely been disturbed by military presence. The village nestled in the rolling countryside that was occasionally interspersed by precipitous hills, heavily forested with Spanish, white, and black oak, and infrequent hickory and scrubby chestnut.[2]

The first recorded appearance of a military detachment occurred on December 12, 1776. Fatigued and with many sick, Major Irving led a contingent of militia to the site of the future historic encampment. After a short rest they resumed their march. Four months later William Dewees, resident manager of John Potts's forge and mill, appealed to the Pennsylvania Supreme Executive Council for a sergeant's guard to protect his property. Although somewhat isolated from military raids, Dewees, a former colonel in the States Quartermaster Department, was uneasy with Loyalists in the region. He expressed grave concern over who would be responsible for providing provisions, arms, and ammunition for the guard. As he was apparently dubious about the conduct of Continental troops, Dewees requested they not be sent.[3]

Early in September, 1777, Dewees again became apprehensive for the safety of his property. He protested that a never ending procession of wagons were depositing military stores at the forge. His objections were ignored until every building in the vicinity of the forge overflowed with supplies. When intelligence reached Washington of this cache,[4] he immediately directed Dewees to transfer them to a less exposed area. To coordinate his instructions he sent Lieutenant Colonel Alexander Hamilton, Captain Henry Lee, and six dragoons to destroy any items that Dewees could not remove.

Howe's baffling maneuvers had not hoodwinked Washington. It was obvious that without possession of Philadelphia the British commander would be confronted with a gloomy alternative—either a fatiguing land withdrawal across New Jersey or a dangerous attempt to board their transports in the Delaware River at Chester followed by a hazardous winter sail to New York. Washington believed Howe would attempt a crossing of the Schuylkill at a ford nearer the city, probably Swede's Ford (Norristown). However, of more and immediate importance to Washington was to safeguard the removal of the stores at Valley Forge. In the event Hamilton needed assistance, instructions were issued to Generals Anthony Wayne, William Maxwell, and Pennsylvania militia General James Potter to deploy their brigades in the vicinity of Valley Forge.[5]

Unknown to Washington, a British agent, possibly a Loyalist sympathizer, had witnessed the unusual activity at Dewees's mill. His report to Howe included a portion of the material stored at the forge buildings "3800 Barrells of Flour, Soap and Candles, 25 Barrells of Horse Shoes, several thousand tomahawks and kettles, and Intrenching Tools and 20 Hogsheads of Resin in a Barn." Upon receipt of this information, Howe dispatched a detachment of light infantry to take possession of the reported stores. Hamilton and his small detail, unable to complete their assignment, narrowly escaped capture by fording the Schuylkill.[6]

The next day, September 19, Cornwallis's advance column passed through Valley Forge and camped at Bull's Head near French Creek. For two days British troops engaged in removing "rebel stores." On the 21st the main army under Howe reached the village and continued on to Moore Hall. For the next two days desultory fire fights were engaged in with Americans on the north bank of the river. Howe was fully cognizant that to achieve an early occupation of Philadelphia he must quickly gain a foothold on the north bank of the Schuylkill. To attain his objective it was necessary to deceive Washington. A number of feints were made at various fords. To further the deception Howe ordered a bridge: "...to be made across the Schuylkill at this place [probably near Pawling's Ford] where the River is 120 yards and got in great forwardness, intending to deceive the enemy." When only sporadic minor opposition developed at the fords, Howe realized that Washington would not offer a challenge to his crossing the river. Shortly after midnight on the 23rd the entire British Army made an unopposed passing of the shallow waters at Fatland Ford. On the north bank the army reformed and proceeded to Egypt Road and then moved to East Norriton where they established headquarters. Before departing from Valley Forge, Captain John Montresor, of the engineer corps, noted that they set fire to the forge and other buildings.[7]

At East Norriton the impact of the advantage gained by the army's movements of the prior week was self-evident to Howe. With Washington and the Continental Army north of his position at Pottstown, Howe controlled the roads leading to the "rebel capital." Although the British commander's movements were usually sluggish, he wasted no time in placing the army in motion toward Germantown. The latter village would become the temporary headquarters of the main army, while Cornwallis, with 3,000 British and Hessian troops, would take possession of Philadelphia. Cornwallis was to predispose the inhabitants to receive a winter garrison of about 18,000 soldiers, to locate adequate quarters for the army, and improve the city's land and river defenses.

A preoccupied Howe's composure was suddenly jolted by intelligence from New York State reporting the Americans had administered two serious setbacks to Burgoyne's army. Nevertheless, an overconfident Howe and an undaunted Burgoyne were equally convinced of the ultimate success of the invasion force. To relieve the pressure of the Americans opposing Burgoyne, Howe ordered Sir Henry Clinton, commandant at New York City, to make a diversionary foray up the Hudson River. With this order, Howe promptly dismissed the thought of any danger to Burgoyne and turned his attention to solidifying his position in Pennsylvania.

Meanwhile, Washington had taken post at Pennypacker's Mills along the Perkiomen Creek, where he planned an offensive patterned after that which he had employed the previous Christmas night at Trenton. On October 4, the Continental Army was to march in four columns, which hopefully with proper timing would deliver a coordinated attack on the center and flanks of the British position in the village of Germantown.[8] Unfortunately, this ambitious stratagem was to fail. A combination of bad roads, an impenetrable fog, scarcity of ammunition, and a serious tactical blunder at the Cliveden house, snatched from Washington's grasp any hope of victory.

Forced to withdraw from the battlefield, the Continental Army straggled up Skippack Road to Pennypacker's Mills. A Pennsylvania Lieutenant, James McMichael, described how the exhausted men were prostrated willy-nilly at the Mills noting that as he "...marched in twenty-four hours 45 miles, and in that time fought four hours, during which we advanced so furiously thro' buckwheat fields, that it was almost an unspeakable fatigue." However, despite the hardships and the ignominious defeat, Washington did not envision it as disastrous, claiming instead it had been a proving ground for his "young" and inexperienced soldiers. In another letter he expressed his confidence in the Continental Army noting "...they can confuse and Rout even the Flower of the British Army, with the greatest ease, and that they are not that invincible Body of Men which many suppose them to be."[9]

At Pennypacker's Mills Washington's strategy was translated into a plan to contain the British within the immediate environs of the city. A reconnaissance was conducted to locate a strong defensive position that would act as a springboard from which the Army could harass the British and, also, take advantage of any opportunity that was presented to open a full scale offensive. The site selected was the Whitemarsh hills approximately thirteen miles north of Philadelphia. With the destination chosen, Washington completed regrouping the army and ordered a forward movement by easy states, arriving on November 2 at Whitemarsh, a position the French Major General Francois-Jean Marquis de Chastellux later termed so strong Washington must have been directed there by "divine guidance."

While enroute to Whitemarsh, Washington headquartered for several days at the home of Peter Wentz, situated in the lee of Methacton Hill. At this camp he received word of Burgoyne's surrender to General Horatio Gates at Saratoga. An elated Washington immediately declared a day of rejoicing. The brigades were assembled on the parade ground where a feu de joie was delivered to honor the victory. Each chaplain was directed to offer "short discourses" to their respective brigades.

For six weeks Whitemarsh, a mixed camp of brush huts and tents would be a microcosm of what hardships the troops would experience in a few weeks at Valley Forge. As the weeks passed Washington's confidence in the fighting ability of the Continental soldier did not diminish. However, he was frequently disappointed when a consensus of his general officers contended it would be foolhardy to attack a numerically superior professional army defending virtually impregnable fortifications. These critical opinions were expertly summed up by a former French officer and first commandant of the American Corps of Engineers, General Louis Lebégue de Presle Duportail who "...declared that in such works [the British] with five thousand men he would bid defiance to any force that should be brought against him."[10]

Any possibility of taking the offensive was tabled in late November when intelligence reached Washington that unusual military activity in Philadelphia presaged Howe's taking the offensive. With this information Washington dismissed any thought of dislodging the British from the city and concentrated on the defense of his Whitemarsh position.

On October 22, Howe wrote to Sir George Germain requesting permission of the King to return to England. He was aware that his conduct of the war in America was under constant criticism by His Majesty, Germain, and others in the government. Anticipating being recalled in early 1778, Howe decided that a victory would stand him in good stead before a court of inquiry in the House of Commons.

On December 4, Howe with a force estimated at 12,000 moved up the road through Germantown and camped at Chestnut Hill. Although there were minor skirmishes, Washington refused to be lured from his impregnable stronghold. A frustrated Howe declined all suggestions to make a frontal assault, instead he decided on a circuitous maneuver that would bring him to Washington's left flank on Camp Hill. Shortly after midnight on the 7th, the British marched down Main Street (Germantown Avenue) to Abington Road (Washington Lane) where they filed to the left and passed over to York Road. At the junction of the latter road and Church Road, he dispatched General Sir Charles Grey's column over to Limekiln Road. Howe continued up York Road to Susquehanna Road in Abington. Aside from a few minor fire fights, one inconclusive engagement was fought at Edge Hill between Grey's column and an American contingent of Continentals and militia commanded by Colonel Daniel Morgan.

Foiled by his inability to entice Washington down from his stronghold, Howe gloomily reflected on the fruitless conclusion of his campaign. With winter approaching and concerned for the troop's welfare, Howe hurriedly regrouped the army for a return to Philadelphia.

The presence of the British Army had temporarily distracted Washington's attention from the distressing conditions at the encampment, and a decision relative to the site of the winter quarters. He was saddened by his inability to relieve the sufferings of the troops. Most of the brush huts had collapsed, as one soldier recalled "...any hogsty was preferable [to them]." The few remaining tents had been turned over to the regimental doctors to serve as improvised hospitals. To add to their woes the troops were in dire need of provisions; another soldier recounted that conditions were so bad they scavenged the neighborhood and found a carcass that had escaped the hogs and dogs. They cooked the entrails which caused when eaten considerable agony, from which they eased this discomfort by a "violent disgorgement." Others were without any semblance of a uniform, while hundreds had neither shoes nor blankets.

Before the end of November there was unmistakable evidence that the surrounding countryside had been virtually stripped of all provisions and forage, and could no longer support the continuance of the encampment. To Washington's amazement it was reported the Continental Congress believed that ample provisions and supplies existed in the neighborhood. The supposition that a bounteous larder was available to the army may have influenced Congress to ignore Washington's repeated urgings for aid, as only a trickle of provisions and clothing had reached camp.

Several exasperated brigade commanders, who had witnessed the futility of the Commander in Chief's entreaties, were skeptical that any relief would be forthcoming from the Continental Congress. An impatient few decided to take independent action and appealed to their state governments for aid. General Anthony Wayne was one of the brigadier generals who petitioned his State Assembly. In Wayne's case the Pennsylvania Continental Line regiments were destitute of every article of clothing. His importunings were received with studied indifference. The problem was referred to the Pennsylvania Security Council who appointed commissioners in each county to collect clothing. But little reached camp, most having been diverted to local militia units. Finally Wayne's patience was exhausted and he employed a Lancaster merchant, Peter Zantzinger to purchase clothing to cover the nakedness of his soldiers.

Zantzinger's efforts were fraught with frustrations. Although he located quantities of cloth and coats, there was no money to purchase them. Shunted between different members of Congress, he was finally advised to request the assistance of James Mease, Clothier General. Later, through a second hand report, Zantzinger was informed that Mease would pay for the cloth "on sight of Genl. Washingtons order." Apparently Washington was never advised of this proposal to clothe the Pennsylvania troops, as Wayne was still badgering state authorities throughout the winter.[11]

It was obvious that a continued use of the encampment was untenable and a withdrawal from the area would eventually be necessary. Washington began to develop plans for a sudden but orderly move. General John Sullivan was directed to hold a council of the general officers and submit their consensus on an order of march and possible temporary camp sites across the Schuylkill River. Early in December Sullivan submitted an "Order of March, Dec. 1777" to Washington. On December 10, no longer threatened by a British attack, Washington implemented Sullivan's report directing all brigades be ready to march the next morning at 4:00 A.M.

The brigades were to file right from their camp positions and take the road to Matson's Ford (Conshohocken); the baggage wagons and "Park of Artillery" were to follow the road to Swede's Ford (Norristown). Detailed precautions were taken to protect the flanks of the army on the march with large detachments of infantry and cavalry covering all road leading toward Philadelphia on both sides of the river. It was planned to establish the first night camp near the road to Lancaster.[12]

"Washington as Commander in Chief," a 19th century photograph of a painting owned by Robert E. Lee. (Thomas Publications.)

Marked with Blood

WHILE THE ARMY was camped at Whitemarsh the ever present shortage of provisions and clothing was overshadowed by the pressing need to choose winter quarters where the hungry and bedraggled troops would have an opportunity to rest and regroup in preparation for the next year's campaign. Lieutenant Colonel John Laurens, aide-de-camp to Washington, succinctly confirmed the need for a winter encampment in a letter to his father Henry Laurens, President of the Continental Congress: "Our army in particular requires exemption from fatigue in order to compensate for their want of clothing. Relaxation from duties of a campaign, in order to allow them an opportunity of being disciplined and instructed; warm quarters, that it may appear in the spring with undiminished numbers and in the full prowess of health, &ca." As expressed by Laurens, Washington and Congress had, also, recognized the need for "discipline and instruction," with the latter appointing Thomas Conway, Major General and Inspector General of the army. [1]

A concerned Washington was fully cognizant that the lateness of the season did not favor a delay in selecting a site. Further, it had to be situated where militia and Continental detachments could contain and harass British foraging parties, while providing a strong defensive position and an area where forage and provisions were plentiful.

In late November a committee of Congress was sent to Whitemarsh to hold: "...a private confidential consultation with General Washington, to consider of the best and most practical means for carrying on a winter's campaign with vigour and success, an object which Congress has much at heart." No one was more aware than Washington that the thin fabric which held the army together was the spirit of the men, and their loyalty to him. Now, even that allegiance was beginning to waver. Recent events had convinced Washington of the futility of attacking the British defenses at Philadelphia. He explained to the committee that no reliance could be placed on area militia, and with the present condition of the army the results of an attack would be disastrous. Rather the most pressing need was to find winter quarters that would: "...afford supplies of provisions, Wood, Water and Forage, be secure from a surprise and best calculated for covering the Country from the Ravages of the Enemy...."[2]

After conferring with the Commander in Chief, the committee met with the generals of the army and was advised that discontent pervaded the army, where hundreds of officers had openly avowed to resign their commissions unless their grievances were redressed. Their complaints included the demand for a half-pay pension system and a "pensionary establishment" for the widows of officers lost in the service. The committee returned to Yorktown (York) but not before agreeing to present to a full Congress the logic of Washington's opposition to a winter campaign and to request action be taken to comply with the officers' claims of injustice.[3]

At the same time rumblings of dissatisfaction were starting a ground swell of insubordination among the rank and file. Many states had encouraged enlistments for three years or for the duration of the war, with certain guarantees to provide regular supplies of clothing, wages, and price fixing, at stated or current prices, of necessities for their families. Few of these conditions had been honored. When heartbreaking news was received from home revealing the suffering of loved ones due to inflation and the failure of states to fulfill their promises, many officers feared there would be wholesale desertions.[4]

The Congressional Committee, after several meetings with Washington, was convinced that he would always consider the military subordinate to civil authority. However, they recognized that while Washington desired to accede to Congress's directives, he was determined that military decisions must rest with the Commander in Chief in the field and not in the halls of Congress.

Apprehensive over the conditions in the army, he called several Councils of War to consider winter quarters. At these conferences the small cities in the interior of the state were quickly dismissed from consideration. They were already overcrowded with refugees from Philadelphia, the Continental Congress, Pennsylvania legislative personnel, and army hospitals. Therefore, Washington proposed several areas that might answer the army's requirements and the region's defense needs.

Washington suggested a selective choice of locations. While there is some evidence to believe he had a preference for a general area, there was no indication of this in his proposals. Washington requested written opinions of each general that included a chain of cantonments between Lancaster and Reading, the vicinity of Wilmington, or the Great Valley south of the Schuylkill River. After receiving their comments,

Washington convened several Councils to discuss their varying points of view and to consider any alternate suggestions. Most of the generals buttressed their judgment with detailed reasons for a particular location, coupled with a critique on the hazards of all sites. Their qualified selections favored either the Lancaster-Reading line or Wilmington. However, unanimity did not prevail as a few approved different locations such as Reading to Easton, Germantown, hutting in any defensive position, while Pulaski preferred a winter campaign.[5]

On November 30, General John Cadwalader wrote to Joseph Reed concerning the army's future and a dangerous morale problem that was surfacing at the Whitemarsh encampment: "Many of the officers are for going into winter quarters on the line from Lancaster to Easton.... By the best information these towns are crowded with inhabitants from the city...The general officers will set an example of going home. The field officers will follow....Captains and subalterns will expect the same indulgence, and the soldiers will apply for furloughs, and if refused will desert....the army will be dispersed [and the] country on every side will be left to be plundered, and vast numbers will apply [to the British] for protection." Possibly influenced by this letter, the next day Reed gratuitously offered suggestions that Washington considered militarily sound.[6]

Within twenty-four hours a frustrated Washington, dissatisfied with the responses of the generals and apparently not personally committed to any specific site, wrote to Reed: "I am about fixing the winter cantonments of this army, and find so many and such capital objections to each mode proposed, that I am exceedingly embarrassed, not only by the advice given me, but in my own judgment, and should be very glad of your sentiments on the subject, without loss of time." Although occasionally critical of Washington, Reed recalled that during the first year of the Revolution, when he served as the Commander in Chief's secretary, Washington always candidly admitted his shortcomings and was amenable to suggestions that were contrary to his opinions. Although their relations had become somewhat strained, Washington did not hesitate to consult with the Pennsylvanian when he considered Reed's knowledge superior to his own or those of the generals.[7]

After patiently studying his exchange of ideas with Reed, and reexamining the various generals' observations, Washington quietly exerted his authority and chose an area extending along the south side of the Schuylkill River, a few miles above Swede's Ford (Norristown). Although Washington had selected the region that included Valley Forge for the winter encampment, it was not mentioned at this time in the general orders or his correspondence. Apparently, he was reluctant to reveal his decision, rather intending to wait until the army was safely encamped south of the Schuylkill. At that time he planned to reconnoiter the vicinity of Valley Forge for an exact location.

As the Continental Army moved out of Whitemarsh over the road leading to Matson's Ford (Conshohocken), Washington sorrowfully watched the tattered scarecrow lines that comprised the brigades pass his observation post.

Initially, Sullivan had designated Potter's militia brigade, accompanied by Colonel John Lacey and Bucks County's recently recruited militia detachment, to take the van of the march. However, it was apparent to Washington that with the newly constructed British military bridge at Middle Ferry (High—now Market Street), Philadelphia, the enemy could make quick strikes in force along the Continental brigades' strung out of line of march. For over two months Potter had patrolled the roads on the south side of the Schuylkill, harassing British foraging parties and disrupting the traffic of farmers trying to sell their products in the city. Washington realized that Potter was thoroughly acquainted with the area, and was the logical choice to cover the roads and keep him apprised of any British move in force, that could interfere with the army's movement. He, therefore, countermanded Potter's assignment and ordered him to return across the river to delay any British detachment, thereby affording Washington time to deploy the army's brigades.[8]

At Matson's Ford a raft bridge had been emplaced to permit the passage of the army over the Schuylkill River. After crossing the river Potter quickly pushed his brigade down Old Gulph Road, scouting each access road above the Middle Bridge. His advance was not uneventful, as his pickets were engaged occasionally with the British. Alert to any unusual enemy activity, Potter soon discovered that his van was in contact with a superior enemy force. Cornwallis, with a column of nearly 4,000 troops had crossed the bridge on a major foraging expedition.

Cornwallis was surprised at the sudden appearance of Potter's brigade. Potter was equally startled by Cornwallis's presence on Old Gulph Road, as he had anticipated, at most, only a detachment of brigade strength. His small brigade numbered 800, including many militiamen who had never been under fire. Under the circumstances, Potter realized that his inexperienced militia could only offer a delaying action against so superior a professional force.

Nevertheless, Potter was determined to provide Washington with time to cross safely at Matson's Ford. He adopted a tactical plan that would utilize three intersecting ridges on Old Gulph Road. He divided his command into two detachments with orders for the first unit to take a position on the front ridge. They were directed to deliver several volleys and then retire in good order, passing through the second line to the third ridge and regroup. After the passage of the first unit, the troops on the second ridge were to close ranks and after a number of volleys retire to the third ridge to join the first unit. At this position Potter planned to have the reformed brigade present a united front to engage the British.

When the engagement opened a fierce fire fight developed, with the raw recruits and other militia offering a surprisingly stubborn resistance. However, the fight was soon taken out of the militia. At sight of the British and Hessian troops advancing in overwhelming strength with fixed bayonets, Potter's men panicked. At this stage of the Revolution, the threat of "cold steel," or bayonet, frequently created terror and confusion among American troops. Potter and Lacey attempted to rally the frightened troops, but it proved fruitless. Disorganized, they poured through the woods and the defile that led to Matson's Ford bridge. In their fright many had cast away their muskets and accoutrements in an effort to lighten the load for their flight. Reaching the bridge they streamed across to comparative safety on the north bank of the Schuylkill.

As major general of the day, Sullivan had assumed command of the advance brigades of the army. With two brigades of Maryland troops and part of Wayne's two Pennsylvania brigades, he had crossed the bridge at Matson's Ford when British troops suddenly appeared on the precipitous hills above their position. Sullivan was in a quandary—had the British been alerted to the line of march of the Continental brigades? Were these merely the advance units of the main British Army attempting to intercept the Americans along the heavily wooded narrow road passing through the defile?

Uncertain of the answer to these questions, Sullivan immediately ordered the Continental brigades to wheel about and return to the north bank. As this command was being executed, Potter's panic-stricken militia emerged from the woods, closely pursued by superior elements of British troops.

When all the Continentals and militia units were safely across, Sullivan directed that sections of the bridge be dismantled to prevent the enemy from continuing the pursuit. By this time Washington had arrived in the vicinity of Matson's Ford, where a hasty conference was called to consider the army's next move. As the line of march had only been decided at a council the previous night, it seemed inconceivable that Howe could have been alerted to the Continental Army's movement, nor had he time to move out to confront Washington's brigades. John Laurens wrote that Washington, with his usual good judgment, quickly asserted that the British, on the opposite river bank, was probably a foraging expedition, and that the confrontation had been accidental. Intelligence was soon received that confirmed this statement.

On December 15, Potter wrote a succinct account of the engagement to Thomas Wharton, Jr., President of the Pennsylvania Supreme Executive Council. He noted that Washington had commended his brigade in general orders: "But the cumplement would have been mutch more substantale [substantial] had the Valent Generil Solovan Covered my Retreat with two Devissions [Divisions] of the Army, he had in my Reare...." As Lacey recalled the action, the pressure of an overpowering British force had finally penetrated the militia defenses: "I tryed, as well as Potter and many of the other officers to rally them but in vain—the Enemy advancing we gave them a fire or two when a Genl. rout insued—every one making the best of his way—many of the men threw away their guns, that they might be less cumbered [encumbered] in running—...."

Despite Potter's criticism, his troops were badly disorganized and fleeing in disorder, as described by Lacey, and would have been impossible to rally. Therefore, Sullivan's decision reflected sound judgment; to have opposed Cornwallis with his outnumbered division would have trapped Sullivan in a veritable cul-de-sac. The strength of Sullivan's force is corroborated by Lieutenant Thomas Blake, who recorded in his journal that two brigades (of Continentals) had crossed the bridge, when the British were observed taking possession of the heights. Washington stated that after one division: "...and a part of the Second had passed, they found a body of the Enemy, consisting, from the best accounts...of Four Thousand Men...possessing themselves of the Heights on both sides of the Road leading from the River and the defile called the Gulph..."[9]

With the British on the opposite bank and the bridge impassable, it was obvious that an alternate passage of the river had to be found. Under the order of march on leaving Whitemarsh, the artillery and wagons carrying baggage, provisions, and the less serious sick and wounded had been directed to proceed to Swede's Ford. As a bridge was under construction at that ford, Washington ordered the brigades to reverse their line of march and file left through Hickorytown (Plymouth Meeting Mall) and move about three miles west to Swede's Ford.

When the army arrived at the ford, Washington ordered the brigades to form a semicircular encampment fronting on the partially constructed bridge. As he reviewed the temporary quarters his distress was heightened by the suffering of the men. Even if the bridge had been ready, they were in no condition to cross to the south bank. Hungry and thinly clad the soldiers cast their eyes longingly back on the road, hoping to see the wagons containing their provisions and tents.

The next day. December 12, the bridge of thirty-six wagons laid in the river and planked with "fence-rails" was completed. At best it was a rickety structure that provided unsteady footing forcing the army to cross in single file, while the wagon train, when it arrived, had to ford the river.[10]

However, before Washington could order any movement by the army,

16

he had to attend to a number of vexing problems. Several brigade commanders complained that their ranks had been thinned by malingerers who had attached themselves to the hospital and baggage guard, under the pretext of being too weak for active duty. Others were known to be hiding in neighborhood houses and in the brush huts at the Whitemarsh camp. Washington directed each regiment to send a detail, under command of a field officer, to search for any stragglers and return those fit for duty to their respective units.[11]

At the same time it was brought to Washington's attention that his orders for taking care of the sick at the Whitemarsh encampment had only been partially carried out. The surgeons had been ordered to provide wagons to transport the seriously sick and wounded from the improvised regimental hospitals, brush huts, and private residences to Reading and Bethlehem. Those not requiring hospitalization, if able to walk, were to join their regiments, while provision would be made for those too weak to carry their accoutrements or packs. Unfortunately, information from Whitemarsh indicated many shirkers or sick remained at the old camp. A subaltern from each brigade with a detail of dragoons was instructed to return to Whitemarsh and report to Doctors Jabez Campfield (sometimes referred to as Campbell) and George Draper at Hope Lodge—the headquarters of the Medical Department during the encampment. With the assistance of the doctors, they were to roundup all the soldiers belonging to their respective units and, if fit for duty, escort them back to their regiments—otherwise transfer them to military hospitals at Reading.[12]

To Washington the need to rectify the infractions of discipline had been important but, were, nevertheless, distracting when preeminence had to be given to establishing winter quarters for the army. Time was a luxury not at his disposal. He had previously selected the general area along the Schuylkill, west of Swede's Ford, without specifically pinpointing Valley Forge as the site of the encampment.

Now the abject condition of the men, as they huddled around the camp fires at the ford, only accentuated the need for an immediate decision. Washington had some knowledge of the Great Valley and Valley Forge region. In September the army had made interim camps at Yellow Springs, Warwick Furnace, and then on the nineteenth crossed the Schuylkill at Parker's Ford. Hamilton and Lee had provided additional details about Valley Forge and the Valley Creek area. With this information and the urgency of the situation, Valley Forge became Washington's choice for the encampment.[13]

On December 12, his decision made, Washington ordered the first brigade to cross the bridge at 6 P.M. Matthias Holstein, a young boy living in Swedesford[14], recalled in later life the measures that had been taken

The Continental Army on the march to Valley Forge. Nineteenth century drawing by Felix O.C. Darley. (Dover Publications, Inc.)

to protect the troops as they moved to the south bank. The engineers[15] had directed the construction of small breastworks on both sides of the river, while dragoons patrolled the perimeter of the line of march.[16]

The first units began to cross the shaky bridge at 6 P.M. moving out in "Indian file." Because of the unstable condition of the bridge progress was slow and tedious, with the last troops not reaching the south bank until 3 A.M. Local tradition claims a number of soldiers were drowned in the crossing. It is known that at least nine soldiers are buried in the church cemetery at Swedesford.

The crossing was a harrowing experience as recorded by Lieutenant James McMichael: "At 6 P.M. we marched to the bridge, which we crossed in Indian file, and at 3 A.M. encamped near the Gulph, where we remained without tents or blankets in the midst of a severe snow storm." John Laurens wrote: "...[from] want of provisions—I could weep tears of blood when I say it—the want of provisions render'd it impossible to march." Another soldier stated: "It is amazing to see the spirit of the soldiers when destitute of shoes and stockings marching cold nights and mornings, leaving blood in their foot-steps! yet notwithstanding, the fighting disposition of the soldiers is great."[17]

Washington's plan becomes obvious when a study is made of the general orders. On December 13, as the troops arrived at the Gulph, speculation was rife as to the future movements of the army. All uncertainty was soon dispelled when the men were instructed not to pitch any tents. Washington, contemplating only a one night camp at the Gulph, issued orders to bring up axes from the wagons, so the men could build fires and erect brush huts as shelter against the pelting snow and rain. There was considerable flurry throughout the camp as officers were directed to examine all arms and accoutrements, have provisions "drawn, and cooked for to morrow and next day," and a gill of whiskey issued to every "officer, soldier, and waggoner." Inasmuch as the "weather being likely to be fair...The army is to be ready to march at precisely four o'clock to morrow morning." Unfortunately, for the weather forecaster, dawn on the fourteenth would break with a downpour that drenched the men huddled in their huts and made the roads impassable.[18]

Washington was determined to move out to Valley Forge as soon as the weather cleared and the roads would permit the movement of the wagons. A chafing Washington waited impatiently for four days as the heavy rains continued. On December 15, there appeared to be a break in the weather, and orders were issued for the baggage wagons to move out the next day at 7 A.M. with the army to follow at 10 A.M. On the sixteenth the wagons with the army's tents were to leave for Valley Forge and "pitched immediately" for the convenience of the soldiers. Unfortunately, again the weather failed to cooperate.[19]

VALLEY FORGE

Although all orders unmistakably indicate Valley Forge as the site of the winter encampment, it is not officially designated in the orders. By December 13, Valley Forge was well known by civilians and soldiers as the destination of the army. John Miller, a resident of Germantown recorded in his journal on the fourteenth that "General Washingtons headquarters is now at Valley Forge." On the fifteenth, John Laurens stated "the precise position is not as yet fixed upon...probably be determined this day." On December 17, General Enoch Poor wrote "we march in a few days for Valley Forge." Various brigade and regimental orderly books and soldier's journals have the army at, or will soon be, near Valley Forge from the sixteenth to the nineteenth—the actual day the army arrived. These differing dates are confusing but, undoubtedly, reflect the activity of the army's several postponed preparations to march.[20]

On November 1, Congress had set December 18 as a day for public "Thanksgiving and Praise." To comply with the observance of Congress's declaration, Washington delayed until the nineteenth the march to Valley Forge. In the general orders for the seventeenth he extolled the courage and perseverance of the troops in support "...of the measures necessary for our defence we shall finally obtain the end of our Warfare, Independence, Liberty and Peace." He further stated it was essential "...to take such a position, as will enable it [army] most effectually to prevent distress and to give the most extensive security; and in that position we must make ourselves the best shelter in our power....These cogent reasons have determined the General to take post in the neighbourhood of this camp...." Although not specifying the armed services, Congress recommended that all patriots observe the day of thanksgiving, as Washington stated with "...our grateful acknowledgments to God for the manifold blessings he has granted us."

The army was directed to remain in its present quarters and the chaplains instructed to conduct divine services before their respective regiments and brigades. After the solemnity of the day, orders were issued to reinstate the marching orders of the fifteenth for the next morning, which directed the wagons to move out at 7 A.M. and the troops three hours later.[21]

Temporary camps and the drudgery of the march had not allowed Washington to forget that a number of pressing questions had to be resolved before they became problems. The winter encampment must be a springboard from which detachments of brigade, or greater strength, could be dispatched to intercept any British incursion into the countryside. Details of Washington's plan to encircle Philadelphia would not be announced until the encampment was established and steps were taken to house the troops and provide for their well-being.

Closely correlated to his containment plan was the impelling need to improve American intelligence. Washington had become perceptive of the inadequate, and occasionally misleading, information received at the Battle of Brandywine. At Whitemarsh he started to make changes that would improve his "spy system." Washington believed the implementation of his plans of containment and better intelligence would blunt the criticism that had begun to surface in Congress and Pennsylvania.

What had been rumors since mid-November had become obvious rumblings of discontent over his decision to seek winter quarters for the army. Annoyed, Washington's indignation reached a boiling point when he reviewed the pitiful condition of the troops. The paucity of virtually every commodity needed to support the army demanded the immediate and dramatic attention of all Americans interested in sustaining an armed force, and the personal comfort of the soldiers. Washington needed nothing more than the pathetic sight of the blood stained imprints of the troops on the march to raise his wrath against the lack of concern demonstrated by many citizens.

A few days after setting up headquarters in his marquee at Valley Forge, Washington wrote to the President of Congress, Henry Laurens, venting his bitterness at the irresponsibility of the Commissary and Quartermaster Departments, the inattentiveness of Congress, and the indifference of Pennsylvania authorities. His vitriol poured forth without restraint on those who thought the army could conduct a winter campaign with its present shortages: "...as if they thought Men [the Soldiery] were made of Stocks and Stones and equally insensible to frost and Snow and moreover, as if they conceived it [easily] practical for an inferior Army under the disadvantages I have describ'd our's to be wch. [which] by no means exagerated to confine a superior one...within the City of Phila...." With equal acidity he assailed the feeble efforts of Congress and Pennsylvania to furnish desperately needed "Cloaths" to the troops adding: "...not one Article of wch, by the bye, is yet come to hand, should think a Winters Campaign [and] the [army] covering these States from...Invasion...so easy....I can assure those Gentlemen that it is a much easier and less distressing thing to draw remonstrances in a comfortable room by a good fire side than to occupy a cold bleak hill and sleep under frost and Snow without Cloaths or Blankets; however, although they seem to have little feeling for the naked and distressed Soldier, I feel superabundantly for them, and from my Soul pity those miseries, wch. it is neither in my power to relieve or prevent."[22]

Despite Washington's protestations, from mid-October to early January, 1778, he would continue to be irritated by the self-centered interests of many civilians and the jealousies of a few officers. His frustration was revealed in letters that were sprinkled with the question, why can't man forget their personal ambitions and interest and unite for the good of the country? At this time the inability or indifference of Congress and Pennsylvania authorities to provide for the soldiers threatened the country with the dissolution of its army.

While Washington was at Whitemarsh Congress had advised him to live off the countryside. They assumed that the area was a land of plenty, whereas it had been stripped of provisions and forage. Pennsylvania officials and civilians had closed their ears to the pleas of Wayne, and other officers of the Pennsylvania Continental line regiments, requesting recruits to fill out the ranks, clothing, and provisions. The amateur strategists underestimated the strength of the British Army, and optimistically overestimated conditions in the Continental Army.

At citizen's meetings they suggested calling out the full militia strength of Pennsylvania and neighboring states. They forgot that in October an optimistic Washington had wanted to attack the British, and when he appealed for additional militia support only a few weak contingents reached camp. Many were without arms or accoutrements, county lieutenants having kept the better armed units to defend their frontier against Indian attack. Washington did not have a reserve arsenal of muskets, and with a serious shortage of provisions, had to order the useless men to return home. The petitioners made a major miscalculation when they supposed the militia could be called out in December, and have time to train to combat readiness. Also, to attack a professional army of nearly 18,000 troops strongly entrenched behind a series of redoubts, fraised and fronted by abatis would have been suicidal. In the eighteenth century, with defenses similar to those at Philadelphia, it was accepted military practice that the attacking force should be double that of the defenders.

Nevertheless, the memorialists continued to protest to Congress against Washington's taking up winter quarters. When rumors began to circulate that he planned to encamp at Valley Forge or Wilmington, the outcry increased, claiming that such encampment sites would leave the area north of the Schuylkill and New Jersey open to the ravages of the British—if Washington had remained near Whitemarsh the clamor would probably have been reversed for the area south of the river.

Individuals added their concern over the prospect of the army going into winter quarters. Thomas Wharton, President of the Pennsylvania Supreme Executive Council, wrote to Elias Boudinot, Commissary of Prisoners, stating: "I hope our troops may not retire to winter quarters and leave our country open to the ravages and insults of the enemy." A member of Congress, Abraham Clark wrote General "Lord" Stirling expressing deep concern that if the army went into winter quarters at Wilmington, the country would be unprotected.[23]

Except for the expressed opinions of a few members, Congress reserved its comments on the controversy over a winter campaign until they received the report of the committee that had visited Whitemarsh in early December. On the 15th the Committee's detailed report was read to an assembled Congress. The Committee reported that Washington had been advised of Congress's wish for a winter campaign but, after consulting with his generals, concluded that to take the offensive was an "...enterprize too dangerous and not to be hazarded but in case of absolute necessity." As promised before departing from Whitemarsh, the Committee recommended against a winter campaign. In their judgment the condition of the army supported Washington's determination to seek winter quarters to rest and regroup, stating: "That until sufficient reinforcements can be obtained, such a post should be taken by the Army as will be most likely to overawe the Enemy, afford supplies of provision, wood, Water, and Forage, be secure from surprise, and best calculated for covering the Country from the ravages of the Enemy, as well as provide comfortable Quarters for Officers and Soldiers."[24]

With the reading of the report it was ordered: "To lie on the table." After four days of deliberating its Committee's report, the wisdom of Washington's decision to seek winter quarters became evident to Congress. If the Continental Army was to survive the winter to fight another campaign, it must rest, reform, and be disciplined into an effective fighting machine. There was persistent pressure by Pennsylvania authorities to have Congress order Washington to remain in the field and attack the British lines at Philadelphia. Congress was, undoubtedly, aware of Washington's preference for a winter encampment as it had been bruited around the army and Yorktown for over two weeks. Congress was on the horns of a dilemma, a political face-saving accord had to be reached.

On December 19, Congress passed a resolution they hoped would satisfy everyone. Washington was requested to advise them: "Whether he has come to a fixed resolution to canton the army; and if he has, what line of cantonment he has proposed; in particular, what measures are agreed on for the protection of that part of Pennsylvania which lies on the easterly [north] side of [the] Schuylkill, and the State of New Jersey." By not giving a direct order, Congress was hopeful Washington would not consider it an encroachment on his authority as Commander in Chief. Concurrently it was the hope of Congress that this directive to Washington, coupled with a copy of the Pennsylvania Assembly's remonstrance, would appease all Pennsylvanians.[25]

While attending the Thanksgiving service, Washington's thoughts were directed to the final preparations needed to move out of the Gulph. Simultaneously, he formed a plan for containing the British Army within their works at Philadelphia. General William Smallwood was ordered to take the division of two Maryland brigades, formerly commanded by Sullivan, and occupy Wilmington, Delaware. He was directed to place that city and vicinity in the "best posture of defence" and prevent incursions by the British into Delaware. As an added responsibility, he was instructed to intercept and capture any British ships passing the post. President of Delaware, George Read, was requested to reinforce Smallwood with all available militia detachments. Sullivan, with another division, was to temporarily remain at the Gulph until final plans for the disposition of militia and Continental units for encircling Philadelphia had been completed. General John Armstrong's Pennsylvania militia brigade was to remain north of the Schuylkill to cover the area near the former Whitemarsh encampment.[26]

On December 18 Washington, anxious to expedite the orderly establishment of the camp at Valley Forge, ordered all Colonels or commanding officers of regiments, with their company captains, to divide the men into "squads of twelve, and see that each squad have their proportion of tools...." To stimulate the soldiers' interest in building their winter homes, Washington offered twelve dollars to the squad in each regiment that finished its "hut in the quickest and most workmanlike manner...." As a further incentive one hundred dollars would be awarded to the officer or soldier who would submit an adequate substitute for boards that would be cheaper and more expeditiously made.

The soldiers' huts were to be of uniform size, fourteen by sixteen feet on the "sides, ends and roofs made with logs..." Each wall was to be six and a half feet high. To make the roofs weatherproof the men were to use "split slabs, or in some other [undetermined] way;...." The walls were to be plastered with clay on the inside, and a fireplace of clay eighteen inches thick placed in the rear of each hut. Doors made of split slabs or boards were to face the regimental streets. After completing the instructions for construction of the soldiers' huts, Washington suggested housing for the officers. One hut was to be assigned to each general officer, the staff of each brigade, field officers of each regiment, the staff of the regiment, the commissioned officers of each company, and one for every twelve non-commissioned officers. The officers' huts were to form a line in the rear of the regimental street.

These precise instructions covering the detailed dimensions, materials, and the occupants of each hut were probably only intended as guidelines. A number of changes would be made when construction actually started. Many generals and their staffs would eventually find quarters with families residing near the camp. Washington stated he would live in his marquee until all men were hutted. However, after a few days, circumstances connected with the volume of work of his aides-de-camp and his numerous duties as Commander in Chief, made it mandatory that larger army headquarters be established in a nearby house.[27]

On December 20, after an uncomfortable night at Valley Forge, the major generals accompanied by Duportail and his engineers were to survey the site of the encampment to render it as "strong and inaccessible as possible." The engineers marked out the area to be occupied by each brigade, and then directed the field officers, who had been appointed to supervise the site of their brigade, on the details of their duties to ensure that there would be uniformity and order in the layout of their area and the construction of the huts.[28]

After receiving their instructions for erecting winter housing, the army was happy to hear the order to move out of the Gulph for Valley Forge. The Gulph camp would not remain a cherished memory to the soldiers; as one officer wrote, he had lived in a "brush camp" which had to be rebuilt "almost every night." For five days they had patiently endured heavy snow, followed by a torrential downpour, and then biting cold. The men had grappled with hunger as the unpredictable and inefficient commissary and quartermaster systems had only provided a trickle of provisions. Although faced with the uncertainty of the future and the chore of erecting their huts, the soldiers knew, at least, they would have shelter. Drenched and shoeless, many men would again mark their march with blood, as the soft slush of the previous day had turned the road into a succession of icy ridges.[29]

As they trudged along the Gulph Road the thoughts of many turned to home, and the despondent prospect of being away from loved ones. Many had not heard from their wives and families for months. Brigadier General Jedediah Huntington may have best expressed the devotion of the brave veterans of the Brandywine, Germantown and Whitemarsh when queried on the possibility of leaving the service because of homesickness for his wife, he wrote: "...my dear Country is the first earthly Object of my affection and Love, to my Country, I consider myself united in Strongest Bond and to her by Gods Assistance I will be faithful." Huntington added that to help him endure the hardships of winter and the loneliness away from his Nancy, would Colonel Joseph Trumbull have a pencil sketch made of Nancy as a comfort to him over the long dreary months ahead?[30]

The men in the ranks knew that Washington had declared that man for man they were the equal of any British or Hessian soldier. Most soldiers were determined that the Commander in Chief's confidence not be misplaced.

As Washington beheld the panorama of what would be the winter encampment, he perceived that if the Continental Army failed to survive the winter, the cause of independence would be lost—unless France and other European powers believed that the Americans would field an army for the next campaign, they would table any thought of entering the conflict as an ally. With the nucleus of a dedicated soldiery, he was confident that with a winter at Valley Forge of rest, regrouping, and discipline, the Continentals would emerge as an effective fighting force in the spring of 1778.

Chapter

II

Men Unable to Stir

THE AFTERNOON OF December 19, was overcast and raining as Washington, accompanied by his aides, Duportail, the French engineers with others of the general staff—flanked by a detachment of the Commander in Chief's Guard[1]—rode up the glacis that would become the encampment's outer line of defense. As they crested the slope and viewed the bleak forested area, all thoughts must have turned to the monumental tasks ahead if the army was to survive for next year's campaign.

No one was more aware than Washington that the months to follow would be a crucial test for the men of the Continental Army. He had not considered the Battle at Germantown a defeat, but rather a proving ground for his "young Troops." After the battle his correspondence revealed an unrestrained optimism as he extolled the superior fighting ability of the Continentals, when compared with their British and Hessian counterparts.[2]

In the meantime, a compassionate Commander in Chief was hopeful that the huts he had ordered constructed would keep idle men occupied, and later provide protection from the snow and cold weather. Worried, Washington wondered as he looked back at the straggling line of march marked by the blood of hundreds of shoeless soldiers, and the sick being supported by their comrades, how many of these threadbare and hungry men would be able to report for the next day's work details.

Washington's mind probably wandered, as he realized that little Congressional assistance could be expected soon to relieve the army's hunger and shortages. For the indefinite future officers and men must find whatever shelter available in tents or makeshift brush billets, and share similar privations. Equally disturbing were the rumblings of discontent in the ranks, that had now reached an alarming stage that forebode wholesale desertions. The ragtag veterans were aware of the repeated promises of the government to provide provisions, clothing, shoes, and blankets, that had never been received. To paraphrase a statement by

Washington, they had visions of Congressmen comfortably ensconced beside warm firesides, indifferent to their sufferings.[3]

Since leaving Whitemarsh, an apprehensive Washington had observed a steady increase in desertions, especially among foreign born soldiers. His concern was exacerbated by the knowledge that the enlistments of many men would terminate at the end of December, including several entire regiments. Also, distressing was the threatened resignation of hundreds of angry officers. Most of these officers who had served faithfully for over two years were now receiving reports that their families were starving. They were prepared to return home and confront those authorities who had failed to honor commitments to provide for their loved ones.

As a realist, Washington was aware that unless immediate steps were taken to address the wretched conditions existing in the ranks, year's end would find the army reduced to a skeleton force, thereby, precluding any possibility of generating a campaign in 1778. Despite such adversities, his optimism of October and November remained steadfast in the belief that the "young Troops" were capable of delivering a successful surprise stroke against the enemy garrison in Philadelphia. Already forming in his mind were the rudiments of an offensive move, but, for the present, he would not reveal his intentions to anyone. The attention of the officers and men must not be distracted from the priority at hand; the urgency to construct garrison and hospital huts for a possible lengthy encampment at Valley Forge.

After issuing final instructions relating to the first night's bivouac, Washington rode across the terrain of the designated encampment area toward Valley Creek where members of the guard were setting up his marquee.

At dawn on December 20, the bleak landscape at Valley Forge was the scene of bustling activity. Washington's solicitude for the comfort of the men was manifest when his first directive had called for the immediate construction of huts for their shelter. Complying with his order Duportail and his engineers, accompanied by the major generals of the army, rode over the terrain and marked out the position for each brigade, while tentatively designating sites for the fortifications needed for the camp's defense. As a follow-up, the engineers instructed the assigned brigade field officers on their duties as supervisors of the various regimental street layouts and hut building.[4]

Although scarce all available axes were distributed throughout the army for cutting firewood, with the added admonishment that care should be taken to conserve a part of each fallen tree for hut construction. As a tree was chopped down sixteen to eighteen feet of its trunk was to be reserved for building purposes.

Marquee believed to have been Washington's headquarters at Valley Forge during the first days of the encampment. (Valley Forge Historical Society.)

In an effort to make the soldiers' quarters more comfortable, the Quarter Master General was directed to "use his utmost exertions" to scour the countryside for the largest quantities of straw obtainable. The straw was primarily intended for bedding; however, if no other satisfactory method of roofing the huts could be found, a portion should be diverted for that purpose. In accordance with Washington's offer to reward any soldier for a better system of roofing, he appointed Major Generals Greene, Sullivan and Stirling as judges to test any techniques submitted.[5]

Apparently the field officers in charge of building the huts had encountered numerous difficulties. It soon became obvious to Washington that most of the officers were unskilled in construction methods. To assist them, the engineers were instructed to make models of huts and prepare "directions about placing them." Colonel Richard Kidder Meade, one of Washington's aides-de-camp, was designated to act as liaison between the French speaking engineers and the field officers.

With these directives, Washington was satisfied that work on the huts would proceed as rapidly as conditions permitted. He now turned his full attention to camp security, and accessibility to all surrounding areas. He was aware that Valley Forge, as the winter encampment, had been a controversial choice. Certain American and French officers thought it was a desolate location, ill-adapted to defense, and too distant to contain the British Army within Philadelphia's defenses. On Christmas day Major General Baron de Kalb would epitomize these sentiments in a letter to a friend in France, Comte de Broglie writing: "On the 19th instant the army reached this wooded wilderness, certainly one of the poorest districts of Pennsylvania; the soil thin, uncultivated, and almost uninhabited, without forage and without provisions! Here we are to go into winter quarters, i.e., to lie in shanties, generals and privates, to recruit, to re-equip, and to prepare for the opening of the coming campaign, while protecting the country against hostile inroad." While de Kalb's comments paraphrased the opinions of several fellow officers, they also reflected unfamiliarity with the country (although he had traveled throughout the colonies for four months in 1768), and the public outcry that Washington, by taking winter quarters, had abandoned the countryside to British incursions.[6]

Undaunted by certain negative opinions, Washington was confident that the natural strength of Valley Forge, coupled with Duportail's defense plan, would provide security for the camp. The testy Frenchman, unable to obtain able-bodied men to work on the fortifications, believed that his efforts were being hampered by a lack of cooperation on the part of various brigade commanders. The brigadier generals, acting under direct orders from Washington to give priority to the construction of huts, were directed not to release men for other duties unless by order of the Commander in Chief. Duportail appealed to Washington to unlock the impasse, but the latter, although sympathetic to the engineer's problems, remained determined that the comfort and well-being of the soldiers must take precedence.

It was occasionally difficult for Duportail to accept decisions that differed with his concept of military defenses. However, his disagreements with Washington on the adequacy of fortifications were rare, but as will be seen such a dispute would occur in the spring of 1778. For the moment it was agreed a meeting of the general staff was necessary to counsel on other matters of security for the camp. Of prime importance was the accessibility to the camp. Would the encampment be vulnerable to attack? If so, from what direction was it likely to come? Other questions considered were the adequacy of roads permitting rapid deployment of the brigades, or the need to quickly evacuate the camp in the event of a disaster. It was agreed that Duportail's entrenchments, or the outer line, when finished would offer security on the east.

It was known that four roads either crossed through Valley Forge or started in the camp site. Nutts (now Route 23), Yellow Springs, and a very rough road that passed over Mt. Misery offered satisfactory communication with the west and southwest. In addition. a good road for the eighteenth century, entered the camp from the south. Deep concern was expressed that no escape route or contact was available to the north side of the Schuylkill River. That region was considered necessary for movement of troops,and equally important as an area that could provide a bountiful supply of provisions and forage. Fatland Ford was the obvious crossing location; the British Army having forded the Schuylkill there in September. While it normally offered a shallow passage, it was treacherous and not always fordable in winter.

Without hesitation Washington ordered a bridge be constructed near the ford and asked for a volunteer from the major generals to oversee the work. Why wasn't Duportail, an experienced military engineer, asked to design and supervise the building of the bridge? Was it the Frenchman's difficulty in communicating because of a language difference, his intractable personality, or Washington's desire to keep the chief engineer free to plan and superintend the encampment's land defenses? Speculations aside, Washington's request was greeted by Major General John Sullivan:" "...having obligingly undertaken the direction of a bridge to be built over the Schuylkill..."[7]

The bridge was to be located a short distance downstream from Fatland Ford and a small island that had formed a part of that ford. In 1878, when celebrating the Centennial of the Continental Army's evacuation of Valley Forge, the lines of a redoubt could be traced on the eastern tip of this island.[8] Eventually this gun emplacement, and a larger redoubt—designated today as the Star Redoubt—stood on the brow of an elevation overlooking the bridge site, and a picket guard post would provide the span's defenses.[9]

Washington was aware of the hardships that would affect hut construction by his order assigning skilled artisans to Sullivan, a condition that would be worsened because the army had few proficient carpenters. Nevertheless, he ordered "Four carpenters and five expert axmen" from each division be relieved of their duties on the huts and directed to report to the bridge site. Other soldiers detached from duties on the huts, initially from Sullivan's division, were ordered to serve as members of daily fatigue parties consisting of a subaltern,[10] sergeant, corporal and twelve privates. Within a few days it was decided that there should be larger details on duty at the bridge. On Christmas day a routine was established whereby alternating units from the various brigades would assign picket parties of "a Capt. Subaltern, and 40 men" to Sullivan. The bridge guard would vary, but by early spring was set as: "...Guard at Bridge...a Captain, two Subalterns, three Serjeants and thirty six Rank and File where of one Subaltern, Serjeant and sixteen rank and file are to be posted on the other side [north]...." To use as headquarters, a guard house was erected on the south side of the river.[11]

At the time axmen and carpenters were assigned to Sullivan, their numbers were believed to be adequate to build the bridge. It soon became evident that any hope for an early completion of the structure would require additional workmen. Washington was sympathetic to Sullivan's plight, and while recognizing the urgency of establishing communications with the north bank of the Schuylkill River, he adamantly refused to endanger the speedy erection of the huts by releasing more soldiers for the bridge project. His rides over the encampment had stirred his empathy for the hungry, freezing soldiers huddled around smoky campfires of green wood. It was manifestly clear that he couldn't redress their hunger pangs, but he could reaffirm his pledge to give precedence to the prompt building of their shelters.

Washington was aware that a possible solution to Sullivan's problem rested with over 100 Continental soldiers serving on the galleys of the Pennsylvania Navy on the Delaware River. During October and November 1777, the little navy was an integral part of an interdependent Delaware River defense force that, also, included land fortifications—principally Fort Mercer on the New Jersey bank and Fort Mifflin on Mud Island about 500 yards off the Pennsylvania shore—and river obstructions called Chevaux-de-frise.[12] Since October 1, almost daily brushes with ships of the powerful British Navy had thinned the ranks of the galley crews. Commodore John Hazelwood, commander of the combined fleet of State and Continental navies on the Delaware River, and the State Navy Board appealed to Washington for men with maritime experience to replace their loss of manpower.[13]

On October 29, Washington responded by sending slightly over 100 soldiers from the line regiments of Generals Muhlenberg, Weedon, Woodford, Scott, 2nd Maryland, McDougall, and a large contingent of North Carolina Continentals to Fort Mercer where they reported to Hazelwood.[14]

In mid-November, the Delaware River fortifications including Forts Mifflin and Mercer, were abandoned after a valiant defense. Soon after the fall of the land defenses, the main elements of the navy escaped upstream to Trenton.[15]

With these depressing developments, Washington expected a prompt return of the soldiers serving on the galleys. After six weeks of excuses and considerable foot dragging, he issued orders for their return. On the arrival of the first contingent, they were immediately assigned to work for Sullivan at the bridge.[16]

In response to an enquiry from the Pennsylvania General Assembly, Sullivan described the foundation of the bridge platform as piers or boxes filled with stones. It is apparent that these piers—although smaller—were patterned after the large bins or hoppers used to place the chevaux-de-frise in the Delaware River bed. Sullivan believed that if the bridge was properly maintained it would serve Pennsylvanians until the "lumber decays," adding this could be achieved by: "Filling up the Piers or Boxes with Stones, also, a number of Stones to be Thrown Round the Boxes to prevent the Sand washing away Round the sides."[17]

In a somewhat more graphic manner, two officers with the British Convention army offered descriptive vignettes of the bridge's superstructure.[18] Hessian Lieutenant and Adjutant August W. Du Roi the Elder, of Prince Frederick's regiment, passed through Valley Forge on December 16, 1778, on his way to a prisoner of war camp in Virginia. Du Roi noted that: "We crossed the Schuylkill on the Sullivan Bridge which is 228 paces long and rests on 9 wooden pillars. The current is very swift, on account of which fact many stones had to be sunk to keep the pillars in place."[19]

Like Du Roi, Lieutenant Thomas Anburey, a grenadier officer in the British 47th regiment crossed the bridge on December 16, and spent a two day bivouac in the huts of the old encampment. Anburey offered a vivid account of the decorations on the bridge arches: "I imagine it was the intention of the Americans that this bridge should remain as a triumphal memento, for in the center of every arch, is engraved in the wood, the name of the principal Generals in their country; and in the middle arch was General Washington's with the date of the year; this bridge was built to preserve communication, and to favor retreat, in case they were compelled to quit their encampment."[20]

The bridge's denouement was written in February, 1779, when Colonel John Bull of the Pennsylvania Militia began to dismantle the structure. Whether, at this time, a rapid deterioration of the piers and platform had started is unknown. According to Du Roi and Anburey the bridge was in serviceable condition in mid-December, 1778. The intervening weeks of severe weather and the river's swift current may have caused some damage, but it is more likely the Pennsylvania Supreme Executive Council considered the bridge nonessential, whereas timber was desperately needed at Fort Mifflin. The fort was being rebuilt on the ruins of the original Fort Mifflin after being destroyed by the British, and Bull had been directed to restore the barracks, ramparts, and reconstruct the gun platforms. By late February, Bull was floating timbers from the bridge downstream. As a footnote to this project, by 1781, controversy, inadequate funding, and indifference to the need for a Delaware River fortification would witness the cessation of all work at the fort until the next decade.[21]

The early days of the encampment had become the watershed of the war for Washington. A number of organizational breakdowns in the army had surfaced that demanded immediate attention. The Quartermaster and Commissary Departments[22] were in total disarray, and frequent criticisms reached headquarters of the horrendous conditions at the military hospitals. An imperative need was an effective Inspector General. In late November Congress had appointed General Thomas Conway. His assignment, coupled with the accompanying rank of Major General was deeply resented by the officers at Whitemarsh and later at Valley Forge. Virtually ostracized at the latter camp, Conway never functioned as Inspector General. It had become increasingly apparent to Washington and Congress that the only solution rested with a mutual exchange of recommendations for rebuilding the army. On Christmas Day, in accord with this suggestion, Washington wrote to Elbridge Gerry: "...that the method suggested by you, of having a Comee. [Committee] of Congress to consult with me, or a Comee. of my appointing (for it would be impossible for me to give that close attention which the nature of things would require) on the best regulations, arrangements and Plans for the next Campaign will be approved."[23]

Washington's appreciation of the urgency to attend to a shakeup in the army could not dampen his enthusiasm to take the long awaited opportunity to make a surprise strike on the British Army in Philadelphia. However, if this offensive could not be mounted within a few days, the worsening weather would obviate any hope of taking the field before spring. Impassable roads would place insurmountable obstacles on logistical support, or moving the artillery.

Washington's strategy, although undated has been correctly ascribed to December 25, relied on a simultaneous attack by two wings of the army on the British defenses, thus forcing Howe to divide his underestimated force to defend on two fronts. The left wing under Stirling was to assault the northern approaches to the city, guarded by a line of eleven redoubts, all fraised, and connecting entrenchments fronted by abatis. Sullivan and the right wing were to cross at the Middle Bridge and Ferry, and push through the center of the city and take control of the enemy's shipping while releasing all American prisoners. To prevent intercourse between the city and Loyalists in the countryside, Major John Jameson, of the 2nd Continental Dragoons, was ordered to establish dragoon patrols on each road leading into the city.[24]

For several days before committing his plan to writing, Washington mulled over whether to act independent of the general staff. He was aware that the proposal was contrary to his insistence on a winter encampment instead of a winter campaign. However, it was consistent with his frequent desire to assume the offensive in November. Washington did not wish to divulge the project prematurely and, therefore, decided against convening a Council of War; rather, he chose to discuss with Knox and Sullivan on the feasibility of proceeding as planned.

Knox's cooperation was vital, if the artillery could not take to the field immediately any attempt to assail the British fortifications would be futile. Whereas, Sullivan was ordered to act as an intermediary with the other generals. He was to discuss with them, individually, Washington's plan.[25]

Sullivan had been briefed on the unwritten plan a number of days before Christmas and, as will be seen, about the same time Howe moved out Darby Road with a large column. Having knowledge of Howe's move the generals Sullivan consulted apparently considered the proposed attacked modified. On December 26, when Sullivan completed his assignment, any of the general's opinions on the original plan of attack was academic. Sullivan's report indicated that the attention of the generals was concentrated on an attack on the British position at Darby. He emphasized the expressions of loyalty by the generals and their deep concern for the personal attacks on Washington. In his letter Sullivan wrote he had only consulted those generals believed capable of advising on the Commander in Chief's plan in the "army's present circumstances." Their consensus was: "...that they can by no means advise for or against an attack. They are fully convinced that General Howe has his whole force with him; that, if your Excellency thinks your force sufficient to cope with his, they are willing to risk their lives and fortunes with you in the attempt." Not vacillating, but preferring to defer to Washington's decision, they had added: "...if you fail the people who are now so fond

35

of censuring, will change their clamor, and censure you for not attacking him when he was within a mile [Whitemarsh] of you, and your army more numerous and in better condition than at present." On the other hand Sullivan personally "...weary of the infernal clamor of the Pennsylvanians..." believed an attack was worth the risk.[26]

As will be seen, Washington would develop an efficient espionage system in Philadelphia, but for some inexplicable reason his intelligence reports consistently underestimated the size of the British garrison. Actually, Howe had an effective strength of British and Hessian rank and file of approximately 17,000;[27] whereas, Washington repeatedly stated the enemy's force totaled 10,000. Regardless, a confident Washington impatiently waited for intelligence of Howe committing a tactical error that would offer an opportunity to attack the British lines at Philadelphia.[28]

Washington was aware of the desperate conditions facing the British Army and the city's residents. His intelligence had alerted him to unusual activity at Howe's headquarters, and of troops being readied for the field. On December 20, word reached Valley Forge that the British were building a pontoon bridge across the Schuylkill River at Gray's Ferry. At four o'clock the following afternoon intelligence was received that most of the enemy's garrison had been supplied with three days rations, and were preparing to move over the bridge early on the twenty-second.

It had become obvious to Howe, that unless the army could roundup livestock to supplement their meager rations, and forage for the horses, starvation would threaten the city. Both Commanders in Chief were cognizant of the large quantities of hay on the islands in the Delaware River and of the cattle that grazed in the adjacent marshes.

On December 21, Captain Sir James Murray wrote of the city's pitiful conditions noting: "Here we have almost a second part of the Boston blockade; in the midst of a plentiful country, the little provision that is smugld [sic] in through the Rebels Lines & Spies, is sold very dear, and indeed many in the town would starve were it not for the help from the Army Rations & from the flour which Mr. Washington allows wives & families of his adherents to have through his lines."[29]

At dawn on the 22nd, Howe, with a large column consisting of over half the city's garrison, crossed the pontoon bridge. Marching out Darby Road, they established a position extending for over four miles, to act as a screen to protect the parties engaged in collecting forage.[30]

Meanwhile, satisfied with the accuracy of his intelligence, Washington ordered an immediate concentration of the Continental brigades. Each commander was to collect, or recall, any officers or men on detached command. The cannon were to be assembled at the artillery park ready to move the next morning at nine o'clock. Anticipating Howe's objective,

Extract from Washington letter to president of Congress. December 23, 1777. (John F. Reed Collection, Valley Forge National Historical Park.)

he instructed General James Potter with his Pennsylvania Militia Brigade, and Colonel Daniel Morgan's Continental riflemen to adopt any "mode" they deemed expedient to remove or destroy the hay on Tinicum and other islands along the Delaware River shore. Before Potter and Morgan could accomplish their mission, the van of the British column reached the Blue Bell Tavern on the road to Darby. While engaging in a series of fire fights, the Americans withdrew to a position near the road to Lancaster to await further orders.[31]

By the 22nd, Washington envisioned an opportunity to strike a blow at Howe's divided force. His hopes were quickly shattered when he reviewed the condition of the soldiers as he wrote the President of Congress: "...the Divisions which I ordered to be in readiness to march and meet them, could not have moved." He stressed the lack of everything, especially provisions necessary to sustain the troops on the march. Discouraged, but still willing to risk an attack on Howe's extended line, he directed each brigade: "...to furnish a good partizan captain, two Subs [subalterns], three Serjeants, three corporals and fifty privates, all picked men...," to act in consort with Jameson's dragoon details and hang on the flanks of the British column to cut off any of the enemy's detached parties.[32]

Later, on the same evening, reports reached headquarters of the vulnerability of Howe's spread out position. With this information and still hopeful of success, Washington was spurred to make another attempt to mount an attack. As a preliminary to the main assault, Washington ordered General John Armstrong, of the Pennsylvania militia, to mount a diversionary attack against the British lines north of the city. He hoped Armstrong could prevent the enemy troops in the city from reinforcing Howe's column at Darby. On the 23rd the militia contingents formed in lower Germantown and marched against an advance British redoubt. They drove in the enemy pickets, but found their small artillery guns could not match the fire power of the British cannons. Armstrong recognized the almost impregnable British position and ordered a withdrawal. Washington's hopes and preparations would come to naught when he quickly discovered more serious conditions prevailing in the army than was evident earlier in the day. On the 23rd, unable to mask his discomfiture, he wrote to Henry Laurens, President of Congress: "...when, behold! to my great mortification, I was not only informed, but convinced, that the Men were unable to stir on Acct. of Provision, and that a dangerous Mutiny begun the Night before, and [which] with difficulty was suppressed by the spirited exertions of some officers..." To describe the "Melancholy and alarming truth" in back of the troops recalcitrance, Washington stated there wasn't any livestock of any kind and only twenty-five barrels of flour in the entire camp.[33]

On Christmas Day, Washington apparently abandoned any serious intention to take the offensive against the British lines at Philadelphia. Years after the cessation of hostilities, General Henry Knox detailed the preparations that were made for David Ramsey who was writing a history of the American Revolution. Knox implied that Washington's good judgment, reluctantly, finally recognized the utter ruin that would follow a defeat. Knox wrote that Philadelphia had been rendered impenetrable, protected as it was by a superior army and defenses. Be that as it may, Washington probably cherished a lingering hope that an opportunity would present itself to attack the enemy. On Christmas or the day after, Washington consulted with Major John Clark, one of his major sources of information on the activities of the British Army. Clark advised that an attack on Howe's force along Darby Road would be abortive as: "...they can be easily and readily reinforced from the main army." Although Clark was misinformed about the size of Howe's force, it influenced Washington's decision to confine any aggressive action to the detached details that hovered on the British flanks to prevent widespread incursions into the countryside. Colonel Tench Tilghman confirmed the presence of these units containing British activity outside their lines. In the General Orders of January 18, 1778, Washington prefaced his instructions to the Commissary and Quartermaster agents at Valley Forge which might be considered the denouement of his plan: "As the Army is now in all probability stationary for the remainder of the winter..."[34]

By December 27, Howe was aware that the foraging expedition must be terminated. The troops assigned to gathering hay and livestock had carted over 2,000 tons of hay and driven 450 sheep and 180 head of cattle back to Philadelphia. For three days heavy snow had laid its blanket over the troops' improvised bivouac. Under the existing conditions there was a grave danger of sickness facing the shivering soldiers huddled along an extended line on the Darby Road. Howe was adverse to adding more disabled men to the over 3,000 sick and wounded already crowded in the city's makeshift hospitals. To compound his problem, a rumor was circulated that Washington, with a large force, had advanced to the neighborhood of the Lancaster road. On the 28th, Howe ordered the troops recalled to the city without bothering to verify the rumor and, unquestionably, unwilling to engage the Americans under the prevailing weather conditions. The foraging parties were to pass over the Gray's Ferry pontoon bridge, after which the structure was to be dismantled. The detachments on active duty, covering the area in advance of the foragers, were to cross the Middle Bridge.[35]

With the British foraging foray winding down Washington was apparently resigned to the impracticality of mounting an offensive, but his writings reveal that he still harbored a hope that if the troops could be supplied with provisions and clothing, his plan could be revived. Was this the so-called Fabian general who had a month earlier insisted on a winter encampment for the impoverished Continental Army, and resisted any suggestion to consider a winter campaign? In all probability his silence about his strategy in December was merely an extension of the optimism manifested in October and November. Overconfident Washington would not learn until later of the odds which would have confronted the army in an attack on the British fortifications. Even after he was informed that the Continentals would have been vastly outnumbered, he remained sanguine that his strategy was sound. Washington's underestimation of the size of Howe's army ignored the military axiom that an attacking force should outnumber the defenders two to one.

It was obviously clear to Washington that for the immediate future he must put aside any thought of military action. Any lingering doubt that Philadelphia instead of Valley Forge could be substituted for the winter encampment had quickly vanished.

Chapter

III

Log Town[1]

THE VALLEY FORGE encampment represents the transition of the Continental Army into a disciplined effective fighting machine. For three months the troops suffered a succession of hardships including no meat or provisions for periods up to six days. Despite such conditions most of the troops remained loyal as capsulized by the statement of Captain William Gifford "...what can't brave Americans endure Nobly fighting for the rights of their injured Country[?]" This trying time would be followed by three months of relative plenty.

With the approach of Christmas, Washington had outwardly, at least, put aside any thought of taking military action. He was determined that the rank and file have as pleasant a day as their makeshift quarters and scanty fare permitted. It was manifestly clear that easing their suffering would not promise a bountiful or festive occasion. Nevertheless, orders were issued to insure that, at least on this day, each man would receive his allotted ration and a gill of whiskey or rum.[2]

Facing the bleak reality of the worsening conditions, Washington decided to revive the spirit of the officers by renewing, on Christmas day, a custom he had initiated in early November 1777. At that time he had exhibited an eagerness to become better acquainted with as many Continental officers as possible by extending an invitation for those on general field duty to dine with him each day at three o'clock. As a gracious host, these convivial occasions permitted him to judge the personalities and leadership qualities of those officers upon whose direction the fate of the American cause rested. Unfortunately, the hardships incurred on the march from Whitemarsh to Valley Forge had interrupted these friendly and informative gatherings, now to be resumed.[3]

The expenditures of Patrick McGuire,[4] Washington's Steward, divulge the meagerness of the menu that was offered at the Christmas dinner. McGuire records no disbursements for the Commander in Chief's table from December ninth through the twentieth. This was the period when

41

the army was on the march to Valley Forge. However, his entry for December twenty-fourth itemized all purchases for the preceding two weeks. These expenditures totaled £9 11/ —about twenty dollars— and included butter, vegetables, fowl, and meat. As the Commissary's cupboard was bare, little help could be expected from that quarter.[5]

Whatever the quantity or quality of food available, it had to satisfy the hungry appetites of up to twenty-five adults for four days. The Christmas dinner table was graced by distinguished company including the Marquis de Lafayette, Baron de Kalb, Major General John Patterson, Lieutenant Colonels Thomas Paxton and Robert Ballard, and Brigade Major Simon Learned. Also in attendance were seven aides-de-camp,[6] Captain Caleb Gibbs and Lieutenant George Lewis (Washington's nephew) of the Guard.

In addition, the skimpy fare had to provide for about ten servants of Washington and the headquarters staff. It does not require a vivid imagination to visualize the crowded conditions trying to serve this number of guests in the small headquarters house. Several weeks later, after the army was hutted, Washington would have a log hut constructed adjacent to his quarters to relieve the congestion. Washington could not furnish all the amenities necessary, such as sufficient tableware, as his knives, forks, and spoons were with the missing baggage. Nevertheless, it is reasonable to assume that while the snow storm laid its white mantle on the hills of Valley Forge, the diners enjoyed their plain fare.

Following a less than festive Christmas, the Continental soldiers, shivering in their tents, awoke to a four inch blanket of snow. Meanwhile a concerned Washington was anxious to accelerate hut construction. Disregarding the inclement weather, he rode away from headquarters to conduct a personal inspection of the camp—a habit he followed throughout the war. This was probably a carryover from his daily tour of his Mount Vernon farms.

After nearly ten weeks of the camp treadmill, it became obvious that the pressure of the officers's field assignments made it difficult to fulfill their duties and be present at the headquarter's daily dinner. Recognizing that his previous directive had placed the officers in an embarrassing position, on March 4, 1778, Washington proposed: "As the Field Officers of the day are often so busily employed in visiting the Guard the day they are on duty as not to be able to wait upon the General, He desires the pleasure of their Company to dine with him the day after when relieved."[7]

The instructions Washington had previously detailed for building the huts were for the average Continental soldier. The directives were issued because he knew most of the men lacked carpentry, or any type of construction skills. Purposely, the plans were designed as a prototype of the average hut or cabin seen throughout rural America. Washington undoubtedly anticipated some deviations from his guidelines. Valley Forge would become the first winter camp that housed the army in huts, arranged in the semblance of a line or streets.

His inspection on the day after Christmas was not expected to see total compliance with his order. He knew that the army was made up of a cross section of men from the thirteen states, with the human admixture of loyal and industrious, and a smaller number inconstant, indolent and malingerers. His tour of the camp confirmed the progress, or lack of it, by the various regiments. The slothfulness of some units was described by John Laurens when he wrote: "The North Carolinians are the most backward in their buildings, and want for sufficient energy to exert themselves once for all, will be exposed to lasting evils."[8]

Who were these young soldiers that were about to construct their homes for the winter? What were their average age, peacetime vocations, and physical descriptions? Why had they enlisted in an army that offered few comforts or advantages? Knowledge of the soldiers at Valley Forge is usually limited to the lonely sentinel standing wrapped in a tattered blanket with his feet encased in rags or an old hat. For the first ten weeks of the encampment this picture is a reasonably accurate portrayal of their condition. Valley Forge was not the coldest winter of the war, but it is unlikely that during this period, with the temperature rarely passing the freezing mark, that the young soldiers cared or thought about the severity of the weather or conditions of other years.

Occasionally history is the beneficiary of a bit of ephemera, that had been intended for private use. Through such a fragment of transitory data, the winter encampment at Valley Forge becomes more understandable.

A member of a prominent Quaker family, named Pemberton, maintained what he designated as "Meteorological Observations near Philadelphia, January 1777-10 May 1778." Twice each day Pemberton recorded the temperatures inside and outside his Bucks County home, the barometric pressure, and a description of the prevailing winds and weather. The highest outside temperature from December 19, 1777 to January 1, 1778, was 37 1/2 degrees with the lowest 6. Meteorologic data was usually recorded at eight o'clock a.m. and two o'clock p.m. In the month of January only four days reached the low 40's, although Pemberton recorded a heat wave on the 29th of 55 degrees. During the first six weeks there were thirteen days of rain or snow; with the Delaware River ice clogged from December 30 to January 8, when the river was partially opened to navigation. These meteorological observations confirm the climatic hardships which could not have offered much comfort to the oft times hungry, partially naked soldiers constructing their huts.[9]

The statistics of a recent demographic study have provided vital information about the personal and physical characteristics of the Valley Forge soldier.[10]

It was a young army Washington had at Valley Forge with the average age between twenty and twenty-four, intermixed with a sprinkling of men over thirty. The militia system of Pennsylvania, New Jersey, Delaware and Maryland usually called up men for short terms of three months and often included a scattering of older militiamen, a few in their sixties and seventies. Although militia units were not bivouacked at Valley Forge, they did play an important role in harassing British foraging parties and interrupting intercourse between Loyalist farmers and the British Army in Philadelphia.

As reflected in the demographic compilations, eighteenth century America had few men towering over six feet. The soldiers in Washington's army averaged between five feet six inches and five feet eight inches, with a scattering over or under the average. Further support for the study can be found in the construction of the huts at Valley Forge, where the doors were installed in walls six feet high.

Virtually every vocation existent in Revolutionary America was represented at Valley Forge. Farmers, or husbandmen, predominated, especially in states principally devoted to agriculture. Most of the men so classified have been assumed to be farm laborers. However, it is evident that a significant number were small landowners. Encouraged by the bounties offered, they saw a way to supplement the returns of their farmland. Washington seems to have corroborated this, when he stated that native born soldiers with a stake in the land would be more dependable in support of the American cause, than those born in Europe. In order not to cause any dissension in the ranks when choosing members for his Life Guard, he picked only native born Virginians, but directed that this selection be done quietly.

Second to those with farm backgrounds were a large number of artisans. They usually came from urban areas and covered occupations in textiles, wood-working, leather, metal-working, stone masons and miscellaneous crafts. The demographic study concludes that because of their youth most of them were probably apprentices. Also, there was a scattering of ship chandlers, ropemakers, clerks, bakers, brewers, and an occasional lawyer, surgeon's mate, scrivener, and schoolmaster. One category that was noteworthy in New England were men with maritime experience. However, the rate of desertion in this group was more noticeable, as the lure of financial gain beckoned for service on privateers.

Many times the question has been raised as to what motivated young men to enlist in an army that was haunted by neglect, hunger, nakedness, and with pay frequently months in arrears. To the foreign born, whose immediate prospects were marginal at best, the bounty offered to serve in the army seemed to open up an opportunity for a form of employment. In the early years of the war these foreigners had not developed a patriotic attachment to the United States and, particularly at Valley Forge, became disenchanted with the hardships at the camp and deserted in greater numbers than native born soldiers. Over 1,000 fled to Philadelphia compared to only 300 native Americans.[11]

Similar to their foreign born comrades, many native Americans were actuated by bounty offers, while others were inspired by a love of country; some sought the excitement of army life, and early in the conflict many resented Parliament's infringement on their rights. Regardless of motive most of these young recruits would develop a loyal hard core that held the army together. Their loyalty to America and devotion to Washington never wavered at Valley Forge. A number disclosed their sentiments during the encampment and then as veterans later in life. Major Callohill Minnis of the 1st Virginia stated: "...the commander-in-chief whom every soldier venerates and loves manifested a fatherly concern and fellow-feeling for their [soldier's] sufferings..." He added they knew Washington exerted everything in his power to relieve their hardships. On January 5, 1778, Lieutenant Colonel John N. Brooks wrote: "...nothing but Virtue has kept our Army together thro this Campaign. There has been that great Principle the Love of our Country, which first called us into the Field & that only, to influence us." Like Brooks, most soldiers blamed the Continental Congress—which he styled the "General Court"—and authorities of the various states for neglect of the army. Being less caustic, William Webb, Paymaster for the 3rd New Hampshire, wrote to his father and brother bemoaning the vicissitudes of camp life at Valley Forge. After outlining the various trials at camp, he admonished his family in a postscript: "I should be glad if you would be careful of speaking about the bad Fare of the Army, As it might be a *Discouragement* [italics Webb's] to the Men to enlist..." In later years Samuel Downing, private in the 2nd New Hampshire, commenting on his comrade's devotion to Washington declared: "We loved him. They'd sell their lives for him." These expressions of patriotism and loyalty are a capsule of many similar statements by men of the army.[12]

Harold Selesky's excellent demographic survey is the only reliable study on literacy in the Continental Army at Valley Forge. Regretfully, this compilation suffers from the loss or destruction of numerous records during the last two centuries. Nevertheless, it establishes a pattern from which the question of literacy is answered. The premise for defining literacy rests on the signatures of soldiers who had "to acknowledge receipts of wages, bounties, clothing, equipment and billeting money..." Despite some shortcomings it is evident from an extrapolation of the

45

demographic compilations that most men could at least write their names.[13]

The claim of illiteracy at Valley Forge has been based in part on the scarcity of letters written by the rank and file. This critique is not valid, if it is recognized that paper and ink were virtually unattainable to the non-commissioned officer or private. Throughout the Revolution paper was a very scarce commodity and when available was rationed in limited amounts to the brigades and regiments. At Valley Forge when a small quantity was received, Washington directed that "Paper to be issued by the Quarter Master General in the following proportion 2 quire to each Brigadier or officer commanding a brigade, 1 to each Brigade Major and six to each Regiment." With paper needed for Brigade and Regimental orders, musters, orderly books, and other brigade administration, such infrequent and small quantities left little or none for personal use. Apparently Washington had directed General Jedediah Huntington to locate paper for the army. Huntington wrote four days before the paper was distributed that: "We are poorly Supplied with Paper for use of the Troops—the General [Washington] has given me Leave to get it where I can & he will pay for it."[14]

Paper could occasionally be purchased at exorbitant prices from sutlers. However, the hungry, cold and underpaid soldier, preferred food or rum.

The racial background of the first American Army had been predominantly Anglo Saxon from New England. Now after two and a half years the army had become more cosmopolitan, as units from each of the thirteen states joined to form the Continental Army. Nevertheless, in December 1777, the ancestry of most soldiers was still English. At this time, there were, also, other patriotic native born soldiers in the ranks, including Scotchmen, Welshmen, Jewish Americans, Indians, and about 750 Black Americans. On Christmas day Jonathan Todd, Surgeon's Mate in the 7th Connecticut, wrote that a black soldier named Jethro from Guilford, Connecticut: "...belonging to Capt [Stephen] Halls Compy [company] Died in his Tent the first man that hath died in Camp belonging to our Regt." Jethro is one of the earliest soldiers recorded who gave his life for his country at Valley Forge.[15]

The entry of regiments from each state brought a significant number of men of European extraction—some relatively recent arrivals. The largest of this group were first and second generation Scotch Irish and Germans serving in Pennsylvania and Virginia regiments.

These young soldiers were observed starting to build their huts by Thomas Paine, who wrote: "I was there when the army first began to build huts. They appeared to me like a family of beavers, everyone busy; some carrying logs, others mud, and the rest plastering them together...a

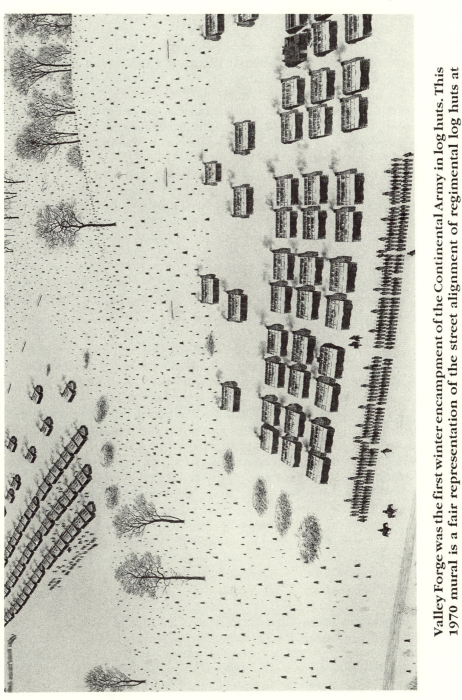

Valley Forge was the first winter encampment of the Continental Army in log huts. This 1970 mural is a fair representation of the street alignment of regimental log huts at Valley Forge. (Morristown National Historical Park.)

curious collection of buildings, in a true rustic order."[16]

During the first three months of the encampment, the army experienced periods of hunger and want, frigid and stormy weather, and bore with patience a lack of many articles of clothing and shoes. One observer noted that on New Year's day 1778, 2,000 were without shoes and some sentries were seen standing in old hats to keep their feet warm. Similarly, two soldiers from Maine, Corporal Josiah Chute and Private John Swett serving in the 11th Massachusetts Regiment stated that during the severest period of frost and snow, they were the only men of their company with shoes.[17]

In the construction of huts, while there was only a handful of proficient artisans, further frustrations occurred when a search of the Quartermaster's stores disclosed a deficiency of tools, especially axes. As one visitor to the camp recalled, even those available were of poor quality being "leaden edged." This defect was exacerbated by a shortage of wagons and horses. The horses in camp had become unfit for duty, owing to overwork and a shortage of forage.

The men felled trees and cut logs of sixteen and eighteen foot lengths. The remainder of the tree trunk was not to be wasted; smaller branches adaptable to making abatis and fascines were to be stockpiled for use on the soon to be constructed fortifications, with the residue to be taken by the men for firewood. Occasionally, necessity forced all members of the mess to assist in dragging timbers to their designated hut site. This duty became more arduous as the supply of trees in the vicinity of camp became exhausted forcing the men to go a greater distance for others.

Washington's instructions for hut construction had been a virtual prototype of the average log cabin built in Colonial America. In building a hut or cabin of round logs, ax handles usually served as a measuring instrument. It was believed: "...not necessary, or even desirable, to strip off the bark, which, left in place *[sic]*, served to protect the walls from decay."[18] It is improbable that hewn or partially hewn logs were employed in the construction of the rank and file quarters. However, they were used for varying purposes in the huts of officers and brigade hospitals. A riving tool called a froe (frow)[19] was used to split flooring, boards, and shingles from hewn logs. The froe was also used to cut fraise pickets for installation on the redoubt's ramparts.[20]

On New Years day 1778, Washington stated that: "A considerable number of Froes and some Axes are ready to be issued..." This may have made such instruments available to some of the men.[21]

Unlike most American log huts built for permanent habitation, those at Valley Forge were pitted, that is dug out to a depth of one to two feet below the surface of the terrain. There is no evidence Washington issued instructions to pit the huts. In lowering the hut floor below the frost line and banking the base of the outside wall with mud and earth, it prevented a loss of heat and made for a warmer and more comfortable shelter. However, the disadvantages of pitting far outweighed the benefits, as it contributed to excessive dampness in the huts. Washington became convinced that the use of sunken floors, coupled with the wide us of "sod and turf" to roof huts had been the chief cause for an inordinate high rate of sickness at Valley Forge.

He reaffirmed this opinion on December 14, 1778, as winter camp was being established at Middlebrook, New Jersey. In the General Orders of that date he noted that:

> Much of the sickness among the Troops seems to have been occasioned by the improper method in forming many of the Hutts last Winter; Some being sunk in the ground and others covered with Earth; To avoid consequences of a similar nature as far as in our power from occurring again, The Commander in Chief directs, that all the officers on the grounds see that their men observe the Instruction of the Quarter Master General [Nathanael Greene] in the formation of their huts. That they be roofed with boards, slabs or large shingles; That the men be not suffered to dig into the ground (except so far as to level the surface) or to cover their huts with earth or turf.

The latter had, also, been an unwise expedient and added its contribution to the dampness. This order clearly manifests Washington's alertness to the dire health problems of the previous encampment at Valley Forge. He had earlier brought this condition to the attention of the President of Congress stating: "...we have had more leisure to make some little preparations, for Winter quarters, I hope they be in a more comfortable situation than they were in the preceeding Winter." In January 1779, Lieutenant William Gifford commented that their quarters were excellent compared to those at Valley Forge, adding that he nevertheless did not regard the winter there as a hardship and: "I would do it again and again if it were for the good of America."[22]

Although the mistakes in hut construction would subsequently be recognized in late 1778, the urgency of immediate shelter for the troops took precedence. The health danger inherent in the dampness caused by sunken floors and sod and turf roofs was probably the result of ignorance or unfamiliarity with hut and cabin building. As mentioned, the efforts of the men were hampered by a reported shortage of tools. It is known that a limited quantity of implements was available but, also, there were questions about their quality. However, on December 22, Colonel Mark Bird, of the Pennsylvania Militia at Reading, dispatched a shipment of 500 picks, 1,000 spades, and 1,000 shovels to camp—useful tools in digging the sunken floors. As previously noted, Washington announced a supply of froes and axes were available. These tools may have been supplemented by additional items in the armys quartermaster's stores.[23]

In construction a foundation of semi-dressed stones was placed in each corner of the sunken area, with an occasional stone, if available, midway between the corners. The first tier of logs was placed on these stones. Each succeeding layer was laid in cross sections, crudely notched and overlapping a few inches at the corners. Space between the logs, that formed the walls, was wedged tightly with small pieces of wood and stones, mixed with local clay soil, called daubing or chinking. Bunks lined the inner side walls, with a chimney and fireplace in a corner of the rear wall. The scarcity of stone and the urgency to complete the huts forced some deviations from Washington's order to line the fireplaces with eighteen inches of stone.

Most officers started to construct their huts at the same time the rank and file—Thomas Paine's "busy beavers"—were building their quarters. Officer's huts, other than the commanders of brigades and regiments, varied little from the basic cabins of the troops. However, a number of interior changes were made including board floors, one or two windows and an occasional division of the hut into two small rooms. Although it cannot be satisfactorily substantiated, the soldiers probably covered the doors of their huts with cloth, or any materials they could beg or borrow, to keep out the blasts of cold winter winds.

On January 19, 1778, Sergeant Jonathan Todd in a letter to his father probably epitomized the typical officer's hut. He wrote the hut was constructed as directed by the Commander in Chief, "18 feet Long & 16 broad...." His cabin was divided into "two Rooms [with] two Chimneys at opposite corners of the house—the Floor is made of split loggs as is the Partition of the Door."[24]

Following the completion of their huts, most of those soldiers sufficiently clad and physically able were assigned to guard and fatigue details or duty at Sullivan's bridge. A number were directed to assist in building "flying hospital huts," shelters for prisoners of the Provost, scores of auxiliary structures for the armorers, blacksmiths, commissariats and quartermaster's stores, and other needs of the army.

As the days passed a deeply concerned Washington began to receive continual reports of a worsening sickness—probably camp or putrid fever—among the troops. At the time dampness in the huts was not recognized as the principal cause of this condition. The severity of the medical problem called for the immediate building of brigade hospitals, probably similar to the "flying hospital huts" designed for regiments. The danger of contagion was rife in the close confines of the huts necessitating the speedy transfer of the sick to a facility where they could receive proper attention from the doctors. In addition, Washington decided that all soldiers who had not been vaccinated against smallpox should be, with all additional regiments or recruits to receive similar medical treatment before reaching Valley Forge.

On January 9, Washington directed each major general and those commanding brigades to assign a location for a hospital to be erected near each brigade: "...as soon as the men can be possibly spared from working on the huts..." Four days later, with the sick reaching alarming numbers, he ordered: "Two such hospitals are to be made for each brigade in their rear, as near the center as may be; and if the ground admits of it not more than three, nor less than one hundred yards from it." The hospitals were to be fifteen feet by twenty-five feet, at least nine feet high, and to be covered with boards or shingles. A window was to be made on each side with a fireplace at one end. On January 13, after mature reflection, Washington considered the dampness in the hospitals a jeopardy to the sick men, and ordered no dirt floors or sod roofs.[25]

To add further anguish to his duties as Commander in Chief, Washington was alerted to the crowded and unsanitary conditions at the Provost's quarters in an old log barn where large numbers of soldiers and civilians were confined. Many had been detained for unreasonable periods on minor infractions while awaiting trial or court-martial. To relieve this inhuman treatment, he ordered the Quartermaster General to erect as many huts as needed. A location was to be selected between or near the outer or inner lines.[26]

The larger huts of generals and colonels were patterned after the smaller quarters of other regimental officers. These structures had to accommodate aides-de-camp and provide space for performance of their many duties. Some aides may have been housed in their superior's quarters or in a smaller adjacent hut. Frequently the generals' and colonels' quarters were the scene of brigade and regimental courts-martial.

An interesting example of the building of a brigadier's hut was that of Brigadier General Charles Scott. The erection of Scott's quarters was entrusted to Colonel James Wood's 12th Virginia Continental Regiment. Major Samuel Hopkins of Wood's regiment was assigned to supervise a work party composed of a sergeant and fifteen soldiers. Hopkins was ordered to consult with Scott to determine the general's wishes for the hut's dimensions and appointments. This directive seems to indicate that the huts of brigadiers were fabricated in accordance with the individual general's desires and requirements. To ensure compliance with Scott's instructions, the Brigade Quartermaster was to oversee the work of Hopkin's detail. Most brigadiers like Scott, Huntington, and Varnum, at least, lived part of the time in huts. In late May General Henry Knox advised his brother that he was in "...My Hut in the centre of the [Artillery]

51

Washington's Headquarters at Valley Forge. (Valley Forge National Historical Park.)

Park." Apparently some generals preferred to be quartered near their commands, although others resided for a period in houses designated as their headquarters.[27]

On December 20, 1777, General Jedediah Huntington wrote his brother: "I am going to build me a House in the Woods, what do you think of the Armys making two thousand Log Houses[28] in all the Regularity of an Encampment." One month later he noted: "...one Business crowds so close upon the Huts of another as to forbid Recreation. The Brigadiers are become Sope [soap] boilers, Oilmen, Armourers—Tanners—Shoemakers and the Lord knows what..." In April Huntington's hut was occupied by General James Varnum, whose headquarters had been turned over to the Orderly Officer. During the last two months of the encampment courts-martial and Courts of Enquiry were held at Varnum's hut.[29]

When Washington occupied the Isaac Potts house at Christmas, it instantly became evident that it was inadequate to accommodate the staff and his multifarious duties as Commander in Chief. His desire to become better acquainted with the field officers of the day, by inviting them to dinner each afternoon at three o'clock, obviously aggravated the cramped conditions. He ordered the construction of a log dining cabin to relieve this condition and provide a more relaxed atmosphere at these dinners. By January 9, work on this structure was underway according to Gideon Savage of Captain William Mills's company of Artillery Artificers. Savage recorded in his diary that he was "Working at General Washington's Quarters." Intermittently through February 12, his diary carried succinct entries stating "Still working at the Generals." There are no entries after the twelfth, but the dining hut was probably ready for occupancy shortly thereafter.[30]

Martha Washington arrived at Valley Forge after February 1, but before the ninth. On the first, Washington wrote to John Parke Custis (Martha's son): "Your mamma is not yet arrived, but if she left Mount Vernon on the twenty sixth ultimo, as intended, may, I think be expected every hour." In anticipation of Martha's imminent arrival, Washington dispatched his aide Lieutenant Colonel Richard Kidder Meade to escort her to headquarters. Fitzpatrick believed she arrived at camp on February second or third. At least she was at Valley Forge before the ninth when Lafayette at Flemington, New Jersey, wrote Washington: "Will you give me leave to inclose my most affectionate respect to your lady." On March 7, Martha, in a letter to Mercy Warren, noted the efficacy of the dining hut: "The General's apartment is very small, He has had a log cabin built to dine in, which has made our quarters much more tolerable than at first."[31]

In reading the letters, diaries, and journals of officers and soldiers, a

Twenty Fifth Page.

From here we marchd to the Valley
Forge in order to take up Winter
Quarters here we built huts in the
following manner   the huts are
built in three lines   each line
four deep five yards asunder   the
huts eighteen by sixteen feet long
six feet to the eves built of loggs
and covered with staves   the chimney
in the east end the door in the
South side   the Officers   huts in the
rear of the mens twelve men in
each hut and two cores of Officers
in a hut

Ensign George Ewing's description of hut construction.
(*George Ewing, a gentleman, a Soldier of Valley Forge.*)

lucid picture unfolds of their hut building experiences. Most of their accounts reflect a close adherence to Washington's instructions. On December 19, 1777, Joseph Clark recounted that: "...the Valley Forge...we immediately struck up temporary huts covered with leaves." Clark does not indicate the precise location of these quarters, but is the only diarist who mentions living in brush huts until the permanent winter shelters were erected. Lieutenant Thomas Blake noted that the ground was staked out to build huts of round logs, most being covered with straw and earth. An observant Ensign, George Ewing, furnished a more detailed description of the camp layout. He recorded that the huts were eighteen by sixteen feet, with the exterior walls six feet to the roof; adding the huts were in three lines with twelve men in each hut, and to their rear a street of two "cores" of officers to a hut.[32]

A somewhat satirical Second Lieutenant Archilaus Lewis reported that: "...we have built us huts to live in which are comfortable and as long as I can get a jackknife and Gimblet [Gimlet] with Timbers, I Shall never dispair of having a Home." In his usual verbose manner, Surgeon's Mate Jonathan Todd gave his father a clear likeness of his hut-mates and their quarters. With Todd were an adjutant, Quartermaster, chaplain, paymaster, and two doctors. He said they had one ax, and no other tools, to build their "log hut," adding it was eighteen by sixteen feet. The hut was divided into two rooms, with two chimneys at opposite corners, with the floor, partitions, and doors made of split logs, the roof was slab topped by turf and earth. A statement by Lieutenant James M. McMichael confirms that there were varying numbers of officers in the different huts. His shelter had "Captain Robert Gray, Mr. Garman and myself."[33]

Many other accounts offer similar descriptions of the soldier's experiences in building their "Log Town" but, surprisingly, virtually all declared the crude huts were warm and comfortable. Lieutenant James McMichael recalled that on January 14, Colonel Walter Stewart "summoned" all officers of the 13th Pennsylvania Regiment to dine with him. This "day in civil jolity" was followed by several days of dinners "in rotation from the senior to the junior officers," at their respective quarters. Like McMichael, George Ewing describes the camaraderie that prevailed in the officers' huts, especially those of officers from regiments of neighboring states. Ewing, although absent from the camp for six weeks in February and March, happily relates the visitation of friends and relatives, some remaining several nights. Other officers had occasional visitors or spent a convivial evening at the theatre, in comradeship, or partaking in a game of cards.[34]

The rank and file had few visitors because of the crowded conditions of their huts. In 1795, Henry Woodman was informed that "inferior officers had single huts." This privacy was especially enjoyed by sergeants, who occasionally had a female companion, either his wife or, contrary to orders, a camp follower.

Many officer's wives and area women were engaged in dispensing cheer to the soldiers. However, Martha Washington was the most faithful visitor as virtually every clear day she was seen entering the various huts to offer comfort to the men. Once, accompanied by a sixteen year old neighbor of headquarters, she entered the hut of a dying sergeant whose young wife was with him. Later in life the young girl, then Mrs. Westlake added: "His case seemed to particularly touch the heart of the good lady, and after she had given him some wholesome food she had prepared with her own hands, she knelt down by his straw pallet and prayed earnestly for him and his wife..."[35]

The comment in Loyalist's letters to government officials in Great Britain had a tendency to underplay the ability and determination of the Americans to carry on the war. Pennsylvania's foremost Loyalist and Superintendent General in occupied Philadelphia, Joseph Galloway, predicted a total dissolution of the American Army by the spring of 1778. He was sanguine that Washington's: "miscreant Troop...[was] mouldering and must moulder to nothing before Spring." In another letter he advised Lord Dartmouth that the Americans were existing at Valley Forge in "very uncomfortable Lodgings," that their men and horses have been "reduced to the greatest distress." The consequence of these sufferings had resulted in "much Disease and great Desertions."[36]

When the Continental Army marched out of the Valley Forge area in June 1778, they left the hospital and other huts filled with hundreds of sick. They were attended by regimental officers, surgeons and their mates, with convalescents and selected camp followers as nurses. In early October the last of the recovered sick, except for a number of malingerers, were dispatched singly and by detachments to rejoin their units.

The final days of the old encampment were recorded by American, British and Hessian officers, who later bivouacked in the old huts, and by a visit of George Washington to the camp.

Six months after the Continentals marched out of a forward position near Valley Forge, Burgoyne's Convention army—that had surrendered at Saratoga—passed through the area on their way to prisoner of war camps in Virginia. For two days they occupied the camp's huts. After reconnoitering the Valley Forge position, Lieutenant Thomas Anburey was desirous of learning more about the conditions that existed in the old encampment. He was quartered at the house of a Valley Forge Loyalist, who provided him with a graphic description of the life of the American soldiers during the previous winter. Anburey detailed the crude construction of the huts, their discomfort in the inclement weather, and the subsequent excessive sickness caused by these hardships. A sickness or "camp disorder" had paralyzed the army's effectiveness. His Loyalist host particularized the lack of shoes, stockings, and other clothing with the resultant nakedness of the troops. Such conditions caused a "wasting away" of the men and contributed to the "extreme mortality" in the camp hospitals. Anburey was told there were at least eleven hospital huts. He repeated the intelligence submitted by other British intelligence sources, that numerous desertions occurred at Valley Forge. Anburey's informant mentioned the devastating losses of horses—a fact confirmed by Washington—a condition that rarely made enough horses available to move the artillery in an emergency.[37]

Du Roi made similar notations, stating: "...huts, about 3000, are built in lines, and are made of beams covered with glue. These huts had been built in three weeks and...looks like a badly built town."[38]

Nearly three years later, Lieutenant Enos Reeves arrived in the vicinity of Valley Forge where he: "...dined near Moor Hall, came thro' our old encampment, or rather first huts of the whole army. Some of the officers's huts are inhabited, but the greater part are decayed, some are split up into rails, and a number of fine fields are to be seen on the level ground that was cleared, but in places where they have let the shoots grow, it is already like a half grown young wood."[39]

These observations were the last recording that huts remained standing at the former encampment. A later visitor has left impressions of the site in the eighteenth century. While attending the Constitutional Convention, a reflective George Washington, rode out to the old camp sites around Philadelphia. On Tuesday, July 31, 1787, he recorded: "...I rid over the [whole] old Cantonment of the American [Army] of the Winter, of 1777 and 8, visited all the Works, wch. were in Ruins; and the Incampments in the woods where the grounds had not been cultivated." Nearly three weeks later he: "...rode up to the White Marsh, traversed my old Incampment, and contemplated on the dangers which threatened the American Army at that place." The visits to these closely linked encampments were undoubtedly filled with evocative memories of the trying days in the fight for American Independence.[40]

Henry Woodman wrote that his father frequently related a cherished chance meeting with Washington in 1796. The elder Woodman recalled that while ploughing a field that was formerly a part of the front line of the encampment, an elderly dignified gentleman, dressed in a plain black suit, accompanied by a black servant;[41] engaged him in conversation about the methods of agriculture used by farmers near Valley Forge. In their dialogue, both men soon revealed their presence in the Continental Army during the memorable winter of 1777-78. Then the man in the black suit introduced himself as George Washington. Somewhat aghast, Woodman apologized for not recognizing his former Commander in Chief because he was not in uniform and his appearance had altered through the years. Washington, acknowledging the change, responded his second term as President would soon expire and he would be leaving Philadelphia, probably never to return. Woodman is the only source to mention this visit of Washington to Valley Forge. However, this is not out of character for Washington who had an all consuming love for husbandry, and a never diminishing desire to visit the scenes of the glories and trials of his Continentals. It is unfortunate that this encounter with Woodman cannot be verified as Washington's diaries for 1796 are missing.[42]

With the men safely ensconced in their winter quarters, attention was quickly diverted to the pressing need to effect camp security and relieve shortages in provisions and forage.

Chapter
IV

Trying Time

AS THE ARMY approached Valley Forge, Washington was optimistic that the fundamental courage of his soldiers would survive the winter if their hardships were alleviated. Changes would be brought about by his persistent importunings and directives. He beseeched assistance from the Continental Congress, various states, and the reorganized Quartermaster and Commissary Departments. Slowly, through their combined efforts, a trickle of the needed commodities reached an adequate if not overabundant flow. To Washington it was manifest that in some areas that army had to become self-sufficient. His concern was for such items as shoes, candles, soap and, to a degree, the conversion of cloth into uniforms. Even if these articles were available, the scarcity of horses and wagons would make it difficult to transport them to camp. Washington combed the ranks for tailors, shoemakers, and artificers—those qualified he would exempt from service in the line. Some states adopted a similar policy and excused men from military duty if they would volunteer to work in a service capacity. Pennsylvania made this gesture by exempting wagonmasters from militia duty. Most of the soldiers had been farm hands or small landowners, therefore virtually every hut had those familiar with soap and candle making with at least one adept at cooking in each mess. Apparently the soldiers in each hut quickly discovered the best cook in their midst, as one soldier noted "...onely I was chose cook for our room consisting of 12 men..."[1]

By March 1778, with little improvement in the drudgery of their existence, Washington applauded the firmness and resolve of most soldiers to the cause for which they were fighting. Under the circumstances, he expressed amazement that the army had not mutinied and dispersed throughout the countryside, adding that such an occurrence would have happened "in most other Armies." He recalled vividly the ragtag, undisciplined army that marched to Valley Forge. Washington's faith in his Continentals would eventually be justified, but he could not in March have envisioned the transformation that would take place before the summer campaign. After overcoming the vicissitudes of the winter and undergoing a rigorous program of drill and discipline, the same soldiers would emerge as a prideful and efficient fighting machine.[2]

Who can better describe the conditions at Valley Forge than those who lived through that fateful winter of 1777-78? Their letters and journals offer a poignant word picture of the struggle for survival of the Continental Army. From the Commander in Chief through the men in the ranks, there is a singular unanimity in their descriptions of the sufferings, yet a firm resolve to face the common cause.

Washington's anger mounted as he witnessed the carelessness and indifference of a number of officers to the needs of their men. Since Whitemarsh he had berated the inattention of those officers who neglected to daily oversee the men's "necessaries."

The orders of Lieutenant John Irvin, adjutant of the 2nd Pennsylvania regiment, vividly summarizes the unhappiness and anger of Wayne and other general officers with those line officers guilty of irresponsibility to their duties. His graphic condemnation of the conduct of these inattentive officers noted that sick soldiers were "...Suffering from Want of Necessaries or proper Care or Attention Either in the Officers or Surgeons." Irvin, with annoyance, describes the needless personal disputes among officers. Acknowledging Wayne's awareness of such pettiness, Irvin wrote: "The general suffers very Sensible pain that the officers of the army are insensible to the good of the service...he Wishes the Officers of this Army to Consider themselves a band of Brothers Cemented by the Justice of the Common Cause: that a perfect harmony might Subsist Among them. And that they Would Settle all personal Disputes Amongst themselves in an Amicable Manner...." In conclusion Irvin warned that more attention must be directed to the cleanliness and comfort of the men—such as making certain the men have their hair cut regularly. These sentiments echo the repeated appeals by Washington for all concerned to subordinate personal differences to unity for the common cause.[3]

Pennsylvania was not alone in its disenchantment with their officers. Virginia was equally disturbed by the return home of officers who had resigned during the early days at Valley Forge. When they reached Virginia they quickly discovered "...that every man, who remains home is making a fortune, whilst they are spending what they have, in defense of their Country." Thomas Nelson wrote Washington that no "spark of Patriotic fire" remained to induce these officers to rejoin the army. They were determined to remain home to enhance their personal fortunes. With these conditions, and the prevalence of wet, cold, hunger, and partial nakedness, Thomas Paine's pithy statement that these were "the times that try mens souls" could apply to the Continental Army at Valley

Forge.[4]

An overview of the "trying time" is graphically portrayed in the writings of rank and file and officers. Their statements, when bemoaning hardship, were also critical of the indifference and inability of weak civilian bodies and army service departments to relieve their suffering. Despite these gloomy prospects, many accounts evince a positive attitude toward the future of America. Sprinkled throughout the writings are steadfast expressions of love of family and country, a faith in God and an unfaltering confidence in Washington, "so good a Man as his Excellency."

When the weary army marched into Valley Forge on December 19, 1777, it became apparent that no provisions were on hand to feed the troops. Ignoring their hunger the soldiers, who had suffered through periods of want before, angrily received the disquieting knowledge that an abundance of foodstuff was in supply throughout Pennsylvania. However, there were no teams or drivers obtainable to transport a single barrel of flour. To exacerbate the situation, a few more fortunate—at least their less lucky comrades thought so—had a limited supply of beef and flour. Unfortunately it was found to be inedible. A committee of inquiry had been appointed by Baron de Kalb to investigate the rumor that these items available to the brigades of Generals Ebenezer Learned and John Paterson had spoiled. The officers' report stated that the beef was "not fit for the Use of human Beings, unwholesome and destructive to nature for any person to make use of as food;" while the "flours being sour is almost of no use." The provision shortage and much of the noxious food available laid the groundwork for the intermittent empty larders that confronted the hungry soldiers until mid-March.[5]

A composite of the writings from camp form a vivid account of the daily routine of a squad of twelve soldiers in any hut. We can visualize the almost naked occupants of a hut huddled around the fireplace in an effort to escape cold blasts of winter. This would have been a comfort difficult to find as the soldier's huts, unlike the officers, had neither doors or windows. The acrid smoke of the green wood caused a constant burning of the eyes. Adding to their aggravation was the necessity that the men venture over a half mile from camp to obtain firewood and then, under grueling physical conditions, carry or drag the logs back to their huts. As at Whitemarsh, many soldiers preferred, against specific orders, to use the small branches trimmed from trees or saplings placed in front of their position as abatis.

When summoned for guard or fatigue duty, messmates would unselfishly lend whatever scanty items of clothing they had to those going on assignment. Usually this forced the lenders to remain confined to their hut until the return of comrades from duty. There was an equal shortage

Nineteenth-century drawing by Felix O.C. Darley depicting the hardships at Valley Forge. (Dover Publications, Inc.)

of shoes with a number of sentries standing in old hats as substitute footwear.

The intolerable conditions in the huts and the absence of food for days at a time, capsules their travails at Valley Forge. Washington was aware of the despondency of the men who believed they had been neglected by their country, but still believed it worth fighting for. The lowering of morale contributed to the uncleanliness at camp, aggravated by officers' inattention to maintaining a wholesome atmosphere in their unit's bivouac areas. Washington, concerned with the health of the army, realized that unless corrected these conditions posed a hygienic problem. Although empathizing with the men's anger over their conditions, Washington knew the camp had to be regularly policed to ensure a clean area—unfortunately these orders were never continuously obeyed. Of immediate and equal importance was the need to attack the root of the problem, by bending every effort to awaken the country's conscience to the deplorable state of its army.

Albeit, while Washington, his generals and a number of patriotic civilian authorities lamented the situation at camp, it was manifest that it would take time to galvanize a sluggish citizenry into recognizing their obligations. Several observers considered the delay a product of indifference, and by some a purposeful disobedience of orders. Nathanael Greene summarized what he considered "a restrained indictment" of the existence of such conditions at Valley Forge, claiming it was a "lasting symbol of suffering and hardship." Greene's observations were the consequence of witnessing the early collapse of the clothier, quartermaster and commissary departments.[6]

The adversities of the army's life at Valley Forge would be repeated time and again throughout the Revolution. Most veterans of the army who survived the winter of 1777-78, candidly referred to that period as the turning point of the war—from despair and distress an army was born. As Greene campaigned in North Carolina in 1781, many of his troops, who had served at Valley Forge, reflected on their present suffering as a capsule of that trying winter.[7]

Writings emanating from the encampment have left us an animated series of portrayals of the trials and tribulations of the army. These accounts depict the heartfelt solicitude of the officers for the men, as well as an overview of the soldiers' just complaints.

A compassionate Lafayette wrote: "The unfortunate soldiers were in want of everything; they had neither coats nor hats, nor shirts, nor shoes; their feet and their legs froze till they grew black and it was often necessary to amputate them...The Army frequently passed whole days without food..." On this point Lafayette agreed with Washington that "the patience endurance of the soldiers and officers was a miracle." Von

Steuben remarked on the "simplicity" of the men's clothing, because they were "literally naked," adding there was little consistency in the makeshift garb of the officers, either as to make or color. Exasperated, Steuben caustically noted that the officers mounted guard in a non-descript dressing gown made of an old blanket or woolen bed cover. The Prussian could have ironically mentioned that the trappings of the men consisted of a patchwork robe and hats substituting for shoes.

As they inspected their commands most colonels of regiments help-lessly viewed the pitiful lot of the men. Writing home they implored governors and anyone who could exert influence to redress the horren-dous conditions. Colonel Philip Van Courtlandt, of the 2nd New York, appealed to Governor George Clinton to help his soldiers who were suffering "beyond description" for want of every article of clothing. He reported that seventy men in his regiment were unfit for duty, of whom twenty "have no breeches at all." When obtainable they used blankets to cover their nakedness. Others were destitute of shirts, stocking or shoes which left him with thirty men fit for duty. Bemoaning the large number of sick and lame, he predicted the entire regiment would soon be incapacitated. The crippled and laboring who were able had to go over a half mile to wood and water with "bare legs in snow and mud."

In a similar vein, on February 12, Colonel Richard Butler, of the 9th Pennsylvania, wrote to Thomas Wharton, President of the Pennsylvania Assembly, that the soldiers in his regiment: "...are totally naked for body Cloathing & not a blanket to Seven men, I have been obliged to retain the Tents to Substitute for blankets to keep them from the Inclemency of the Season at night..." He added all Pennsylvania regiments were in a similar pitiful condition. Butler's retention of the tents was a desperate act, contrary to Washington's orders to collect all tents after the huts were erected, and then cleaned and stored for the forthcoming 1778 cam-paign.[8]

Lieutenant Colonel Samuel Carlton advised General William Heath (stationed at Hudson River) that it was heartrending to witness soldiers mounting guard or go on fatigue with naked feet on snow and ice; stating with bitterness that "It would grieve the heart even of that Cruel Tyrant of Brittain."[9]

Only one brigade reported their men enjoyed more comfort than most of their counterparts. Major Richard Platt, aide-de-camp to General Alexander McDougall, advised the general, who was stationed along the Hudson River, that his brigade was the best clad in the army. Because the other brigades were almost naked, Platt noted McDougall's brigade was forced to furnish over a quarter of the guard and fatigue duties required at the camp. Ironically, in contrast to the prevailing shortage of cloth in the army, his brigade, according to Platt, had an excess of £600 of cloth which the troops did not need or want.[10]

Contrary to Platt's note of optimism, Colonel Henry B. Livingston, of the 4th New York, complained his soldiers were naked and in a starving condition. After blaming the commissaries for these problems, he harshly criticized their negligence for causing the death of all regimental horses. In summarizing his grievances, he described the pathetic state of his regiment: "...all my men except 18 are unfit for duty for want of shoes, stockings and shirts, breeches and coats...and are becoming exceedingly lousy." The same could be said for all the other brigades.[11]

An observant, Thomas Jones, said there was a steady stream of generals and line officers to headquarters where they registered dissatisfaction with the distressful conditions in their commands. Second Lieutenant Archilaus Lewis, 1st Massachusetts, was sharply critical of the Massachusetts authorities that permitted entire regiments, including his own, to be "...naked, barefooted and destitute of Money to help themselves." Sardonically he denounced those safe in their own domiciles, stating "I shall wish myself at home...why should we trouble or concern ourselves...let them lookout for themselves..." Although Lewis's anger was possibly a tongue in cheek comment, it was apparently nearly mutinous.[12]

A more patriotic appeal for understanding was addressed by Lieutenant Colonel John Cropper, 11th Virginia, to his wife. He beseeched her to understand why he did not apply for a furlough. Cropper explained that he couldn't abandon his duty in: "...saving my distress'd Country, tottering at this time on the brink of ruin; My dear! Excuse your husband for doing what he thinks is right! Excuse in him an overfondness for his Country's cause! Don't think him insensible of a husband's affection or the distress of an absent wife..."[13]

That the failure to provide the bare necessities for the soldiers created health and hygienic problems is partly described by General Lachlan McIntosh who stated his brigade had been decimated by the death of fifty men between late January and early March.

Equally disturbed was General Enoch Poor who was crestfallen by the sight of the sufferings of the men in his brigade. Empathizing with the men, Poor could not bring himself to punish those attempting to desert. Another general, Jedidiah Huntington, commenting on the troops being forced to live on half allowance for many days, expressed gratitude for the presence of the Congressional Committee in camp. He hoped their influence would rectify the shortages.[14]

General John Paterson implored Colonel Thomas Marshall, home on leave, to exert his prestige with the Massachusetts Council to supply the states regiments with clothing, declaring that conditions are ten times worse than when the colonel left camp. Paterson asserted: "Out of Seven

Hundred and fifty six Rank and file present (excluding those on command or in the hospital) I have four hundred and fifty returned unfit for Duty for want of shoes an other clothing—"[15]

Among a number of soldiers there was a reluctance to worry those back home with the privations at camp. In certain instances if they enumerated the difficulties at camp, they would admonish their loved ones not to reveal their distress. Such a revelation would discourage enlistments and bring embarrassment to the Commander in Chief.

On the other hand, a number of soldiers after suffering through periods of hunger and cold, with no foreseeable relief in sight, gave vent to expressions of utter despair. Others, with Spartan resolve, drolly accepted the austere conditions in camp. Ebenezer Wild somewhat lightheartedly wrote that they had only two kettles to prepare meals for an entire company. With equal witticism he said "the meat was broiled over the fire, spitted on a bayonet, and the bread was baked in the hot ashes." Hopefully, at least, the latter problem was corrected with the arrival of Christopher Ludwick's bakers.[16]

As noted, some soldier's letters were written without a grievance or mention of a hardship that might cause anxiety to those at home. Samuel Harris wrote an affectionate letter to his "Beloved Wife with the Blessing of God I am in Good Health." He concluded with the wish "that we shall be Contanted [contented] with our Lots in Life."[17]

Before concluding this chapter and exploring what was done to address the hardships at camp, three quotations poignantly drop the curtain on the suffering and fortitude at Valley Forge.

One chronicle is a searching version of a Massachusetts officer, who describes in detail the deficiency of everything needed for their comfort, and his embitterment with the neglect and indifference of the civilians. He lambasted them for ignoring the brave defenders of America encamped at Valley Forge. Captain Joseph Hodgkins, of the 15th Massachusetts—with his quaint orthography—offers a delightful appraisal of his experiences.[18] Hodgkins wrote:

> I am in grate hast as the Barer is waiting I must just inform you that what our soldiers have suffred this Winter is Beyond Expression as one half has Ben Bare foot & all most Naked all winter the other half Very Badly on it for Clothes of all sorts and to ComPleat our misery Very shorte on it for Provision not Long since our Brigade drue [drew] But an half Days a-Lowance of Meat in Eight Day But these Defeltis [difficulties] the men Bore with a Degree of fortitude Becoming soldiers But I must say one word to the people at home who I fear have Lost all Bowles [bowels] of compassion if Ever had any for the Country Towns have Provided Clothing for their men and Brought them to Camp But as there has Ben none from the seaport Towns I fear they have Lost all there Public Spirit I would Beg of them to

Rouse from there stupedity and Put on som humanity and stir themselves Before it is too Late I would not [?] have them think hard of maintaining there soldiers for what the soldiers has suffered the past year Desarves a Penshon During Life...

As a postscript Hodgkins implored his wife to "have some shirts for me against I get home for I am all naked."

A moving climax is offered by Thomas Wharton, Jr., President of the Pennsylvania Assembly. Wharton wrote to Washington on March 10 expressing his compassion and consolation for the resolve of the troops: "The unparalleled patience and magnanimity with which the army, under your Excellency's command, have endured the hardships attending their situation, unsupplied as they have been through an uncommonly severe winter, is an honor which posterity will consider as more illustrious than could have been derived to them by a victory obtained by any sudden and vigorous exertion."[19]

In reply to critics on the problems at Valley Forge, a pungent opinion of those captious individuals is contained in a letter of Washington. It served as a denouement to the camp's troubles. In commenting on the "dreadful situation" of the army, he wrote it is more alarming than can be conceived and "to form a just idea, it would be necessary to be on the spot."[20]

Chapter

V

Barefoot and Otherwise Naked

T HE LACK OF adequate clothing in the army was evident from the day in June 1775, when Washington reviewed the tatterdemalion militia companies. However, of immediate importance to Washington was not the uniformity of dress, but the molding of himself and the inherited aggregation of militiamen into an effective fighting machine. The difficulty of properly outfitting the army would gradually worsen over the next two and a half years and finally reach a crisis at Valley Forge.

During the first year of the Revolution, Congress had ignored the need to cover the nakedness of the troops. After the Declaration of Independence, it became manifestly clear that if the United States was to conduct a successful war against Great Britain, a permanent army must be organized. Finally in October 1776, in an effort to encourage men to enlist for the duration of the conflict, a clothes bounty was offered to all recruits. An unusual provision was included in the bounty offer which displayed Congress's casual approach to the affairs and conduct of an army—if the enlistee preferred he could have money equivalent to purchase his own outfit. This completely disregarded uniformity of dress in the army.

The clothes bounty authorized by Congress for those who rejected the money offer was for: "two linen hunting shirts, two pair of overalls, a leathern or woolen waistcoat, two pair of breeches, a hat or leathern cap, two shirts, two pair of hose, and two pair of shoes." Like all good intentions to aid the troops, these items seldom reached them.[1]

Meanwhile, Washington sensible to the scarcity of cloth and its excessive cost had been reluctant to advocate a standard uniform for the army. In July 1776, with many soldiers in a naked condition, he suggested that they be outfitted in hunting shirts, which Congress adopted in three months. Washington recommended the shirts be supplemented with long breeches of similar cloth "Gaiter fashion about the Legs." If these overall type uniforms were obtainable, he thought they would be desirable for summer and winter with "under Cloathes" added for comfort during the latter period. With tongue in cheek Washington added that this garb would strike terror in the enemy, believing all Americans were marksmen.[2]

Eleven months later a dawdling Congress acknowledged that all provisions of the bounty had not been fulfilled. They had been unable to procure a sufficient quantity of cloth to tailor all the hunting shirts needed. Congress recommended a substitution of regimental coats without specifying where the cloth could be obtained, nor the style or color as a step toward standardization.[3]

Many of the troops that marched into Valley Forge were equipped as suggested by Washington, while several thousand others he considered virtually naked. As the war progressed most soldiers would have been delighted to have overalls and hunting shirts.

Among the changes that would take place at Valley Forge was a concerted effort by Congress and Washington to influence the states to outfit their regiments. Most states did faithfully provided uniforms and other accoutrements for their regiments. Their compliance decreased the responsibility of Congress, and reduced the cost of outfitting the remaining non-state supported Continental units which consisted of sixteen regiments, the artillery and cavalry as reported by Washington.

In mid-November 1777, Congress had taken what they considered an optimistic and aggressive action in response to another plea by Washington for assistance. On the 14th they resolved to inform the Commander in Chief that they had written to France for "cloathes complete for eighty thousand men." They had been assured that France would send these uniforms before winter set in. Congress, enthusiastically, noted they had "adopted various other means for importing cloathing." Needless to state, none of this promised largess was ever received by the suffering troops at Valley Forge. At the same time, Congress distributed a copy of Washington's return of the clothing needed to the eastern and middle states requesting their cooperation in filling it. In a rare mood for Congress, Washington was granted the "power vested in him" to impress at "a reasonable price" any clothing needed from the disaffected citizens. Sardonically, Congress expressed the opinion that the "well disposed" people would be pleased that Loyalists would have to furnish the army with clothing.[4]

While enroute to Valley Forge, Washington's compassion had been aroused by the "bareness" of many soldiers. Unable to accept the distress he witnessed on the march, orders were issued to officers from each regiment to scour the countryside for clothing. He was aware that this action would be unpopular and possibly stir a public outcry. Nevertheless he had only taken this measure after the area residents ignored the

Clothier General's appeal to "private Persons" for clothing. At the time Washington was unaware that Pennsylvania had started a program to gather clothing for the army. As a conflict of effort resulted, the Assembly directed two of its members to visit headquarters and apprise the Commander in Chief of the state's action. With this information, Washington, not desiring to interfere with the state's collection program, immediately ordered all Continental officers to return to their regiments.[5]

The recently reorganized Board of War, ignorant of what had transpired, imperiously reprimanded Washington for exceeding his authority. An embittered Washington made a moderate but firm response to the Board noting that:

> Nothing but the absolute necessity which the army lay under for want of Cloathing induced me to send out Officers to make Collections; the Cloathier General represented it to me as impossible for him to procure what Articles were in the Hands of private Persons and I therefore, by Virtue of the Powers with which I was vested by Congress, granted Warrents to different Officers to impose which the holders would not willingly part with; but I, at the same time, directed them to give orders upon the Cloathier General, to be paid for at a Reasonable rate. Since the State of Pennsylvania have undertaken to collect what things are proper for the Army by Commissioners of their own. I have recalled all the Officers sent out by me.[6]

During Washington's embroilment with the Board of War, Congress had again acted on the former's suggestion to urge the states to become involved in outfitting their regiments. Although previously petitioned, several states had dragged their feet without any clothes reaching the camp. In December 1777, unable to arrive at a unanimous decision and hampered by indifferent attendance at Congressional sessions, they implored absent members from Connecticut, New York, Pennsylvania, Maryland and South Carolina to hasten to Yorktown. A bolstered membership was required to act on the needs of the army. To stimulate their return, Congress emphasized that the program to outfit the troops had been fraught with great waste, incompetence and faithlessness.[7]

A month later Washington was further incensed when the Board of War again raised the question of his overstepping his authority. They wanted to know what had happened to clothing collected in Pennsylvania for the use of their regiments and those issued to the "Army in general." Calmly, Washington responded that he assumed the problem must have been misrepresented to them—and then slightly irritated, he reiterated that no clothing had "ever [been] received...on general account."[8]

While still smarting under the rebuke, Washington wrote to Wharton outlining the dire need that had prompted him to dispatch officers to collect clothing until withdrawn at the Assembly's request. He was mystified! What had happened to clothing that had been gathered by the state, as none of it had reached Valley Forge? As he had no quarrel with Wharton, he softened his comments by alluding to the moderate success enjoyed by Wayne in obtaining a "tolerable supply" of clothing for his two brigades. Then on another bright note he reported that Colonel Lutterloh had located a considerable quantity of clothing near Reading. If this information was accurate, he requested Wharton to speedily send it down the Schuylkill River to camp, thereby saving labor and expense over land transport.[9]

Putting aside his irritation with the Board of War, Washington addressed his attention to the more pressing problem of awakening the states to their responsibilities. Hopefully, a personal appeal to the governors would help untangle the bureaucratic redtape that had frozen their efforts to outfit their troops at Valley Forge.

Among Washington's first correspondents was Patrick Henry, Governor of his native state, Virginia. Henry responded promptly by collecting a quantity of garments for the state regiments. Washington gratefully acknowledged receipt of the outfits and assured Henry they would be distributed to the Virginia troops as he requested, although the clothes received would not cover the nakedness of all Virginians. With a daily worsening situation, Washington made another appeal to Henry for any garb that would provide cover for the men—especially needed were shoes, stockings and blankets, without which it would be "impossible to gauge the Suffering of the Troops."[10]

By late January, Washington proposed the possible standardization of the army's uniforms. In a letter to Governor Jonathan Trumbull of Connecticut, he urged that there be no delay in forwarding a uniform for Connecticut's regiments. As the scarcity of regimental coats had delayed shipments of complete uniforms, he suggested that a garment patterned after a "Sailor's Sea Jacket" would be more practical. Apparently enthused with his thought, he said it should fit close to the body and if doublebreasted, add warmth in the winter. Washington added that a small cape and cuff of different colors would distinguish the various corps. As speed was essential, he advised Trumbull that the cloth could be sent to camp for fabrication by army tailors.[11]

The tailors Washington referred to were a part of his plan to make the army self-sufficient as much as possible in some articles. He directed the Commanding Officer of each regiment to make a return of the tailors in their commands. The tailors were to be on detached service, but would remain inactive until a uniform pattern being designed could be furnished them.

Within hours the Board of War heard of Washington organizing a company of tailors. Without knowledge of his intentions, the Board dashed off an order for him to send the tailors to Lancaster to manufacture clothing. Probably seething from another interference in his function of command, Washington quickly composed a lengthy letter about conditions in the army. Perhaps to cool off, he penned this letter over a two day period, but stated firmly that as the army had been reduced by sickness, the detachment of troops on command and the expiration of enlistments in several units, he could not further weaken the army. Under the circumstances the tailors would "Work either in Camp or at some place Contiguous to it."[12]

Another difference had developed when the Board of War questioned the distribution of the clothing specified by the states for their regiments, new recruits, and soldiers in army hospitals. Washington explained that while Virginia was providing some clothing their regimental requirements remained deficient, and the state would resent any tampering with the designated supply of clothing for Virginia soldiers. On a brighter side, Connecticut had furnished their regiments with an abundance of clothing and were retaining the extra quantity for their future needs. Unfortunately, Washington pointed out, the other states had not matched the efforts of Virginia and Connecticut. He bemoaned the fact that the trickle of clothing reaching camp was a mere pittance of what was needed for the hospitals, American prisoners of war, and the dire want of any garments for between three and four thousand men in camp.[13]

As the weeks passed the flow of clothing to camp became erratic and searching for a prime target for the charge of incompetence fell on James Mease, Clothier General. Mease should not be blamed for all the disasters that plagued his department in the attempt to clothe the troops. He had been thwarted by apathy and a lack of cooperation by several states and individuals. Also, he had the misfortune of being frustrated by what a contemporary described as "bureaucratic negligence."[14]

Mease became the butt of calumnious remarks over the loss of convoys of clothing destined for Valley Forge. Caravans and individual wagons, frequently without a military escort, were stopped east of the Hudson River occasionally by soldiers of Israel Putnam's command who looted the wagons of part or all their contents. Washington had reproved Putnam demanding that wagons intended for Valley Forge not be stopped for any reason. Later in February Washington was horrified to learn that Putnam's troops were in as appalling condition for want of clothing as those at camp. When advised of this situation, he took immediate steps to alleviate Putnam's distress by urging Congress to take action "affording your relief." Mease was ordered "to furnish a proportion of Cloaths for the use of the men under your command." In an effort to soften his previous admonishment Washington wrote: "In the prohibition I made, some time since, I only meant to hinder any breach being made upon the Cloathing intended for and coming to this Army...But I did not suppose the Clothier would have been inattentive to the wants of the Troops with you."[15]

Rumors, on occasion, reached headquarters that quantities of clothing had been purchased for the army, but rarely arrived at Valley Forge. Some of these shipments had unaccountably disappeared, but others had been stopped by roving bands masked as American militia or disaffected persons, who plundered the wagons of any articles of value. If the misfortunes that befell these caravans were not frustrating enough, reports of natural disasters exacerbated the gloom in camp. Accidents occurred owing to poorly constructed wagons breaking down and being abandoned by the drivers. Others were delayed or damaged by poor roads and the capriciousness of rivers. One such accident happened to a company of wagons and their cargo that sustained heavy damage in attempting to cross the Susquehanna River.[16]

With Sullivan in Rhode Island and McDougall stationed in the Hudson River Valley, Washington solicited their cooperation to locate the mysteriously missing wagons of clothing. He cautioned them, if success- ful, to send them across the Delaware River at "East-Town" (Easton) and not at the usual crossing, Coryell's Ferry (Lambertville). He anticipated grave danger from British troops at the lower crossings.[17]

Washington was discouraged by the failure of the expedients that had been taken to stimulate the gathering of clothing by representatives of the Clothier's Department. Frustrated and in a pique, he wrote a long letter to the President of Congress in which he unburdened himself of the futility of trying to work with Service Department representatives who were not in camp. In his indignation he added there was no reason these departments should be scattered throughout the states. Somewhat calmer he expressed hope the recently departed Congressional Commit- tee from camp would make recommendations to reorganize the army. For the first time he gave evidence of his displeasure with the Clothier General, declaring to his astonishment it had become common knowledge that the New England states alone could furnish enough materials "to cloathe 100,000 Men." Obviously annoyed with this infor- mation he wrote: "If this be a fact there is a fatal error somewhere, to which may be attributed the death and desertion of thousands."[18]

Possibly Washington's letter was prompted in part because of the many expressions of displeasure with conditions at Valley Forge by officers and civilians, that had reached headquarters. General Enoch Poor registered a strong letter of protest with Meschech Weare, President of New Hampshire. He stated the roads of New England were "crowded

73

Extract from letter of Paul Zantzinger to Brigadier General
Anthony Wayne explaining the difficulties in obtaining sup-
plies for the troops. (John F. Reed Collection. Valley Forge
National Historical Park.)

with wagons carrying clothing" that never reached camp. Poor added that the presence of these wagons had probably led state officials to believe the troops were well supplied. Wishing to convey an accurate portrayal of the lot of his brigade, he painted a graphic statistical picture of the clothes available to the New Hampshire regiments: "...only one coat to each 100 soldiers, waistcoats 6 to 100, Breeches 4 to 100, shirts 2 for 9, shoes 1 out of 3, stockings 1 out of 5, blankets 2 out of 100." To emphasize that this pathetic condition was common throughout camp he noted "...our army still remains in their ragged suffering situation."[19]

Letters of officers to families back home reaffirmed Poor's description of life at Valley Forge, arousing the indignation of entire communities and instigating petitions to state legislatures to investigate why their men were suffering. Citizens of Bridgewater, Massachusetts were aghast to hear that soldiers from their town were naked, as one company had only two men fit for duty because of this condition. In their letters, the officers had indicated they believed "themselves neglected" and that clothing provided by Massachusetts had been "Dealt out to the men of other states."[20]

These and other failures to provide outfits for the soldiers caused Mease to be characterized as incompetent. Initially Washington had not severely reprimanded Mease, but finally, his patience exhausted and disturbed with the Clothier General's absence from Valley Forge, he revealed his displeasure on matters governing this activity. He reminded Mease that headquarters was in the dark concerning his operations; how much, if any, clothing had he gathered; were officers uniforms available; and who was satisfying the constant outcry of merchants demanding their bills be paid? Washington was obviously irked at being dogged and badgered on these categories of Mease's responsibilities.

To further aggravate the situation, Mease had installed a clerk at camp to carry out the functions of his department. The incompetency of this individual placed a heavy burden on Washington and the headquarters staff. Becoming acerbic, Washington wrote that if Mease wanted to remain in office he must insist that the Clothier General establish his quarters at or near Valley Forge, where affairs of his department could be quickly resolved. Mease had been spending considerable time at Lancaster, and Washington added that, if necessary, he would not object to a qualified and active deputy being stationed there to supervise the tailoring of clothes.[21]

In late April and early May, despite administrative confusion and the apathy of certain state and Continental officials, a moderate quantity of clothing began to arrive at camp. Included in this flow of apparel were some garments from France. Nevertheless, dissatisfaction over the persistent shortages of any articles to cover the men's nakedness existed in several brigades. Typically, Wayne had been engaged in a running dispute with the Pennsylvania Assembly and Mease since Whitemarsh, over the failure to clothe his brigade. This unfortunate brouhaha remained unresolved when the army moved out of Valley Forge.

With the advent of spring, well clad recruits began to arrive at camp in sharp contrast to the number of hardened veterans who still suffered after months of varying degrees of undress.

When the army arrived at Valley Forge, an eighteenth century custom that charged soldiers for the cost of their uniforms had aggravated the bitterness of the clothing shortage. In November 1775, Congress had ordered the deduction of one and two-third dollars from the pay of each recruit. This sum was to be repeated each month until the cost of his uniform had been satisfied. By 1778, an indifferent application of this order, caused in large part by the nakedness of the army, was evident among all brigades. Most authorities, shocked by the deplorable condition of their regiments, made no attempt to charge the soldiers for the meager supply sent to camp, while others continued to exact payment. To many soldiers the only way to escape their nakedness was to purchase any handy garment or blanket from a sutler or merchant—if fortunate to have enough money. [22]

As early as January 1778, Baron de Kalb presented a graphic picture of the results of this parsimonious policy. Writing to Henry Laurens, he asserted that "half the Soldiers in the army, who have still Blankets, will tell you, they got them with their own money." He acknowledged that he understood that some states were fraught with many difficulties that prevented them from providing for their regiments. However, he contended that the "neglect, ignorance or carelessness of officers of all ranks" rendered a disservice to the men who conditions were lamentable, because of improper attention to training them of their responsibilities in caring for their possessions. He had witnessed instances of soldiers selling "as soon as got, Stockings, Shoes, Blankets and even arms under pretense of being their property." De Kalb's observations epitomized the dilemma that confronted every effort to solve the needs of the troops at Valley Forge. [23]

The exertions of Washington, Congress, the Board of War and others concerned by the clothing shortage would be hampered by the vicissitudes of indifference, greed and thievery that would continue throughout the period of the encampment. The negligence in several states was obscured by the mistaken belief that the army was fully outfitted.

Since 1775, the scarcity of foot wear of any kind had been a source of grave concern to Washington. In July, 1777, he issued explicit orders to Mease to collect as many pair of shoes as the countryside could offer, stating even "...if we had 50,000 pair it would not be too many." He added that shoes gathered at Peekskill, New York, that had been destined for the main army were never forwarded. Those shoes that had reached the army were ill-fitting and entirely too small for the troops. Of greater discouragement was that the shoes received at Peekskill were French pumps that tore to pieces when wet.[24]

When conditions had not improved by October, an exasperated Washington ordered brigade commanders to select men capable of making "Mockasins" for their units. Commissaries were directed to cooperate by removing the skins off the heads and legs of bullocks to be furnished for that purpose.[25]

In early November, a still annoyed Washington admonished General Israel Putnam to stop appropriating for his use the shipments of shoes destined for the army at Whitemarsh. Still fuming ten days later, he offered ten dollars to the officers or soldiers who would submit a drawing of "the best substitute for shoes, made of raw hide." Later in the month Daniel Morgan's corps was ordered to report to Nathanael Greene in New Jersey to assist in defense of the Delaware River, but was forced to remain in camp as only 170 men had shoes.[26]

The march to Valley Forge and the first weeks at camp had been marked by blood from the lacerated feet of the many shoeless soldiers. Washington was displeased at the seeming negligence of the civil authorities, and the lack of compliance with those designated to make footwear for the army. Burning with anger he empathized with the plight of the soldiers as they painfully performed their duties.

While some improvement would occur, it became gradually evident that the basic failure to supply the army with shoes would continue throughout the entire period at Valley Forge. Some purveyors of shoes and other articles of clothing had become disgusted with what they claimed was the negligence of the states in fulfilling their obligations to reimburse them for items delivered to the army. Samuel Hunt, a New Hampshire supplier, wrote he had forwarded all the shoes he could find, but refused to send socks claiming he hadn't been paid for previous clothing sent to the army.[27]

Repeated orders were issued to ensure that all hides be saved with the prospect that they could be bartered for leather to manufacture shoes. For this purpose Washington authorized a rate of exchange of five pounds of raw hides for one pound of tanned leather. It was hoped that a sufficiency of leather would also be available to make "cartouch boxes." Earlier, anticipating that the shortage of leather would worsen, Washington directed all commissaries "to Save all horns of the cattle and have them separated from the bones..." The horns were to be stored by the Quartermaster General for possible conversion into powder horns as a substitute for the cartouch boxes. Procrastination by the commissaries and others involved in this function, usually resulted in shortages of the horns. Even when prompt attention was given to the problem, it would require several months to tan the hides and produce dressed leather. Nevertheless, this method offered the only assurance that a continuing supply of shoes would eventually be available to the army.[28]

The problem of supply was exacerbated by the cupidity of individuals, especially near Germantown, who preferred to take their hides into Philadelphia for British hard money rather than worthless Continental currency. Another source of irritation to Washington was the extravagant waste of hides by the various brigades.[29]

Shoe factories were established in outlying counties where they were considered safe from British raiding parties. Apparently some shoemaking was done at Valley Forge as Sarah Platt Potter stated her father was in the army and made shoes for the men at the camp.[30]

Many items that were vital to the health and welfare of the troops, but not readily available to the army, included soap and candles. Washington in his campaign for cleanliness was conscious of the importance to provide any necessity that would improve camp morale. A large number of officers and men in the Continental Army were husbandmen, frontier settlers or, like Washington, large land owners. Their relative isolation in private life had forced them to produce specific commodities, not readily accessible, for the convenience of their families. Washington was aware that with this background the army could provide, at least, their minimum requirements of soap and candles.

The Commander in Chief's directive to conserve ashes gathered from the hut fireplaces was understood and appreciated by the soldiers as an attempt to improve their condition. On January 12, he ordered all company orderly officers to supervise the removal of the ashes and have them deposited in a designated area. A shelter, or small hut, was to be constructed about twenty yards in front of each regiments's position. This cover would keep the ashes dry and free of moisture to prevent premature leaching.

Extreme care had to be exercised so that dirt did not become mixed with the ashes. All hard "Oyle" (fat) from the hooves of cattle was to be saved for the production of tallow. The effort was temporarily aborted when the soldiers assigned to make the tallow discovered there were no kettles of the size needed in camp. Although delayed by the shortage, the quartermasters eventually obtained a supply of kettles sufficient to permit the men to leach water through the ashes to produce lye. The lye was then blended with the tallow and boiled to produce an alkaline substance used to make soap—at Valley Forge it was soft soap. Tallow was also used in the process of molding candles for lighting the dreary huts.

As a background on the use of soap in the army, in the fall of 1775 Congress resolved that twenty-four pounds of soft soap, or eight pounds of hard soap be issued to each 100 men per week. This would provide each individual soldier with 1.28 ounces of hard or 3.94 ounces of soft soap. It is unlikely that under existing conditions at Valley forge Washington made any effort to comply with this resolution, rather, as the soap was produced by the different regiments, and depending on the quantity available, it was doled out to the soldiers.[31]

A Fight for Survival

FROM THE DAY the army marched into Valley Forge until the reorganization of the Quartermaster and Commissary Departments in March 1778, no correlation existed between supply and demand. As the army neared the chosen campsite several brigades were destitute of provisions, while in Pennsylvania's back country there was an abundance of foodstuff that could have sustained the army for several weeks. Thomas Jones, Assistant Commissary of Issues, a concerned Pennsylvanian attempting to rent horses and wagons asserted not one barrel of flour could be delivered to camp because no wagons were available.[1]

Jones's statement pinpointed the crux of a supply dilemma that faced the army in the early months of the Valley Forge encampment. Makeshift expedients would not sustain the hungry, ragtag army and would hamper its mobility. Without an adequate logistical system, the army would suffer from an extreme shortage of every necessity and materiel of war—even when those articles were obtainable in the outlying countryside. It has been rightly claimed that logistical support represents half the effectiveness of an army.

At this time the missing logistic ingredient was a brigade of fresh horses and well-constructed wagons. What remained of the Quartermaster Department's horses were spavined or otherwise crippled, and incapable of the rigorous demands of draft animals. Deputy Quartermaster General, Colonel Henry E. Lutterloh had implored President Thomas Wharton, Jr., of the Pennsylvania Assembly, to provide teams to transport the provisions, forage, and other supplies—including the much needed straw for bedding in the huts and regimental hospitals—for an army bordering on the brink of dissolution. He called Wharton's attention to the worsening conditions, pointing out that the surviving horses were "Worn out." In the same disabled condition were the few officer's mounts that had survived the recent military actions, while Pulaski's cavalry had been sent to Trenton for replacements and regrouping. This horrific situation traumatized a camp littered with the carcasses of horses and the noxious stench of offal.

It was quickly recognized that the prime suppliers of horses and wagons must be the nearby Pennsylvania counties, where owners and farmers with teams had already expressed reluctance to rent them to the army, even with the presence of a British Army in their state. Adamant, many farmers contended that in the past when acceding to similar requests, they had experienced the shocking "wear and tear on the waggons," and in return were offered no recompense for their loss.

Obviously, a volunteer system to recruit teams would not be effective. To overcome the lack of cooperation by owners, the Pennsylvania Assembly decided to put their official stamp on the rental program by enacting a law that would establish mandatory quotas for each county. The owners would receive thirty shillings a day for a wagon with four horses and a driver. An immediate hue and cry was heard from farmers objecting to the price set in depreciated Continental currency, when they could receive three or four pounds hard money in the private sector.

The law also authorized the appointment of a Wagon Master in each county and Assistant Wagon Masters in the various townships. Even with the authority granted by the law, Wagon Masters encountered unrelenting opposition. Dejected state authorities opened what became an extensive and animated but fruitless correspondence to bring compliance with the law. Nothing would move the recalcitrant farmers and owners. The state's delegates to the Continental Congress were instructed to importune that body for financial support.[2]

In an effort to carry water on both shoulders, Pennsylvania's Supreme Executive Council attempted to justify the actions of all involved in the controversy. They wrote two letters, one on March 9 summarizing their anxiety over the distress of the soldiers. Writing to Joseph Jeffries, Wagon Master for York County, they ordered him to collect fifty wagons and report to George Ross, Deputy Quartermaster, who would supply forage as their cargo. The letter continued ordering Jeffries to: "...exert yourself to forward them immediately, as the army are *[sic]* suffering beyond description for the want of them. If you stand in need of assistance I beg you to employ as many as necessary, for the Waggons must be had...Assembly are about passing a supplement to the Waggon Law...." authorizing the impressment of teams.[3]

The next day a distraught Council wrote to Lutterloh[4] stating they had wholeheartedly cooperated with the Quartermaster Department but their efforts had been misunderstood and abused. They "imputed to another cause" the reason for the lack of cooperation, saying it rested with the department's representatives who had displayed little compassion or understanding of the rights of the farmers. In more detail they acidly defined their irritation by claiming that: "Numbers of good people of this State, whose waggons have repeatedly been in the service, as well as many other, I [we] are informed, who have had their forage, &c., taken from them by the Q. Masters & their Deputies, are not paid, nor do they see the least hopes of obtaining their Monies. This injurious treatment...is the cause why there is a backwardness in furnishing Waggons,...a matter so serious, that unless a remedy is soon applied, it will be out of the power of Council to put the Laws in execution, unless the army is called upon to assist them—." Not content with this harangue Council threatened the troubled Lutterloh stating they might bypass him and the Commander in Chief and call to the attention of the Continental Congress the transgressions of the rights of civilians by Quartermaster Deputies.[5]

In the meantime, the Congressional Committee at camp was aghast at the steady worsening plight of the army. With approval of Washington, they ordered Lieutenant Colonel Alexander Hamilton to direct Lutterloh to gather the necessary horses and wagons and forward them filled with provisions and forage to camp. In writing to Lutterloh, February 20, Hamilton implored "For God's sake, my dear Sir, exert yourself upon this occasion, our distress is infinite." Trying to fulfill his duties as Deputy Quartermaster, a badgered Lutterloh quickly dispatched Hamilton's letter to Secretary of the Assembly Timothy Matlock, adding: "In the neighborhood of the Camp are no Waggons, all are worn out and our own Teams [horses] cannot go along being so worked down...Consider the Distress of the army..."[6]

Other voices were being raised in protest over the constant bickering, when supplies were available and urgently needed by hungry soldiers. Ephraim Blaine, Deputy Quartermaster, advised Wharton that flour, whiskey, and forage were available in large quantities in the western counties, with no wagons for transporting them. Blaine's comments were repeated by others who recognized the dire need to impress teams and drivers from reluctant owners if the troops were to survive.[7]

On the other side of the dilemma were the chapfallen Wagon Masters who found that neither appeals of patriotism, persuasion, or threats were going to fill the various counties's quotas of horses or wagons. Concurrent with their frustration, the effort of the Supreme Executive Council had been nonproductive. It was obvious that the owners were undaunted, having been left with memories of broken promises that transcended all appeals to ease the supply condition. A number of factors hampered the efforts of the faithful and conscientious Wagon Masters. In certain counties a sizable number of Loyalists and members of pacifistic religious sects were aided and abetted by a few unscrupulous Wagon Masters in concealing their teams from the Quartermaster and state authorities. There were, also, reports of vandalism, encouraged by the

Major General Nathanael Greene by Charles Willson Peale.
(Independence National Historical Park Collection.)

duplicity of the wagon drivers.

Finally, a nonplused Assembly and Council vented their displeasure on the conduct of all concerned by advocating the enactment of a law to protect the farmers from those who impressed teams without consideration for the owner's needs. The proposed law would broaden the authority to permit the army to confiscate teams and establish a more equitable rate of compensation for those taken.

While no law was forthcoming, in February the Quartermaster Department directed their deputies in Pennsylvania and adjacent states to cooperate with any army detachment sent to recruit teams. Their orders were to give full recognition to the needs of farmers and permit them to retain any teams necessary for their subsistence. With these instructions troop details scattered through Pennsylvania and Delaware, where they enjoyed varying degrees of success. As an example, Captain Henry Lee with a company of dragoons roamed over northern Delaware, principally New Castle County, where they recruited several hundred teams and wagoneers, of whom about one-third were black men. Unfortunately most of the teams met with misfortune and never reached camp.[8]

Conditions began to improve with the advent of spring and the forceful leadership of Nathanael Greene as Quartermaster General. Greene, with the cooperation of Pennsylvania authorities, warned owners who were still hiding their teams that they faced prosecution to the fullest extent of the Pennsylvania State law. As a frightening gesture, the owners were cautioned that their neighbors and friends had been offered a handsome reward to reveal anyone who was not cooperating under the law.

In this transitional period attention was directed to New England where wagoners were offered an enlistment bonus for volunteering to serve for three years. In New Jersey an active campaign was initiated to recruit "good wagoners" for the Continental Army who were skilled in driving teams and caring for cattle. They were to serve for one year and receive ten pounds a month, and if they served faithfully, after six months they would receive a bounty of a suit of clothes.[9]

Dissatisfied with the endless delays, Washington could not wait for tomorrow to alleviate the supply deficiency; nevertheless, he remained adamant in his resolution not to interfere with the laws of civilian authorities. Finally, with affairs at a desperate state, Washington was forced to take immediate action. Having complete confidence in Nathanael Greene—not yet Quartermaster General—and Lutterloh, he directed that they reconnoiter all areas of Pennsylvania and Delaware for teams to transport supplies to Valley Forge. He personally appealed to other governors of states from Virginia to New England.

As a guideline for Greene and Luttlerloh, Washington ordered them to adhere to the instructions he had issued on December 20, 1777, for appropriating horses. On that date he had admonished the Deputy Quartermaster to not take any horses "absolutely necessary" to the families for drawing such commodities as fuel required for the winter. All details relating to the horses should be noted on a receipt specifying their age, size, color, and marks. They were to be delivered to Smallwood's Wilmington Headquarters accompanied by the owners, where impartial observers would affix a fair value for each horse.[10]

Of equal concern to Washington was the grave scarcity of wagons needed for the long hauls of army supplies from the various states. An example of the gravity of this shortage was evident when Greene discovered a large supply of hay existed along the New Jersey coast, but he had to order it destroyed because he lacked the wagons to bring it to camp.

Acting under orders, Lieutenant Colonel Tench Tilghman, a Washington aide-de-camp, with the support of Governor William Livingston made a personal reconnaissance to determine the quantities of provisions available in New Jersey. The state's legislature enacted a law to establish commodity prices destined for the army. Livingston considered the law enforceable only if the commissaries were vigorous and attentive to their duties. However, Livingston did not believe the law would be respected because Congress expected local governments to correct conditions, considered by that body as state responsibilities. Opposing Congress's allegation, he maintained the people had rights that Continental authorities were violating by confiscation and regulations. Frustrated by British forays in northern New Jersey where large quantities of grain lay exposed to any marauder, Livingston expressed concern because farmers would willingly sell to the enemy, rather than face confiscation.[11]

In the middle sector of New Jersey, near Trenton, Tilghman found ample supplies with no means to forward them to Valley Forge. He discovered several caches containing 671 barrels of fish, 450 of pork, and 190 of bread; adding, a more thorough search would have easily uncovered 10,000 barrels of pork. A further hunt of the area disclosed that many patriotic farmers were salting their beef, but unfortunately, like flour, had no way of forwarding it to Valley Forge stating "The country is full of flour and the only thing is to get it to camp." Another reconnaissance that was equally futile was carried out by Major John Jameson. Dispatched to Virginia in search for horses, Jameson encountered a lack of cooperation and returned empty handed.[12]

The shortage of provisions and other necessities created widespread despair among the Deputy Quartermasters over the failure of Pennsylvania to fulfill its promise to maintain a regular supply of wagons. They constantly harassed the state authorities, hinting that the army might be forced to adopt a policy of impressment. Blaine contended that there was enough flour and whiskey available to fill over 200 wagons, but none could be located. Moderating the tone of his letter, he acknowledged that the "hardness" of the roads would probably prevent one wagon from reaching Valley Forge. In late April, Colonel Benjamin Flower, traveling in the interior parts of the state along both sides of the Susquehanna River, observed that the roads were "Intolerably bad." He believed a wagon would be fortunate to carry two-thirds of a normal load without breaking down and asserting that in addition to the almost impassable condition, the roads were only twenty-five to thirty feet wide. [13]

Another frustrating disclosure occurred in February when of the various Commissary magazines for food and supplies that had been established by Washington to served the camp, only two had ample stores. One magazine was at Dover, New Jersey and the other at Head of Elk. However, the remoteness of their locations, coupled with a shortage of wagons, rendered it impossible to transport their supplies to Valley Forge. [14]

Meanwhile in Pennsylvania, Greene was encountering one disappointment after another, with most citizens who owned teams or provisions and other supplies, on the verge of hysteria. People of all political persuasion were fearful of discrimination or retaliation regardless of which army they cooperated with. Many disaffected and patriotic farmers resorted to hiding teams, forage, provision, and straw in the woods and swamps. To further disturb Congress, a disquieting rumor was being circulated that Howe was successfully purchasing cattle in the western counties. [15]

At first sympathetic to the hardships of the farmers, Greene gradually became embittered with what he considered their indifference to the plight of the army. Baffled, he advised Washington that although distressed by the condition and crying of the people, he was "like Pharoh I harden my heart." Greene reported capturing two men in the act of carrying provisions to the enemy in Philadelphia, and wrote "I gave them an hundred [lashes] each by way of Example." Exasperated by insubordination, desertion, indiscriminate pillaging of farmers and intercourse with the British, commanders commonly meted out punishments of one hundred or more lashes. Dejected, Greene acknowledged that the numerous small patrols he sent out to collect horses, enjoyed a limited success. But at the end of his patience, Greene wrote "I determine to forage the Country very bare—nothing shall be left...." Committed to the role of despoiler, he destroyed a large quantity of hay on Tinicum Island in the Delaware, and action that also forced the British who were in equal need of forage, to eventually bring boats loaded with hay down from Rhode Island. [16]

With the coming of spring Washington was confident that there would be inevitable improvement in the flow of supplies. Sanguine about the forthcoming summer campaign, he took steps to accumulate and store adequate supplies to provide logistical support when the army evacuated the camp. Forge Master General Clement Biddle was ordered to appropriate enough wheat fields near camp to serve as forage grounds, with each brigade assigned an area in proportion to its strength. In addition, magazines were directed to be established to accommodate the anticipated flow of supplies and equipment.[17]

Washington's optimism was partially fulfilled as the roads improved and more wagons became available, but never a sufficiency to supply all the needs at camp.

However, with the loss of logistical support, Washington was aware that every exertion must be employed to gather cattle and flour. Without these essentials the army would probably dissolve. He remembered that since 1775, when an optimistic ration allowance was granted of beef, fish, pork, soft bread or flour, hard bread and, on special orders, whiskey, it became an unfilled promise as the army's wants were never satisfied. With chaos in the Quartermaster and Commissary Departments, Washington realized that he must take the initiative to resolve the hunger at Valley Forge.

He recalled that before marching out of Whitemarsh the army had stripped the surrounding countryside of cattle, grain and any other items considered edible. These shortages had made it impossible to store up enough provisions to sustain the troops as they moved forward, or during the first days at Valley Forge. Unless provisions were speedily obtained, the future would represent a grueling life for the soldiers. To alleviate this condition, Washington immediately took action that he hoped would bring a sizable herd of cattle to camp. He wrote to General Israel Putnam to forward as many cattle as possible from both sides of the Hudson River.

Alas, in direct violation of Washington's order, Putnam had diverted cattle destined for Valley Forge to the use of his command. Unhesitatingly, a wrathful Washington reflected his displeasure with this insubordination, and angrily called Putnam to task stating the main army's meat supply was exhausted and the troops were in a "starving condition." He admonished Putnam to obey orders and directed all cattle intended for the main army to Valley Forge. He asked why were they "diverted into other Channels?" Washington explained that he had been reluctant to order cattle from distant states, but because of the plight of the army he had no choice.

Although exasperated with the apparent indifference shown to the needs of the army, Washington endeavored to soften his anger by asserting that "...for the future, I beg you will consider it as explicitly contrary to my intention that any cattle ordered for the use of this Army should be stopt short of their destination." Any attempt to temper his dissatisfaction vanished when he informed Putnam that he was aware the latter had a ready and ample substitute of salt provisions and should use them for his troops.[18]

On the same day Washington wrote to Governor Jonathan Trumbull entreating him to galvanize the people of Connecticut into action, otherwise the army was in danger of disbanding. However, he did not labor under any illusions, realizing that Trumbull could do little to ease the needs of the army. Nevertheless, as the situation was so critical, Washington begged Trumbull to exert his efforts to dispatch cattle to Valley Forge and "thereby prevent a Melancholy and alarming Catastrophe."[19] This communication had barely cleared headquarters, when Colonel Ephraim Blaine,[20] reported that the area in Pennsylvania, for which he was responsible, was exhausted concluding that with "the most vigorous and active exertions," the provisions available would not sustain the army through the month.

Accompanying Trumbull's letter, the express carried another frustrating message for Henry Champion,[21] stating the "army is the most Melancholy that can be conceived." Out of despair he repeated that the vicinity of the camp was virtually exhausted of beef and provisions and there was no transportation to bring what was available to the army. Little assistance could be expected from Maryland or Virginia, with the Chesapeake Bay controlled by British men-of-war. Washington referred Champion to Colonel Blaine and urged them to cooperate in gathering all the cattle to be found and drive them to camp without delay, thereby freeing the army from "calamitous consequences."[22]

The condition of affairs in camp had become so ominous that virtually all Washington's correspondence on February 6 and 7 was directed to those responsible for supplying the troops or interested authorities who, by extra exertion, could alleviate the suffering. Rather dolefully he entreated William Buchanan[23] for assistance noting that: "The spirit of desertion among the Soldiery, never before rose to such a threatening height, as at the present time."[24]

Washington's blandishments brought some success during February, as Champion obtained a small herd of cattle. Acknowledging Champion's contribution, Washington requested that he search for salt meat, as it would be a welcome supplement to the soldiers' diet. Conversely, Washington said his attempt to draw cattle from New Jersey, Maryland, Pennsylvania and Virginia had been fruitless, with the disappointing few that reached camp being "very thin, and no improvement expected before fall."[25]

Greene, who had previously been directed to scour the back country of Pennsylvania for horses and wagons, was now given an additional assignment. Word had reached headquarters that British raiding parties had been carrying off the property of "good People of the State" along the Delaware River south of Philadelphia. He was ordered to remove all horses, cattle, sheep and "provender" within fifteen or twenty miles of the Delaware River between the Schuylkill River and Brandywine Creek, however, if it was too hazardous to remove these items, he was to burn or destroy them. Greene was cautioned that all residents were to receive certificates that were to be honored in payment by the Commissary or Quartermaster Generals. None of these directives brought in a bountiful supply of provisions.[26]

In February one bright prospect appeared on the horizon when Washington received information that ample cattle and forage could be found in southern New Jersey. But caution must be employed as a significant Loyalist population in that area had taken steps to prevent confiscation of cattle by American troops. The swamps and pine woods of South Jersey offered excellent places of concealment. However, Colonel Joseph Ellis of the New Jersey militia asserted that patriot sympathizers in the region knew where many of the steers had been cached, and would direct American foraging parties to their whereabouts.

Greene's assignment to bring order out of the chaotic condition surrounding Pennsylvania's effort to procure horses and wagons was now broadened to included the direction of Captain "Lighthorse Harry" Lee's foraging activities in Delaware and a proposed expedition by General Anthony Wayne to southern New Jersey. It had become vital to the survival of the troops that Wayne and Lee collect all the cattle and forage obtainable in those two states. On February 16, Lee was ordered to proceed to Dover, Delaware and Head of Elk, Maryland and gather "all the flesh provisions" in the magazines in that area. With his usual dash and aggressiveness, Lee enjoyed moderate success and was directed to make certain all those "tolerably fit for slaughter" were immediately driven to camp. Conversely, rather than expose the lean cattle to a further loss of weight, they were to be left in Chester County where forage and grass were plentiful until they would "fatten up" for consumption.[27]

All intelligence indicated Wayne's excursion into New Jersey would be confronted with danger from opposition by Loyalist farmers and, even worse, the threat of interception by superior British troop detachments. Washington and Greene were determined that every precaution would be taken to prevent a leak of plans concerning Wayne's movements. To ensure the strictest secrecy all preliminary sessions were private and held at headquarters. The discussions at these clandestine meetings were not committed to writing, with Wayne receiving verbal orders from Greene.

The first intimation in writing was found in an ambiguous note Greene dispatched to Wayne on February 12, alluding to the planned raid in New Jersey.[28]

Regrettably, the British received early information and prepared to send a large detachment of troops to New Jersey when their informers located Wayne's point of embarkation and proposed landing in New Jersey. Washington and Howe seemed to always receive early intelligence of each other's moves.

Wayne quietly proceeded to assemble the units of the brigade that was to accompany him to New Jersey. On February 20, Greene informed Washington that Wayne had crossed the Delaware the previous night. Wayne's instructions were to cross from New Castle, Delaware to Finn's Point in New Jersey. This order of crossing was selected as being shorter and the safest from possible detection by the British. Captain John Barry, who had borrowed four guard boats from the out of service Pennsylvania Navy to prey on British shipping below Wilmington, was ordered to ferry the contingent over the river. No cumbersome equipment or wagons were taken as the boats were too small and would have added to a hazardous crossing.[29]

Wayne and Barry were instructed to cooperate in destroying all hay they could not successfully remove. In addition, they were admonished to take a record of all farmers whose cattle or forage was appropriated for subsequent restitution. Many New Jersey farmers, including American sympathizers, were disinclined to take worthless promises to pay, and hid their livestock and hay deep in the pine woods. Albeit, scattered units of Continental soldiers, New Jersey militia and Barry's sailors enjoyed a limited success.

With the final confirmation that Wayne was in New Jersey on February 24, Howe dispatched Lieutenant Colonel James Abercrombie, with a force of 2,000, across the Delaware landing at Billingsport. Abercrombie immediately put his detachment in motion to intercept the wily Wayne. The British planned a pincers movement ordering Colonel Thomas Stirling with Simcoe's Queens's Rangers, totaling about 1,300 men, to cross to Cooper's Ferry and head for Haddonfield, believing if Wayne tried to move north he would discover he was caught between Stirling and Abercrombie. Meanwhile Wayne assisted by a small New Jersey militia company under Lieutenant Colonel Joseph Ellis, could only assemble a combined force of 500.

Not losing sight of his objective, Wayne collected 150 cattle and a number of wagon loads of hay in the Salem area. He realized that to linger in any one locality would run the risk of being trapped by Abercrombie. Leaving Salem, guided by patriotic citizens, he traveled over interior roads to Woodbury where he had been advised that farmers and

Gloucester County militia had gathered an additional eighty-five cattle. An adroit Wayne, attempting to avoid a confrontation with Abercrombie, took a circuitous route to Haddonfield, from which town Stirling had surprisingly withdrawn after ravaging the area. Under existing circumstances, Wayne's progress had naturally been slow, as modern authorities believe that at the time cattle on the hoof could have made only abut eight miles a day over the existing poor roads.

In his effort to locate Wayne, Abercrombie moved to Salem, where local American farmers warned him that large numbers of militia were gathering on his flanks. Whether alarmed by this report and their possible merger with Wayne, the British officer decided to hastily evacuate the area and embark his detachment to return to Philadelphia. While his expedition was unsuccessful, he returned with the encouraging news that South Jersey had an abundance of cattle and forage. This knowledge to an army with an almost empty larder became a great temptation. In March, Lieutenant Colonel Charles Mawhood led a major junket to the Salem area and removed large quantities of supplies for the British Army.

Ellis' principal contribution to the safety of Wayne's cattle drive was to locate remote areas, where for a few days the herd could be rested and fattened. After a series of rest periods, Wayne eventually arrived at Burlington where he welcomed the addition of 100 cattle, raising his herd to 335.

Unknown to Wayne two large droves of cattle and supplies were on the march to Valley Forge. A detachment under Lieutenant Colonel Isaac Sherman, of the 2nd Connecticut, reached the Delaware River near Coryells Ferry (Lambertville). They were driving a herd of 130 cattle and after crossing the river Sherman asked Brigadier General John Lacey, of the Pennsylvania Militia, for assistance. Lacey said he could not mount a corporal's guard and therefore could not spare a man. Unknown to Sherman a detachment of British dragoons and "embodied Refugees" were hurrying to overtake him. As he neared Skippackville (modern Skippack) the dragoons surprised the herd and its escort, effecting a complete rout. A large number of prisoners and the 130 cattle were taken back to Philadelphia. The British version of the incident was printed in the *Pennsylvania Ledger* of February 25: "Yesterday afternoon a party of dragoons of the royal army and Cap't Hovendon with a party of Pennsylvania dragoons returned to town, having left it the night before about eleven o'clock. They had been at least Thirty miles up the Skippack road, and, having taken one hundred and thirty head of fine cattle, brought them in with prisoners."[30]

On February 23, in another effort to supply Valley Forge with provisions, a division of wagons in charge of John Hunt, wagonmaster, started for camp. Fearing for the safety of his wagons, Hunt appealed to

Governor Livingston for a military guard. Livingston was granted authority by the Privy Council of New Jersey, to embody several units of Hunterdon County militia to escort the train to Valley Forge, unless relieved by another unit in Pennsylvania. Apparently these wagons reached camp as no British or American records mention their capture or dispersion.[31]

Meanwhile, Wayne, after resting his troops and herd near Burlington, divided his command dispatching a strong detachment across the Delaware to Bristol. They were to patrol the west bank and parallel his drive to Trenton. A short distance north of Trenton was Howell's Ferry, where Wayne planned to ferry the cattle across the river (modern Yardley). From this point a road led directly through Newtown, to the Warrington-Doylestown area and then towards the Schuylkill River and Valley Forge. Unaware of Sherman's fate, Wayne considered this route far enough removed from British marauding parties to permit him to safely reach the encampment. Fortunately the herd reached the north bank of the Schuylkill without incident.[32]

In an effort to coordinate commissary operations on the north bank of the Schuylkill, Colonel Ephraim Blaine suggested for a depot "two Rooms in Old Mr. Pawling's" near Pawling's Ford.[33] He planned to maintain his quarters at Pawlings until a proposed bridge was constructed. As his letter is dated after the completion of Sullivan's bridge, it was undoubtedly the same span Steuben suggested opposite Washington's headquarters. Under most circumstances the Schuylkill near Pawling's Ford was shallow enough to drive cattle over safely and probably influenced the decision not to build this bridge.

Most cattle were herded to Valley Forge in small droves, rarely exceeding 100 head. They came from the New England States, New York and New Jersey, with lesser numbers from Pennsylvania, Delaware and Maryland. Blaine's selection of the Pawling property for his depot was its isolation from the main encampment, and a better pasture to graze and fatten the cattle for slaughter. Possibly, he did not wish to tempt the hungry soldiers. However, with the scarcity of beef during the first months, it is unlikely that there were many cattle in the pasture at anytime. Local tradition claims the encampment slaughter house was a short distance west of the Pawling property.

Closely allied with the meat shortage was a provoking problem with the army butchers. They were civilian personnel hired to slaughter, dress and distribute meat to the various brigade quartermasters. In a surreptitious manner and free of supervision, the butchers were greedily bilking the hungry soldiers. Certain parts of the slaughtered cattle, such as heads and plucks[34] that should have been delivered to company quartermasters were being sold at exorbitant prices to any soldiers who had money—albeit, depreciated Continental currency. When brought to Washington's attention, he bitterly denounced the heinous practice of taking advantage of the suffering troops. On January 13, in his general orders, he directed that all heads and plucks in camp be gathered and put up in packages of eight pounds. Company quartermasters were instructed to apply in turn for their allotted quantities of these bundles to supplement the meager allowance of other foodstuffs for their men.[35]

While beef was vital to the soldier's fare, the staff of life—bread—formed the other basic item on their diet. Congress had made a number of attempts to provide a regular supply of bread to the army, but all were unsuccessful. In early 1777, Congress, chagrined by these failures and of being a repeated target of the army's criticism, resolved to hire a company of journeymen bakers. Of equal importance was the hiring of an exceptionally qualified baker to direct the activities of the company. There is evidence that Congress already had that individual in mind—Christopher Ludwick. On May 3, 1777, Congress passed a resolution naming Ludwick "superintendent of bakers, and director of baking, in the grand army of the United States." At the same time, Congress declared that no person would be permitted to bake or sell bread to the army without a license. Those who applied for a baker's license and were approved would be allowed seventy-five dollars a month and two rations a day.[36]

The urgency to maintain a constant source of bread made it imperative to establish magazines to store flour for ready use. To provide for these storage areas Congress, on July 23, 1777, directed the Commissary General to install them at Yorktown, Lancaster, Downingtown and Valley Forge.[37]

With the threat of a British invasion of the Delaware Valley, implementation of Ludwick's recruitment program was temporarily tabled. Ludwick had discovered that most local bakers were serving in the state militia. Congress suggested he apply to the State Supreme Executive Council to secure their release from militia service. With the British Army on Philadelphia's doorstep, there was panic in the city, and Ludwick apparently postponed any effort to recruit bakers. Congress, anxious to leave the city and settle the seat of government in Yorktown, suggested Washington live off the country.

While Congress appeared indifferent, a certain concern manifested itself in late November when it sent a Congressional Committee to Whitemarsh to check on the suffering. Besides acting as an investigative body, they were to determine if the magazines ordered constructed in July were supplying the soldiers. Washington's heartrending description of conditions and William Buchanan's report on the magazines, revealed that only two might be in existence with little to sustain the army on their march to the winter encampment. Apparently only those at Lancaster and Yorktown were "supposed" to have 1,000 and 5,000 barrels of flour, respectively. However, Buchanan acknowledged they were not sufficient and he was uncertain about their condition.[38]

By January 1778, there was no evidence of improvement as the search continued for an adequate supply of flour, so essential for the army's survival. Ample quantities existed throughout Pennsylvania, but there was no means to bring the flour to Valley Forge.

Congress issued instructions to the Board of War to purchase 15,000 barrels of flour in Massachusetts and turn them over to the Deputy Quartermaster General of Issues. The Board was also empowered to purchase, charter or hire as many vessels to ship all the flour that could be procured in Virginia. If the quantity of flour in that state was insufficient, the deficiency was to be made up by importing rice from South Carolina. All the accumulated flour and rice was destined for the Valley Forge area to be stored in yet to be built magazines. Quantities were to be drawn by the bakers who were to be hired as needed. Unfortunately, as will be seen, it frequently happened their intentions were merely an exercise in bureaucracy. The optimistic endeavors never reached fruition, and it would be over six weeks before any bakers reported to camp.[39]

These directives may have stimulated Congress, for after lengthy debates it revived its desire to recruit a baker company. On February 27, Christopher Ludwick was named Director of a baker company to be recruited. He was ordered to proceed to Valley Forge as soon as the complement of the company was complete. Ludwick's unit was to consist of three sub-directors, twelve foremen (one for each brigade) and sixty bakers. Fortunately he encountered no difficulty in raising the allotted number as they arrived at camp with a full roster on March 2.[40]

Ludwick and the baker company were immediately assigned to set up their quarters in a building euphoniously designated the "bake house." Before the arrival of Ludwick, the writings of Washington, other officers and orderly books had denoted the structure by that name. Over the past 200 years the bake house has been remodeled several times and used for varying purposes, leaving us with an imperfect description of the Revolutionary structure. During the early weeks of the encampment it was the site of general courts-martial. When Ludwick moved in, these functions were transferred to large officer's huts and a few buildings in the camp. Most of the bakers were dispatched to the different brigades where they served during the encampment. Ludwick, with a small complement of bakers, established themselves in the bake house where they prepared bread for headquarters, and to assemble a reserve for emergencies, and later to sustain the army on its march across New Jersey in pursuit of the British. In colonial times bread was frequently improperly baked and was referred to as "soft bread" by the soldiers, and, in some instances, as "beaten biscuit."

The selection of Ludwick for the post of Director was in part due to his known skill as a gingerbread baker and, equally significant, the high esteem which he enjoyed among Pennsylvania German farmers. Congress was convinced that his acceptance by these farmers would permit him access to large quantities of grain stored in their barns. A recent biographical study of the German baker suggests his success taxed his "best powers of cajolery." Of the grain he obtained, a quantity was stored at Valley Forge, although the main depot was set up at Reading.[41]

Except for there being manifest improvement in the supply of bread for the troops, little is known of Ludwick's activities during the remaining weeks at Valley Forge. What we know is taken from a contemporary biography written by Benjamin Rush. He records one incident that shows an honest and sincere patriot. Ludwick's commission as Director was presented by a Committee from Congress. They proposed that at Valley Forge, he furnish a pound of bread for every pound of flour. Unacquainted with the German's high standard of morality and the techniques of baking, the Committee was obviously unaware that the weight of bread increases by adding water and leaven. He quickly reflected his honesty when replying that he did not wish to get rich by the war; rather, he would supply 135 pounds of bread for every hundred-weight of flour.[42]

Although known to be abrupt in discourse, but never offensive, his present was welcomed at dinner by most officers, including Washington. On many occasions he spent several hours with the Commander in Chief discussing the baking department and the general state of the provisions needed for feeding the soldiers.[43]

Wood was an indispensable ingredient in the health and welfare of the soldiers at Valley Forge. This commodity, also, became a necessity for the various bakers scattered throughout the encampment. A 1965 study indicates that between 80,000 and 100,000 cords were used for all purposes over a five month period. Unfortunately this report is computed on 900 huts which does not account for the huts constructed in April and May, when reinforcements began to arrive at camp. These huts were ground level structures designed for a short use until the weather moderated permitting a move into tents. Planned as makeshift huts, they had neither flooring, nor fireplaces, nor windows. The study predicated the quantity of wood on the amount used in the reconstructed huts we see today, and the belief that each cabin would consume a half cord each day for cooking and heating. Therefore, adding the wood needed to construct these shed-like huts and those built during January and February, a larger quantity of wood was probably consumed during the army's encampment at Valley Forge. Nevertheless, the estimate provided by this research confirms the fact that soldiers were seen dragging logs from a distance exceeding a half mile—thus stripping virgin timber convenient to most huts.[44]

Through its industry the army had been able to cope with several shortages of essentials that plagued the camp. With the disorganized conditions in the Quartermaster and Commissary Departments, little relief could be expected for the need to provide a steady flow of provisions to ease the suffering at Valley Forge. A constant fear persisted that the current alarming increase in camp sickness would be intensified by the unbalanced diet prevalent among the men. Fresh vegetables and salted fish were vital for a healthier diet, but were virtually unobtainable in the adjacent states. Early in February the Congressional Committee at camp directed Congress's attention to the monotonous fare, and recommended that "very great Quantities of Vinegar" be procured to counteract its ill effects, and insure it neither became epidemic, or repeat the current wave of camp sickness in the winter of 1778-79. They, also, suggested that large amounts of "old corn" could be purchased and kiln dried in southern New Jersey to substitute as Indian or mush meal.[45]

The Committee decided to conduct an inspection of the magazines in the Valley Forge area and confirm whether they were fully stocked with flour and provisions, as previously reported. Unfortunately, after a close scrutiny it was found that all the foodstuffs in the magazines had mysteriously disappeared. An explanation of the discovered deficiency was demanded of Colonel Ephraim Blaine, Commissary of Purchases. Blaine was completely baffled, stating he was unaware of this shortage, inasmuch as the responsibility rested with the Commissary of Issues. Naturally Blaine's disclaimer did not satisfy the Committee. Piqued over the apparent lack of cooperation within the Commissary Department, Francis Dana, of the Committee, conducted a personal investigation of conditions in the camp by visiting every brigade. He discovered that every regiment had been without flour, bread, fish or flesh for four days. On the fifth day most soldiers received three-fourth pound of salted pork, while others only a half—not a day's allowance. Dana's findings solidified the determination of the Committee that a complete reorganization of the service departments was essential.[46]

The Committee's letter to Laurens stirred Congress to review all criticisms of the Quartermaster and Commissary operations received over the past year. As early as April 1777, accusations of abuse of authority and dishonesty had been received. Washington later joined the chorus of censors expressing displeasure with the Commissaries, asserting he had "by remonstrating, by writing to, by ordering" appealed for assistance, but had been ignored. Contrary to his desire, he had been compelled to act as the army's Quartermaster and Commissary and, with the catastrophic situation at Valley Forge, order detachments from each brigade to report to Charles Stewart, Commissary of Issues, to scour the countryside for life saving provisions. Stewart and Blaine, with a few other dedicated deputies, were laboring under grave handicaps.[47]

Assistant Commissaries were charged with "raising the price of articles they purchase by bidding upon each other, under an idea of receiving commissions or compensation proportioned to the sums they spend." Other Purchasing Commissaries were reproached for being oversensitive of their authority, by refusing requests for payment of provisions or supplies, without their prior authorization. Such callousness resulted in the starving soldiers going several additional days without sustenance. A flagrant abuse occurred when a Purchasing Commissary considered his prerogative was usurped as reported in a letter of Major John Steel Tyler to his superior Colonel Henry Jackson, of the 16th Additional Continental Regiment. In his words, after witnessing for days the suffering of the men in the regiment, and after three days without any food, he offered to go into the countryside to purchase provisions. He asserted his suggestion was appreciated. Tyler took a detail from the regiment and after going about five miles from Valley Forge, he bought twelve head of cattle and gave receipts for them to the farmers. A Purchasing Commissary refused to honor the receipts because his prior approval had not been obtained. This officious individual appealed to the Pennsylvania Supreme Executive Council, who without authority over Tyler, ordered him to assume full responsibility for payment of the cattle. Tyler considered this demand wrong, as he had conducted himself as an officer and gentleman concerned about the welfare of his men. No record can be found of the outcome of this brouhaha, nor why a Continental Army Commissary petitioned state authorities to intervene, thereby extending the men's famine to an additional five days.[48]

In another instance an unidentified person took a quantity of provisions to an officer commanding the outpost at Radnor Meeting House and, when presented with the receipt, a Commissary refused to pay without a general order. A compassionate Alexander Scammel, Adjutant General of the army, petitioned John Laurens at headquarters to "Please put me in a way to get the honest fellow rewarded." Laurens quickly complied ordering the Commissary General of Purchases to honor the receipt.[49]

On the other hand, Regional Deputy Quartermasters believed their efforts were hampered by official negligence. Nettled, they complained their endeavors were unappreciated, laying the blame on what they described as indifferent public authorities. Occasionally their duties were forestalled by careless paperwork and a scarcity of forms needed to issue the release of supplies. They were aware that the hunger of the troops had worsened by these unnecessary roadblocks that prevented deliveries to Valley Forge. Also, they were always without funds, and what was received was too little and in depreciated Continental Currency which the farmers were reluctant to accept, considering it worthless promises to pay. Giving vent to their own frustrations, the deputies expressed deep resentment over their long overdue compensation.[50]

The establishment of magazines for forage and provisions were vital to the current and long range survival of the army. Washington and Congress were puzzled by the seeming indifference of local citizens and authorities, and the laissez faire attitude of certain New England legislatures to this urgency. To aggravate the situation some appointed service department assistants wasted little time, upon taking office, in making independent decisions contrary to their instructions.

It was hoped a dynamic leadership in the reorganized Quartermaster and Commissary Departments would bring order to their operations. Early in February a consensus prevailed that the army could not survive the winter. To address this possible calamity, Congress and Washington agreed that magazines should be established in the middle states to provide the hoped for flow of supplies.

As a beginning Colonel Clement Biddle, Commissary of Forage, was ordered to install fodder magazines in states from New York to Virginia. They were to be placed at distances considered safe from British raiding parties, with Valley Forge the central location for control of operations. However, it was soon apparent that in the debilitated condition of the army, Biddle would have to table the start of establishing magazines.[51]

The Supreme Executive Council of Pennsylvania, in cooperation with Congress, agreed to build a chain of backup magazines from New Jersey to Maryland. On February 6, a Council Circular announced the appointments of Robert Lettis Hooper, Jr., Jonathan Mifflin and Nathaniel Falconer as Superintendents of the magazines. Their duties were broadened to include the operations of all planned provision depots and those in process near camp.

Within ten days the project collapsed, like a house of cards, when Congress declared the three superintendents were charged with malfeasance of office. The Congressional Resolution asserted that: "Hooper, Mifflin, and Falconer are guilty of making contracts contrary with commissaries authorized to store 30,000 barrels in magazines on each side of the Susquehanna." They fixed prices in violation of the laws of Pennsylvania and contrary to instructions of the Board of War. They made contracts at much higher prices than allowed by law and directed quartermasters to accept such "illegal rates." Congress ordered the three superintendents suspended.[52]

Washington had been forced to assume the role of acting Quartermaster before the appointments of Nathanael Greene and Jeremiah Wadsworth as Quartermaster General and Commissary General respectively. The depressing problem of feeding the soldiers extended back to the Whitemarsh encampment during November and early December, 1777. All forage in the countryside near Valley Forge was exhausted and farmers refused to grind the grain that remained in their barns. As always, Washington was adverse to exerting the "vigorous exercise of military power." With the citizens jealous of "military power," it was an evil to be avoided. In January he advised Congress that it would never be advisable to "procure Supplies of Cloathing or Provisions by coercive measures." Further, he was convinced that under the use of aggressive measures the quantities would never fulfill the army's wants; instead they would create "the alarm and uneasiness...among our best and warmest friends." Washington realized that temporary changes would only aggravate rather than ameliorate the suffering, but hopefully a reorganization of the Quartermaster and Commissary Departments would bring a regular flow of provisions. With this in mind, he directed William Buchanan, Commissary General of Purchases, to form "with all possible expedition" magazines in the rear of the camp to stockpile provisions for the duration of the encampment, adding each depot should be stocked with thirty days provisions.[53]

A month later, with worsening conditions, he wrote pleading letters to several citizens for assistance to ease the crisis. Compassionately, he noted there was "a famine in camp...naked and starving, we cannot enough admire the incomparable patience and fidelity of the soldiery." He acknowledged that if all the beef and pork in Pennsylvania, New Jersey and Maryland were available to the encampment, it would not last one month. In confirmation of Washington's prediction, Colonel Ephraim Blaine estimated that "700 cattle...should last about one week." In his report, Blaine indicated that "one hundred barrels [of flour] is needed each day...."[54]

Blaine's judgment on the cattle and flour requirements to sustain the army for one week was supported by John Chaloner, Deputy Assistant of Purchases, who on March 17 reported he was attempting to supply 160 cattle each week; but as recruits were arriving at Valley Forge it would be essential to increase that number to 200. Chaloner observed that his efforts were handicapped by Washington's appeals to the states who had stripped their areas of livestock. To make conditions worse, some of the beef available was discovered inedible. It was an arduous and futile task for the Deputies and Assistant Commissaries of Purchases to attempt collection of cattle in the optimistic numbers indicated by the letters of Blaine and Chaloner. The average eighteenth century farmer had limited livestock holdings and the Commissaries were frequently greeted by indifference and hostility. Added to their woes were the hazards of slow progress in herding the cattle long distances, especially those from New England and Maryland over the bad roads of the time.[55]

In early March as the grievances continued to mount against the operations of the commissaries, Congress took steps to ease the herculean task confronting Jeremiah Wadsworth before he assumed the post of Commissary General. To appease the uneasiness that prevailed among the Assistant Commissaries of Purchases over their inadequate and often infrequent compensation, they were granted varying allowances on all provisions bought for the army, based on the price of each item. A contingent resolve stated that if they exercised good judgment and were able to save money on the purchases, they would be allowed ten percent of the savings.

Three weeks later, and four days before Wadsworth reported to Valley Forge, Congress modified the payment arrangement for the Commissary Department. A revised scale of remuneration allowed the Commissary General a half percent on all moneys received and expended by his department. Deputy Commissaries were to get the same percent for expenditures in their districts, while Purchasing Commissaries, pursuant to the orders of Wadsworth and the Deputies, were to be granted two percent of the amount they paid for provisions.[56]

Although satisfied that the passage of the compensatory resolutions would make service in the Commissary Department more attractive, Congress recognized that other obstacles remained to smooth out the operations of the department. Its attention was drawn to a conflict of interest between the Commissaries and some states, where they were competing in the purchase of provisions. Confused farmers complained of the practice, but naturally honored the highest bidder. The evil of this practice was that the food destined for the troops at Valley Forge was delayed or, in some instances, never reached camp. As in Pennsylvania, the state and Commissaries were engaged in bidding for the same supplies of wheat and flour. To stop this practice Congress, on April 17, passed another resolution directing Thomas Wharton, Jr., and the Pennsylvania Supreme Executive Council to discontinue the purchase of these products, and prepare a return of what they had gathered for Wadsworth and the Board of War.[57]

On the same day Washington, unhappy with conditions in the service departments, wrote to Wharton declaring that the difficulties in gaining supplies had resulted from the bad choice of deputies: "...who have not only personally abused the inhabitants, but have defrauded them of a great part of their dues." However, he added, he believed that with Greene and Wadsworth at the helm of those departments, conditions would improve.[58]

Greene, appointed March 2, assumed his post of Quartermaster General on March 23, following several fruitless weeks on a roving assignment to improve the flow of provisions and forage to camp. Rebuffed and ineffective after importuning many authorities and civilians, an angry Greene vented his displeasure with the complacency he encountered. He was aware, however, that urgency did not permit him to indulge personal frustration. With time at a premium, any intention to reorganize the Quartermaster Department had to be put in abeyance. All priorities would be directed to ease the needs of the men. In an attempt to soothe the dissatisfaction that prevailed among the deputies, he decided to solicit their continuance as employees of the department. Most accepted his entreaty, although a few declined reappointment.

Throughout the remaining weeks of the encampment, the pangs of hunger would be eased but the men's appetites were never satiated. During this period many soldiers, dissatisfied with their meager diet, wandered into the countryside to find any kind of nourishment. It soon became apparent they could extort, buy or obtain a gift of foodstuffs by claiming they were under orders from Washington. Infuriated by the misuse of his name, Washington directed all officers to take any measures necessary to stop these excursions; however, no evidence exists that the officers succeeded as the soldiers continued to leave camp for provisions.[59]

Greene and Washington were discouraged by the gloomy reports of John Ladd Howell, a quartermaster employee, that grave danger was manifest over the safety of large quantities of provisions in Delaware and Maryland. Writing to Governor George Johnson, of the latter state, Howell asserted that over 35,000 barrels of vegetables, beef, fish, wheat, flour, pork, bread, salt and lard were scattered in different storage depots in the two states. In addition, there were 3,500 bushels of beans, corn and oats. He lamented that no transportation was available to send these commodities to Valley Forge. Also fearful that these provisions might fall into enemy hands, he asked and received permission to store them in Cecil County, Maryland.[60]

A bonanza that eased the food supply for the troops in the spring of 1778, was the large quantity of shad that was taken from the Schuylkill River. In Colonial days the river in the vicinity of Valley Forge abounded with these fish, providing a major activity for rival groups of fisherman. Inhabitants for miles around gathered on the banks of the river with branches of bushes, stakes and a variety of tools to march abreast upstream driving the hapless shad before them. Others on horseback cornered them in a fenced enclosure embedded in the river bed. Tradition claims that tens of thousands of fish, mostly shad, were taken by this method each spring. As the shad came upstream to spawn each spring other fishermen above the future camp site charged them with monopolizing the catch, whereupon bloody clashes usually occurred.

In Philadelphia Loyalist sympathizers alerted the British to the windfall of shad that would be available to the Continental Army. Charles Blagden, a British Army Surgeon, relates to what extent they would go to cut off the American's food supply. British soldiers were instructed to build barricades in the Schuylkill to prevent fish from going up the river. Unfortunately, Blagden did not indicate the method used; it may have been the building of a sturdy weir. Although the surgeon thought the effort was successful, his surmise is suspect as a bountiful supply of shad was caught by the American soldiers. Not surprisingly, those benefiting the most were the regiments stationed near the river.[61]

Most studies of the encampment have referred to the scarcity of water for drinking, cooking or washing. Units stationed on or near the perimeter of the camp probably used Trout Run on the east, Valley Creek on the west or the Schuylkill River—however, access to these water ways in the first months of the encampment would have been difficult because of the rough terrain. Other troops not near these streams had to depend on small springs scattered throughout the camp; also, evidence exists that snow was melted when available. One authority claims there were "only two wells at extreme ends of the encampment," however no citation is mentioned. Washington appears to dispute this statement in his general order of March 19:

> The Commander in Chief directs the officers to be very attentive to the Water their men drink. The little springs about Camp from which they have been accustomed to supply themselves during the winter will in their present state become extremely impure and pernicious in the approaching warm season; as it is a matter essential to health it is expected that officers will without delay take measures to provide good water for their men by having the springs opened and cleaned and Wells sunk in proper places with barrels to preserved them taking care to have them frequently emptied and cleansed to prevent an accumulation of Filth.[62]

Private Elijah Fisher graphically describes the condition of the creeks and springs encountered at most encampments after repeated use, noting so many "dippin and washin—it was Dirty and muddy." Always interested in the health of the soldiers and recognizing that cleanliness was a necessity, Washington on May 14, when the water in the streams was warmer and more sanitary, excused the men from exercise on Friday afternoons. He announced that this time was allowed them for washing "Linnen and cloathing" adding "The Serjeants who conduct the Squads to bathe are to be particularly careful that no man remains longer than ten minutes in the Water."[63]

While money was scarce among the troops, a number had retained their bounty, others saved a portion of their meager and infrequent pay, with a few receiving gifts from home. During the winter a number of parasites were observed hovering about the encampment. These conscienceless sycophants considered the men with money a profitable object for their unregulated wares, especially liquors. The presence of cheap whiskey may be the source of recent contentions that drunkenness prevailed at Valley Forge, however there is no documentation proving excessive drinking among the soldiers.

By March a number of these avaricious black marketeers were reported operating in and near camp. As these unprincipled merchants did not have brigade commanders' approval, they were both unauthorized and unregulated. Despite these restrictions numbers were seen infiltrating the encampment selling their products at prices exceeding those established by the general officers. Most distressing was the disclosure that some of these peddlers were sergeants and soldiers in the army. A futile effort was made to curtail black market activities by ordering all not licensed by a brigade commander to leave camp.[64]

As early as January 20, anticipating these nefarious black market operations, Washington had directed all general officers and brigade commanders to convene at Sullivan's headquarters "to consider the expediency of opening a public Market in camp." If a consensus agree, they were to determine where the markets should be situated, days of operations, a rate schedule of all approved items to be sold and the assignments of guards to preserve order. In affixing fair prices for products, it was suggested that area farmers be consulted in helping set prices. There was little doubt that the emphasis of Washington's order would bring a negative response to the opening of markets.[65]

Nearly three weeks elapsed before Washington announced that the first market would open at the "Stone-Chimney Picket" with business held at the same location each Monday and Thursday. At the same time he stated that every Tuesday and Friday a market would be open across the Schuylkill River, on the north side of the Sullivan's bridge, with a third market near the Adjutant General's office on Wednesday and Saturday. A committee of General Officers published a handbill that set the prices to be enforced at each location. Another notice detailed the regulations that would govern the functions of the farmers participating in the markets and the concurrent responsibilities of the army. To impress the individual soldier, commanding officers of each brigade directed that the market regulations be read at the head of each regiment.[66]

Although the markets were functioning smoothly, by April flagrant violations of the posted orders were observed. Washington was chagrined by reports that these malefactors were members of the army. Officers and soldiers were apprehended trying to circumvent the regular markets by leaving camp to purchase similar products at a lower price and returning to sell them at a lower price than permitted the farmers. Washington ordered an immediate stop to this breach of faith with the authorized markets and their vendors. Incensed, he threatened dire punishment for any officer or soldier making such illegal purchases. Farmers who conducted business with these violators would have their stocks confiscated, with the items or their value awarded the soldier or civilian who acted as informer.[67]

Washington was constantly irked by the misconduct of authorized sutlers. At Whitemarsh they had considered it more lucrative to move beyond what they believed was the jurisdiction of the army and opened tippling houses of ill-repute, dealing in large sales of liquors at high prices and women. With this background, Washington was determined to adopt strict regulations governing the sutler's activities at Valley Forge.[68]

He appointed a board of General Officers to study the methods under which the sutlers would be permitted to operate in the encampment. Approving the board's recommendations, on January 26 Washington issued orders that endorsed their provisions. Each brigade would be limited to one sutler, whose operations were to be closely watched by two officers appointed by each Brigadier. As the main commodity to be dispensed was liquors, they were to be strictly regulated at established prices. Rum and spirits were accepted by eighteenth century armies as a stimulant and were usually doled out to the men during a campaign, or after a battle to relieve the fatigue.

Because Washington and the General Officers placed little confidence in the sutler's adherence to any rules laid down for their operation, severe penalties were to be levied on all violators convicted by a brigade court-martial. Common offenses were charging prices above those established, adulterating liquors and using deceptive measuring methods. The penalties were usually the forfeiture of a quarter of the sutler's stock, not exceeding thirty gallons, or an equivalent monetary value. The informer was to receive a quarter of the value or its equivalent in liquor, with the balance given to a person appointed by the Brigadier to be distributed one gill per day to all non-commissioned officers and privates of the brigade, or, if money, in equal proportion.

Under this ordinance the brigade sutler was permitted to sell leaf tobacco at four shillings per pound, Pigtail at one dollar per pound and hard soap at two shillings per pound. However, sutlers were more interested in the more lucrative liquor sales. The sutler was prohibited from selling any commodities that were to be sold in the public market soon to be opened at a few locations near camp.[69]

In mid-February, Washington directed a strict inquiry be held into the rumor that sutlers and outside persons were selling "spiritous liquors" contrary to regulations. He was especially disturbed by the report liquor was being sold near the picket lines and on the perimeter of the encampment, rather than at the locations assigned the merchant. Any liquors discovered during this investigation were to be confiscated.[70]

A month later further violations were reported: rum, French Brandy, Gin, Spirits and Cyder Royal were being sold "at the most exorbitant rates." Sutlers had taken advantage of these items which had been omitted from the pricing order handed down on January 26. All officers commanding brigades were ordered to meet at General Woodford's quarters to establish prices for these items. In concurrence with Washington's order, the Brigadiers set prices on sundry liquors.[71]

The repeated effort to control the operations and prices of the sutlers' wares continued to vex Washington. Finally, on April 16, he issued a sweeping order to reaffirm the old directives and cover new conditions. Washington found it necessary to reissue his firm order that each brigade was to have only one "Sutling Booth," all others were to be evicted. The sutler was restricted in his sale to the officers and men of the brigade to which he had been assigned, at prices set by the Commander in Chief. Any violation of this order would result in his entire stock being confiscated. Also, he would be ejected from the camp and never granted permission to serve as "a sutler in the Army again."[72]

Still exasperated, Washington was determined to drive all unauthorized sutlers and vendors a distance from the camp that would be inaccessible to the troops. He forbade unauthorized individuals from selling any liquors in camp or within seven miles, threatening to seize their entire stock for use by the army and destroy their booth or houses.

Realizing that civil authorities and others had occasion to visit the camp, he permitted the construction of a hut to "accommodate Travelers and Strangers that have business at camp." The Quartermaster General was authorized to allow one or more houses of Entertainment" for such visitors, but under no consideration could they "vend their liquors to any person belonging to the Army."

As a conclusion to his order, Washington warmly reminded all commanders of brigades that a strict accounting must be maintained of the names and activities of all sutlers; and if any changes should occur they must be promptly reported to headquarters.[73]

Despite all orders, some sutlers considered the opportunity for a more lucrative income worth the risk of detection. As in prior years a number opened tippling houses at locations considered to be beyond Washington's authority. Unfortunately for these unsavory individuals, they misjudged Washington's relentless determination to close and destroy all unauthorized sutler's business. Apparently most recognized Washington's unfaltering resolve to close down all violators and operated within the provisions of their franchise.

State of Defense

I N JANUARY 1778, with work on the huts nearing completion, Washington ordered that all brigadiers under the direction of the engineers begin construction of the camp's fortification. From the first reconnaissance of the Valley Forge area, Washington and Duportail had been in accord on the strength of its natural defensive characteristics, but it was apparent that some sections of the proposed lines were exposed and required the addition of redoubts. As will be seen, Duportail's plan to build redoubts only would lead to a bitter dispute with the general staff.

At about the same time and beset with many problems, a troubled Washington directed his attention to redressing the discontent and rebellious spirit that existed in the ranks. The growing unrest among the troops had begun to manifest itself during the march from Whitemarsh to Valley Forge. Late in December at least two abortive attempts to mutiny were quickly quelled. That the men responded so readily to the importunings of their officers reflected a continuing loyalty and dedication to the Commander in Chief and the cause for which they bravely and faithfully fought at the battles of Brandywine and Germantown. Nevertheless, there was no abatement of their anger and distrust at what they termed the failure of the Continental Congress to provide for their welfare.

Although Washington realized the potential dangers created by these acts of insubordination, he was equally aware that the only lasting corrective would be a complete reorganization of the army before the next campaign. The first three months at Valley Forge would be the most critical period for the maturing Continental Army. With the Quartermaster and Commissary Departments in utter chaos, the troops had had to rely largely on their respective states for sustenance. Despite the unrest of the men, Washington's faith in the fighting capabilities of his young Continentals never wavered. However, for the soldiers to develop a sense of personal pride in their role as fighting men, a competent Inspector

General must be found to replace the absent and disgruntled Conway.

Aggravating an already untenable situation was the public misconception of the number of effectives in the Continental Army. The paper strength of the army at Valley forge was reported at 22,000, whereas there were only 12,000 available and fit for duty. Even the latter figure was misleading as it included many soldiers who were physically exhausted, hungry and in varying stages of nakedness.[1] The dilemma for Washington was compounded by certain regimental officers purposefully filing false muster rolls. These officers were reluctant to report that a greater number of soldiers than usual had been granted furloughs. Washington was hesitant to believe that the muster rolls were being deliberately falsified, but rather he felt the officers were unfamiliar with the paper work involved. In a quandary, a disturbed Washington realized that such misleading returns shrouded the true strength of several regiments. On January 25, to obviate the continuance of inaccurate returns, he ordered the preparation of a standard form to be distributed to all muster officers.[2]

Hopefully, these new forms would provide accurate information on the number of rank and file fit for the duties and tasks needed to make the camp secure and habitable for the winter. As early as Christmas, disquieting civilian outcries filtered into headquarters adding to the uncertainties that plagued Washington. They were complaining that armed Continental soldiers, singly and in groups, were marauding through the countryside. These looters had no respect for their victim's political sympathies, robbing Patriot and Loyalist alike.

An exasperated Washington condemned such "cruel outrages and robberies" although he realized that the seed for the soldier's riotous conduct was the same hunger pang that had nearly precipitated a mutiny. Regardless of his empathy for the men, he must not allow these crimes to go unpunished.

A determined Washington issued orders designed to confine the men to their quarters when not on assigned duty. He directed that passes could only be issued by regimental commanders. He also insisted that non-commissioned officers and privates could not bear arms except when on duty. To ensure that all rank and file were accounted for and in their huts, frequent roll calls were to be made each evening.[3]

A relevant problem that annoyed Washington was the abnormally high number of men reported on furlough. From December 1777, through April 1778, over a thousand soldiers were absent from camp, despite the frequent admonitions of the Commander in Chief, that furloughs be granted only if absolutely necessary. On April 8, 1778, as this situation snowballed, Washington's irritation manifested itself when he wrote to Major General William Heath: "It is shameful to see the number of Men that have been admitted to Furlough. In some Brigades they amount to nearly as many as the men present and fit for duty."[4]

By late December 1777, in an effort to control this promiscuous practice, he had directed that furloughs for non-commissioned officers and privates be issued only by their brigade commanders. Washington recognized that this was an added burden for the brigadiers, but repeated violations by regimental officers demanded drastic action. At the same time the major generals were ordered to adopt stringent regulations affecting the issuance of passes, and to personally be responsible for granting furloughs to officers below the rank of major. Washington reserved the right to review and authorize all requests submitted by officers above that rank. These orders were ignored, possibly out of sympathy for the homesick men, as leaves continued to be granted until late April.[5]

Washington's order appears to have been ignored as he quickly became harassed by numerous petitions for leave from major generals down through the ranks of all officers, with such requests citing the appalling conditions at camp, the "depreciation of our Money," petulant disputes over seniority and promotions, to a simple appeal to visit family. Brigadier General Anthony Wayne wanted to return home, but Washington admonished him not to leave the "camp or its vicinity." Similarly he denied Brigadier General James M. Varnum leave because he did not think himself "...warranted in suffering the Army to be deprived of its best bulwark, good Officers." This was in April, 1778, when Washington believed the season was approaching when the British might attack the camp.[6]

In a different vein, Washington implored Brigadier General John Glover, who had left Valley Forge earlier, to return to camp. He emphasized the need for Glover's presence in camp as many officers were preparing to resign, adding that: "The spirit of resigning which is now become almost epidemical, is truly painful and alarming." Washington continued with the observation that "This spirit, [prevailed] among many of the best Officers, from various inducements." He beseeched Varnum to put everything aside for the "common cause."

More depressing to Washington was the request by Major General John Sullivan for permission to return home to Rhode Island. On February 14, 1778, he replied expressing his dissatisfaction with Sullivan's lack of consideration and indifference to the cause. Washington desired to allow "every indulgence" to the "principal Officers" to visit their families, and then somewhat petulantly stated: "...I can very well form a judgment of the necessity you are under, by my own Affairs, left near three years ago at a very short notice." In denying Sullivan's request he described the worsening conditions in camp, stating there were only two other major generals present, several brigades without brigadiers, and many regiments without a field officer. Ironically, Congress would shortly order Sullivan to command the Continental forces in Rhode Island.[7]

The Continental Congress was cognizant of the dangers that existed in the casual granting of furloughs and leaves of absence. They resolved that the Commander in Chief's orders must be obeyed or the malefactor severely punished. Even with this added support Washington witnessed a continued flood of requests for furloughs. It would be mid-May before these petitions would taper off to an acceptable number.[8]

Brigadiers were directed to order all absent soldiers return immediately to man the works under construction.

Initially, Duportail had been satisfied that his staff of French engineers, with cooperation from the line regiments, could build the needed fortifications. Unfortunately, this was not to be, as controversy began to surface when some units provided less than enthusiastic support to the engineers. Lieutenant Colonel John Laurens, aide to Washington, had been assigned to Duportail as interpreter. Laurens attended all the meetings between the Commander in Chief and the Frenchman, and accompanied Duportail on his contacts with other army personnel to translate his various memorials and orders. There is no evidence that Washington, at this time, issued any written instructions to Duportail.

Even though Duportail enjoyed the respect and confidence of Washington, he had antagonized some of the very officers with whom he should have established an amicable relationship. He was irascible and impervious, and apparently treated with disdain those he considered to be unprofessional American Officers. On March 9, 1778, Laurens advised his father that: "The repeated cavils of some general officers have driven the engineer in his own defense to substitute lines to redoubts in fortifying the camp." Laurens added that the changes increased the labor of the soldiers engaged on building the fortifications.[9]

On January 15, Washington, disturbed with the peevish quarrels and the slow progress of construction, directed Generals Greene, Stirling and Lafayette to consult with Duportail "on the proper means and number of men necessary to execute the works in the different Wings and Second line." They were to express his displeasure with the slothful response of the brigadiers and to appoint proper officers "to Superintend and push forward the defense."[10]

With pettish differences jeopardizing army morale, Washington turned to the proposition that a separate Engineering Corps was needed, with rank equivalent to a brigade of the line. In 1776, Colonel Rufus Putnam, a surveyor, had served as Washington's chief engineer and submitted a plan for an Engineer Corps. However, Congress, in tabling the proposal, apparently considered that Putnam was unqualified or that the army did not need an engineering corps.[11]

On January 20, after consulting with Washington and gaining his approval, Duportail prepared a memorial respecting establishment of an Engineer Corps for presentation to Congress. After detailing the advantages to the army of having a professional engineering team to choose camp sites and prepare the proper type of fortification for their security, Duportail then added an outline for the Corps personnel.

The Corps should be composed of at least four companies of sappers.[12] These men must be superior and vigorous men, preferably carpenters and masons. The work would be exceedingly hard as they must learn the construction of field works, make fascines, palisades, and properly face works with sod and turf. With this arduous work their pay should be higher than that of an "ordinary foot soldier." Non-commissioned officers should be able to read and write and be of good character. Each company would be commanded by a captain accountable only to the Chief Engineer. Duportail emphasized that the need for this control by the "Head Engineer" was necessary, and then testily observed that otherwise: "...if the Major Generals had a right to employ them [Sapper Companies] as they pleased, each, from a desire of fortifying his Camp in his own way, would ask for Sappers and they would all be taken from the Engineers."[13]

Washington unqualifiedly endorsed Duportail's plan and enthusiastically submitted it to Congress, with a copy to a Committee of Congress sitting at Valley Forge, for consideration of problems confronting the army and recommending a proposal for reorganization. He was aware of the need for an immediate engineering department—a vital first step in any improvement in the army. Confident, he assumed Congress would act promptly and endorse the proposal. As added support the Congressional Committee at camp endorsed Duportail's plan. On February 8, in anticipation of its approval, Washington asked all officers desirous of accepting commissions in the companies of sappers to be raised, to report to the Adjutant General's Office. The applicants must have all "necessary qualifications, such as the knowledge of practical Geometry and drawing." To fill out the Corps Duportail needed three captains, three first lieutenants, and the same number of second lieutenants.[14]

Regardless of the urgency, any hope Washington had for a prompt endorsement by Congress was doomed to disappointment. A vacillating and sluggish Congress would not act until May 27, when they authorized the raising of three companies of engineers.[15]

Washington gradually came to the conclusion that no decision would soon be forthcoming from Congress. As a realist he quickly turned his attention to one of the camp's most pressing problems—the defenses! Evidently, Generals Greene, Stirling and Lafayette had successfully combined importunings with an occasional tongue-lashing to emphasize the

Commander in Chief's displeasure with certain brigadiers' lack of cooperation with the engineers. The brigadiers were cognizant that the General's instructions would not brook a rebuttal. They expressed a willingness to start construction immediately on their section of the line. In a spirit of cooperation, some brigades completed their works quickly and with pride. However, as was characteristic throughout the war, there were units whose gifts of patriotism and dedication did not reach the same proportion as those of other regiments. The soldiers were slovenly in their habits and evinced little interest in improving the comfort of their quarters or the security of the camp. One observer noted the lethargy of one specific brigade. On January 1, John Laurens wrote to his father that: "The North Carolinians are the most backward in their building, and for want of sufficient energy to exert themselves once for all, will be exposed to lasting evils."[16]

Undoubtedly, Washington regarded the excessive amount of time he had to devote to arbitrating personal issues as a distraction from duties at headquarters. His aides-de-camp were overworked and needed his attention to resolve the many problems relating to camp routine and security. While he would petition Congress for permission to augment his staff, additional aides were not immediately available.

As will be seen, of equal importance was the need to confine the British Army within their lines and disrupt all intercourse with Loyalist farmers bringing produce to the city.

It was also necessary to recall to active duty soldiers who had been assigned to tasks that could be filled by civilians. One example that plagued the army was the breakdown in the administration of the Quartermaster and Commissary Departments. The chaos created by this situation had forced the army to assume many logistical duties. At Valley Forge the shortage of horses—with those in camp broken-down and emaciated—combined with a paucity of wagons and wagoners intensified Washington's insistence that this function be handled by civilian employees attached to the Quartermaster and Commissary Departments.

The administration of the army necessitated daily contacts with Congress, other civil authorities and detached military units on command. For this purpose a courier service was established. However, with few army horses available and a reluctance to assign soldiers to this duty, Washington employed civilian riders who had their own mounts. Concern was expressed at headquarters for the safety of the express riders, and that expenses be adequate for the risks they took. As they carried letters and documents of a security nature, they were constant targets of British soldiers and Loyalist sympathizers. General Nathanael Greene was directed to investigate the conditions and expenses of this service. John Erskine reported to Greene that he had checked their tavern bills and compared them with similar rates prevalent in Philadelphia. Erskine added that a very "honest fellow" had furnished him the latter rates. He found that the riders when "travelling" expended upwards of fifty dollars per day and were allowed thirty dollars when idle. As they were engaged between a half and two thirds of the month, their pay and expenses would total about nine hundred dollars. With the constantly depreciating Continental dollar this did not seem sufficient recompense for their service, considering the risk of losing their horses and possibly their lives. There is no record that Congress acted on Greene's recommendation to increase the compensation of express riders.[17]

General William Smallwood, with the Maryland brigade stationed at Wilmington, bemoaned his inability to establish communications with Delaware authorities and army foraging units. In response to Smallwood's complaint, Washington benevolently admonished the Marylander that he could correct this deficiency "...for Expresses hire them from the Country." Washington always referred to the couriers as expresses.[18]

Washington also favored a position that had obvious natural defensive characteristics. Since his service as a Colonel in the Virginia militia during the French and Indian War to the recent encampment at Whitemarsh, he had emphasized the choosing of this type of position. At such times he usually supplemented the natural defensive conformation by adding abatis or brush, and buttressing weak points with earthen works often fraised and reinforced with fascines and gabions.[19]

The affect of these works on the cautious Sir William Howe and other British officers was evident at Whitemarsh in early December 1777—two weeks before the Continental Army marched to Valley Forge. A British officer noting the "felled trees" on the Whitemarsh hills, reasoned that any attempt to storm the heights would be a disaster, causing irreplaceable losses.[20]

Before issuing an order that would force cooperation between the generals and the engineers, Washington and Duportail surveyed the outer line position and concurred on the works to be constructed. The line was on an elevation approached by a gradual glacis. When cutting trees for hut construction on the glacis, the men were instructed to leave the stumps and fill the intervening space with branches and brush. This helterskelter brush defense was not a pure abatis which would have had the branches sharpened to spear points, but as Duportail wrote: "...they must pass over that space of ground thick set with obstacles—without being able to fire a single shot."[21]

While effective, the abatis and brush demanded constant attention. At Whitemarsh Washington was forced to order the filling in of spaces in the brush where the wood had rotted or been carried off as firewood by the soldiers. The same condition would later exist at Valley Forge. On

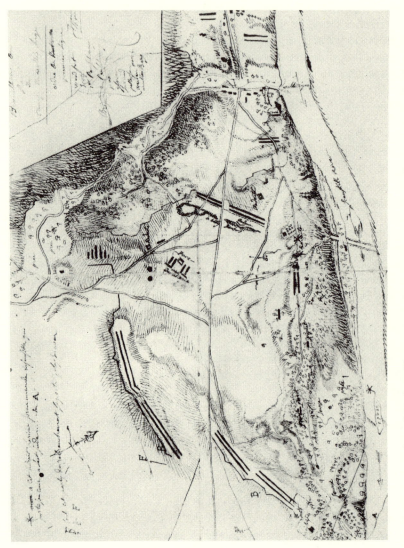

Contemporary sketch of Valley Forge encampment attributed to Brigadier General Louis Le Bégue de Presle Duportail. Probably drawn by his cartographic engineer Lieutenant colonel Jean Louis Ambroise de Genton Chevalier de Villefranche. (Historical Society of Pennsylvania.)

April 2, 1778, Washington ordered that as all: "...Stumps and brush in front of the New Lines afford an excellent obstacle to the approaches of an Enemy, it is expressly forbid that any part of it should be burnt by the fatigue parties or any others for distance of Musquet range in front of the Lines." He added that there were sufficient stakes, or fraise, available at the camp for use on the works.[22]

Washington and Duportail had agreed that the line defenses should be reinforced at weak points by the erection of redoubts. However, as previously indicated, controversy had developed between the generals and Duportail over the absence of entrenchments, or breastworks, along the entire outer line. Apparently, Washington was forced to act as mediator to speed up construction, by acceding to the brigadier's demands.

Displeased with the haggling and realizing the need to compromise, but recognizing the urgency, Washington decided he must take the initiative to expedite work on the defenses. On January 13, pushing aside but not ignoring other problems, he ordered each brigade to furnish five men, accompanied by an officer, to parade the next morning on the left wing at nine o'clock. They were to report to General John Peter Muhlenberg and assist the engineers in tracing the planned fortifications. Muhlenberg's position on the extreme left of the front line was considered most vulnerable to enemy attack. After these lines were traced, other brigades were to assist the engineers in performing the same function fronting their position.[23]

The order to assist the engineers in tracing the planned defenses was quickly followed by the aforementioned directive to Greene, Stirling and Lafayette to warn the brigadiers that they must expeditiously cooperate with the engineers. However, a week later on January 20, Washington was not satisfied that work on the breastworks and redoubts was progressing as speedily as desired. Fearful that Howe might take advantage of the exposed situation on the left, Greene was ordered to place General John Paterson in charge of the work. Paterson was to use every soldier not on duty in the brigades on the left wing to report every morning at nine o'clock, until the works were completed. Greene wrote the commanders of the fatigue parties should carefully observe that: "His Excellency the Comdr in Chief Desires the Officers to Exert themselves to put the Camp in a Defenceable Condition as soon as may be."[24]

Even with these orders and admonishments, the work proceeded at what Washington considered a snail's pace. Finally, on January 27, another order emphasized the imperative need for a more rapid compliance. General Enoch Poor's instructions to his New Hampshire Brigade mirrored those issued to all brigades, declaring: "It is necessary the Camp should be put in a State of Defense immediately, as soon therefore as

Work is allotted to each Regiment, which shall be done in Proportion to their Strength the Genl intreats the Commanding officers of Regiments to exercise every effort possibly in their Power to compleat it. The least Delay may prove fatal—"[25]

Various officers reported on the progress made in constructing fortifications, with several exhibiting an unbounded faith in the camp's impregnability. Such confidence is exemplified in a letter of Captain William Gifford to Lieutenant Colonel Benjamin Holmes of the New Jersey militia. Writing on January 24 he noted: "The Army is Divided into Two lines front & Rear besides Corps de Reserve, and possessing very Commanding & defensible ground, we are fortifying the Camp as fast as possible, tho' we are under no apprehensions of a visit from the Enemy, Tho' such a report is current in Camp, but I am very sensible they know better things, if they shou'd come & trust in God we shall be able to give them a warm reception, perhaps a total defeat..." After commenting on New Jersey's failure to provide for their men and some hardships in the huts, he added "...what can't brave Americans endure Nobly fighting for the rights of their injured Country." On the same day, Gifford's sentiments were echoed by an anonymous New Jersey officer who wrote: "...the advantageous situation of the camp, and the bridge over the Schuylkill, not only made us secure in camp, but enabled us to act with advantage against the enemy in almost any route."[26]

In a more pragmatic manner, Major Richard Platt advised General Alexander McDougall: "We are fortifying our Camp by Redoubts in front of the first & second lines..." Other officers were equally terse in a description of their work as Lieutenant Thomas Blake noted "each brigade was ordered to build a breast work in front of their own huts."[27]

Unfortunately, few rank and file have left accounts of the adverse conditions under which they labored in building the works. There is little doubt that their exertions were fraught with numerous difficulties. In the last half of January with the soil frozen and but a few dull and leaden tools available, their toil must have been disheartening. Dr. Philip Syng Physick, a prominent Philadelphia physician, visited Valley Forge at this time and commented that the cannon being "frozen solid in the mud," they would have been incapable of working if the camp were attacked.[28]

According to Woodman, the soldiers digging the trenches threw the excavated earth to their rear, thus forming a second breastwork. He noted that in 1800 the trench was "considerably filled up" and the embankment formed by the excavation remained about the same height as originally built. Fifty years later, Woodman observed that the defenses were in a "tolerable good state of preservation." Woodman's observations on the relatively shallow entrenchments coincided with those of the British Lieutenant Thomas Anburey, who was at Valley Forge in December 1778, as he caustically noted: "...the ditches were not more than three feet deep, and so narrow, that a drum-boy might with ease leap over."[29]

The construction of the outer-line of breastworks was partially completed in February, but other works such as the redoubts and redans and inner-line defenses would drag on, and not be finished until late May.

Concurrent with the building of the manmade fortifications, it was acknowledged that several other measures had to be taken to ensure the camp's security. Of primary importance, a vigorous program of exercise and drill had to be introduced to the army. Both Washington and Congress were aware that an experienced and efficient Inspector General had to be found. On December 13, 1777, Congress promoted Brigadier General Thomas Conway—an Irish mercenary who had served in the French Army—to Major General, over a number of senior American brigadiers, and then promptly named him Inspector General. Although Congress had only exercised its right to make promotions of this rank, they had not consulted the Commander in Chief on Conway's appointment.[30]

Conway reported to Washington at Valley Forge, but immediately encountered a frigid reception by the generals in camp. Although an excellent field commander, his promotion over their heads, and his known low opinion of most Americans, angered the officers. Neither Congress nor Conway had properly gauged the temper of native born officers who had been bypassed in rank by foreign officers. In addition, Conway's abrasive personality had not engendered a spirit of camaraderie. An indignant Major Richard Platt, aide to General Alexander McDougall, voiced the opinion of most officers when he wrote his superior that Conway had been "...hanging about Congress, till he got promotion." He later noted that "...The Brigadiers have thrown in a Remonstrance to Congress respecting Genl Conway's promotion." However, when they did not receive an answer, General Jedediah Huntington echoed Platt's statement adding that the only reason a number of general officers had not resigned was because of "their patriotism."[31]

Due to the officers' disdainful attitudes, Conway stated it was impossible to perform the duties of Inspector General. Ignored by Washington and unacceptable to the general staff, he quickly left Valley Forge to report to Congress. There is evidence that Conway's attitude did not help the situation. He believed his appointment by Congress had mandated him to establish a "field agency" reporting to the President of the War Board, Major General Horatio Gates.

Conway's miscarriage as Inspector General prompted him to write Washington in an endeavor to justify his conduct. On December 29, 1777, he wrote the Commander in Chief emphasizing that his only objective was to serve the American cause and to make the "troops fitt to exercise [Washington's] ...orders." Conway contended that the rank of Major General was an absolute requisite when assuming the post of Inspector General.[32]

Washington replied the next day, believing that Conway's letter had only expressed his frustrations with his reception at camp, stating he assumed that Conway was ready to begin the function of Inspector General. In a dispassionate but reserved manner, he assured Conway that the general officers did not resent his appointment as Inspector General, but rather were angered by their being superseded in rank when he was appointed as Major General. Washington reaffirmed that only Congress could name general officers, and that he "shall always afford every Countenance and respect to those appointed by that body." He reminded Conway that he had taken similar affront when the "Baron" de Kalb had been appointed by Congress to Major General.[33]

Troubled by Washington's letter, Conway instantly answered that he had only intended to coordinate the activities of Inspector General and to prepare and print a set of regulations on maneuvering and discipline, warning that the present state of the army demanded immediate attention. At somewhat greater length, Conway tried to justify the rank of major general as the acceptable designation for those selected as inspector general in European armies. He concluded by asserting that: "By the complexion of your Letter, and by the two receptions you have honour'd me with...that I have not the happiness of being agreeable to your Excellency." Conway added that he could not expect the support of the various officers in performing his duties as Inspector General, and not wishing to be a disturbing influence in the army, reiterated he was "very readdy" to return to France to rejoin the French Army where he "will Meet with no frowns." Apparently in a fit of pique, Conway was attempting to shift all responsibility for relinquishing his assignment. He never intended to return to France and quickly departed for Yorktown to seek another post.[34]

Displeased, but inasmuch as he had not been consulted on Conway's appointment, Washington decided to direct his attention to other pressing needs of the army and camp security. Disquieting information had reached headquarters that many muskets and bayonets had rusted or were broken and would be useless in the event of an enemy attack. As this condition had to be quickly rectified, orders were issued that "all armorers and blacksmiths" were to immediately repair and place in usable condition every musket, bayonet, and other equipment.[35]

As vital as the manmade defenses were to the security of the camp, it was absolutely necessary that a well-disciplined and completely reorganized military establishment be also ready for the coming summer campaign. While the search for an inspector general continued,

Washington and Congress agreed to dispatch what Joseph Reed styled a "Committee of Congress for the Reform & Re-establishment of the Army" or more commonly referred to as the Committee of Conference, to Valley Forge to study the weaknesses and strengths of the military. On January 10, Congressmen Francis Dana, Joseph Reed, Nathaniel Folsom and John Harvie were chosen to serve on the Committee. Two days later three members of the Board of War were selected, namely Major Generals Horatio Gates and Thomas Mifflin and Colonel Timothy Pickering, but for personal reasons were excused from serving. Eight days later, January 20, Congressmen Charles Carroll and Gouverneur Morris were chosen to replace them. Arriving at camp, they established their headquarters at Moore Hall about two miles west of Valley Forge.[36]

On January 13, Elbridge Gerry advised Washington on the appointment of the Committee and its broad responsibilities. The congressman and Commander in Chief had agreed in previous correspondence on the need for members of Congress to become involved in the reorganization of the army. Gerry outlined in general terms:

> A Committee is appointed from Congress & the Board of War [members of the Board of War would ask to be excused from serving on the Committee], who in Concert with your Excellency have full powers to form & *execute* a Plan for reducing the Number of Battalions now in the Service; to recommend the necessary Appointments of General officers, to determine on the necessary Reinforcements for the Cavalry, Artillery, & Infantry & report their opinions on the Mode of obtaining the same; to remove from office any officers of the civil Departments [Quartermaster, Commissary and Medical Departments] of the Army for Negligence, Incompetency, or Fraud, & appoint others untill the Sense of Congress can be known; to report all just Causes of Complaint relative to rank, confining it nearly as may be to the military Line & for other purposes mentioned in their Commission.

Gerry expounded in detail on what the officers of the army considered the pressing question to be resolved—the need of a provision for pensions and a similar consideration for the widows of officers slain in the service of their country.[37]

Only upon their arrival at camp did the Committee become aware of the myriad of unanticipated problems that confronted them. After a conference with Washington, it was agreed that the first step would be for the Commander in Chief to submit a particularized account of the evils existing in the army and his recommendations for correction. Following this meeting, individually and as a Committee, they visited every area of the Valley Forge encampment holding discussions with the officers and men, and understandingly listening to their complaints. The hungry men grumbling that they had been abandoned by Congress and their states, unburdened their gripes to the Committee. A by-product of these animated discussions was the startling revelation, that in their hunger these very same men would: "...disperse in the Neighborhood & take indiscriminately the provision laid in by the Inhabitants for the Winters Support of themselves & Families." The Committee noted that the specter of starvation engendered "Mutiny, Desertion, and a Spirit of Depredation & Plunder..." Washington, although sympathetic with the men's distressing condition, had unsuccessfully tried to curb the depredations by ordering severe punishment for those absent from camp without leave. However, it had become manifestly clear that the penalties involved were more bearable than the pangs of hunger.[38]

While a hard core of soldiers were dedicated to the American cause and devoted to their Commander in Chief, numerous Americans looked askance on establishing or strengthening a regular army. Prior to the Revolution the colonies had based their defense on short term militia called up to thwart any incursion into an individual colony—principally against threatened Indian attacks. Many men serving in the army at Valley Forge and elsewhere throughout the states, were no less loyal than their comrades, but vehemently opposed a standing army, believing instead in a strong militia. Colonel Joseph Ward[39] epitomized this position in a letter to Samuel Adams writing that he: "...considered *Standing Armies* dangerous to Liberty, ...at some particular times a *necessary evil but* an *evil* and a capital one...*A good Militia* is my Doctrine...As long as he is able he will fight for a formidable Militia, —to render Standing Armies unnecessary..."[40]

On January 29, Washington forwarded to the Committee a detailed and comprehensive plan of the needs of the army and suggestions for its betterment. The preamble to this submission stated that he "would be happy [if] his recommendations were conducive...to remedying the Evils and inconveniences we are now subject to." In addition he expressed hope that together they could put the army on a more respectful footing. As a mild admonishment, he refreshed the Committee's memory on the known unrest among the officers who had enlisted at the beginning of the struggle with Great Britain, but were currently uneasy about possible future provisions for their service, especially a workable pension arrangement. Washington's plan covered every facet of army organization including size of regiments, state quotas, rank, promotions, and an evaluation of the importance of each arm of the military establishment.

The presentation was favorably received by a sympathetic Committee. It had been obvious when they reached camp that a complete reevaluation of the army, its logistical and support units and of redressing the complaints of officers and men was imperative. Their headquarters at Moore Hall was also the post of Colonel Clement Biddle, Commissary

General of Forage, who on February 12, was named temporary superintendent of the Commissary and Quartermaster Departments by Nathanael Greene. This provided the Committee with an excellent opportunity to review the chaotic conditions in these two departments.[41]

With Washington's report as a benchmark and after their interviews with army officers, it became obvious that the Commander in Chief had a firm grasp on the military's needs. An early authority on the Continental Congress stated that the Committee had little rapport with Washington and other officers or with their colleagues in Congress. Edmund Burnett wrote that the Committee was "as successful in muddling as it was enterprising in meddling." He contended that the Committee, contrary to their instructions, virtually ignored Washington. In fact some Congressmen "positively refused" to serve with the Committee, knowing that with their past criticisms of the army, they would not meet with open arms at Valley Forge. Today with more research material at our disposal, it appears to be an unfair critique on members of the Committee. Naturally there were disagreements, but all were eventually satisfactorily resolved. Washington remained adamant that the military must be subservient to civil authority as exemplified in his carefully phrased, but forceful recommendations for any reorganization as requested by the Committee. Despite Burnett's criticisms of the lack of cooperation, Washington frequently met with the Committee, usually at their headquarters in Moore Hall. Their concern for the Commander in Chief is reflected in a letter to Washington suggesting that as: "The travelling is so bad that we wish you wou'd not attempt to meet us while it continues. We shall employ ourselves in that part of our business which can be done without your personal attendance."[42]

With Washington's evaluations and suggestions before them, the Committee was prepared to fulfill their assigned instructions. But, as Joseph Reed noted, their task to "Reform & Establishment of an Army" had encountered numerous diversions that introduced them to disorder and confusion, making their efforts almost impossible. Reed also declared that his "three years Connection with the Army" with observations of life in camp, confirmed his belief that had there been more intercourse between the army and Congress, and more frequent and longer attendance at camp of Congressional representatives, it "would have prevented some Errors and Mistakes which have happened." He concluded such lack of harmony could lead "God forbid" the nation to "political Suicide." These minutiae of misunderstanding were noted in certain Congressional correspondence of what was termed the ease with which the British had occupied Philadelphia, assuming the mistaken belief that the Continental Army was "double to that of the Enemy."[43]

The Committee, not daunted by their critics, plunged into both their assigned and unassigned responsibilities.

Although the Committee's priority was to submit to Congress a plan for reorganizing the army before the opening of the 1778 campaign, probably in June, other problems diverted their attention. They had been warned by Washington and Congressional colleagues who had visited the Whitemarsh headquarters in early December 1777, that unless Congress enacted a pension plan, the army faced the loss of hundreds of discontented officers. As has been noted, the officers, most of whom had served since the Revolution began and had seen their fortunes disappear and their families in want, were demanding a half pay pension establishment after the end of the war.

With this knowledge the Committee conducted numerous interviews with officers, and rank and file that revealed angry and adamant soldiers who would not listen to anyone who didn't respect their grievances. After considering their complaints and the horrific conditions in camp, the Committee decided to approve the soldiers' plea and submit a recommendation for a pension plan to Congress.[44]

The question of rank was another issue that clouded their principal purpose at Valley Forge, a dilemma that had frequently confronted Washington. As an example, a bitter dispute existed over the precedence of rank between Brigadier Generals William Woodford, George Weedon and Charles Scott. Jealousy of rank was also evident among the officers below the grade of general officer. Inasmuch as all decisions of rank and promotions rested with Congress, Washington could only appeal to the officers to drop their ambitions in the interest of the common cause. Handicapped by his lack of authority, he entreated the Committee to assist in resolving the disputes. While ultimately these disagreements would be solved, temporarily they would have a discordant effect on camp morale.

Concurrent with the problem of rank was the tendency of Congress to transfer general officers to other sectors without Washington's consent. As will be seen, Congress decided to organize an expedition to conquer Canada, assigning Lafayette to command with the assistance of de Kalb and Conway. This would be followed by an order for Sullivan to assume command of the Continental troops in Rhode Island. Washington protested that no matter how: "...inconvenient and distressing to the Service in this quarter it may be to part with another Major General, yet in obedience to a resolve of Congress I must do it..." He had urged Congress to consider sending either Major General Israel Putnam or William Heath to Rhode Island. They were stationed in a sensitive and strategic area at West Point and the Hudson River Valley, which made them well qualified to fill the Rhode Island command. Apparently the judgment of Congress and its Committee were of a different opinion as they said Putnam and Heath did not "answer the purpose" of that command.[45]

Another condition which seriously aggrieved the Committee during January and February was the egregious scarcity of provisions, especially meat. One Congressman noted that they had been without meat for four days. A frustrated Committee issued a broad appeal to the states to quickly move to remedy the shortage. In writing to Governor William Livingston of New Jersey, Washington stated he would not elaborate on the dire conditions as the Committee had already graphically represented "the distress of the Army for want of provisions" adding that he only considered "the colourings not sufficiently strong."

It was evident that the only permanent solution was to reorganize the Quartermaster and Commissary Departments and to appoint efficient heads of these activities. Early in the search for a competent Quartermaster General, it was soon manifest that everyone favored Nathanael Greene for the position. A reluctant Greene finally agreed to serve if John Cox was appointed Deputy Quartermaster. In a game of musical chairs, Cox consented to act as Greene's assistant if Charles Pettit was named to the third post in the Department. Greene stated his concurrence was only made: "from Public Motives...thinks he might be of some Use in the military Part of this Office but disclaims what may be called the civil Part." He also received assurance that in the event of action he would be restored to duty on the line. With all his conditions granted Greene entered on his duties with his characteristic energy to bring order out of chaos in the Quartermaster Department.

On March 13, Congress, anxious to remove the confusion in the Commissary Department, approved new regulations to govern that activity. Jeremiah Wadsworth was the unanimous choice of Congress and Washington for the post of the Commissary General. In an effort to influence Wadsworth's acceptance, a copy of the regulations was sent to him for consideration and any suggested changes. On April 9, after submitting his comments with three minor alterations, Wadsowrth was named Commissary General.[46]

Many distractions served to prolong the Committee's deliberations. However, after a few weeks of firsthand observations of the depressing conditions at Valley Forge, it became manifest that corrections of these ills were mandatory if there was to be an acceptable plan of reorganization and discipline for the army. Late in March, after formal and informal conferences and a close scrutiny of Washington's recommendations, the Committee drafted a proposal for Congressional consideration. In late May, after a lengthy debate, Congress would accept most provisions in the Committee's plan and issue instructions for the changes to be made in the army.

Chapter
VIII

The Baron Arrives

A BRIGHT SPOT IN the first months at the encampment occurred in February with the arrival of "Lieutenant General" Baron Frederick William Ludolph Gerhard Augustin Steuben.[1] Steuben's rank was a gift from the facile pen of Benjamin Franklin. Franklin, cognizant of Steuben's qualifications, realized that with many foreign officers in America his talents would be hidden; hence the need to elevate the Prussian's rank in his country's service. As a Steuben biographer noted, it was "necessary to sell the Baron" to the people of the United States. Silas Deane, Franklin's associate, echoed the latter's craftiness in a letter to Robert Morris, extolling Steuben's importance at the court of the King of Prussia. Both diplomats considered Steuben's service so essential to the young American Army, that the Prussian was urged to sail immediately for the United States.[2]

Apparently Washington's first knowledge of Steuben was a letter from the Baron, written at Portsmouth, New Hampshire, where the Prussian and his entourage was being feted by the town's citizens. Unlike some of the pompous foreign officers, Steuben's self-effacing letter stated that: "If the distinguished ranks in which I have Served in Europe should be an Obstacle, I had rather serve under your Excellency as a Volunteer, than to be a subject of Discontent to such deserving Officers as have already distinguished themselves amongst you." On February 23, when Steuben reached camp, Washington offered a restrained impression of the Prussian, writing that "He appears to be much of a Gentleman, and as far as I have had an opportunity of judging, a man of Military knowledge and acquainted with the World."[3]

Any uncertainties or misgivings that Steuben would not be accepted by American officers soon vanished. John Laurens was impressed by the modesty of Steuben's offer to serve as a volunteer in the Continental Army. In the first conference between the Commander in Chief and the Prussian, with Laurens acting as interpreter, he was pleasantly amazed at Steuben's reaffirmation that he did not want to give umbrage to American

124

Major General Frederick William August Baron von Steuben by Ralph Earl. (New York State Historical Association, Cooperstown, NY.)

officers. He admitted that he desired the rank of major general with its emoluments, however, he reiterated his happiness in serving as a volunteer under Washington, until Congress considered it appropriate to appoint him to a command in the line. Steuben stated that as a foreigner and ignorant of the American people and their language, he was "totally" unfit to be given the desired rank. At this meeting occurred initial recognition that there was a possibility the Baron could serve as Volunteer Inspector General. Laurens remembered it had been agreed that he was well qualified to correct the obvious lack of discipline and training in the Continental Army.[4]

Washington knew that without Congressional approval, he could not at this time offer Steuben a specific assignment, but in an unofficial capacity the Baron's expertise would be invaluable. He asked him to reconnoiter the encampment, inspect its defenses, delve into the personal conditions of the men and life in their quarters, and review the effectiveness of the various regiments and brigades. It was manifest to Washington that Steuben's observations and recommendations would be the touchstone for pinpointing the responsibilities and duties of the anticipated Inspector General.

The Prussian enthusiastically pursued Washington's instructions, but soon became appalled at the slovenly and disordered conditions throughout the camp. A particular source of irritation was the obvious understrength of a number of regiments and companies, with some unable to mount a corporal's guard. The negligence of officers and armorers had permitted many muskets to rust, thereby rendering them incapable of firing a shot. In addition, Steuben was aghast to discover that half the troops were without bayonets.

Steuben's reports were cogent and detailed, with most findings being discussed verbally in meetings with Washington; with at least three in depth papers prepared for the Commander in Chief's guidance. One was a forceful and critical blueprint of the weakness of the camp with suggested corrections. At several meetings they discussed the uncleanliness of the camp, agreeing that it was a hazard to the health and morale of the army. Washington bemoaned that his frequent orders to clean up the camp, had been treated repeatedly with indifference or disobedience by some brigades. It was agreed that the horrendous sanitary conditions in the camp must be corrected before a course in drill and discipline could be initiated.

The input of a strict disciplinarian like Steuben would serve as a catalyst to cleaning up the offal and debris that cluttered the camp. John Laurens wrote that his influence for improvement in the army was "uncommonly [good] for a stranger." As an aside with tongue in cheek, Laurens advised his father that the Baron's rank in Prussia had actually been "lieutenant general quarter maitre [which] in good English [was]...deputy quarter master general."[5]

On March 13, two months after his first directive, Washington issued orders to clean up the camp. He was chagrined to find certain areas loathsome and littered with "the Carcases of dead horses...that offal [was] near many of the Commissaries Stalls" thus being a deterrent to the good health of the soldiers. In addition, he had observed a large amount of "Filth and nastiness is spread amongst the Hutts...[will] soon be reduced to a State of Putrefaction...." Convinced that these horrific conditions had contributed to the increased sickness among "His brave Soldiery," Washington irritably demanded of the Quartermaster General that he make certain the dead horses be buried, and that the Division and Brigade Commissaries diligently apply themselves to "Bury the offal and damaged provisions..." within the areas of their commands.[6]

Another source of hygienic concern was the condition of the necessaries or vaults. Washington had ordered they be cleaned every week with older vaults filled and new ones dug, and all filth to be buried or "flung into the Vaults" before they were covered. As it was mandatory "to preserve Health in Camp" no plea of ignorance would be accepted, but rather "severely noticed." A decorous Washington was embarrassed at the inability of company commanders to control the filthy habit of the men's relieving themselves wherever nature called. In early May with little improvement noted, he directed regimental commanders "For the sake of decency," to hide their necessaries with "Boughs or Hurdles."[7]

Unfortunately, little attention had been given to orders respecting the slovenly dress of the soldiers. In early April a wrathful Washington upbraided those officers, especially sergeants and corporals, who permitted soldiers to mount guard or appear at drill in unclean dress. Not overlooking commissioned officers, he bitterly reproved them for lack of "order, regularity and obedience in their commands." To emphasize the sanitary condition, Washington called upon all from major generals down through the ranks to corporals, to recognize that: "Nothing does, nor nothing can contribute more to the health of soldiers than a clean Camp, clean Cloathes and victuals well dressed, [adding parenthetically] however deeply involved in rags an Army can be." In conclusion, he noted that it would not have been necessary to castigate any officers if they had given more attention to the needs of their men.[8]

Hopefully, cleaning up the camp debris would subsequently improve morale and permit Washington to shift his attention to initiating Steuben's program of training. To implement the instructions of drill, he ordered a company of 100 chosen men be added to the Commander in Chief's guard, to serve as a model to demonstrate the techniques of Steuben's drill and maneuvers. Sensitive to the criticism that he favored soldiers from Virginia for his present guard, Washington requested that the incoming soldiers be selected from other states. Two days after the order to form a model company, he issued instructions that would staff the Inspector General's Department. As the first step, he directed the formation of a "uniformity of discipline and maneuveres [and] ...form a Body of Instructors." The program was unquestionably the result of Steuben's advice, but deliberately made no mention of the Baron, as Washington was waiting for the proper time to make an official announcement of his assuming the Inspector General's function. The Instructors mentioned were to report to the Inspector General to coordinate his draft of procedures. Washington also requested that "Brigade Inspectors" be appointed to train their respective brigades after preliminary instruction from the Instructors.[9]

Washington emphasized that only those officers with exceptional qualifications and "...whose activity, Intelligence, Address and decided Taste for the kind of employment," be accepted. Preferably the post of Sub-Inspector (or Instructor) should be chosen from the rank of Colonel, with majors selected as Brigade Inspectors. However, as the summer campaign was only a few months away and time imperative, Washington stated that if qualified officers who desired the posts were not available the choice could be made from those of a higher or lower rank.[10]

On March 22, after observing the current forms of drill practiced by the different brigades, and the ragged execution of them by the rank and file, Washington quickly ordered their discontinuance. New regulations were issued that all future drill routines would emanate from the Inspector General's headquarters.[11]

Washington's apprehension about the success of the project was evident when he personally participated in the selection of the Sub-Inspectors. Steuben asked for an exception, requesting the appointment of a highly qualified foreign officer Jean Baptiste Ternant to fill one of the posts on his staff.

On March 23, with the completion of preliminaries, Steuben issued his first instructions to the Sub-Inspectors, commanding them to have all commissioned officers below the rank of colonel, not on duty, in the first battalion or regiment of each brigade to assemble on the parade the following morning at eight o'clock. Because of confusion about the authority of the Sub-Inspectors and a reluctance by some officers to comply with the order, delays in training the Sub-Inspectors in their specific responsibilities, curtailed their functioning until April 19.[12]

On March 28, after several discussions with the Committee at Camp, Washington finally announced that: "Baron Steuben, a Lieutenant General in Foreign Service and a Gentleman of great Military Experience [has] obligingly undertaken to exercise the office of Inspector General in this Army..." The Baron was gratified that the army had finally acknowledged his status, even as a volunteer, although he and the Commander in Chief knew he had been serving in that capacity for ten days. Nevertheless, Steuben hoped that Congress would act promptly on his desire for a permanent rank. He wrote to Henry Laurens, President of Congress, declaring his dedication to the army and Washington noting that "...If His Excellency thinks, that I may be more Useful to you as a Volunteer, than as a Commissioned General, I shall willingly submit to his Desires."[13]

Unquestionably, Steuben's reaffirmation of his loyalty was sincere, but it was also probably an effort to accelerate the sluggish movements of Congress. Albeit, action on the Prussian's appointment would have to wait until early May. On May 9, Washington announced that "Congress has been pleased to appoint Baron de Steuben Inspector General with the Rank of Major General..." With this resolution Congress also vested Washington with the continuing right to name the Inspectors. Six days later, in a letter to Henry Laurens, Steuben acknowledged his official rank, although he considered the post of Inspector General as "brevet." He stated his work with the army had been crowned with success as: "...Order, Discipline, and that Uniformity So necessary in an Army, begins to take place and to the Zeal of your Officers, and good Disposition of your Soldiers is owing a [more] rapid Progress than any other Army would have made in So Short a Time."[14]

The contents of Steuben's letter summarized the denouement of two months of frustration and constant devotion to molding the ragtag Continentals into an efficient fighting machine. To achieve this state of perfection, many steps were taken beginning in mid-March when twenty men from each battalion were chosen to cooperate with the model company to receive training instructions without muskets. Initial exercises were elementary, including "how each soldier should stand straight & firm upon his Legs without affectation, the Shoulders square and to the front and half back. Head upright & both Arms hanging down the sides without constraint." After several futile attempts to instruct the Continentals in the drill used in European armies, it was clear to Steuben that they were clumsy and could not perform the basic fundamentals of army drills. To achieve any degree of perfection, he decided to exercise the men in the simplest military routines.

Contemporaries recalled that in the early stages of the training, an exasperated Steuben would grab a musket from an awkward soldier, and then personally demonstrate each exercise. As his irritation increased he would hurl imprecations in German and French at the clumsy trainee, then would order one of his inspectors to take over and curse the soldiers in English. As the men became more proficient in the drill, Steuben's outbursts decreased. The soldiers realized that the Prussian's willingness

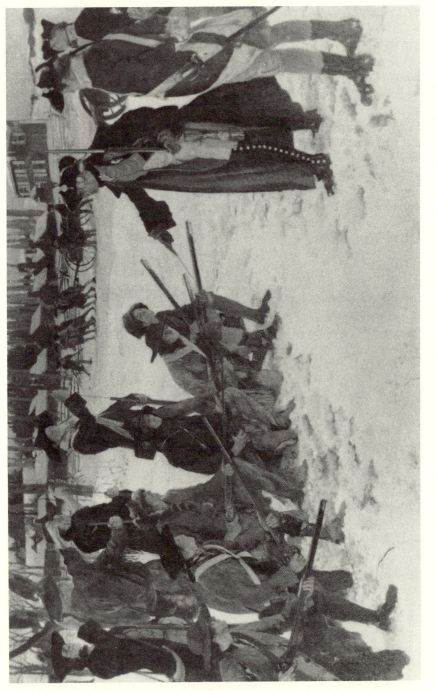

Baron von Steuben drilling recruits at Valley Forge, February 1778, by Edwin A. Abbey. (Pennsylvania State Capitol Building, Capitol Preservation Committee.)

to persevere and personally demonstrate the various drill routines would in time make them a well disciplined army.

Steuben acknowledged the camaraderie he had enjoyed with most officers and rank and file. He advised Henry Laurens that the "good Will I find in your Soldiers and the greatest part of your Officers, Encourages me Exceedingly." In the same vein he wrote Horatio Gates that he had met with a favorable reception from all generals, and Washington in particular who "is willing to Entrust me with the Department of Exercising and Discipline."[15]

When the men were considered to be proficient in the basic exercises and drill, they received training in maneuvers and charging by platoon and company, in using the bayonet and in the cadence required in loading and shooting their muskets. Using the model company and special units as demonstrators, they drilled the men each morning and afternoon. When Steuben and the Inspectors considered they exhibited the necessary skills, they were formed into regiments and brigades.[16]

The drudgery of the constant drilling continued until late May, when the army began preparations to move out of Valley Forge. Meanwhile, several units that had either been indifferent or less attentive to Steuben's instructions were singled out to undergo extra training exercises. In the interim, Washington had been calling on the various states for reinforcements to bolster the army for the summer campaign. Like those assigned to extra training, the newcomers were given a crash program of drill, to qualify them for the arduous military operations ahead. Later, after all brigades had completed their training, the Continentals would move out of Valley Forge with pride and precision.

As previously mentioned, Steuben's manual of arms was not his only contribution to the Continental Army. Washington had urged the Baron to submit his observations and recommendations for improvement of the camp's defenses. Complying with this request, Steuben prepared three documents that covered the Prussian Army organization and a detailed scrutiny of the defenses. His comments in the latter paper, dated March 5, elicited Washington's immediate attention. It highlighted many weaknesses in the fortifications with methods to strengthen them. Steuben was blunt in his criticism of the vulnerability of specific sections of the lines. Washington, after carefully scrutinizing the Prussian's presentation, quickly ordered Duportail to strengthen and complete the outer line works and expand and prepare new redoubts on the inner line. While not referring to Steuben, these orders closely paralleled his opinions and suggestions. Naturally, the sensitive Duportail resisted the orders, resenting them as an infringement on his position as Chief Engineer.[17]

Without designating any priority, Steuben considered certain defenses weaker and more exposed than the rest to enemy attack. In outlining the glaring deficiencies of certain positions, he urged prompt attention to correct certain vulnerable areas. He contended that Sullivan's bridge was badly planned and poorly constructed at an indefensible location. There were heights on the north side of the river that commanded the approach to the bridge but had been left unfortified. Steuben realized the rough terrain and the time available would not permit the erection of a bridgehead to cover that side of Sullivan's bridge. He was adamant in his opinion that any bridge to span the Schuylkill should have been constructed nearer Washington's headquarters. He forcefully advanced the argument that a bridge there would add to the camp's security, and provide an avenue of escape for the headquarter's staff. Not adverse to supporting his proposals, he indicated prompt action could correct the lack of a bridge near headquarters by gathering boats, rafts and planks to build a span at that location. Apparently Washington did not consider this project feasible or necessary as it was never undertaken.

While Steuben considered the left wing of the outer line well planned, he belittled the irresponsibility of those who had left two redoubts half completed. His observations and suggestions were constructive, but evidently he was not aware that the easily offended Duportail had never received wholehearted cooperation from several brigade commanders. Their unwillingness to permit their men to perform manual labor on the defenses had virtually brought the work on certain sections of the line to a standstill. Unaware of Duportail's baffling situation, Steuben continued his criticisms claiming that an oversight had exposed the extreme left flank, leaving it up in the air and open to an attack. To counteract this negligence, he recommended a small work be placed on an eminence near the Schuylkill River. Continuing his relentless critique of the outer line, he denounced the glaring weakness of the unfinished entrenchments or parapets. Steuben remarked that the brush or abatis in front of the incomplete lines had been removed by soldiers for firewood at campfires, or in the hut fireplaces.

Steuben then focused his attention on the sad plight of the inner defenses. He was disturbed at the lack of foresight in planning protection for the large gap that existed between the right flank of that line and the right of the outer line. He stressed concern with the oversight that exposed this section of the camp's defenses. Unfortunately General William Woodford's brigade huts occupied the gap and with the inclement weather, it was not advisable they be moved or torn down. The only solution would be to extend the inner line as far as possible and erect an alarm post near Woodford's brigade. Apparently, Steuben's proposals were major factors in the idea to strengthen the inner line; improvements suggested included building additional breastworks, redoubt number 3 (Fort Washington) and buttressing the front of the line with more brush,

132

fraise work on the parapets, and stakes. As will be seen, Duportail would strenuously oppose these additions to the works.

Turning to an area that would not antagonize Duportail, Steuben severely criticized the concentration of artillery behind the right wing of the outer line. He asserted that in the event of an attack on the left flank the artillery would be immobilized. In its present position the cannon could not be moved because they would either be mired in mud or frozen ground. Even if mobile, a quick movement would be handicapped by a long haul over the one poor road available. To cover this obvious encumbrance, Steuben urged that a battery of artillery be placed in the rear of the left flank of the outer line.[18]

The need to implement the Baron's suggestions became obvious in April and May, as rumor after rumor reached Washington, indicating the possible recall of Howe to Great Britain, to justify his conduct of the war in America. Washington was convinced the cautious Howe would make one last attempt to give the rebels a drubbing. On May 27, General Henry Knox confirmed Washington's assumption in a letter to his brother, stating that "...A Battle at Valley Forge, for they [British] threaten hard to fight bloodily before they depart." To combat any surprise movement by the enemy, Washington overruled all objections, especially those of Duportail, to promptly improve the camp's security. The partially finished outer line was ordered strengthened, with the addition of strong points and parapets on the inner line.[19]

Duportail reluctantly complied with Washington's orders to strengthen the inner line, but in a letter to Stirling he stressed the impracticality of constructing the proposed fortifications, calling such effort "a superfluous exertion of strength." He considered the location of such works indefensible if the British broke through the outer line. In support of his position, Duportail irritably stated that if the enemy reached the extreme range of musket fire and case-shot, they would have to advance over terrain "thick set with obstacles [brush and tree stumps] without being able to get off a responding volley." Such conditions would unquestionably create confusion among the British regiments and force their officers to assume the difficult task of reforming their ranks. Duportail judged that this maneuver would take at least five minutes, during which time the Americans could "fire fifteen rounds with good Aim." He asked if this didn't disconcert and create havoc among the advancing foe "where shall we find better during the Campaign, even seconded by all the assistance of Art?"

He manifested displeasure with Washington's orders claiming they had presented him with a most discouraging situation, inasmuch as most of the original works were either unfinished or not started. Unburdening himself to Stirling, Duportail wrote that many officers and men refused to work on the redoubts, or found excuses to shirk their assignment. With their attitude the Chief Engineer could see little encouragement to building additional fortifications. In describing this lack of cooperation, he noted that "...officers and Soldiers finding such work too long and taking disgust [sic] at it..." resulted in his "never been able to accomplish half a redubt." Harking back to the previous opposition of the general officers to his plan for the camp defenses, he reiterated that if he had been empowered to complete the redoubts, it would not be necessary to erect new works.[20]

There is no evidence that Duportail's depressive remarks were brought to Washington's attention; however, as John Laurens was translating all the engineer's letters into English at this time, his attitude was probably known. Nevertheless Duportail was determined, albeit reluctant, to satisfy the demands of his Commander in Chief. As he started to trace the lines of the proposed fortifications, it was discovered that such a small item as cord for measuring could not be obtained in camp. The responsibility of procuring all needed materials was assigned to John Laurens and General "Lord" Stirling. On April 14, Laurens directed Charles Pettit, Assistant Quartermaster General, to dispatch an express to the nearest supply point or magazine and purchase at least "two hundred fathoms of such cord." It was emphasized to all involved in obtaining supplies that the work of the engineers must not be hampered by the failure to furnish them with whatever articles were needed.[21]

At the same time, Stirling was alerted to the apprehension at headquarters caused by the delay in securing palisades, or abatis, for the front of the inner line. Apparently, someone on the general staff had recommended building a fence as a defensive obstacle; whether or not this suggestion was intended as a facetious comment is not known. It was quickly squelched with the comment that "this odious method was not agreed to." Laurens ordered a supply of rails to be obtained without "injuring anyone," especially civilians. Wagoners were instructed to choose only the soundest rails, and the fatigue party was detailed to cut the logs into fraise (sharp pickets) and palisades. With speed essential, Stirling lost no time in following through on his order, directing Pettit to immediately dispatch six wagons, and if obtainable "twelve or twenty" more, to the former encampment of the British Army near Moore Hall. A large number of seasoned rails were available at that location, and would be more desirable than the use of green wood for pickets.[22]

Exasperated with the progress on the new inner line defenses, Washington vented his anger in an order that stated the work was: "...very carelessly executed in many Parts, and the Representations of the Engineers to the Officers commanding fatigue Parties [having] hitherto been of no Avail, the General calls upon the several Brigadiers to inspect the

134

Part which have been alloted to their several Brigades and order their defects to be remedied..."[23]

In the meantime, a dubious Duportail continued his reconnaissance of the terrain near and on Mt. Joy. After a survey of the mount, he advised Washington that the proposal to build a redoubt was ill-advised and any work on the summit would be virtually indefensible and would not cover the area unless "exceedingly strong"—a condition he did not consider possible. The available fatigue parties, even if cooperative, were too weak to complete such a work; in addition, materials were scarce and a strong force to protect the flanks of the summit was not convenient. To buttress his disagreement with the order for building new works, he wrote Washington that if his original plan for defense of the camp had been pursued, it would have afforded complete protection for all the "declivities" accessible to the British. And further if he had sufficient workmen the only: "...improvement he...[could] make...[would be] to strengthen our Profiles, and increase the obstacles of Brush, Palisades, etc."[24]

While work continued on the defenses, they would never be completed to Washington's satisfaction, although his opinion was not shared by a number of rank and file who believed they were strong enough to resist any attack. On April 26, Ensign Ewing accompanied by Lieutenant Ebenezer Elmer, Surgeon's Mate, walked around the encampment and expressed confidence in the inner line: "...which is Picketed from end to end in front of the huts and abuted in front of them besides breastworks and Redouts on several heiths [heights] on the flank and in the Rear." Washington was probably aware that such optimism prevailed in the ranks, but he did not share this view. Nothing could ameliorate his dissatisfaction with the failure in supplying officers and men to labor on the fortifications. Washington's angry reproof disturbed certain brigadiers, and Stirling asked if the rebuke was directed specifically at him. On May 11, an obviously irritated Washington wrote to him: "I had no particular person in view when I issued an order respecting the slow progress of the Works, at the same time, I acknowledge that I am exceedingly mortified at seeing and beholding the delay of them..." In an effort to soften the sharpness of his reply, he added that he didn't know if the delays had been "Unavoidable, or not...."[25]

Other defensive works added at this time probably originated with Steuben's observations, including his recommendations for additional security to cover Sullivan's Bridge. The redoubt designated as number one, or Star, was built on the eminence to the south side of the Schuylkill. Neither its original location nor configuration is known, but it is believed to haven been in the vicinity of the reconstructed Star redoubt. At the same time, a redan, or gun emplacement, was added to the east end of a small island that formed a part of Fatland Ford, just west of the bridge. The guns of this work facing downstream commanded the approaches to the bridge from boats coming up the river. The lines of this small work were still visible at the time of the Centennial celebration in 1878.

A cautious British commander, Sir William Howe, expressed his opinion about the defenses at Valley Forge. On April 19, he wrote to Lord George Germain that the "...Enemy's...force...has been diminished during the course of the Winter by Desertion..." However, he acknowledged he had not been able to mount an offensive against the "rebel" position, because of the scarcity of "green Forage." In eighteenth century warfare the paucity of forage in winter created serious logistical problems for an army, preventing movement of large bodies of troops. Howe continued, stating that a setback at this stage might counteract "His Majesty's Intentions of preparing the way for the return of Peace..." Apparently, Howe was anticipating the Peace Commission that would reach America in a few weeks.[26]

Before arriving at Valley Forge, Washington realized that intercourse between the British and Loyalist farmers, and containing Howe's army within the city defenses would be important to minimizing local criticism for not engaging in a winter campaign.

IX

Encirclement

WASHINGTON HAD NOT forgotten the brouhaha that occurred when he decided to take the hungry and poorly equipped Continentals into a winter encampment, rather than conduct an offensive campaign against the enemy. Contrary to his announced intention, he had not abandoned the hope Howe would make a tactical mistake, giving him an opportunity to launch an assault on the British lines. If this attack were successful the British would be forced to evacuate Philadelphia in midwinter. However, the plan was aborted in the first week at Valley Forge, when it became obvious the troops were not in condition to take the offensive, coupled with a mutinous undercurrent that threatened a dissolution of the army.

Before construction of the huts or completion of the inner defenses, steps were taken to guard the camp's perimeter against a surprise attack. Concurrently the outposts, patrols and pickets, assisted by militia units were directed to prevent intercourse between the British and the countryside. Lieutenant Thomas Blake offers a succinct contemporary description of the outposts south and east of the encampment. Blake noted that: "The whole army lay there [Valley Forge] except two brigades at Wilmington, down the Delaware river, and also about 300 men at Rednar [Radnor], 7 miles from camp; and 200 at the Gulph Mills [Rebel Hill] about the same distance; each of these two last named parties were relieved every week. There were likewise guards kept about one mile distance from camp, which formed a chain of centinels round the whole encampment, which were relieved daily."[1]

The perimeter defense, or encirclement, south of Valley Forge was entrusted primarily to Continental detachments. Except for General William Smallwood at Wilmington, the other outposts were stationed along the principal roads leading into Philadelphia. On December 19, Washington had ordered Smallwood to take the division lately commanded by General John Sullivan and set up a fortified post in Wil-

The Sentinel Chestnut Tree. In the nineteenth century when the tree was standing the sentry's platform was still visible. (*The Sentry Tree of George Washington.*)

mington. A French engineer was detached to accompany him and super-intend the construction of the necessary works. According to local tradition, Smallwood's encampment was on the highland between Delaware Avenue and the Brandywine [Creek] and Franklin and Clayton Streets. This "land is now [1915] well within the city limits, but in 1777 it was a mile away from the built-up town."[2]

On the same date Washington advised President George Read, of Delaware, of the planned move by Smallwood, and requested that the state contribute militia to the defense of Wilmington, and assist in drawing supplies from lower Chester County, Pennsylvania and northern Delaware. After Smallwood's troops were supplied, the balance of that garnered was to be sent to Valley Forge.[3]

As indicated by Blake, large contingents were placed at Gulph Mills and Radnor Meeting House; also, a smaller unit commanded by Captain Henry Lee was near the intersection of Sugartown and Newtown Street Roads. Colonel Daniel Morgan at the Radnor Meeting House, a veteran frontiersman, probably was responsible for the unique line of "signal trees" to the rear of his post. Tradition, coupled with eyewitness statements have assisted historians in tracing and locating most, if not all, of those trees serving as alarm posts.

Beginning at a lookout post atop Mt. Joy and extending south, closely paralleling but to the west of Baptist Road, these signal trees stretched to the area near Lee's outpost. Most of the trees were large chestnuts with one or two oak. The tops of the trees were cut off to permit the installation of crude platforms or scaffolding. Early in this century some of the trees, or remnants of trunks of others were still standing, but the chestnuts had succumbed to a disease called "San Jose Scale."

Situated where they covered the various roads and open areas, sentinels stood guard day and night, probably suffering from freezing conditions during winter months. Observing any movement by British troops or farmers attempting to carry produce to the city, they quickly relayed their presence to other posts and the members of their squad. Several methods of communicating with other posts have been suggested including gunfire or lanterns; however, these signals could easily have been detected by the enemy. Morgan's background seems to be evident again in this unusual alarm system, with the soldiers probably using the turkey call, which would only alert those familiar with the frontier usage of this method. Each squad posted at a signal tree consisted of up to twenty rank and file, with a subaltern or sergeant. For protection against the elements, they constructed crude shelters or lean-tos, using any material to be found.

One tree has been favored by posterity with a special honor called the "Washington Sentry Tree." Many twentieth century inhabitants pointed out this tree as one of the signal trees still standing on Old Eagle Road. At the time, Henry Pleasants authored a book on the *Old Eagle School and Old St. David's Church*, which has a good photograph of the tree showing what appears to be a section of the platform.[4]

While evidence of the many picket posts has vanished, one described as the Stone Picket Post stood at the intersection of Swedesford and Baptist Roads. During the Revolution this area was called New Centerville. The post derived its name from a rough shelter which was built using the standing chimney and fireplace of a house burned years before the war. As previously noted, the Stone Picket Post was the site of an army market.[5]

The picket squads were usually placed about a half mile apart, which distance the sentinel would patrol until he met his counterpart from the next post.

One soldier, who did not designate the location of his post, has left an amusing account of an incident he experienced as a picket. Isaac Loftus served throughout the encampment and took great delight in regaling his family with the tale of a frightening confrontation he had as a picket. Claude E. Hemsley, a great great grandson, gave his account to Ronald E. Heaton for publication. Although slightly embarrassed, Loftus unquestionably considered his encounter an interesting interlude from the dull routine of a picket. He said the men:

> ...were on half rations, scantily clothed, without shoes and many left bloody foot prints in the snow. Many were sick. The countryside had been foraged for miles to no avail. One dark night he was on picket duty next to a thicket following the hard packed path left in the snow by the previous pickets, when he heard a noise in the thicket. He called out a challenge and on the third challenge he fired. his gun fired instantly, there was no flash in the pan. They beat the drums to arms and the whole camp was up at once. A deploy was thrown out and soon a shout went up that the intruder was found. It was a big fat steer killed by the sentry. The animal was butchered and fires sprang up all over the camp, the sick being cared for first.

How far would one steer go among thousands of hungry soldiers?[6]

The vulnerable sector of the encirclement line was between the Schuylkill and Delaware Rivers. Many factors contributed to Washington's reluctance to disperse an already weakened army suffering from hunger and cold, by placing Continental outposts between the two rivers. Smallwood had two Continental brigades at Wilmington, but needed adequate reserves of healthy and well equipped militia to furnish rotating garrisons at outposts south of his position. It was also necessary to have sufficient manpower to construct winter quarters and for fatigue duty. Another distressing situation as 1777 drew to a close was the threat of large-scale resignations of officers and the imminent expiration of enlistments among the rank and file.

Under limitations confronting him, Washington dubiously accepted assignment of Pennsylvania militia to defend the high risk area. Available for this responsibility was Major General John Armstrong's Division of 3,500. However, Armstrong had transferred three battalions, totaling about 1,000 men, to Brigadier General James Potter patrolling across the Schuylkill facing Philadelphia. These numbers are deceptive because most of the militiamen's three months service was about to expire, and all were anxious to return home. Unexpectedly, their opportunity came in early January when the militia infrastructure suddenly collapsed. Armstrong resigned, claiming his age made active service a hardship; Potter was granted an indefinite furlough because of illness in his family, and Brigadier General William Irvine who was a prisoner of the British in Philadelphia.

Without a general officer most militiamen took advantage of the situation and vanished, taking with them their muskets and accouterments. The Supreme Executive Council was at a loss to fill the vacancy left by the sudden departure of the general staff. On January 9, a desperate Council appointed twenty-two year old Colonel John Lacey, Jr., of the Bucks County Militia, as Brigadier General. Lacey was obviously inexperienced for a general command. His problems were many, as he had inherited a reduced force, many without muskets. Nevertheless, the young general was determined to prevent any contact between the country and the British in Philadelphia. Assembling his small force, Lacey detached patrols to cover the roads leading into the city; and to conceal the size of his command, or a surprise by British detachments, he instructed outposts to change their location every few days.

Washington next turned his attention to New Jersey, where he recognized that the small militia unit under Colonel Joseph Ellis could do little more than observe British movements. It was apparent that the area with its large stocks of forage would be a tempting target for the enemy. To reinforce Ellis, he dispatched Colonel Israel Shreve and the undermanned 2nd New Jersey Continental Regiment to New Jersey. Even with an augmented force, Ellis and Shreve were too weak to patrol the east bank of the Delaware River between Cooper's Ferry [Camden] and the head of Delaware Bay below Salem.

Although patrols and outposts girded the city, Washington realized that it would be impossible to forestall the British from making occasional incursions into the countryside for forage. In areas where forage could not be removed, he ordered it destroyed, particularly northeast of the city in Frankford and Smithfield [Somerton]. Nevertheless, Washington hoped that the precautions taken would limit the British garrison to provisions brought in by their shipping.

Two American naval captains, tired of inactivity and not being provided with funds to pay and provision the Pennsylvania Navy crews, decided to engage in privateering in the lower reaches of the Delaware River. Captain Nathan Boys, of the State Navy, requested the loan of two guard boats (half galleys), and his counterpart in the Continental Navy, Captain John Barry, borrowed two armed barges. The State Navy Board manned each guard boat with an officer and ten seamen, while Barry was granted permission to recruit crews from the Continental Navy. The boats were rowed downriver to Cooper's Creek from where they were taken overland to the vicinity of Salem and refloated. Boys and Barry proposed to lie in the mouth of small creeks that dotted the area and prey on unsuspecting British merchantmen. Barry would later ferry Wayne's contingent over to New Jersey.

Another guard boat commanded by Captain Robert Collings was later sent overland from Burlington to the Salem area. William Bell Clark states that three additional guard boats were dispatched to join the flotilla. These small boats operated successfully for a time. Unfortunately, the boats invariably capsized in rough water. This occurred when the river became partially choked with ice, forcing them to be taken out of service.[7]

It was apparent that all preparations to contain the British in Philadelphia would be fruitless, if Howe suddenly adopted aggressive tactics and sent large foraging parties into the countryside. However, if Howe elected to use small patrols, Washington knew he could spare enough troops to strengthen threatened areas.

To each commander in chief it was manifest that the mobility, and even the survival, of his army depended on an adequate supply of forage and straw. For Washington the appalling lack of straw as bedding had become a serious health hazard in the hospitals and huts.

On April 19, the always cautious Howe wrote to Lord George Germain, Colonial Secretary for the American Colonies, that he had hoped to make a strike at the rebels at Valley Forge, but could not take the field for a "want of green forage." Earlier he had admonished the army woodcutters supplying the barracks not to overwork the horses as they were "in very poor condition." As noted, Captain John Peebles recorded that the garrison used 800 cords each week. The need for such large quantities of firewood kept the woodcutters out every day, weather permitting. As the wooded areas near the lines were stripped of trees forcing longer and consequently fewer trips by the exhausted horses, conditions in the city worsened causing considerable suffering for the garrison. Elizabeth Drinker, a Quaker lady known as a reliable observer wrote "I am told it [forage] will last but a little time, for 'tis said twenty four tons per day are used."[8]

An important key, to whatever objective Washington hoped for, was the intelligence system he had developed in 1777 and refined at Valley Forge. To serve as "chief of spies" Washington and General Nathanael Greene, after careful consideration, chose Major John Clark, Jr., aide to Greene, as the officer best to serve in this post. With complete confidence in their selection, Washington gave Clark discretionary authority in his hazardous assignment in selecting and screening a network of loyal operatives. Through the first weeks at Valley Forge, the ubiquitous Clark clandestinely entered the city and rode throughout the surrounding area garnering intelligence from his spies, and making detailed observations of British activities. All accumulated data was forwarded to Washington for scrutiny as he assumed responsibility for sifting through the reports and eliminating what he considered heresay, or misinformation. To Washington's dismay, information reached headquarters that the strenuous pace Clark demanded of himself had undermined his health. Chagrined at the possible loss of Clark, Washington received approval to offer him the post of Auditor of the Continental Army at Valley Forge, until he had sufficiently recovered to return to active duty.[9]

To supplement Clark's efforts, Washington ordered Major Allan McLane with a picked troop of dragoons to patrol north of the city, reporting directly to him. He assigned Lieutenant John Craig,[10] of the 4th Continental Dragoons, to move further east to the Frankford neighborhood.

The encirclement of the city was complete, however, Washington was aware that the thin line of Continentals and militia was honeycombed with roads that could not be guarded. Many farmers would be apprehended, while others escaped detection by avoiding patrolled roads and taking to the fields and dense hardwood forests north of the city. Washington believed some of these holes could be plugged by encouraging loyal farmers to act as agents. He had recommended to Clark that he "grant permission to all those who want to go into Philada....on whom you can depend and from who you expect any intelligence in return." Washington was concerned that if most roads leading to the city were closed, it would restrict his ability to send secret agents through British lines. Conversely, it was essential that intercourse with the British be limited. Intelligence had been received that the enemy was being forced to increasingly depend on their shipping for provisions and forage.

British troops in Philadelphia were on reduced rations and many civilians, especially the poor, were starving. An unknown informant advised Washington that "Every day increases the price and scarcity of Provisions, Heavens only knows what will become of us, if you don't relieve us by routing them." The ease of bypassing any security adopted by Howe is illustrated when Continental officers at Valley Forge needing an article for personal use, could appeal to Clark or McLane to have an agent purchase the desired item at one of the city's shops.[11] Alexander Scammel wrote McLane that "I am suffering for want of a good Leather ink pot, and a good penn knife—If you have an Opportunity wish you would send into Philadelphia and procure these Articles...." Scammel added that his preference was for a double ink pot with provisions for a pen on each side.[12]

Washington always tried to ensure the secrecy of reports reaching headquarters, realizing that Clark and McLane's system was operated by amateurs. He was also cognizant that a number of spies could be double agents, but he judged the advantage gained, was a risk that had to be taken. To protect his informants, Washington instructed them to relay any message "unsigned" by reliable friends of America direct to him. Some agents signed their letters, from which he took care to cut out the signatures, a few of these can be found in the Washington Papers. Several of these unknown correspondents, who had reported to Washington at Whitemarsh, were instrumental in warning of Howe's planned offensive against his position.[13]

With a large Loyalist population in Bucks County, Lacey frequently apprehended many people seeking to sell their products to the British, as it had become impossible to barter or sell, especially with worthless Continental currency. South of Valley Forge, Morgan and Smallwood were equally active, but with less traffic and fewer British patrols. Meanwhile, Lacey became despondent with the insubordination of his militia and their small numbers, usually sixty or less. The size of his area made it impossible to cover all roads. He had a plan that could enable his small command to control traffic. General Lachlan McIntosh, visiting his outpost, agreed that under existing conditions the only solution was to force everyone living between Lacey's outposts and the British lines to move into the interior parts of the county. McIntosh agreed to present the proposal to Washington, who obviously did not approve, believing it would cause unnecessary and indiscriminate hardships to friend and foe alike.[14]

In April all detachment commanders were instructed to treat the villages of Germantown and Newtown as neutral ground, while representatives of both armies were meeting to arrange a prisoner exchange.

Lacey and McLane were chagrined with their failure to intercept brazen and boastful farmers who gloated over the ease with which they had repeatedly penetrated American outposts. Lacey advised Council that "It was distressing to See the Numbers of people who flock to the Enemy with Marketing...I have taken Several of them who were going to the Enemy with Barrels of Meal on their Backs." His disappointment increased as he seized a number of young men going to Philadelphia to enlist in British Provincial Regiments. Lacey considered all Loyalists inimical to the American cause. Some of those whom he considered dangerous were sent to Valley Forge for court-martial and punishment. Most were convicted, some receiving 100 lashes; others were confined in the Provost each night and forced to serve fatigue duty during the day for one month. Several, whose violations were considered less of a threat, were fined and their provisions confiscated. Because of mitigating circumstances, several were acquitted. Could those released have been working as American agents and ordered freed on Washington's order?[15]

McLane experienced similar encounters with those who boasted that it was easy to pass through American lines. During their interrogations most revealed a callous indifference to any possible punishment. One, Enas Thomas, said he had been in the city six times carrying twelve pounds of butter each time, and on another occasion driven a cow to Abington. Equally contemptuous, Joseph Long admitted going into the city twice; the first time with 107 pounds of butter, and again with fifteen pounds of butter and two fowl. John Keyser claimed he had also been in the city twice, one time with two lambs and fifty pounds of meal. The punishment received by these offenders is unknown.[16]

After a few weeks it became obvious that an unexpected loophole had developed in the attempt to establish a tight security cordon by both armies. Howe and Washington, in a chivalrous gesture, had permitted women to enter and leave their lines without being interrogated or searched. American prisoners in the Walnut Street prison were hungry, ill-clad, and living in extreme squalor. Before an agreement could be worked out for each army to furnish their prisoners of war with provisions and other necessities, Howe, who had been unable to spare food, welcomed the women who brought food to the American prisoners. The ladies found a pleasant attraction in the city when a large number of merchants from New York followed the army and set up shop in stores and residences abandoned by Americans who fled the area. They offered an enticing and varied selection of items not available to American women from rural areas. These allurements coupled with a desire to visit friends and relatives on both sides of the lines, saw many women avail themselves of the unrestricted privileges their visits permitted.

For a time this permission seemed to be innocent and not violative of the barriers placed against farmers and spies entering or leaving the city. Neither Howe nor Washington had seen any danger in women carrying small amounts of grain or other provisions to friends, loved ones and prisoners. Suddenly, intelligence reached both headquarters that a large number of women were transporting quantities of provisions and returning with intelligence on the activities in Philadelphia and Valley Forge.

Lacey informed Washington that trading in produce was "chiefly carried on by women." To worsen the situation, youths accompanied the women in order to enter the British lines. In the last weeks of the encampment, when it was evident that the British planned to evacuate the city, women requested permission to leave escorted by "Quakers or Peasants." These latter were actually Loyalist Provincial Officers seeking to flee the city.[17]

December 30, 1777, Howe placed limitations on ingress and egress through the troop barriers. Five roads gave direct access to the city by way of the British fortifications, in addition to the military bridge constructed across the Schuylkill. To prohibit unauthorized persons from passing these barriers, Howe ordered them closed "between Evening gunfiring [taps] & half an hour after gunfiring in the Morning [Reveille] Except those carrying intelligence of the enemy." A few days later, January 7, 1778, he closed the barrier at the "top of Second Street & on the Ridge Road" to limit unwarranted passage. In three days he again took measures to prevent people from slipping out of the lines under cover of darkness. Anyone on the streets without a "Lanthorn was to be turned over to the Field officer for punishment." These precautions were followed by a proclamation that no one could leave the city without a pass from headquarters.[18]

An interesting incident that reflected the lengths to which women would go during this time to assist a loved one is found in the records of the Von Myers family. Lieutenant Henry Myers, Sr. was attached to the staff of Lieutenant Colonel William Bradford, Jr., Deputy Commissary of Musters, at Valley Forge. Receiving a promotion to captain, Myers wrote to his wife, Catherine, in Philadelphia, asking her to bring him new regimentals. Apparently she made a new uniform and secured a pass from Howe's headquarters to visit her half sister living between the lines, whose husband was a Loyalist. Donning the regimentals and sword, she put on her dress and easily passed through the barrier, delivering them to her husband at camp.[19]

As time passed the encirclement became moderately successful. Punishments meted out to those seized attempting to enter or leave the city and the loss of their property acted as a deterrent to many farmers. Washington was emphatic in his orders that while such traffic must be stopped, the inhabitants should not be abused. His determination mitigated by compassion was stressed in instructions to Captain Stephen Chambers of the 12th Pennsylvania Regiment:

> To induce your men to be more active and zealous in the execution of their duty; everything which may be *actually* taken going into, or coming from the city, shall be the property of the captors. But to prevent an abuse

146

of this privilege, by making it a cover for plundering the inhabitants, it must always be managed under the eye of a commissioned officer, and no forfeiture must be made, but where the fact is clearly ascertained . One principal object of your command is to protect the county, it is therefore peculiarly your duty to prevent any violence on the persons or property of the inhabitants, being perpetrated by your party.

This order was unquestionably prompted by the numerous reports of mental and physical abuse of citizens by various patrols.[20]

During the spring, although not seriously affecting the life or activities at Valley Forge, the British conducted several seize and destroy missions. In March, desperate for forage, Lieutenant Colonel Charles Mawhood led a foray into southern New Jersey, where Abercrombie had discovered an abundance of forage in February. Mawhood, with a force slightly over 1,200, escorted by a number of small armed boats of the Royal Navy, sailed for the Salem area. He spent nearly two weeks gleaning forage and grain, while detachments roamed the county ravishing and also wiping out pockets of resistance. One contingent ruthlessly killed a number of militiamen who had surrendered, thereby placing a blot on the honor of the British Army. Nevertheless, Mawhood's cargo was welcomed by the British garrison.[21]

On the last day of April, a force of 850 under Lieutenant Colonel Abercrombie, including Captain John Simcoe's Queens Rangers, moved out of the city intent on surprising and destroying the pesky Lacey and his militia. Abercrombie, maintaining the utmost secrecy, marched under cover of darkness to Huntington Valley, where he divided his command into two columns to envelop Lacey's camp. As often happens with separate detachments, they did not converge at their designated position at the appointed time; however, without waiting, Abercrombie struck Lacey's camp like a bombshell overrunning the sleeping and unprepared militiamen. Bewildered, the Americans offered little resistance and many were cut down attempting to surrender. In a manner uncharacteristic of most British Army units, Abercrombie's troops committed atrocities more infamous that Mawhood's men in South Jersey. Lacey's vivid report to the Executive Council depicts the savage acts committed by the British: "Some were Butchard in a manner the most Brutal Savages Could not equal, even while Living Some were thrown into Buckwheat Straw and the Straw set on fire, the Close [clothes] were Burnt on others, and scarcely one without a Dozen Wounds with Byonets [Bayonets] or Cutlasses." Lacey's account was verified by area residents who visited the so-called battlefield.[22]

In May, Howe was advised that the galleys of the Pennsylvania Navy had been scuttled, leaving many boats and ships unprotected, including the partially constructed frigates *Washington* and *Effingham*, in the creeks between Burlington and Bordentown. A skeptical Howe believed there were still four state galleys patrolling the Delaware above Burlington that represented the only deterrent to destroying all American shipping. The force he ordered out was considered capable of overcoming the firepower of any opposition the Americans could offer. Major John Maitland, with the 2nd Battalion of light infantry and two field pieces, embarked on eighteen flatboats on the night of May 7. Captain John Henry commanded a formidable squadron that included five galleys, two armed schooners and four gunboats, which would not have been powerful enough to confront the state navy, if it had not been scuttled. Maitland and Henry conducted a systematic mission that destroyed all the shipping found in the area, while some malicious elements in their command set fire to several private residences, an action that both British officers deplored. After two days, the joint commanders, being satisfied that their mission was completed, returned to Philadelphia.[23]

Although several skirmishes occurred south of the encampment, one that mixes documentation and tradition stands out as an exemplary example of heroism. Captain Henry Lee and his dragoons had been a persistent thorn to British patrols, and Howe was anxious for an opportunity to eliminate this troublesome annoyance. Learning that Lee was camped on the farm of James Scott at the intersection of Sugartown and Newtown Street Roads, Howe thought he had an excellent chance to corner him. He ordered out a company of 200 dragoons, with instructions to take a circuitous route over back roads and effect a complete surprise. Fortunately for the Americans, as the British emerged from a wooded area, one of Lee's dragoons spotted them in time to sound the alert. Unknown to the British, most of Lee's troops were at another farmhouse. His small garrison included five troopers and two other officers, Major John Jameson and Lieutenant William Lindsay. According to tradition, the Americans quickly retired into the house and barred the doors, while the British commander—some claim it was Banastre Tarleton—sounded a parley, threatening to burn the house and its occupants. Lee was reported to have replied that only a fool would attempt to burn a stone house. With his small force, Lee planned his defense by having his troopers keep up a steady musket fire and pass from window to window to conceal their few numbers. Their fire was so deadly that the British retired to regroup. As mentioned, most of the details are based on tradition. It is claimed that Lee repeated a stratagem that completely confused the enemy. He leaned out a window shouting for the men to continue their fire as he could see the approach of infantry reinforcements. Uncertain and confused the British retired in some haste. As in most reports casualty figures vary, but the most reliable place the British at four killed and three wounded, while Lindsay with a shot in the hand was the only American injured. Washington confirmed the salient aspects of the engagement in his general orders. Regardless of details, the skirmish would catapult the dashing Lee into prominence and add a "cubit to his fame."[24]

Uncounted rumors reached headquarters that the British planned to evacuate Philadelphia, often with many different variations of the same account. Washington was perplexed as to what Howe and his replacement, Sir Henry Clinton, had designed for the upcoming campaign. He had apparent doubts about the accuracy of the many accounts and what was happening in the city. On May 18, in an effort to rectify any misinformation he had received, Washington advised Lafayette that his:

> ...march towards the enemy's lines is designated to answer the following purpose: to be a security to this camp and a cover to the country between the Delaware and Schuylkill, to interrupt the communication with Philadelphia, obstruct the incursions of the enemy's parties, and obtain intelligence of the motions and designs. This last is a matter of very interesting moment, and ought to claim your particular attention. You will endeavour to procure trusty and intelligent spies, who will advise you faithfully of whatever may be passing in the city...

Washington added that a variety of accounts state the British are preparing to evacuate the city; and cautioned Lafayette that his "detachment is a very valuable one" and its loss "would be a severe blow to the Army."[25]

Within hours of Lafayette's arrival at Barren Hill, his position was known to Howe. As usual Howe was dilatory, postponing any action for twenty-four hours. The fun-loving Howe was preoccupied with plans for a Meschianza, an extravaganza to honor him before he embarked for England. On the 19th he ordered General James Grant, with 6,000 rank and file, to take a roundabout route and come up in the rear of Lafayette's position, while another column of about the same strength, personally commanded by Howe, would strike the enemy's position in the front. Even though Howe had relinquished command of the British Army in America to Sir Henry Clinton, he had reserved the right to lead this last assault, which he was confident would be successful—hopefully it would vindicate his conduct of the war in America. The prospect of capturing Lafayette represented laurels Howe could not resist; otherwise why employ a force of 12,000 troops, the flower of the British Army in America, to overwhelm a force of about 2,200? The British hierarchy consisted of Howe, Clinton, Knyphausen, and every British general but Leslie, who was in command of the front line fortifications. They planned a gala celebration in the city to honor the capture of Lafayette. An ebullient Howe believed the taking of the French nobleman would be a feather in his cap and he could triumphantly return home to the accolades of the English people and government.

At 9:00 p.m. on the nineteenth, Grant moved out of the lines and up Old York Road. At the junction with the road to Whitemarsh (Church Road), he filed to the left. Then at the intersection of North Wales (Bethlehem Pike) and Skippack Roads, he marched northwest to Broad Axe,[26] turning left over modern Butler Pike to Manatawny or Ridge Road, where he belatedly took position in Lafayette's rear. Unfortunately for Howe, he had selected his most sluggish and indecisive general for this mission. Grant would arrive at his designated position after his wily quarry had escaped. Equally procrastinating, Howe delayed his departure until 5:30 a.m. on the twentieth. As his column approached Chestnut Hill, he was informed that Lafayette had fled the trap.

C. Stedman's is the only contemporary account that mentions General Sir Charles Grey leading a detachment out Ridge Road to harass Lafayette, while the larger columns converged on Barren Hill to complete their mission. Grey's skirmish with the Americans is the only recorded military action in Howe's chimera for a major coup.

An example of comic relief happened near Barren Hill supposedly involving a confrontation between British dragoons and a group of forty-five Oneida and Tuscorora Indians attached to Lafayette's command. The popular version of this incident depicts both parties fleeing in terror. According to this account the Indians were startled by the brilliant red coats, while the dragoons were terrified by the Indian war whoops, and all panicked and fled in opposite directions. A surprising aspect of this confrontation is the assumption that the Iroquian Indians had not previously seen British red coats.

Lafayette's escape was the result of Grant's lethargy and Howe's overconfident belief that the Frenchman was surrounded, with no avenue of retreat remaining. There was a back road that led to Matson's Ford, which Grant had failed to cover. Lafayette, with an advance warning of the snare that was slowly encircling his position, quickly filed to the right passing through a dense woods and reaching Matson's Ford, crossed over to the south bank of the Schuylkill. Thus came to a climax, created by a comedy of errors, the only aggressive move by American troops during the encampment. For the number of troops involved, casualties were small, although it has been asserted a number of Americans were drowned while fording the river.[27]

Occasionally, farcical events occur in war to relieve its more sombrous aspects. During the last week of December 1777, David Bushnell, America's pioneer builder of submarines, devised a method which he believed would destroy British shipping and anchored in the river and at the wharves of Philadelphia. He developed a number of underwater mines connected with buoys, or kegs, in which the motion of the water was expected to explode them against the hulls of the ships. Unfortunately for the fondest hopes of Bushnell, the plan proved abortive and unworkable. However, it did generate several ludicrous accounts. American reports painted a terror-stricken citizenry racing through the city streets, with nervous British troops firing wild volleys at the floating mines and "some shadows." Not surprisingly, little reference to this incident is found in British sources, but it did inspire patriot Francis Hopkinson to write his famous poem "The Battle of the Kegs."[28]

Chapter

X

Poor Fellows in Hospitals

WASHINGTON'S ATTENTION HAD not been diverted from the plight of the sick and wounded; rather he was chagrined at the sight of "well clad" men entering a military hospital and found to be "in a manner naked when they got well and cannot return to their Regiment..." Nettled, he ordered every effort be exerted to apprehend the culprits guilty of stealing the clothing of the sick and to make certain they were severely punished. On December 26, further instructions were issued forbidding the admittance to hospitals of sick and wounded soldiers "without a List of the Regiment and Company they belong to and of every Article of their Clothing..." These lists were to be authenticated and signed by the company's commanding officer "and Transmitted to the Surgeon of the Hospital." In addition, careful attention was to be taken that the arms and accoutrements of each patient were to be sent to the Adjutant General. Washington's concern was for the continuing loss of these items to an army already destitute of most necessities.[1]

Three days later, Washington directed a "Circular to the States" that divulged the shocking fact "that not less than 2898 Men [were] unfit for duty by reason of their being barefoot and otherwise naked." He emphasized that these soldiers unfit for duty were only those at camp, adding: "Besides this number sufficiently distressing of itself, there are many others detained in Hospitals and crowded in Farmers Houses for the same causes." Such numbers unfit for duty—about 4,000—immobilized the army. Washington implored the states to take vigorous steps and exert their authority to ensure the delivery of "Shoes, Stockings and Blankets" to their troops, without which the army will have little "prospect of success."[2]

On New Years Eve, after having maintained a constant vigilance over the sick, an harassed Washington wrote to Governor William Livingston of New Jersey that "I sincerely feel for the unhappy Condition of our Poor Fellows in the Hospitals." He bemoaned his helplessness to ease their sufferings because of "exceedingly scanty and deficient Hospitals Stores." Unable to conceal his frustrations, he lamented "Our sick naked, our well naked, our unfortunate men in captivity naked!" He was hopeful that placing a field officer at each hospital would "prevent some of the inconveniences" and bring relief to the sick and wounded.[3]

Washington was in a dilemma over what should be done to correct the ills in the Medical Department. His constant review found many Hospital Store employees derelict in the performance of their duties and cases of flagrant mismanagement in some hospitals. To guarantee that each sick soldier receive proper care, Washington ordered all surgeons to make a report each Monday on all patients in their charge to the Surgeon General.[4]

As was his custom, Washington personally inspected the encampment, and with additional evidence existing, he expanded his observations to include a visit to many of the hospitals in the Valley Forge vicinity. On one occasion Dr. James Craik wrote that Washington visited the Yellow Springs Hospital where he spoke"...to every person in their bunks, which exceedingly pleased the sick." With over 300 patients at Yellow Springs, Washington's care to talk with each sick soldier revealed his gentleness and heartfelt compassion. In turn, most soldiers responded with a sincere devotion to their Commander in Chief.[5]

About this time Washington took his first steps to guard against a possible smallpox epidemic at the encampment. Years earlier he had accompanied his ailing half-brother Lawrence Washington to Barbados, where Washington contracted a mild case of the disease. With this experience, Washington had become a staunch advocate of inoculation as a deterrent to the deadly disease. On January 6, he ordered a detailed return, to be made by the Regimental Surgeons, of all men "who had not had the small pox." This data would be the base for his ultimate decision to ensure that every soldier at Valley Forge had either had the disease or been inoculated.[6]

Three days later, Washington instructed the Major Generals and officers commanding brigades to select suitable ground near each brigade to construct regimental or "flying hospitals." As previously described, these flying hospitals were "to be fifteen feet wide and twenty-five feet long." They were to be roofed with boards or shingles with no sod or dirt, as he believed the latter would cause dampness, adding to the misery of the sick. A window was to be placed on each side, with a chimney at one end. Two hospitals were to be erected by each brigade not less than 100 yards from the center of its position. It was obvious that these dimensions would seriously limit the capacity of a flying hospital. Their principal objective was to care for those not seriously ill, while others with severe or contagious ailments were to be quickly transferred to larger military hospitals near the encampment. When Washington ordered everyone who had not been afflicted with small pox be inoculated, the flying hospitals were taxed beyond their limit. Many sick soldiers remained in their huts, thus, exacerbating an already over-crowded and dangerous situation.[7]

Many complaints were directed to Washington concerning the horrendous conditions in the hospitals scattered throughout northern New Jersey and the vicinity of Valley Forge, due to the lack of order and discipline by the patients. The most irascible of the critics was Dr. Benjamin Rush, considered by most scholars as the best physician in Colonial America. Rush later became the hero of the Yellow Fever epidemic in Philadelphia. Rush's portrayal of the filth, unsanitary conditions, inadequate medicine and supplies and understaffing was a reasonable description of many hospitals. However, he ignored the emergency in the winter of 1777-78, when the rapid increase in those requiring hospital care overtaxed the existing facilities and forced the improvisation of poorly staffed makeshift hospitals.

Contentious and querulous, Rush did not confine his criticisms to the system and its problems, but directed his animus in a personal attack on Dr. William Shippen, Surgeon General, demanding a Congressional investigation of Shippen's conduct and belligerently condemning questionable areas as malfeasance. As a former Director of Medical Administration for Congress, Rush's request was put before that body but, after examining a number of witnesses, Congress dismissed the charges. Most of the members of Congress looked upon this feud as burdensome to morale in the various hospitals. Richard Peters, Secretary to the Board of War, in writing to Robert Morris, probably epitomized the reactions of most members of Congress, saying "If the Jealousies which seem to exist...continue to rage much longer I don't see how any Man of Feeling or Sentiment can continue in a public Department...The Enemy will prevail more by *our* Animosities than they have yet been able to do by *their Arms.*"[8]

Not content with his inflammatory condemnation of Shippen, Rush attempted to drag Washington into the controversy charging him with condoning Shippen's mismanagement of the hospitals. On January 12, Washington, in an effort to state his position without mentioning Shippen, outlined to Rush his feelings on the hospitals' operation. His letter of this date was in answer to Rush's of December 26, a delay that probably irritated the impatient doctor. Washington acknowledged that if Rush's contention that "...the present medical department is as you say a bad one, no time ought to be lost in amending it..." He pointed out that those closest to the operation, namely the surgeons and physicians, should know the department's "defects." Washington expressed regret that he was not in a position to supply the "necessary apparatus of an Hospital as we ought to be..." But he quickly admitted "we might do much better." He also apprised Rush that he had taken measures to ease conditions by having a field officer stationed at each hospital to oversee the well-being of the sick. Washington's letter closed with the statement "I shall always be ready to contribute all in my power towards rendering the situation of these unhappy people...as comfortable as possible." It is unlikely that this letter satisfied Rush. Also, no one could have conceived the large number of improvised hospitals nor the exigency that conditions at Valley Forge would demand.[9]

Later in the month Washington would work closely with Congress, through its Committee at Camp, to submit recommendations for reorganizing and improving the army. With the Rush-Shippen dispute before them, the Committee was unquestionably alert to the need to carefully review and analyze the problems in the Medical Department. They held several briefings with Washington on what he considered a cure for the evils that fraught the system, and requested he present comprehensive recommendations on how to improve the army and its medical facilities.

On January 29, Washington submitted a detailed analysis of problems in the army with suggestions for its reorganization. This presentation, covering forty pages, succinctly referred to the needs of the Medical Department. He reaffirmed that since the beginning of the war there had been "...difficulties and imperfections in this department." He repeated he had neither the "leisure or opportunity to examine [them] with a critical eye." However, he readily acknowledged he was aware of the pernicious wrangling between the main hospitals and the regimental surgeons. The latter complained that they had been ignored in the distribution "of medicines and other necessaries." This shortage had created a serious problem in the "slight cases, and in the first stages of more dangerous complaints." It was claimed that the avoidance of their request for medicines had caused unnecessary deaths. Deploring the careless apportionment of medicines, Washington advocated prompt Congressional action to resolve the problem. Regardless, in the interim, he declared regimental surgeons should be allotted a reasonable quantity of medicines because "...the accommodation of the sick [at Valley Forge] and the preservation of men's lives are the first and great objects to be consulted..." He lamented the ill effects of a system that sent those with a "slight indication of disease to distant hospitals." Forced transfers increased the severity of many cases of sickness and caused unnecessary deaths.[10]

Even without the Rush-Shippen dispute or the Committee at Camp's report, the appalling need to bring order to the medical system had reverberated through the halls of Congress for some time. Unless immediate measures were taken to reorganize the Medical Department, Congress was aware that continued sick conditions would have a cataclysmic effect on morale in the army. On February 6, spurred by these exigencies, Congress enacted a series of resolutions to regulate the military hospitals of the United States. The first appointment was to name a Director General to oversee operations of all hospitals between the Potomac and Hudson Rivers. Congress relieved all officers currently exercising authority in hospitals of their powers. Regrettably, the new regulations would not be implemented in time to relieve the dreadful conditions at Valley Forge hospitals. Albeit, Washington would take advantage of the resolves to direct the establishment of the first military hospital of the Continental Army at Yellow Springs, as distinguished from many makeshift hospitals in churches, meeting houses, and residences.

Under the jurisdiction of the Director General, organizational personnel were to be selected, and rules governing the hospital operations were to be instituted. He was to name a Deputy Director General for each district after they had been determined, and to cooperate with the Physician General and Surgeon General in all affairs of hospital administration. Each Deputy was to name one or more assistant deputies, who would be responsible to see that every hospital was fully equipped with furniture, utensils, apparel, medicines, instruments, dressings, physicians mates, nurses and other necessaries, such as herbs. Besides overseeing that these administrative requirements were fulfilled, the Director General was to visit frequently "every hospital, examine the qualifications and performance of hospital officers, and report [his] findings to Congress." As an added responsibility, he was empowered to discharge those employees judged supernumerary.

A ward master was to be added to the staff of each hospital, where he was to be responsible for every article of clothing and personal effects of each soldier admitted to his hospital. Congress concluded the resolutions by setting a pay scale for hospital officers.[11]

Meanwhile, Washington and hospital officials were faced with the day to day need to redress the suffering throughout the encampment area. Their duties were complicated by the indifference of many soldiers who ignored their personal hygiene and this contributed to the increased high instance of illness. Numerous admonitions were issued to Regimental Officers and Quartermasters to make certain the men used the vaults [latrines] and not ease themselves about the camp, or any other place, "otherwise the Camp will be insufferable from the Stench when the warm weather comes." Unfortunately, even though the Quartermasters regularly filled the vaults and dug new ones, many men disregarded orders.[12]

Despondent over their lot, or careless, other soldiers were indifferent to the cleanliness of their surroundings, necessitating the issuance of orders to remove all filth from their huts. Although Washington understood the reasons for the low morale, it was essential that the malefactors be punished.[13]

A number of soldiers have left graphic, sometimes satirical, accounts of conditions affecting the health at the encampment. Possibly the most melodramatic was a Surgeon in the Connecticut Line, Dr. Albigence Waldo, who left a description of Christmas at the camp: "We are still in tents, when we ought to be in huts—the poor sick, suffer much in tents in this cold weather. But we now treat them differently from what they used to be at home, under the inspection of old women and Doct Bolus Linctus. We give them mutton and grog—and a capital medicine once in a while—to start the disease from its foundation at once. We avoid Piddling Pills, Powders, Bolus Linctus Cordials and all such insignificant matters whose powers are only rendered important by causing the patient to vomit up his money instead of his disease. But very few of the sick men die." A few days earlier Waldo had described their scarcity of food, recalling "A general cry thro' the Camp this Evening among the Soldiers, "No Meat! No Meat!"—the Distant vales Echo'd back the melancholly sound—"No Meat! No Meat!" Imitating the noise of Crows & Owls, also, made a part of the confused Musick. What have you for Dinner Boys? "Nothing but Fire Cake & Water, Sir." At night, "Gentlemen the Supper is ready." What is your Supper Lads? "Fire Cakes & Water, Sir."[14]

During the first three months, conditions that filled the flying hospitals and many improvised military facilities were the consequence of inedible and insufficient provisions. There was also a paucity of clothing to protect the men from the cold. Lafayette believed that inadequate safeguards against the cold was a major factor in the increase of sickness. He wrote: "Blankets were at a premium. The troops slept in shifts. The wakening soldiers crouched about the campfires as others took their disturbed place beneath the inadequate covers." The son of a Chester Springs surgeon, Dr. Bodo Otto, writing in a whimsical mood, described the monotony of their diet "For breakfast, we have bacon and smoke; for dinner smoke and bacon; as for supper, smoke." Baron de Kalb lamented that no one was troubling himself to relieve the many soldiers infected with the itch. Many of the tongue-in-cheek protestations by the men were a way to vent their displeasure with conditions that they realized would not be quickly rectified.[15]

During the encampment Washington's attention was never diverted from the needs of the sick. Paramount among his concerns was the ever increasing number of incapacitated soldiers, and the mushrooming number of hospitals on both sides of the Schuylkill. He was perplexed by this rapid growth of improvised hospitals, and concerned as to where adequate staffs and medical supplies could be obtained. The exact number of military hospitals is not known, but over fifty have been identified. Shippen and Scammel listed over twenty-two but did not include all the numerous meeting houses, churches, and private residences that had been commandeered as facilities for the sick. In Chester County, George Thomas noted that "...several neighbors are in distress by having their Barns turn'd into hospitals and filled with sick." Another authority claimed most places of worship, numerous barns, and some residences for fifteen miles south and west of the encampment were taken to house the sick.[16]

Unhappily, mismanagement and indifference added to the haphazard fashion in which the sick were transferred from one hospital to another. No attention was directed to whether a specific hospital could accommodate additional patients. And admixture of contagious cases and those recuperating from an illness worsened the surgeon's problems. The men so indiscriminately assigned were victims of "A contrary practice" which Washington believed caused "the Death of many men." Another distressing condition brought to Washington's attention involved the large number of men who were carried on the rolls of hospitals for several months after their death or discharge. Lieutenant Colonel William Bradford, Deputy Commissary General of Muster, believed many of the latter had deserted. Every effort to correct these mistakes was frustratingly ignored. Bradford reported an alarming number of sick were moved "from place to place," with no records maintained of their transfer. In some cases he found "hospital books" lost, thus making it impossible to know what had happened to many former sick and wounded.[17]

Exasperated by the non-compliance of his orders, Washington directed each Regimental Surgeon to visit every hut in his regiment and compile a list of all occupants. Forms were available to record the physical condition of the men, with special notice of those needing hospital care. He insisted that they were "to spare no pains for the help of the sick untill they can be sent to the Hospl'." Threatening punishment for failure to comply with these instructions, he demanded a check must be made each morning, noon, three o'clock and at taps.[18]

Washington requested that the encampment be canvassed to determine how many soldiers had had smallpox the natural way, and was amazed to discover that a surprisingly large number would have to be inoculated. At this time in America most citizens had an unyielding aversion to inoculation, believing it gave the patient "pain and grief." However, their opinion would not deter Washington's determination that all who had not been afflicted with the disease undergo inoculations. Otherwise, he was convinced, the army faced an epidemic. He readily admitted that he understood his "Countrymen['s]" fear that "consequences [could make them] so apparently ill, must result from it."[19]

Before mid-March everyone in the army had been inoculated. The more sagacious soldiers were aware that the recuperation period would be easier and possibly shorter if they observed the doctor's instructions and "made certain to get Fresh air every day." One discreet soldier wrote that he had been "reduc'd far more from *Fever Ague* than smallpox." Others reported they survived the "smallpox inoculation," with "little discomfort [and] with the loss of only a few [soldiers]." Others less prudent had lolled around their huts indifferent to the surgeon's instructions. These foolish men adopted the view that "eating and drinking" would carry them safely through their convalescence. Their lackadaisical attitudes brought many to a point where "seeming to be out of danger [they] had by overeating and drinking lost their lives." Even obedience to careful living did not protect some from suffering. A number died from "want of straw to raise them from the damp earth." Others were delayed from receiving their inoculation because of a scarcity of straw upon which they could rest during the early days of recovery. One source claimed that the incidence of smallpox was found prevalent in the civilian population close to camp and the hospitals.[20]

To enforce the advice given the men on their eating, drinking and exercise, the Captain of each Company was to parade his men, when weather permitted. He was, also, to assure that the soldiers and "tenders" (nurses) received training "on their conduct, eating, drinking and keeping in the air." It was hoped these training sessions would encourage the men to comply with an orderly regimen of diet and exercise.[21]

In 1779, Dr. Albigence Waldo, in a departure from his whimsical journal, wrote a studious treatise on the effects of the smallpox inoculation at Valley Forge. In his study he stated "above four thousand, Officers and Soldiers were inoculated with the Small Pox." His calculation of the number inoculated is confirmed by the statements of others at camp. Dr. S. Tenney asserted that between "3 and 4,000" were inoculated, while John Chaloner declared the number to be "near 4,000."

Waldo wrote that while the quality of the patient's diet was life-supporting, they had little "else but Beef & Flour." Evidence exists that the Deputy Commissary Purchases made an exhaustive search for Indian meal and rice. Waldo added that the only medicines available were "Tartari Emetici [Tartar Emetic]" and "Jalap,[22] generally mixed together and even two or three times." He believed few deaths occurred among those who observed their diet and exercise. However, for others there appeared "a secondary fever which would mostly turn putrid." Waldo was convinced that most victims perished because of the "uncommon fatigues" and the "unwholesome provisions for which this Campaign of 1777 was remarkable."[23]

Because of the number of cases involved, smallpox received the most publicity, but when the surgeons reviewed their crowded hospitals, they were distressed by the other dangerous diseases prevalent in the army. Other illnesses that prevailed during the encampment were camp or putrid fever and dysentery. Eighteenth- century armies suffered from a type of malignant dysentery, of which little is known today, that disabled and killed many. Equally virulent was the pernicious camp fever which Dr. Rush described as a form of typhus. These diseases were communicated to a large number of soldiers suffering from a minor ailment who, after transfer to another medical facility, were exposed to the contagion of dysentery and fever. With these illnesses rife, the sick contracted them through the reuse of blankets, clothes, straw and the dampness and chill of their accommodations. To what degree venereal disease existed at Valley Forge is uncertain as it was discreetly omitted from most surgeons reports. However, it was known to be a concern to the army throughout the war.

To combat discomfort and pain, the questionable practices of the eighteenth century were the only hope for the sick. Most medical men of the time had great faith in a purgative-cathartics-emetics, blistering, bloodletting, opium and bark or other herbs. Strong reliance was also placed on diet, especially rice, meal and milk, and to a lesser degree, meat. Little could be accomplished when medical science depended on these as cures. In the early months of the encampment, Dr. Rush, although prejudiced, aptly stated that the "Hospitals are the sinks of human life in the army." Frequently, even with the dubious use of such medicines and methods, the former became scarce, necessitating the dispatch of members of the Medical Department to various states for supplies to fill the medicine chests. Truly for the survival of the sick, "Those were the days of faith."[24]

Regrettable circumstances during the first quarter of 1778, were lack of adequate facilities and the Rush-Shippen imbroglio that caused confusion in the Medical Department. These distractions hindered the physicians in their efforts to control the spread of contagious diseases. Among the overlooked casualties were the number of physicians and attendants, who perished, thus decimating the staff of a facility. In places of worship converted into hospitals, members of the congregations volunteered as nurses, while the clergy sought to comfort the suffering of the dejected and helpless wretches. Reports from these institutions disclosed the mournful fact that there was a high incidence of mortality among these angels of mercy. One example of such losses among these unsung heroes was reported for the Bethlehem Hospital (Moravian Seminary) where during January 1778, camp fever was fatal to five members of the congregation and their assistant pastor. The scarcity of "tenders" (nurses) became to critical that a search was conducted to

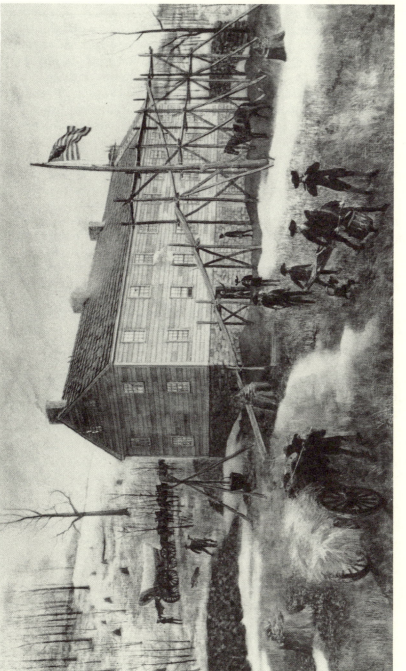

Yellow Springs Hospital by Barclay Rubicam, first Continental Army Hospital. (Historic Yellow Springs Archives, Chester Springs, Pennsylvania. Courtesy Dr. and Mrs. Henry A. Jordan.)

enlist females to serve.

With the advent of spring, a vigorous attempt was made to clean up the hospitals and make them more habitable. While we can only conjecture, it is possible the appearance of Washington on one of his inspection tours spurred the program. As he toured the Yellow Springs facility, he found clean and healthful accommodations. The Yellow Springs visit was not an isolated instance as those of the Reverend James Sproat, Hospital Chaplain. Sproat revealed that most of the facilities were "very neat and clean, and the sick seem to be well attended." Sproat's custom on arrival in the area was to first visit and converse with all the sick, and then preach in the wards or at a local church for those able to attend. His visits covered a wide range of facilities situated in places of worship and barns. At Yellow Springs he delivered several homilies in three converted barns which he found were "clean and airy."[25]

The lore of Valley Forge is enhanced by the report of a diary kept by a family named Hartman. This diary records that German farmers in the area collected "meat, flour, potatoes, cabbage and other foods, together with straw and clothing" and delivered them to Washington. On their return trips the wagons were loaded with sick soldiers for the Yellow Springs hospital.[26]

Meanwhile, Washington's concern had not been diverted from the care of the sick. He was gratified by the improvements, but he believed a constant vigil should be maintained to prevent backsliding.

On April 14, while on an inspection through the lines, he expressed pleasure that some brigadiers had obeyed "his orders respecting the Neatness and Purity of their Camp." His apprehensions and fears were that other brigades would not comply with the order for cleanliness. To his chagrin, they were confirmed as he found "the smell was in some places intollerable, owing to the want of Necessaries or lack of them...." Incensed, he directed that all "Dirt and Filth as well that in Front, Rear and between the Hutts as there shall be found on the Parade and before the doors raked together and burned or buried." Any soldier who shall "attempt to ease himself anywhere but at a proper necessary" was to be punished with five lashes. To eliminate any excuses of urgency or privacy, Washington ordered the "Necessaries to be hid with Boughs or Hurdles, the last tho' more troublesome at first will allways serve as they can be easily removed."[27]

Apparently disturbed by the lack of control by the officers assigned to hospitals and certain surgeons, he took the unusual step of ordering General Lachlan McIntosh to make a survey "of the state of each hospital." Justified or not many surgeons became so involved in caring for patients that they overlooked hospital conditions. McIntosh's directive was long and detailed. It included preparing a list of all patients, their regiments and companies and "as nearly as possible" enumerating how many had died or been discharged. He was to make a complete examination of the books of "Directors, Surgeons, [and] Commissaries." Washington was dissatisfied with the failure of the Congressional resolutions to relieve the conditions at the Valley Forge hospitals. Displeased, he ignored the resolves and ordered McIntosh to determine the number of hospitals needed, to fix the locations for each one, and to recommend an operational setup for every facility. To broaden the scope of his investigation, he was to ascertain whether the soldiers serving as guards, tenders of the sick or waiters on Officers and Surgeons were excessive. As many as could be spared were to be sent back to their respective regiments. Another difficult assignment was for McIntosh to decide how many sick were fit for duty and return them to camp. It was also left to his discretion to decide if any soldiers were "unfit for Service;" those so classified were to be discharged. McIntosh's assignment had been sweeping and could not have been completed before he was ordered to take command at Fort Pitt, on the Pennsylvania frontier. He did enter on his duties, as Reverend James Sproat reports meeting him on April 18, at the Schaefferstown hospital. He probably made a verbal report to Washington before his departure for Fort Pitt.[28]

On the same day that Washington issued his instructions to McIntosh, he advised officers commanding the various hospitals that McIntosh's orders were to be obeyed "as coming from Sir [Washington]." The officers were also informed that McIntosh was "to inspect into the economy and management...and the Military order and government observed at each...hospital."[29]

Of grave concern as winter progressed were the conditions in the huts and the health of the troops. It was disclosed that the huts were littered with debris and were dank and smoky, creating a situation that caused many soldiers to contract fever and various other minor ailments. Insufferable conditions had incapacitated many soldiers, rendering them unfit for duty. Their disabilities could be calamitous, as rumor after rumor continued to reach camp that the British were planning to evacuate Philadelphia. With such intelligence, Washington issued almost daily orders for the army to be ready to move out on a moment's notice. Other warnings were directed to the Regimental Surgeons to have every man capable, ready to march. In turn the surgeons and hospital officers informed Washington that when the army abandoned Valley Forge, at least 1,000 sick would have to remain confined to the hospitals. After this startling disclosure, it was discovered that the Regimental hospitals' medicine chests were virtually empty. Without hesitation Washington directed each division as selected, to apply to the Yellow Springs Hospital, or to John Burns Cutting, Apothecary General of the Middle Department currently quartered at the same facility, for chests and medicines to meet their needs.[30]

As a further deterrent to any increase in sickness, in the spring Washington adopted measures to improve the personal cleanliness of the men. Regiments with the highest incidence of illness in their huts were ordered to move into tents. To improve their lot, other units were ordered to remove the caulking from the chinks in the walls, to permit the passage of fresh air and to build two windows in each hut. As a move to improve sanitary conditions, Washington excused the soldiers from exercising on Friday afternoons. They were limited to ten minutes to bathe and wash their clothes, owing to the number of soldiers in camp.[31]

Valley Forge's unsolvable puzzle involves the question of how many unnecessary deaths occurred among the sick and wounded during the six month encampment. Equally enigmatic are the places of all interments and, in some cases, the numbers buried in unmarked individual and mass common graves. Some historians assert that the number of deaths in the Valley Forge area was nearly 3,000, however, this is an estimate and cannot be verified. A number of identified burials dot the countryside churches, barns and residences, with some honored by monuments indicating the number interred. Others, such as the Valley Meeting House, can only be gauged by tradition because of the Quaker custom of not making records of any war connected activity. A study by a member of the Valley Meeting House estimates that about 300 were buried in an unmarked section of the church yard, called "the buried over section."[32]

Early scholars have poured through the records of churches and private residences with their barns, but regrettably some are incomplete or never existed. One example of how vague and uninformative these records are can be found in the hospital at Lititz, where there were reports of a number of burials. One visitor stated that before his arrival on December 21, 1777, 110 soldiers had died and been interred; obviously most of these deaths occurred before the army entered Valley Forge on December 19. At the hospital in the Moravian Seminary at Bethlehem, it was estimated that during the winter of 1778 over 500 died and were buried on the grounds. Most of the deaths at this facility were soldiers wounded at Brandywine and Germantown, who had not been transferred there from Valley Forge. Some surgeons and visitors from camp have left records of the deaths of soldiers covering a limited time, making it difficult to obtain precise figures and to sort out those that overlap. Most prefaced their comments with the word "about."

Another distressing and unknown casualty list is that of physicians, nurses and members of the church congregations who succumbed to the fever contracted from the sick soldiers. Tradition, coupled with some records, indicates that a good number of individuals offered care and comfort to sick soldiers.

Over the years and particularly at the turn of the last century, interested citizens have searched within the lines of the encampment for a bit of sacred ground that contained the remains of the unknown heroes of the war. In some instances the searchers unsuccessfully looked for mass graves. Some antiquarians discovered rough headstones scattered over the slopes of Mt. Joy extending to the Schuylkill toward Port Kennedy and across Valley Creek opposite Washington's headquarters. William M. Stephens, an active participant in these searches, reported that in 1901, he watched as workmen dug a path to the Waterman monument—the only marked grave in the Park. They were surprised as three distinct graves were uncovered "with the bones of the soldiers in perfect condition and three bodies to a grave." An effort was made to preserve the remains, but they disintegrated when exposed to the air.[33]

Weedon has left us the only description of the honors paid to officers buried within the encampment: "The Funeral honors at the Interment of Officers, are for the future to be confined to a solemn procession of Officers and Soldiers in Number Suitable to the Rank of the Deceas'd with revers'd arms. Fireing on these occasion, is to be abolish'd in Camp."[34]

A recent report issued by a National Park historian indicates where the locations of eleven burials have been identified within the encampment. However, all of the studies and observations cannot account for the catastrophic loss of life in the army while at Valley Forge. Time and the absence of specific written historical citations, will continue to leave unsolved this tragedy of the Valley Forge encampment.[35]

The problems of hygiene and the disposition of the sick who were left at the encampment when the army evacuated Valley Forge will await the last chapter.

Camp Medley

A POTPOURRI OF happenings and army routine activities occurred during the encampment, offering a unique mixture of humor, compassion, pathos and military regimen. Most of these incidents were seemingly of minor consequence to the discipline and organization of the army, but each had its peculiar niche in the daily routine.

Courts-Martial

Throughout the six months at Valley Forge, Washington was troubled by the large number of courts-martial. Daily one or more officers or soldiers appeared before either a General, Brigade or Regimental tribunal on charges ranging from desertion, conduct unbecoming a gentlemen, scandalous remarks, disobedience of orders or other violations. Washington, as Commander in Chief, reserved the right to review and approve or reverse all decisions handed down by the courts-martial. After carefully scrutinizing the sentences rendered it became apparent to him that many officers of impeccable past service had been judged out of prejudice. He believed conditions at camp, and the stress of the service, occasionally caused a frustration that led them into unusual behavior. Determined to put a stop to the influence of personal animosity in court-martial decisions, he issued an order indicating his awareness of the painful situation an his wish that "...the Officers of his Army...consider themselves as a band of brothers cemented by the Justice of the Common Cause, that a perfect harmony might subsist among them..."

Washington added that he hoped all personal disputes would be amicably resolved before airing them in a court-martial or bothering him with "private dissentions," as the inclusion of these differences entered as a record in public files would eventually "reflect disgrace upon themselves and the Army."[1]

Religion

Such injustices and the lack of a spiritual motivation had surfaced during the last campaign. Representing the army Chaplains, Reverends Francis Allison, John Ewing and William Marshall petitioned Congress to make bibles available to all members of the army. Congress appointed a committee to investigate the feasibility and cost of printing 30,000 bibles. After consulting several American printers it was deemed that none could publish this number, especially with the cost of "paper, binding, &c... £10,272 10/." A note of skepticism crept into their report at this point when it became obvious that Congress would have to advance the money for publication, with its only hope for reimbursement coming from the "sale of the books." However, Congress agreed "that the use of the Bible is so universal, and its importance so great," that 20,000 copies could be imported from "Holland, Scotland or elsewhere." Unfortunately, the final disposition of this resolution is unknown.[2]

It appears that there was a scarcity of chaplains to conduct daily prayers and divine services each Sunday. To fill this gap, Generals Wayne, Scott and others petitioned Congress to appoint recommended chaplains to specified regiments.[3]

Washington's input into the printing of bibles for the army cannot be determined, but his orders indicate frequent directives to conduct regular worship service in each brigade and regiment. His irritation increased when reports reached headquarters that vice and gaming were becoming common in camp. At the same time he felt that a lack of spiritual guidance had developed a laxness in attending divine services. In an effort to counteract the spread of these perceived evils, Washington issued instructions that all regimental commanders; "Let Vice and immorality of every kind be discouraged as much as possible in your Regiment: and see, as a Chaplain is allowed to it, that the Men regularly attend divine Worship. Gaming of every kind is expressly forbid as the foundation of evil, and the ruin of many a brave and good Officer. Games of exercise, for amusement, may be not only allowed of, but Incouraged."[4]

Two orders of Washington typified his attention to the spiritual needs of his soldiers. One was directed to all brigades, stating:

> The Commander in Chief directs that divine Service be performed every Sunday in those Brigades to which there are Chaplains, those that have none to attend the Place of Worship next to them. It is expected that officers of all Ranks will...set an Example to their men—While we are zealously performing the Duties of good Citizens and Solders we certainly ought not to be inattentive to the higher Duties of Religion—To the distinguished Character of Patriot's it should be our highest glory to add the more distinguished Character of Christians. The single instance of providential goodness,

which we have experienced & which have now almost crowned our Labours with compleat Success demands from us in a peculiar manner the warmest returns of gratitude & Piety to the Supreme Author of all Good—[5]

Another order that symbolized Washington's desire for regular religious observance was that each regiment: "...is to attend prayers every Day when the Weather will permit, just before the retreat beating at Evening—They are to Parade on Regt. Parade at the long Roll beating with their Arms, then March immediately to the Ridge in the Center of Coll Herman Swift's Regt. there to attend—It is expected that officers see that their Men strictly attend—"[6]

Unfortunately, Washington discontinued his diary early in the Revolution thereby obscuring any record of his private habits such as attendance at religious services. In civilian life he was considered a consistent if not regular churchgoer. At Valley Forge the demand on his duties as Commander in Chief undoubtedly encroached on any personal inclinations. However, Washington's frequent and insistent orders that religious observances be conducted throughout the army, clearly reflect his spiritual convictions. There is evidence in the correspondence, diaries and journals of officers and rank and file that he occasionally attended worship service at several regimental and brigade posts.

The army was assembled to celebrate, or observe, specific occasions. On December 18, 1777, the day before the army entered Valley Forge, a special service was held of "Thanksgiving and Praise...to God for the manifold blessings he has granted us." Again May 6, 1778, the army would solemnize the Alliance with France.

While there are not many personal letters of soldiers at Valley Forge, those found are sprinkled with a devout reference to God or Providence. One statement that epitomized their belief is embodied in a letter of Major Albert Chapman, of the 5th Connecticut Regiment, that America, with God's help would be: "Inabled to [do] good in our Day & Generation, may we maintain our Liberties & Rites that God has given us to Inlist ourselves under the banner of Jesus Christ & fight like a good Soldier for him that loved us and gave himself a ransom for our Sins." There is sufficient evidence to indicate that Chapman's belief is representative of most Continental officers, and by the very few letters of the rank and file that have survived, most being from soldiers in the units of New England states.[7]

The Indispensible Ladies

Many women made significant contributions to the welfare and comfort of the troops among them were Martha Washington, wives of officers, ladies residing in the neighborhood of the camp and the ubiquitous camp followers. Other than the implied conduct of the latter, they volunteered their services in many vital areas. Some worked as washerwomen or laundresses, others were nurses, cooks and handy workers. No reliable figures are obtainable for the number of camp followers at Valley Forge, but they were present in large numbers creating quartering and logistical problems. When the British occupied Philadelphia, Commissary Daniel Weir issued 626 rations each day to women. Later, in June 1778, some authorities contend that Sir Henry Clinton was accompanied by 1,500 women in his march across New Jersey. It is believed this increase of followers occurred when about 800 women attached themselves to the army in Philadelphia, most having married British or Hessian soldiers. One Hessian chaplain, living on Shippen Street, reportedly performed at least 100 marriage ceremonies.[8]

The camp followers were, at times, a nuisance to the army when on the march, but their services in camp were admittedly a blessing. A number of soldiers were accompanied by their wives and children during their term of enlistment. It is a disappointment that no records have been found that disclose the housing arrangement of soldiers with families. American Armies through the Indian wars of the latter decades of the nineteenth century usually erected small huts or tents to the rear of the barracks for camp followers. It is possible that some variation of this practice existed to quarter soldiers with wives existed at Valley Forge. As the huts were designed for a squad of twelve soldiers, there is little likelihood that women were permitted to cohabit in those crowded quarters. Washington granted the camp followers a half ration each day, with those having children an additional quarter ration. Neither Washington's orders nor recent archaeological studies make reference to where and how these unknown women were housed.[9]

Camp followers straggled into Valley Forge in the wake of the army. As in most wars a large number of women were attracted by what they believed was the excitement and romance of army life, although at Valley Forge the dishevelled appearance of the poor Continentals must have had a chilling effect on the women's ardor. Scattered among the camp followers were many prostitutes, whose numbers increased significantly later in the spring, their arrival coinciding with the opening for business of the tippling houses, at what they unmistakenly considered a safe distance from Washington's jurisdiction. As expressed by John Laurens, "The camp whores, who have become numerous, are being used as nurses." Alexander Milliver, a soldier at camp, claimed his mother was at Valley Forge and helped the troops as a washerwoman. The services of the washerwomen were a boon to the troops. A plentiful supply of water was obtainable only on the perimeter of the camp; the Schuylkill River

169

and Valley and Trout Creeks all at a considerable distance from most regiment's positions. The men gladly relinquished the chore of washing their tattered clothes. In Colonial days overexposure to water was considered unwholesome, and the men were cautioned to bathe only on orders and for a short period, by spring usually ten minutes.[10]

An unusual visitation by women from Philadelphia brought relief to the men. On New Years Day ten teams of oxen driven by women arrived in camp. The wagons were filled with supplies and 2,000 shirts made by the women of Philadelphia; after delivery the oxen were slaughtered for the benefit of the camp. This incident would seem to be apocryphal except that at the time women were permitted to pass freely through the lines of each army.[11]

More pleasant happenings pervaded the camp when officers and soldiers married young ladies from the Valley Forge area or their personal camp follower. On April 30, a Virginia cavalryman, Captain Berryman Green, was married to Ann Pritchard of Charleston, Chester County, by Chaplain William Rogers. Tradition claims Green's marriage climaxed a series of six weddings by members of his company.[12]

Throughout January women passed freely in and out of the lines at Valley Forge and Philadelphia. Both Washington and Howe considered allowing women to visit relatives, friends and soldiers to be a salutary gesture. They believed that the camaraderie and pleasure of taking small gifts to loved ones was not a violation of security. However, by February 1, the euphoria vanished when many reports of frequent violations of this privilege reached both headquarters. There were indications that incidents of espionage had become a part of each army's intelligence system. To Washington, the most damaging breach of faith was the repeated effort to induce desertion. On February 4, his orders stated "The most pernicious consequences having arisen from suffering persons, women in particular, to pass and repass from Philadelphia to camp under Pretense of coming out to visit their Friends in the Army...but really with an intent to entice the soldiers to desert." He directed all officers to prohibit any intercourse between soldiers and "such persons." Any unauthorized women detected in camp were to be "turned out" unless they were detained "under peculiar circumstances of suspicion," whereby they were to be arrested and punished. These directives did not stop all communications, as women could still, under certain conditions, receive a pass at headquarters.[13]

A by-product of Washington's concern was an incident that happened in Greene's Division. Mary Johnson was charged with "laying a plot to Desert to the Enemy." There is no record to indicate the number of soldiers she tried to involve in her intrigue. The court-martial considered her crime sufficiently heinous to render a verdict of guilty. She was sentenced "to receive 100 lashes and to be drum'd out of the Army by all Drums and Fifes in the Division."[14]

After the arrival of Martha Washington at camp in early February, increased activity became evident for an already busy and overcrowded headquarters. Aghast at the sight of many near naked soldiers, she recruited the services of all the officers' wives in camp to determine what they could do to ease the men's sufferings. From the beginning of the encampment a local resident, Mrs. Bowers, often visited the soldiers with her saddle bags of food. Local tradition asserts that upon meeting Mrs. Washington she taught her how to knit stockings. From this beginning, Martha Washington became an inveterate knitter, ably aided by the other officers' wives. Many neighboring ladies joined in assisting the knitters, among them a young girl of sixteen who later became Mrs. Westlake.

The only known eyewitness account of Martha Washington's activities at Valley Forge was related by Mrs. Westlake to Benson J. Lossing, historian, in the nineteenth century. Lossing faithfully provided a verbatim account of her observation of "Lady Washington's" activities at Valley Forge. Although skeptics have questioned Mrs. Westlake's recall, some credence may be attached to the broader aspects of her account. Similar incidents have been recorded of Martha Washington at other winter encampments during the Revolution. Lossing recorded the following passage from Mrs. Westlake: "I never in my life knew a woman so busy from early morning until late at night as was Lady Washington, providing comforts for the sick soldiers. Every day, excepting Sunday, the wives of officers in camp, and sometimes other women, were invited...to assist her in knitting socks, patching garments, and making shirts for the poor soldiers when materials could be procured. Every fair day she might be seen, with basket in hand, and with a single attendant, going among the huts seeking the keenest and most needy sufferers...giving all the comforts to them in her power." The other area women mentioned by Mrs. Westlake probably included Sarah Walker, Elizabeth Stephens, Priscilla Stephens, Margaret Beaver, Elizabeth Moore, Jane Moore and others. A large number of ladies that resided near the encampment were frequent visitors carrying what quantities of food and clothing they could spare.[15]

Elizabeth Drinker adds a final descriptive touch to the simple yet hectic life at headquarters. Early in April, accompanied by three Quaker ladies, she journeyed to Valley Forge to beseech Washington's intercession with the state authorities in securing the release of their husbands confined at Winchester, Virginia. Mrs. Drinker commented:

> [We] arrived at headquarters about half past one o'clock; requested an audience with the general; sat with his wife (a sociable, pretty kind of woman) until he came in; a number of officers there, who were very

complaisant—Tench Tilghman among the number. It was not long before G.W. [George Washington] came and discoursed with us freely, but not so long as we could have wished, as dinner was served, to which he invited us. There were fifteen of the officers, besides the General and his wife, Gen. [Nathanael] Greene and Gen. [Charles] Lee. We had an elegant dinner which was soon over, when we went out with the General's wife to her chamber and saw no more of him. He told us he could do nothing in our business further than granting us a pass to Lancaster [where the State Assembly was in session].[16]

Indians

At one of Washington's conferences with the Committee of Congress at Camp, a mutual agreement was reached to employ Indians in the army. In writing to Congress, the Committee stated that jointly with the Commander in Chief, they contemplated the formation of a "Flying Army..composed of light Infantry & rifle Men." As one purpose of these troops was to provide protection for the Pennsylvania frontier from raids by Indian allies of the British, they considered it expedient to raise a contingent of friendly Indians to "mix" in this frontier force.[17]

A scattering of Stockbridge and Mohican Indians were already serving in the ranks of several New England Continental Regiments, especially those of Connecticut and Massachusetts. Dr. Waldo recorded inoculating two Indians from his Connecticut Regiment for smallpox. He noted the effects of "Spirits," on one Indian who "rarely passed a day without being intoxicated" and recovered his health, while the other only "indulged himself but once in drinking too freely and died the next day." In 1775, when Generals Richard Montgomery and Benedict Arnold invaded Canada, a few Algonquins joined Moses Hazen's regiment of French Canadians.[18]

A letter of the Committee in Camp preceded, by one week, a report of a meeting to effect a treaty with the "Six Nations" (Iroquois) at Johnstown, New York. The delegation, consisting of the Indian Commissioners and army personnel, were disappointed with the small representation of the Iroquois tribes. Except for the attendance of Oneidas, Tuscaroras and some Onondagas, the other tribes were represented by a handful of warriors, whereas no member of the powerful Senecas was present. Reports estimated 700 to 2,000 Indians were in attendance, the first figure probably being the number of warriors. Chevalier de Pontgibaud said 2,000 men, women and children were regaled with presents, and particularly "fire water." The Americans present acknowledged the cruelty and hostility of all Iroquois except for "the faithful Oneidas & Tuscaroras." Therefore, they suggested that it would be beneficial to enlist members of these tribes in the army.[19]

When the commissioner's recommendations and comments were reviewed by the Board of War, they gave a tongue in cheek endorsement to the project, questioning the cost and advantage in employing Indians. However, they admitted that with Washington's knowledge of Indians, and the Committee in Camp's acquiescence, it might be desirous to adopt the proposal. On this qualified recommendation and the Committee's support, Congress resolved to empower Washington "if he thinks it prudent and proper to employ...a body of Indians not exceeding 400." At the same time Congress decided to explore establishing a similar force for the back county of the Carolinas.[20]

Before Washington could recruit Indians to join the army at Valley Forge, a number of vexing problems surfaced. The friendly Oneidas and Tuscaroras were being harassed and terrorized by the more numerous and powerful Senecas, Mohawks, Cayugas and Onondagas. Echoing similar threats and propaganda, the British tried to convince the "friendlies" that the Americans didn't need their assistance and, to cement their friendship, plied them with numerous presents that Washington could not match. Washington advised Congress that at best the Oneidas and Tuscaroras are "in a state of hesitancy and indecision," but he was certain Congress would "do everything in their power to promote these desirable ends."[21]

After many presents and much cajoling by the officers at Fort Stanwix (present Rome, New York), the Indians reluctantly left their unprotected villages. Finally, in late April under the escort of Louis de Tousard,[22] a French volunteer, "seven and fourthy [forty] Indians" left the fort destined for Valley Forge. On the march Tousard was harassed and delayed "...by some Indians who remained behind to get drinking [liquor] with more ease." Arriving at the encampment on May 14, Tousard, with his charges, reported to Washington. Lieutenant Colonel Jean Baptiste Gouvion, of the Engineer Corps, was expected to "set out" with another party for camp. However, Washington requested Schuyler to order Gouvion to defer his start as he believed with the lateness of the season, the army's "prospects were very different" and that the Indians could not be profitably utilized in the forthcoming campaign. Nevertheless, not wishing to upset the sensitive Indian allies, he hoped it "can be done without occasioning disgust," inasmuch as "The Oneidas and Tuscaroras have a particular claim for attention and kindness, for their perseverance and fidelity."[23]

Although the Oneidas' and Tuscaroras' sojourn at Valley Forge would be of short duration, while there they were involved in some interesting episodes. Chevalier de Pontgibaud recalled what he described as "two singular incidents" involving the Oneidas and Tuscaroras. As aide-de-camp to Lafayette he dined frequently at headquarters. At one dinner he remembered that "...an Indian entered the room, walked round the table, and then stretching forth his long tattood arm seized a large joint of hot roast beef in his thumb and fingers, took it to the door, and began to eat it. We were all much surprised, but General Washington gave orders that he was not to be interfered with, saying laughingly, that it was apparently the dinner hour of this Matins Scaevola of the New World."

As Pontgibaud noted, under more sensitive circumstances, Washington would not brook any interference as exemplified when a "chief came into the room where our generals were holding a council of war. Washington, who was tall and very strong, rose, coolly took the Indian by the shoulders, and put him outside the door. The son of the forest did not protest; he concluded probably that his ejectment was a way of expressing by signs that his company was not wanted."[24]

Peter S. du Ponceau wrote of a pleasant conversation he had with the first Indian he encountered in the United States. One morning as he was walking before breakfast he heard a "French fashionable opera song sung by a powerful voice." He was abruptly surprised to be confronted by a tall Indian in Continental Regimentals with two epaulettes on his shoulders. Du Ponceau was further astounded when the Indian conversed in fluent French and English. The Indian said he had been raised by the Jesuits and had served in the Continental Army since Montgomery invaded Canada in 1775. He explained the epaulettes represented his recent elevation in rank to Colonel. Although disappointed, du Ponceau never saw the Indian again. From the background obtained, the Indian was probably an Algonquin.[25]

To draw the curtain on the Oneida and Tuscarora Indian activities at Valley Forge, on June 21, while on the march to Monmouth, Washington agreed to let them return to New York state. The Indians were apprehensive on account of threatened hostile acts planned by the Senecas. Orders had been received from their "sachems" directing they return at once. As a final gesture of appreciation, Washington hoped "they should be furnished with ample and suitable presents."[26]

Masons

Our search for camp diversions chiefly relies on the letters, diaries and journals of officers, a few soldiers, and some entries in Washington's orders and courts-martial, which unfortunately only provide sketchy descriptions of activities.

An element of camaraderie was enjoyed by officers and men who participated in the meetings of fraternal organizations. Many Masons were scattered through the ranks, and, while possible to identify some officers as Masons, little but speculation remains concerning rank and file members, or where lodge meetings were held.

A number of Masonic historians have researched extensively, but their findings are inconclusive. According to Masonic tradition military lodges held meetings at Valley Forge, some of which Washington attended but, unfortunately, because of the loss of records this cannot be verified. Lodge No. 8 did meet in the vicinity of the encampment, its meeting place is unknown, although some unsubstantiated claims state they met at the King of Prussia Tavern.

On April 10, 1880, a Masonic publication, *The Keystone*, inserted a comment on military lodges, stating: "An interesting subject connected with the Masonic Order during the Revolution relates to the traveling Lodges, commonly called "Military Lodges." They were held under direction of officers of regiments, and the ceremonies were as complete as circumstances would permit. If the membership was composed not only of officers but of private soldiers, the equality of the lodge room was in strong contrast to the military discipline maintained outside of it." It is possible some of these lodges may have held meetings at Valley Forge, but their positive existence has defied the research of Masonic historians.[27]

Music

In the early years of the Revolution the drums and fifes furnished music for most functions and movements of the army. By the drum beat the army "...rose in the morning, assembled, paraded, saluted, marched off, ceased work, and retired for the night." With the fifes they developed the proper cadence for slow parade and funeral marches. Even when at practice, the drummers and fifers relieved the humdrum of camp life. Most brigades and regiments had their own drummers and fifers, usually numbering between two and fifteen musicians.[28]

Later in the war bands would complement the fifes and drums. The bands were composed of up to eight musicians equipped with woodwinds and horns. However, there is at least one instance where a Brigadier desired to form a band at Valley Forge. On February 23, 1778, General John Paterson requested Colonel Thomas Marshall, of the 10th Massachusetts Regiment, to use his influence in recruiting the "German Musicians at Mystick" to form a band for his brigade. If the Germans were reluctant to come to camp, Marshall should procure instruments and "pick of those who can play on them." However, Paterson preferred the Germans and was willing to regale them with presents, assure them he would guarantee their pay and permit them to live with his guard without bearing arms. He stated "Good Music being of Importance in Camp, & the badness of ours determine me if possible to get a band to my Brigade."

The Bake House, pictured here, has had a number of alterations since Revolutionary times. It was frequently mentioned in Washington's General Orders and correspondence during the encampment period. On various occasions the structure was occupied for general courts-martial, Ludwick's bakery quarters and the camp theater. (Valley Forge National Historical Park.)

It is uncertain whether Paterson's wish was fulfilled, but the request suggests the possibility of a band of woodwinds and horns at Valley Forge.[29]

Confusion was evident in camp when the troops exercised and the drummers and fifers whimsically practiced at their pleasure. In early May, Washington changed the hours for exercising the brigades and simultaneously altered the practice hours for the drummers and fifers. He ordered the latter to practice at "five to six in the morning and from four to five in the afternoon, any Drummer that shall be found practicing at any other time than the time mentioned above shall be severely punished." The cacophony created by the widely scattered drums throughout the camp in early morning would not disturb the Commander in Chief. At that hour Washington would be in the saddle to start his camp inspection, a habit carried over from his life at Mt. Vernon, where he rode out at dawn to oversee his farms.[30]

Theater

With the advent of spring a number of plays were planned for the Bake House. One authority contends that Washington sponsored this activity to raise morale among the officers. This is possible, but it must be remembered that he was a devotee of the theater. The earliest record of a play was reported by a disappointed Ensign George Ewing, on April 15: "...this afternoon I received a ticket for the Play to be acted this evening at the Bakehouse in the evening went down in company with Major Bloomfield [Joseph], Lieuts Curtis [Marmaduke], Wayman [Abel, also spelled Weyman] & Kersey [William] but the house was so full that I could not get in then a number of Gent went to Major Parkers[31] hut in the fourth [Regiment] where we spent the evening very merily..." Possibly somewhat remorsefully, as the next day he noted "...my head achd very badly this morning occasioned by my last nights frolic..."[32]

No evidence survives to indicate if another play was presented before May 11, when Joseph Addison's "Cato" was performed to an appreciative audience at the Bake House. On May 14, Colonel William Bradford, Jr. describing the festivities to his sister Rachel wrote:

> ...the Theatre is opened—Last Monday Cato was performed before a very numerous & splendid audience. His Excellency & Lady, Lord Stirling, the Countess & Lady Kitty [Stirling] & Mr. Green [General Nathanael Greene] were part of the Assembly. The scenery was in Taste—& the performance admirable—Col. George did his part to admiration—he made an excellent *die* (as they say)—Pray heaven, he don't *die* in earnest...If the Enemy does not retire from Philada soon, our Theatrical amusements will continue—The fair Penitent with the Padlock will soon be acted. The recruiting officer is also on foot.[33]

177

Bradford invited his sister to visit the camp as it could now provide some entertainment, "The manoeuvering of the Army is in itself a sight that would Charm you." Six days later he advised her the invitation to visit the camp was withdrawn as "...all is hustle and bustle—our plays and other amusements seem to be laid aside & every one is preparing for a sudden movement." Regretfully, with these accounts, the curtain falls on the army theater at Valley Forge.[34]

Recreation

The soldiers engaged in a number of physical activities, and when conditions did not permit outdoor exercise, they resorted to "gaming." Washington viewed these "gaming" diversions as shameful vices and was determined to stamp out all forms of gambling and profanity. On January 8, his General Orders served notice to the army that he: "...is informed that gaming is again creeping into the Army; in a more especial manner among the lower staff in the environs of the camp. He therefore in the most solemn terms declares that this Vice in either Officers or soldiers, shall not when detected, escape exemplary punishment; and to avoid discrimination between play and gaming forbids Cards and Dice under any pretense whatsoever." There are scattered references to courts-martial sitting to judge officers or soldiers for playing cards; however, this was only the tip of the iceberg as many risked discovery by playing cards to blunt the effects of boredom. Washington usually agonized over anything that cast a blot on his beloved Virginia, and we can only assume his feelings when he had to sit in judgment on two officers from that state convicted of card playing. Nevertheless, he concurred with the verdict rendered on Lieutenant John Rust, 10th Virginia, dismissed from the service, and Lieutenant Abraham Tipton, 12th Virginia, who resigned but returned to the service later.[35]

Despite Washington's orders and admonitions, considerable conviviality was evident in many officers' huts. Officers representing New Jersey and Pennsylvania, because of their close proximity to home, received visits from friends and relatives who occasionally spent several days in their huts. On the surface this was an apparent lack of vigilance on the part of regimental commanders, as these visitors with their host officers toured the camp inspecting the fortifications and the positioning of troops. Presumably their patriotism had been vouched for, because the freedom of camp made them as great a risk to security as the women who were prohibited in February from entering the lines.

In their writings, Washington and his generals rarely mentioned the amenities or amusements of camp life; rather they adopted a solemn tone decrying the hunger and nakedness of the men. Most of our knowledge of activities at the encampment are found in the letters and journals of lower ranking officers. Subalterns like Ensign George Ewing, 3rd New Jersey, have furnished us with succinct but graphic pictures of camp recreations.

Whether by invitation or happenstance, Ewing's Uncle James arrived to visit him the day he occupied his hut and spent three days. On January 30, Ewing was the guest of Captain Lieutenant Seth Bowen, 3rd Continental Artillery, and Surgeons Mate Ebenezer Elmer, and they were joined by other officers "who staid very latte and spent the evening at cards."[36]

Obtaining a furlough from General William Maxwell, Ewing left Valley Forge on February 5, and did not return until April 1. Four days later he received orders to mount guard at the Provost [Captain Isaac Farwell] where Ewing noted there were thirty prisoners. Washington had expressed concern that the close confinement of prisoners placed their health in jeopardy. Apparently they were permitted to play ball as a form of exercise. In early May, Sergeant Joseph West was court-martialed for being drunk on duty. At his trial it was mentioned that the prisoners were actively engaged in this form of recreation. Returning from his service as guard, Ewing spent the afternoon playing "base," the American equivalent of the English "Rounders," a precursor of baseball. Later that day he recounted a prank committed by "some Rogueish chaps, who tied a sheaf of straw to the tail of Joseph Andersons B [Brigade] Quartermaster commonly called leg and...five Pound...horse tail and set it on fire and left him run very much offended...he set out for the Genl to enter a complaint."[37]

Apparently the officers in the New Jersey regiments were addicted to practical jokes. Ewing relates an incident that occurred after Brigade exercises when several had a merry time holding rump courts that tried "delinquent" fellow officers who were always found guilty and fined a quart of peach brandy.[38]

Ewing's adventure at the theater on April 15 has been described previously, however, five nights later while on picket duty, he witnessed the "most violent Gust of wind which continued to blow very hard all night a fire broke out on the height just to right of the Camp (Mt. Joy or Mt. Misery) and burnd the most furious I ever beheld during the whole night." Regrettably, Ewing does not detail the consternation this blaze must have caused, nor the army's efforts to contain it.[39]

On April 28, Ewing tendered his resignation to Washington, but volunteered to serve with the 3rd Continental Artillery commanded by Captain Thomas Randall. His choice of the artillery was probably because of his comradeship with several artillery officers.

A recreation that was popular among the officers was "wicket" (cricket). Ewing participated in this sport whenever the opportunity was offered. Probably he enjoyed his greatest thrill on May 4, when "This day His Excellency dined with G. Nox [General Henry Knox Commander of the Artillery] and after dinner did us the honor to play at wicket with us."[40]

The army sought any excuse to find a diversion from the boredom of camp routine. On May 1, the army celebrated "May Day," and we are indebted to Ewing for a vivid description of the festivities. He noted that on the previous night "May Poles were Erected in every Regt in the Camp and at Revelle [Reveille] was awoke by three cheers in honor of King Tamany The day was spent in mirth and Jollity the soldiers parading marching with fife and Drum and Huzzaing as they passed the poles their hats adorned with white blossoms [dogwood ?]."

Ewing was still quartered with his old regiment, the 3rd New Jersey. In a graphic account he recapitulated the regiment's procession and activities:

> first one serjeant drest in an Indian habit representing King Tamany Second Thirteen Serjeants drest in white each with a bow in his left hand and Thirteen arrows in his right Thirdly thirteen Drums & fifes Fourthly the privates in thirteen Plattoons thirteen men each— The Non Commissiond Officers and Soldiers being drawn up in the afforesaid manner on the Regimental Parade gave 3 Cheers at their own Pole and then Marchd of [off] to Head Quarters to do Honor to his Excellency but just as they were descending the hill to the house an Aid met them and informed them that the Genl was Indisposd and desird them to retire which they did with the greatest decency and regularity—they then returnd and marchd from right to left of Lord Stirlings Division Huzzaing at every Pole they pasd and then retird to their Regimental parade taking a drink of whiskey which a generous contribution of their officers had procurd for them they dismisd and each man retird to his own hut without any accident hapening throughout the whole day...in the evening the Officers...assembled and had a song and dance in honour of King Tamany about 12 O Clock we dismisd and retired to rest.[41]

Captain (brevet) Peter S. du Ponceau, aide-de-camp to Steuben, recorded several amusing incidents of which three offer a lighter side to life at Valley Forge. When Steuben's aides proposed to have a dinner, to which they intended to invite other officers, the "Baron" gave his blessing provided that "none (including himself) should be admitted that had on a whole pair of breeches." Du Ponceau must have smiled as he recalled the occasion at which: "the guests clubbed their rations, and we feasted sumptuously on tough beef steaks and potatoes with hickory nuts for our dessert. In lieu of wine, we had some kind of spirits with which we made

Salamanders; that is to say, after fillimg our glasses, we set the liquor on fire, and drank it up flames and all. Such a set of ragged and, at the same time, merry fellows were never before brought together." Steuben frequently spoke of this dinner as one he remembered calling the guests his *sans-culottes.*[42]

Du Ponceau narrated another occurrence that caused him considerable embarrassment. In the spring of 1778, Washington ordered a training exercise involving a "sham fight" between two divisions of the army. One of the divisions was commanded by Steuben, whose aide, du Ponceau, was directed to reconnoitre and report the "enemy" position. Riding out about a quarter mile, the young aide espied what he believed was a body of British troops. Momentarily forgetting that the contending sides involved in the drill were both Americans, du Ponceau dashed back to camp shouting that the British were marching on Valley Forge. Steuben instantly placed his division in motion and marched out to confront the redcoats, when "behold! the sight of red petticoats hanging on a fence to dry," turned out to be the enemy. Du Ponceau misidentifying the red petticoats as British soldiers caused "a great deal of merriment" to his confusion and dismay. Fortunately for the young aide, his misadventure was related to Washington who put him at ease when "in my presence, such was the conduct of that excellent man, that I retired comforted." Du Ponceau thus mirrored the high esteem with which most foreign officers held Washington.[43]

Another happening that the aide thought "strongly descriptive of his [Washington's] honest heart" was related to du Ponceau by Captain Benjamin Walker, who later became an aide-de-camp to the Commander in Chief. As recounted by Walker, he had been engaged for some time to a young Quaker lady whom he would eventually marry. However, at this time, Walker only wanted a leave of absence to visit his beloved. When the General said he could not dispense with his services at present, Walker "insisted, begged, entreated, but all in vain." In desperation Walker exclaimed "If I don't go, she will die," Washington replied "Oh! no women do not die for such trifles." Pleadingly, the young officer asked Washington what he should do, then in rebuttal what would the General do. Seeing the young man's anguish, Washington tried to make a lighthearted comment, saying "Why, write to her to add another leaf to the *book of sufferings.*"[44]

Captain Alexander Graydon, while on parole, visited the encampment and commented on "the army being reduced and in a wretched state." Viewing these conditions, he may have been amazed when he searched out Colonel Walter Stewart, 13th Pennsylvania, and was informed the Colonel could be found at a barbecue on the banks of the Schuylkill. Later he would reverse his opinion of the somber gathering at the river, as it became obvious that officers and rank and file seldom had moments of "hilarity." However, he noted that it was "scarcely necessary to say, that the Commander in Chief was not there." Apparently Graydon knew that Washington rarely attended such affairs unless it involved the entire army.[45]

Tradition has embellished some of the more raucous outbursts of the troops. Stories have been passed down of fights, teasing of recruits and, on occasion, a brawl between regiments of different ethnic backgrounds. One historian states that with the advent of spring the soldiers spent their "leisure moments...[in] practice of feats of strength, dexterity, and devilment." An illustration of the latter occurred when fresh levies from Maryland decided to celebrate St. Patrick's Day. A big, brawny noncommissioned officer gathered a number of cohorts from the Pennsylvania line, who decided the upstart Marylanders needed "taking down a peg." To lay the foundation for their prank, they "whittled a figure four and set it under one side of an old spike-toothed harrow, baiting it with a handful of potatoes." According to legend the Maryland soldiers were rapt with curiosity and one, more inquisitive than the others, asked "what is it for." This was exactly the question the Pennsylvanians were waiting to hear, and the response was instantaneous, "A trap to catch the Irish." Naturally the Marylanders, the majority being Irish and Catholic, resented the slur and a free-for-all developed. As the brawl continued, other men from different units joined in the fray. The story continued with Washington on a tour of inspection of the lines, and seeing the disorder quickly quelled the fracas with a daring bit of horsemanship with the assistance of company officers. Tradition, legend or fact, the troops in idle moments or a state of ennui would seek relief in a form of devilment or bellicosity which could trigger a meaningless brawl.[46]

Continental Lottery

On May 1, 1778, the first lottery drawing of the United States was held at Yorktown, [York] Pennsylvania. In a desperate effort to finance the war, the Continental Congress had resolved on November 1, 1776, to defray the expenses of the next military campaign by holding a nation-wide lottery. A spirit of optimism pervaded Congress as it was expected the lottery would yield $1,568,000. Apparently, after a more sobering second thought, they considered that amount unrealistic, as the resolution is crossed out in the Congressional Journals. It was essential that more mature planning would be needed for which a Committee was formed to prepare "The scheme of the Lottery."[47]

Seventeen days later Congress adopted the Committee's "scheme" for a national lottery. The plan as submitted was considered similar to those designed in the "state lotteries in Europe" and several copycat American lotteries. Congress would issue "100,000 tickets each ticket to be divided into four billets, and to be drawn in four classes..." As directed by Congress, each offering of 100,000 billets included over 70,000 blanks. Only the billets of class one would be actively participated in at Valley Forge, although class two went on sale the last month of the encampment.[48]

The four classes were progressive with the billet of the first offered at ten dollars, and each subsequent class increased by the same amount, with the billets in the fourth class offered at forty dollars. By this formula it was expected one million dollars would be raised by class one, with each succeeding class being increased by a similar amount, thereby making a total of an anticipated ten million dollars from the four drawings. By a unique method fifteen per cent was to be withheld from the amount realized from the sales of billets in each class, or a total of one and a half million dollars as the government's share. By some unusual equation they would, also, hold back certain sums from each of the first three classes to be added to the awards of class four, totaling $1,600,000. It was hoped by making this class more attractive, it would enhance continued participation through all classes of the lottery. This singular arrangement in selling, drawing and distributing the awards are detailed in the footnotes.[49]

The lucky recipients of the minimum prizes had an option to roll over their winnings into the next class, if they exercised this option within six weeks after the drawing; Congress designated those who made this choice as "adventurers." A further incentive was offered to those who were fortunate to receive higher awards. They could elect to take a United States Treasury Bank Note, maturing at the end of five years bearing four per cent interest, payable annually; or pick up pre-emptive rights to purchase billets in the succeeding class. Seven managers were named to supervise the lottery, with the privilege of appointing assistants to sell billets. Individuals and state governments, who sold billets were to receive "1/2 per cent" on the total amount of their collection. A self-assured Congress optimistically set the drawing of class one for March 1, 1777 in Philadelphia.[50]

The popularity of the lottery in the military was attributable to the spirit of gaming that existed in camp and the knowledge that if successful it would bring benefits to the army. Sales of billets were considerably less than anticipated in the summer of 1777, because the army was constantly on the move, uncertain of Burgoyne's objective in New York or Howe's in Pennsylvania. As the latter approached Philadelphia, Congress fled to establish a temporary capital at Yorktown (York, Pa). While there they tabled the lottery program; however, they took the time to tentatively schedule a drawing for January 6, 1778. To absolve themselves of any fault, Congress blamed active military campaigning, the invasion of Pennsylvania, and unsettled conditions in that Commonwealth.[51]

As the years progressed many vicissitudes obstructed the management of the lottery, especially in the third and fourth classes, however these are not pertinent to Valley Forge. The operations were further complicated by a number of changes in managers, largely because of more profitable personal ventures. Some were disgruntled with the low rate or remuneration, as they received only a tenth of one percent of the total amount collected by their assistants. In an effort to appease the managers, in November 1778, Congress resolved to allow four dollars a day for their services prior to February 5, 1778, and five dollars after that date through November. Future compensations would be determined after the drawing of class two. From the beginning of the program, the managers were confronted with counterfeiting and forging of lottery billets and by certain states conducting unauthorized private lotteries. Congress warned the "several states" to prohibit all illegal lotteries, but there is no evidence that such reproofs were more than a protest.[52]

No unsold billets (Congressional designation) were placed in the lottery wheel for class one. On December 18, 1778, Congress resolved that "...it will be more agreeable to the adventurers in the lottery..." if the blanks are included in future drawings. It was Congress's judgment that the "adventurers"—winners of the smallest award—would take advantage of the opportunity to purchase the unsold or not drawn billets.[53]

Optimism prevailed in Congress over the prospect of a successful Lottery that would finance a large part of the military requirements. To its dismay the drawing of class one on May 1, 1778, was a bitter disappointment. Out of 100,000 billets offered 20,433 were marked as prize winners, with a ten thousand dollar first award down to 20,000 twenty dollar prizes. Of the latter, 1,983 billets were not sold; in addition there were unknown thousands of unsold blanks. Although Congress's rosy prognostications were shattered, it was hoped subsequent drawings in classes two through four would be more productive.

After the drawing Congress authorized the printing of a pamphlet listing all the prize winning numbers. Possibly through an oversight, the names of winners were omitted. The few known winners or players at Valley Forge had to be gleaned from private correspondence and other documents.[54]

Among the players was a purchaser of nine billets, for ninety dollars, recorded in Colonel Ephraim Blaine's accounts. Blaine purchased them from Mr. Hillegas (Michael Hillegas, Treasurer of the United States). In May, John Chaloner wrote Charles Stewart that Blaine had three prize drawings, one for five hundred dollars and two for twenty. The most interesting "plunger" was Washington. On February 17, 1779, he ordered furnishings and furniture for his Middlebrook, New Jersey headquarters from John Mitchell, Deputy Quartermaster General in Philadelphia. Apparently as an after thought, he inclosed some lottery tickets, asking Mitchell to check if any "have come up Prizes." Four days later Mitchell replied that "...all your Tickets were in the wheel but one is a Blank." These tickets were for class two, drawn on January 1, 1779. It raises the question, had he possessed similar billets for class one? With his aversion to gambling in camp—although in civilian life he enjoyed a sociable game of cards—he probably considered the lottery worthwhile as it would benefit the army. After the war Washington participated in at least one Virginia lottery. With ten other Virginians, he purchased lottery tickets that awarded half acre lots in the town of Richmond.[55]

As befitted the purpose of the lottery, disbursements were made before the drawing of class one. James Mease, Clothier General, received ten thousand dollars and was named a manager of the lottery. Other funds were sent to the Auditor General and the state of Georgia. The latter grant was to pay for the subsistence of Continental and Militia troops, raised in the state, although the purpose was crossed out in the Journals.[56]

Acts of Subversion

During the period of the Valley Forge encampment, the British made several efforts to undermine the morale of the Continental soldiers and Washington. As insidious as their endeavors were, they only served to strengthen the resolve of most Americans, particularly the army. It cannot be ascertained if Sir William Howe or the British government were privy to these schemes, but they must have been aware of them as they appeared in newspapers which coincided with the release of a spurious pamphlet attributed to Washington.

One of their objectives was to lure the Continental soldier to desert by offering generous inducements to enlist in His Majesty's service, and by picturing a Washington whose faith was wavering in the relevancy of the American cause. To the chagrin of the perpetrators their intrigue would boomerang.

A reflection of the scorn with which the soldiers treated the enemy's plans, was graphically depicted by the Pennsylvania German Battalion of Continentals who noted that: "A most scandalous Performance has made its appearance in the Evening Post of the 3rd of this month bearing all the marks of a genuine Act of Congress setting forth that those brave men who have inlisted or have been draughted to serve in the continental Army for any limited time are nevertheless to be detained during the War...[warning that the] Enemies finding themselves unable to reduce us

185

by the force of their Arms and practicing every insidious art to gain time to disunite us." Continuing, the notice asserted that the men were "offered free passage to Great Britain or Ireland and set free, whereas they are really lured on board ship and forced to serve as seamen or in the garrison of some British posts."[57]

Washington's order was more succinct, but carried an appeal to ignore the enemies "...practicing any insidious Art to gain time to disunite us." He entreated the army to remember the dangers they had encountered together and "are not to be conquered by Artificers which are so easily exposed [and should not be] deluded by traiterous promises of the Enemy."[58]

Congress and Washington were nonplused that their British adversaries would resort to such devious acts to win the war. Therefore, they were amazed when the artful designs of certain Britons stooped to counterfeiting Continental money. With a depreciated currency, the American government was sorely pressed to find funds to meet its needs; thus, by flooding the country with fake bills they might bankrupt the economy.

Sir William Howe and British authorities disavowed any knowledge of these intrigues, despite the blatant offering in New York newspapers for "persons going into other Colonies...any number of counterfeit Congress Notes, for the Price of the Paper per Ream." The notice added that the bills were so genuine they could not be differentiated from those issued by Congress. As the counterfeit currency began circulation, Howe, by his silence, gave tacit endorsement to the trickery.

At Valley Forge two persons were intercepted trying to pass the fake bills, but claimed their innocence, stating they were unaware of its spuriousness. Uncertain of the prisoners' guilt, Washington faced a futile effort to have persons in the city come to camp to testify on their behalf. He was confident that Howe would not allow anyone to give evidence about this nefarious practice, as the British commander in chief had declared that such claims of counterfeiting did not have "the lease foundation in truth." Obviously his acceding to such a request for witnesses would fix the responsibility for "issuing counterfeiting Money upon some of his own party." These shadowy practices were never discontinued, but it served to warn Americans to be on the alert to intercept any persons engaged in passing fake bills.[59]

Washington evinced considerable vexation when spurious letters purportedly written by himself were circulated. They were supposedly written to friends expressing his disenchantment with the American cause. On January 2, 1778, Richard Henry Lee sent copies of some of the letters to Washington writing: "The arts of the enemies of America are endless, but all wicked as they are various. Among other tricks they have forged a pamphlet of Letters entitled 'Letters from General Washington to several of his friends in 1776.' The design of the Forger is evident, and no doubt it gained him a good Beef steak from his Masters." Lee believed that the contents of the letters indicated they were written sometime in 1777.

In replying to Lee, Washington stated: "The enemy are governed by no principles that ought to actuate honest men; no wonder then, that forgery should be amongst their other crimes. I have seen a letter published in a handbill at New York, and extracts of it republished in the Philadelphia paper, said to be from me to Mrs. Washington, not one word of which did I ever write; those contained in the pamphlet you speak of, are, I promise equally genuine, and perhaps written by the same author."

The handbill Washington referred to was prepared by New York printer Rivington and issued in advance of the pamphlet mentioned by Lee. It has been claimed that the letters were written by American expatriates in London, who received a few shillings for their work. However, it is believed that Washington thought they were written by a fellow Virginian, "Jack" Randolph. As soon as he possessed a copy of the American reprint of the pamphlet, he forwarded it to the president of Congress with the comment that it was "Among the many villainous acts practiced by the Enemy to create divisions and distrust."[60]

Chapter

XII

Ally and Allegiance

ON FEBRUARY 16, 1778, France recognized the Independence of the United States, followed by a declaration of war against Great Britain. Because of the difficulties of ocean communication in the eighteenth century, news of these developments did not reach America until April 13. Meanwhile, unsubstantiated reports of a possible alliance were circulating in the United States, raising the hopes of Congress and Washington. The latter was anxious for the culmination of an agreement to counter the adverse effect on public attitude created by false reports disseminated by the British offering "specious allurements of Peace." In writing to John Banister, a Virginia Delegate to Congress, on April 21, he detailed the evils of such proposals that would "...be extremely flattering to Minds that do not penetrate far into political consequences...Men are naturally fond of Peace, and there are Symptoms...the people of America are pretty generally weary of the present War." However, he believed before European powers would permit a British victory, they would conclude the negotiations now going on in Paris and enter the war as America's allies.[1]

Congress wasted little time in ratifying the alliance on May 4. Before this date it was unofficially known in political circles and at Valley Forge headquarters. On April 30, an exuberant Washington congratulated Smallwood "on the most interesting and important intelligence just received." Manifestly ecstatic he announced the "Court of France has recognized us free and independent States." His enthusiasm was evident as he noted that Great Britain was in an uproar, and the European continent was aflame. The following day in a letter to the President of Congress, he begged leave to congratulate that body on the "good tidings." Washington acknowledged that he had not mentioned it to any officers he had seen, but would await the pleasure of Congress before announcing it to the army, and then would omit any part of the alliance considered "sanctified by Authority." Of course, this statement was

Oath of Allegiance subscribed to by officers of the army. (John F. Reed Collection, Valley Forge National Historical Park.)

wishful thinking as the supposedly well kept secret was common knowledge in the encampment.[2]

In his after orders of May 5, Washington, with Congressional approval, detailed the program to be staged the next day to honor the French Alliance. It was declared a day of joyous celebration, with the proceedings orchestrated and planned by Steuben, who considered it an opportunity to exhibit "The visible progress which the troops have already made, under his discipline."[3]

Washington outlined the festivities and activities observing that:

It having pleased the Almighty ruler of the Universe propitiously to defend the Cause of the United American-States and finally by raising us up a powerful Friend among the Princes of the Earth to establish out liberty and independence up lasting foundations, it becomes us to set apart a day for gratefully acknowledging the divine Goodness and celebrating the important Event which we owe to his benign Interposition.

The several Brigades are to be assembled for this Purpose at nine o'Clock tomorrow morning when their Chaplains will communicate the Intelligence contain'd in the Postscript to the Pennsylvania Gazette of the 2nd. instant and offer up a thanksgiving and deliver a discourse suitable to the Occasion. At half after ten o'Clock a Cannon will be fired, which is to be a signal for the men to be under Arms. The Brigade Inspectors will then inspect their Dress and Arms, form the Battalions according to instructions given them and announce to the Commanding Officers of Brigades that the Battalions are formed. The Brigadiers or Commandants will then appoint the Field Officers to command the Battalions, after which each Battalion will be ordered to load and ground their Arms.

At half after eleven a second Cannon be fired as a signal for the march upon which the several Brigades will begin their march by wheeling to the right by Platoons and proceed by the nearest way to the left of their ground in the new Position; this will be pointed out by the Brigade Inspectors. A third signal will be given upon which there will be a discharge of thirteen Cannon; When the thirteen has fired a runing fire of the Infantry [feu de joie] will begin on the right of Woodford's and continue throughout the whole front line, it will then be taken on the left of the second line and continue to the right. Upon a signal given, the whole Army will Huzza! "Long Live the King of France." The Artillery then begins again and fires thirteen rounds, this will be succeeded by a second general discharge of the Musquetry in a runing fire. Huzza! "And long live the friendly European Powers." Then the last discharge of thirteen Pieces of Artillery will be given, followed by a General runing fire and Huzza! "To the American States."

There will be no exercise in the morning and the guards of the day will not parade 'till after the feu de joie is finished, when the Brigade Major will march them out to the Grand Parade. The Adjutants then will tell off their Battalions into eight Platoons and the commanding officer will reconduct them to their Camp marching by the Left.

Major General Lord Stirling will command on the right, the Marquis De la fayette on the left and Baron De Kalb the second line. Each Major General will conduct the first Brigade of his Command to its ground, the other Brigades will be conducted by their commanding Officers in separate Columns. The Posts of each Brigade will be pointed out by Baron De Steuben's Aids. Majr. Walker will attend Lord Stirling—Major DeEponsien [Despinieres] the Marquis De la Fayette and Captain Lanfant [L'Enfant] the Baron De Kalb. The line is to be formed with the Interval of a foot between the files.

Each man is to have a Gill of rum. The Quarter Masters of the several Brigades are to apply to the Adjutant General for an order on the Commissary of Military Stores for the number of blank Cartridges that may be wanted.[4]

As in any event of this consequence, several soldiers recounted their observations of the day's activities that varied slightly from Washington's orders, but added a personal touch to the happenings of the occasion.

The most particularized account of the day is that of an unknown soldier, apparently an officer, who presented a joyous, yet somber and reverent portrayal of the occasion. In a flashback he recalled the dangers the army had passed through and its fight to overthrow tyranny. His pride was obvious as he watched the troops assemble, noting the cleanliness of their dress, and "...brilliancy and good order of their arms, and the remarkable animation with which they performed the necessary salute as the general [Washington] passed."

As a participant in this happy, but solemn occasion, he referred to the mystical numbers used by ancient peoples, noting that the Continental Army's number was thirteen. After the feu de joie, he described that: "The officers approached the place of entertainment in different columns, thirteen abreast, and closely linked together in each other's arms." Their line of march signified the thirteen states "...and the interweaving of arms a complete union and most perfect confederation."[5]

Before this the brigades had assembled at eleven thirty o'clock on the parade where they were reviewed by Washington and the other General Officers. After this inspection, a soldier of the New Jersey Brigade, Joseph Bloomfield, recorded that the feu de joie began. One unknown soldier vividly reported the firings were: "conducted with great judgment and regularity. The gradual progression of the sound from the discharge of cannon and musketry, swelling and rebounding from the neighboring hills, and gently sweeping along the Schuylkill, with the intermingled huzzas—to long live the King of France—long live the friendly European powers, and long live the American States, composed a military music more agreeable to a soldier's ear than the most finished pieces of your favorite Handel."[6]

Ewing's account noted that preceding the feu de joie, thirteen six-pounders had been placed on the heights to the rear of Conway's Brigade, and that after the troops were in position on the parade the flag on Fort Huntington was lowered. This was instantly followed by a cannon being fired at the Artillery Park, after which a salvo from the cannon on the height heralded the feu de joie.[7]

Bloomfield's journal provides some timing on the beginning of the days ceremonies, noting that at nine o'clock "Gen. Washington and his amiable lady & suite...with other general officer's & ladys..." assembled at Maxwell's New Jersey Brigade for prayers and a discourse by the Reverend Andrew Hunter.[8]

The unknown soldier furnished the best description of the entertainment and collation that followed the feu de joie:

> The amphitheater looked elegant. The outer seats for the officers were covered with tent canvas stretched out upon poles; and the tables in the centre shaded by elegant markees [marquee], raised high, and arranged in a very striking and agreeable style. An excellent band of music attended...but the feast was still more animating by the discourse and behavior of his excellency to the officers and the gentlemen in the country (many of them our old Philadelphia acquaintances). Mrs. Washington, the Countess of Stirling, Lady Kitty her daughter, Mrs. Greene and a number of other ladies, favored the feast with their company, amongst whom good humor and the graces were contending for pre-eminence. The wine circulated in the most genial manner—to the King of France—the friendly European powers—the American States—the Honorable Congress, and other toasts of a similar nature, descriptive of the spirit of freemen.

He couldn't "forbear mentioning a little anecdote" related at the camp. A known spy had been observed during the day's activities watching the army's maneuvers. When asked what punishment should be meted out to the culprit, an officer suggested he be ignored, let him return to "his employers" as they would experience more pain from his reports, than to hear of his death.[9]

Despite the jollity of the occasion, the army had been placed on alert to repel a surprise attack by the enemy. Between five and six o'clock Washington pardoned himself and returned to headquarters, to the huzzas of the troops chanting "*Long live Genl. Washington!* & clapping of hands until the Genl. rode some distance." A fitting climax to a day of triumph and justifiable pride in the discipline and conduct of the Continental soldier.[10]

On May 7, while the exuberance of the previous day still lingered, Washington directed the army's attention to the Congressional resolution of February 3, requiring all officers, civil and military, to take an Oath of Allegiance to the United States. Six days previously he had agreed to comply with the request of Congress to proceed with the administration of the Oath of Allegiance and Abjuration to all officers in the line and service departments. He acknowledged he should have offered the oath when first resolved by Congress, however "...there were some strong reasons which made it expedient to defer the matter." Those reasons were the appalling conditions in camp, and Congress's dragging its feet on the reorganization of the army as recommended by its Committee at Camp. Congress's plan for the new army would not be submitted to Washington until early June.[11]

In the General Orders of May 7, Washington reprinted a copy of both oaths for the line and service officers.[12] Printed copies of the military oath were distributed to all Major Generals, with lists of the various brigades and units of the army, to which they would be responsible to administer the oath. Certificates in duplicate were to be prepared with one copy for each officer taking the oath, and the other returned to headquarters. Greene was to assure that all officers in the service functions subscribed to their oath of fealty and to guarantee them exclusion from bearing arms.[13]

Simultaneously, Washington, in a grateful mood, announced that "The Commander in Chief in a season of General Joy takes occasion to proclaim Pardon and Releasement to all Prisoners whatever now in Confinement."

Hampered by delays in obtaining forms, celebration of the French Alliance, and rumors of some opposition to the oath, Washington finally selected May 12 as the day to administer the oath to all officers in camp. The General Officers were to take their oath at eleven o'clock at headquarters and then proceed immediately to take the oath of all officers.[14]

Disturbingly, there was substance to the report that resistance had surfaced in subscribing to the oath. It quickly came to Washington's attention that opposition had appeared in General William Woodford's Brigade. Lafayette, responsible for Woodford's Brigade, discreetly presented to Washington the objections of of twenty-six of its officers. Their remonstrance covered four reasons for resisting the oath. They had served faithfully throughout the war and considered it an indignity and unnecessarily demeaning order. A second reason was one that had previously perplexed Washington, as the officers contended they had been "injured in rank" and it would be an impropriety for them to swear to their continuance in their present posts. Thirdly, they were of the opinion that the oath would "debar" them from resigning, even if it were indispensable for personal or family demands. Their fourth objection was another argument Washington had advanced for postponing the date to administer the oath. Concerned that the much heralded reorganization of the army had not been approved by Congress, they contended that by signing the oath they would be inhibited from procuring a change of assignment or rank "...which the whole army have long, not only most ardently wished for, but conceived absolutely necessary for its preservation."

Washington, aware of Lafayette's quandary, attempted to appease the young Frenchman by answering in detail a partial rebuttal to the officers' protest. He said any officer taking the oath should do so as a "free act of the Mind." Washington insisted that none should be compelled to sign, nor would he interpose his opinion on officers of the Virginia Brigades, to influence their decision. Puzzled, he could not see why such extensive peculiarities were confined to the officers of one brigade. Further, the arguments of rank were specious as the oath was neither intended, nor could it prevent resignations. Considering their fourth objection, it merely mirrored Washington's personal frustration at the dillydallying of Congress in approving a reorganization of the army as he deemed this a "Key to their scruples." After reviewing this point, he believed the officers had been misled and that he could "but regret that they were ever engaged in the measure, [adding] I am certain they will regret it themselves."[15]

The issue seems to have been amicably resolved after the initial objections, as very few officers in the army refused to take the oath.

Chapter

XIII

Controversial Cabal

The most disputatious incident of the Revolution was the so-called Conway Cabal.

When Washington assumed the role of Commander in Chief of the ragtag and bobtail force encircling the British Army in Boston, he was apparently unaware that several New England Patriots had vehemently objected to the selection for that post of anyone not from Massachusetts. Despite discord over rank and precedence, most of the generals facing the British were from that colony.

The lack of order and discipline horrified Washington's orderly sense of military decorum. His bitter comments reflected a militia and command staff rife with insubordination. Such censorious remarks were shortly followed by a number of letters indicating frustration over the indifference and lack of support by Congress and the colonies. He interspersed these lamentations with humble expressions deploring his inexperience and lack of ability. As was to be expected, these comments were merely more ammunition for critics, and evoked harsh condemnation of his generalship.

The intervening years before 1778 would dishearten Congress and lower civilian morale. Except for the brilliant victories, engineered by Washington's stratagem, at Trenton and Princeton, on Christmas night 1776, and January 3, 1777, the army had suffered a succession of setbacks. Nevertheless, Washington's faith in the rank and file never wavered. He stated after the Battle of Germantown, on October 4, 1777, the loss was only temporary and had strengthened the resolve of "young and inexperienced soldiers." His observation also reflected that: "The Enemy are nothing better by the event and our Troops, are not in the least dispirited by it, have gained what all young Troopers gain by being in Action." Bristling with confidence, Washington added "they can confuse and rout even the flower of the, British Army, with the greatest of ease." His faith in the men was returned with a dedication that had carried them through two years of adversity. Washington recognized that the one ingredient lacking was discipline which, unknown to him, would be provided by Steuben in a few months.[1]

On October 17, 1777, the surrender at Saratoga of General John Burgoyne's British and Hessian invasion force, catapulted his captor, General Horatio Gates into the middle of the controversy over Washington's generalship. He immediately became the darling of Washington's detractors. Gates contributed to a temporary schism with Washington by dispatching news of Burgoyne's capitulation direct to Congress, instead of the Commander in Chief. Washington would learn of Gates' victory second hand. On October 30, Washington wrote a congratulatory letter to Gates on the "signal success of the Army under your command...." However, obviously aggravated that he had been officially ignored, he closed with a caustic reprimand:

> I cannot but regret, that a matter of such magnitude and so interesting to our General Operations, should have reached me by report only, or thro' the Channel of Letters, not bearing that authenticity, which the importance of it required, and which it would have received a line under your signature, stating the simple fact.

Gates' bypassing the Commander in Chief strained relations between the two generals. It was natural that Gates' humanly deportment would show gratification to those who believed his success qualified him for command of the Continental Army. He would have welcomed the promotion. There is little substantiation that he acted overtly to supplant the popular Washington, however, his subtle conduct leaves a modicum of doubt.[2]

In the meantime, Dr. Benjamin Rush and General Thomas Mifflin, two former admirers of Washington, had entered the fray. Rush wrote at length on what they believed was the horrendous condition of the troops and the Commander in Chief's inability to win on the battlefield. These vituperative comments laid full blame on Washington for ineptness, exacerbating the growing tension over his conduct of the war. Whatever response Washington made to these acrimonious accusations was confined to private correspondence.

Rush was obsessed with a reforming zeal. Formerly associated with the army, he rendered several offensive remarks describing the filth, shortage of nourishing food and lack of clothing or blankets for the sick and wounded troops. The target of his vehemence was Dr. William Shippen, Director General of the Medical Department. Rush accused Shippen of malfeasance, declaring that he was devoid of ability while his carelessness worsened the plight of patients. He was so incensed that he carried his complaints to Congress, demanding an inquiry into Shippen's conduct, confident that an investigation would at least result in censure of the Director General. After hearing the charges, Congress decided they were unsubstantiated and dismissed them. His appeal to Washington also received no encouragement and apparently turned his resentment on the Commander in Chief.

Congress had retained control of the Medical Department, and made several futile attempts to reorganize an efficient hospital and personal care system. Rush was cognizant of this fact, but turned his spleen on Washington, considering him responsible for the makeshift hospital facilities. He demanded the removal of Shippen from his post; however, this was not a function of the Commander in Chief. Washington had repeatedly tried to get better equipped and cleaner hospitals, but a dallying Congress did not take positive action until 1778.

Rush had a tendency to listen "to malicious or perhaps just nagging tongues...[which] became a personal grievance he harbored." He was a dedicated critic of anything he considered unacceptable "to his ethics or patriotic inclinations." Although a devoted American and one of the county's most distinguished doctors, "his knowledge of the battlefield problems were shrouded in an idealist disapproval of the realities of warfare."[3]

Irascible and with uncontrolled intensity, Rush foolishly wrote to Patrick Henry leaving the letter unsigned. The missive denounced Congressional members because only twenty-one were present for their sessions. However, his prime target was Washington: "A Gates, a Lee, or a Conway, would in a few weeks, render them [the army] an irresistible body of men." He added a quote which inferred that "A great and good God hath decreed America to be free—or xxxxx [Washington] and weak counsellors would have ruined her long ago." Unfortunately for Rush, his handwriting was easily identifiable and Henry, considering his responsibility to Washington, forwarded the letter to Valley Forge.[4]

Rush's anger and vexation overcame his good judgment as revealed in a letter to John Adams, noting that "Gates' army was compared to a well-regulated family, Washington's to an unorganized mob"—another instance where he had accepted unverified comments.[5]

The course of events would change viewpoints, and with a lapse of time old friendships would be restored. Rush's biographer notes that during the Constitutional Convention, and when Washington was President, they were on the "most cordial terms." Rush entertained Washington, favored him with gifts and held many discussions of mutual interest.[6] However, there is a question whether this cordially was skin deep intended for a national hero, or sincere. It is claimed that Rush and John Adams years later, in the nineteenth century, tried to discredit Washington, building their personal dislike of him "on rumor, lies and more important a desire to believe them."[7]

197

VALLEY FORGE

A disillusioned Thomas Mifflin's comments were more, if possible, scathing and vindictive than Rush's. Originally, he had a friendly relationship with Washington, serving with Joseph Reed as his first aides-de-camp. Later in 1775, Mifflin's competency so impressed Washington that Congress promoted him to General and named him as the first Quartermaster General. Cognizant of the importance of his new post, he performed satisfactorily, executing "the orders given him by Congress and by Washington" until the closing months of the 1777 campaign and the army's arrival at Valley Forge. Suddenly, on October 8, 1777, he submitted his resignation, pleading ill health. While his health may have been impaired, he was known to be unhappy with the Quartermaster General's function, preferring a command on the line. Washington was aware of the drudgery and thanklessness of the post, but demurred to Mifflin's wish even though the army needed competency in the Quartermaster Department. The lifeblood of the army was dependent on a regular and steady flow of provisions and supplies. Mifflin returned to Reading to recuperate, and there began a vilifying attack on Washington.[8] The loss of his Quartermaster General forced Washington to act temporarily in this capacity, ordering and cajoling the remaining deputies for specific provisions, clothing or other supplies.

Mifflin's virulent outbursts would be repeated, in a less abusive tone, by a number of concerned Americans including James Lovell, Elbridge Gerry, the Adamses, Richard Henry Lee, and a few others. Most of these critics were dedicated citizens who had natural frustrations, as human beings, over the paucity of victories by the main army. Not directed at Washington personally, but rather at his conduct of the war, several carried on official and intimate correspondence with Washington free of rancor.

Unfortunately for Mifflin, most officers in the army believed that he deserted them in the darkest days of the war. They also considered him the leader of a conspiracy to oust Washington as Commander in Chief. Typical of these opinions were the ones expressed by Tench Tilghman and John Laurens. Tilghman in a letter to John Cadwalader made an implied comment "who is at the bottom of this you I dare say will easily guess. But that you may not be in doubt, it is a Gentleman who resigned important offices at a critical time." Laurens, with less subtlety, advised his father, Henry Laurens, that a certain party was formed against the Commander in Chief with Mifflin at its head. He castigated Mifflin, writing that his "preposterous panegyricks of himself, and the influence of this junto, have probably gained the extraordinary promotion, which has convulsed the army." Laurens was referring to the new Board of War appointments with Gates as President and Mifflin a member. Many in the army and among the civilians believed the Board was created to greatly

198

Major General Horatio Gates by Charles Willson Peale. (Independence National Historical Park Collection.)

restrict the authority of Washington.[9]

Washington was sensitive to acrimonious remarks made by a member of the military. He considered them aware of the frustrating experiences they had jointly encountered, as the army was his "family" and fighting for a common cause. Initially, he had been astounded by Mifflin's vitriol. This was probably exacerbated when in May 1778, Congress restored Mifflin to active service in the line and ordered him to report to the Commander in Chief. Acceding to Congress's wishes, Washington assigned Mifflin command of the division, comprising Wayne and the "late" Conway's brigades. On the "Order of March" his name appeared in the marching directions. Apparently Mifflin had second thoughts, because he did not appear at Valley Forge to assume command when the army moved out the following day. Washington quickly assigned the division to General Anthony Wayne.[10]

On the same day, a humane and sensitive Washington gave vent to his exasperation with sunshine soldiers in a letter to Gouverneur Morris:

> I was not a little surprized to find that a certain Gentleman who some time ago (when a cloud of darkness hung heavy over us and our affairs looked gloomy) was desirous of resigning, now stepping forward in the line of the Army. But if *he* can reconcile such conduct to his own feelings as an *Officer* and Man of *honour* and Congress hath no objection to his leaving his Seat in another department [Board of War], I have nothing *personally* to oppose to it, yet I must think, that Gentleman's stepping in, and out, as the Sun happens to beam forth or obscure is not *quite* the thing, nor *quite* just with respect to those Officers who take the bitter with the Sweet.[11]

Soon after Gates' victory at Saratoga, caustic appraisal of Washington's losses reached a high plateau. He was charged with being irresolute, lacking initiative and following the advice of bad "counsellors" which led him into making strategic mistakes. Certain detractors accused Washington of being partial to the precedence and rights of American born officers, favoring their preference to promotion over more experienced foreign officers. For the most part, objections were directed to a few foreign officers considered arrogant and self-seeking. Congressman Elbridge Gerry declared he could not understand the attitude of American officers who resented the promotion of French officers over them.

About this time the ill-starred Conway was cast into the so-called Cabal. His purported indiscreet letter to Gates placed him in the middle of a controversy. Brevet Brigadier General James Wilkinson, Deputy Adjutant General of the Northern Department had been dispatched by Gates to carry the official notification of his triumph to Congress. Wilkinson stopped at Stirling's quarters in Reading and, in a moment of conviviality, disclosed remarks attributed to Conway in a letter to Gates. Conway praised Gates' superior generalship as compared to Washington. On November 9, 1777, when his outburst was revealed to the Commander in Chief, he sent a terse note to Conway mentioning a disparaging remark imputed to him. Conway's letter was supposed to contain the comment "Heaven has been determined to save your Country, or a weak General and bad Councellors would have ruin[e]d it."[12]

In his approach to Conway, Washington has been accused of being oversensitive; however, this assumption ignores the pressure he was under to hold the army together, to select an encampment site for the approaching winter, or to deal with a recalcitrant Congress.

Although Conway had been a Colonel in the French Army, Washington considered him an able field commander, assigning him a brigade at the Battle of the Brandywine. Unfortunately, as a soldier of fortune, Conway acknowledge that his service in the Continental Army was a stepping stone for preferment in rank upon return to his adopted country, France. An ingratiating individual, he haunted the halls of Congress seeking military advancement. Conway appears to have had little interest in America, as he informed Gates it is "Your Country." His self-centeredness, combined with disdain for native born American officers, earned him the enmity of the army.

A week after Washington's short note, Conway replied, saying that because of the threat of war in France, he was prompted to resign his commission in the Continental Army and return to Europe. Without reference to Washington's letter, he thanked the Commander in Chief for "civilities...while I had the honor of being under you orders..." He begged Washington to accept his warm and sincere wishes for "liberty to America."[13]

However, Conway's resignation would not be accepted by Congress. His concern for the future of France was soon forgotten as Congress named him a Major General and Inspector General of the army. We have seen the furor his appointment created and his cool reception at Valley Forge, not about the post of Inspector General, but rather his elevation to Major General over many American Brigadiers considered by Washington worthy of promotion. It is claimed by some that Congress's resolution in this instance was evidence of an unfriendly gesture to Washington.

Certain malcontents, especially New England Congressmen, saw Gates' victory as an opportunity to display their displeasure with Washington—even though the triumph at Saratoga largely belonged to Benedict Arnold and Daniel Morgan. On December 21, William Ellery wrote to William Whipple, "I wish there was the same spirit in the main army as displayed to the Northward." A cautious Elbridge Gerry responded to General Knox's enquiry on the attitude of members of Congress: "the Alarms that have been spread & Jealousies that are excited relative to this matter, appear to be calculated rather to answer mischievous rather than useful purposes." He assured Knox that he had not detected any "Suspicion of a plan being formed to injure ye [Washington's] reputation."[14]

Any coterie that may have been created by this controversy was misnamed, small and disorganized. Washington's resentment may have unwittingly stirred like sentiments in most officers to Gates and Conway, as they rushed to his defense. A few examples will suffice to demonstrate their fervency. Major John Taylor of Hazen's 2nd Canadian Regiment, witnessed a "*great* vortex of intrigue" in the force collecting at Peekskill for the invasion of Canada. On April 12, 1778, he wrote to General William Woodford that there had been "a great aversion to Serving under him [Conway]." In January 1778, Tench Tilghman, aide-de-camp to Washington, declared "That many of the best officers have taken the alarm and are ready to speak in very plain terms."[15]

In the private sector, Washington received as much or more support than in the military. John Fitzgerald, a former aide-de-camp to Washington, wrote that only one member of the Virginia Legislature supported the condemnation of him and he "was so warmly replied to from different quarters that he has been Silent." On December 30, 1777, Francis Hopkinson (accredited by some scholars as designer of the American flag) and John Wharton sent Washington a few fish for "a reasonable Refreshment," adding their sentiments for "all Manner of Felicity & Success equal to the virtuous wishes of your Heart." Later in the spring of 1778, Henry Laurens, President of the Continental Congress, added a postscript to the nearly forgotten cabal that Conway had sarcastically compared Washington with Frederic the Great, but he believed "Washington in War shall be the equal to Frederic—in many respects he is far superior."[16]

This potpourri of opinions and beliefs were representative of those who approved and opposed Washington as Commander in Chief. However, the army and most members of Congress manifested solid support for him. Conway's reputed remark would probably have ended without comment, if Washington had ignored it. Nevertheless, he cannot be faulted for exhibiting a human frailty, rather it shattered all accusations of his being snobbish and aloof.

Exasperated with Gates for sending a copy of his note to Congress, on January 2, 1778, Washington forwarded all his correspondence with Conway to that body. He readily acknowledged that he "did not receive Conway in the language of a warm and cordial Friend." However, he continued, "my feelings will not permit me to make professions of

friendship to the man I deem my Enemy, and whose conduct forbids it."
A sentiment Washington confessed he "hoped never to repeat...till I am
capable of the arts of dissimulation." Apparently, Washington was still
disturbed by the insidious comment attributed to Conway and the
arrogance he displayed at Valley Forge.[17]

Gates had adopted a questionable stance by sending a copy of
Washington's letter to Congress. On December 8, 1777, Gates implored
Washington to assist in locating "the authority of the infidelity, which put
extracts from General Conway's letters to me in your hands." Rather
desperately he inferred the miscreant could have been a member of
Washington's staff. Gates believed the detection of this "wretch who may
betray me," was imperative as "it could injure the very operations under
your immediate direction." Then in direct contradiction, he said it might
have come "from a member of Congress."[18]

Confronted with pressure to plan and establish the winter encampment, Washington did not reply to Gates until early January 1778. On the
4th, he expressed indignation that Gates' action had forced him, in
self-defense, to send copies of all correspondence with Conway to
Congress. He described in detail how Conway's remark had come to his
attention. Angry and chagrined, Washington resented the implication
that Congress might believe he had used indirect means to learn the
contents of confidential correspondence between Gates and Conway.
Further, he disclaimed any knowledge of a regular correspondence
between the generals. Washington assured Gates that he had behaved
"with an openness and candor, which I hope will ever characterize and
mark my conduct."[19]

Gates' response on January 23, indicated that the frankness of
Washington's letter had "relieved him from unspeakable uneasiness." He
found it difficult to understand to whom or for what reasons Conway
would defame the Commander in Chief. In defense of Conway, he went
into a long explanation of what might have caused such a remark. But,
he quickly countered with the statement it was "spurious," and not
contained in any letter he had received from Conway.[20]

This reply apparently did not appease Washington's wrath. On
February 9, he berated Gates for the obvious contradiction in his letters,
stating he could not reconcile "the spirit and import of your different
Letters." How could Gates declare Conway's remark "a wicked forgery"
and yet assert that it had not appeared in any letter received by him. As
a rebuttal to Gates' defense of Conway's "constant friendship to
America," Washington wrote a lengthy account of the general's haughty,
self-indulgent attitude in the presence of American officers, adding this
was not a sign of loyalty to a common cause.[21]

Ten days later, acknowledging Washington's letter, Gates suggested no more time be wasted on whether Conway was guilty of the remark or not, adding "He (Conway) must be responsible [to Congress]; as I heartily dislike controversy..." He declared he had a violent dislike for misunderstandings "solemnly" noting that his letters "aggregately" nor in any "paragraph" were intended to be offensive to "your Excellency."[22]

Before receipt of Gates' letter, an incident occurred which worsened the dispute between Washington and Gates. Major General Friederich Adolph von Riedesel, commander of the Hessian contingent at Saratoga, asked why Gates had acceded to General Burgoyne's request to have certain British officers "exchanged for Officers of the Continental Army." He was concerned because his request for an exchange of "Officers of his Suite" had been ignored. Washington asked Gates to explain whether such a distinction had been made, thereby permitting him to know how to answer Riedesel.[23]

Washington answered Gates' letter of February 19, in a conciliatory mood, stating he was also "as adverse to controversy as any Man, and had I not been forced into it, you never would have had occasion to impute to me, even the shadow of a disposition towards it." Washington further stressed his complete agreement to "burying them [their differences] hereafter in silence, and as far as future events will permit, oblivious. My temper leads me to peace and harmony with all Men." With this letter the so-called Cabal disappears from Washington's public correspondence. However, as will be seen, regrettably some officers loyal to him would harbor for some time a resentment to Gates.[24]

As previously noted, Gates became President of the Board of War in November 1777. In April 1778, Congress named him to command the Northern Department (Hudson River sector) subject to the direction of Washington. On April 24, the Commander in Chief acknowledged Gates' appointment, and requested he report to headquarters at Valley Forge to discuss "and form some general System" for the army.

In late May, an illustration of Washington's constraint occurred when Gates withheld "728 stand of Arms" badly needed at Valley Forge. This misunderstanding was amicably resolved, as Washington's reaction was moderate and represented a normal military directive. Tench Tilghman had been instructed to write the letter to Gates, but the aide still "burning with rage at Gates' impertinence" for ignoring Washington's original request for the arms, prepared "a stinging rebuke and peremptory order to Gates." Washington, exhibiting his qualities as a gentleman and fellow officer, crossed out all the acrimonious sections of Tilghman's draft "and shifted the rebuke from a personal plane...to the more acceptable line of official duty."[25]

Although the so-called Conway Cabal was not put to rest until late March 1778, Lafayette's observation at the end of 1777, probably pinpointed the heart of any controversy. He wrote Washington that: "There are open discussions in Congress; parties who hate one another as much as the common enemy; men who, without knowing any thing about war, undertake to judge you, and to make ridiculous comparisons [with Gates]." Such judgmental opinions are characteristics of all wars.

With the advent of spring, Conway still remained a controversial figure, until he finally decided the Continental Army offered little opportunity to gratify his personal ambition. His leaving the country was interrupted on July 4, 1778, by a duel with General John Cadwalader. Severely wounded in the mouth, he despaired for his life. Although the wound was not fatal, in a fit of remorse on July 23, Conway penned a short letter to Washington, that he was taking:

> ...this opportunity of expressing my sincere grief for having done, written, or said anything disagreeable to your Excellency. My career will soon be over; therefore justice and truth prompt me to declare my last sentiments. You are in my eyes the great and good man. May you long enjoy the love, veneration, and esteem of these States, whose liberties you have asserted by your virtues.

Was this note a confession of an indiscretion; or a sincere deathbed expression of an individual who had at last recognized a man worthy of his admiration? Conway would recover and subsequently return to France.[26]

205

Chapter

XIV

Moving Out

THROUGHOUT THE PERIOD of the encampment, Washington was compelled to apportion his time among a fruitless search to provide sustenance and comfort for his troops, molding the army into a disciplined fighting force and, lastly, planning an offensive campaign for the summer. Concern for the welfare of the soldiers was always foremost in his plans. After the appointments of Nathanael Greene as Quartermaster General and Jeremiah Wadsworth as Commissary General, some improvement was seen in the supply of necessities. Washington then turned his attention to the vital need of reorganizing the army and the assignment of Steuben as Inspector General to train and discipline the troops. He was constantly conscious of the urgency of having the army ready to move out when the weather moderated and Howe revealed his intentions. Unable to comprehend Howe's inertia, Washington still anticipated that the British Commander in Chief would make a last attempt to crush the Continental Army before it could break camp at Valley Forge.

Shortly after assuming his new post in March, Greene proposed the establishment of magazines at strategic locations to support the army on the march, but at safe distances from British raiding parties. His recommendations were detailed and somewhat aggressively optimistic considering the current scarcity of necessities in camp. Greene suggested that magazines be placed at least forty miles from Valley Forge along the banks of the Delaware and Schuylkill Rivers and near Head of Elk in Maryland. Each of these depots were to stockpile 200,000 bushels of grain, with smaller storage areas to accommodate 100,000 bushels of hay at various locations between Reading and Wright's Ferry on the Susquehanna River. As a final suggestion, Greene advocated depots at Trenton, Allentown and one in southern New Jersey, each to be stocked with 40,000 bushels of hay and grain, twisted into bundles.

On March 31, after giving careful consideration to Greene's proposal, Washington approved the plan in principle, but judged it premature. The country was not in a position, at this time, to endorse such a far-reaching project. When the moment was appropriate, Washington said the magazines should be "tolerably high up, for security," adding he did not believe that Trenton should be considered as it was easily accessible to the British. Unwilling to be entirely negative, Washington softened his criticism by intimating that small magazines were preferable to large ones, and easier to protect. In addition, any proposal should include the means to supply the army in the field for four to six months. Because of Washington's objections and suggested modifications, the project was abandoned. The idea was not forgotten as elements of it were brought back later with the placement of storage depots along the planned route the army would take out of Valley Forge.[1]

Under Steuben's training the army was ready to take the field, but a review of the regimental musters revealed many were under-strength. Washington was constantly frustrated by the lackadaisical attitude of some states in filling existing vacancies in their regiments. He particularly resented the lukewarm compliance by Connecticut authorities, whose regiments were below their authorized strength, and their pretense of complying by sending in recruits that were "incapable of performing the duty of soldiers in any respect," adding this "is intolerable." To strengthen the army, Congress authorized Washington to call up 5,000 militia from the states of Maryland, Pennsylvania and New Jersey. Washington revealed his reluctance to use militia in field operations, by advising President Thomas Wharton, Jr. of Pennsylvania and Governor Thomas Johnson of Maryland, that the militia "shouldn't be called into service a moment sooner than [when] their presence in the field is essentially requisite." He followed with a conciliatory statement that "I am fully sensible of the disadvantages that accrue from drawing farmers and tradesmen from their respective employment, especially at this season."[2]

To add to his woes, over 2,000 soldiers remained in military and flying hospitals. Determined to know how many of the sick were capable of joining their units, he ordered doctors and certain officers to check all patients in the hospitals to ascertain their fitness. Later Washington would outline a procedure to be followed for all those who needed additional medical care and could not accompany the army.

In mid-April, foreseeing the urgency that the army be prepared for a quick move, the Board of War ordered Wadsworth to employ twenty coopers to make casks. Supplies of fresh meat and provisions were almost nonexistent. Therefore, a large number of casks were required to hold salted fish, pork and other provisions. These instructions were closely followed by an order of Clement Biddle to Moore Furman, Deputy Quartermaster General in New Jersey, to prepare depots to house 40,000 bushels of grain, oats, corn, rye, spelt, barley and buckwheat. Furman was also to gather as much straw as possible to substitute for hay. Biddle was well aware that this request was optimistic, but some reports had been received indicating that limited supplies could be obtained in northern New Jersey. Washington, uncertain of Howe's destination, directed Biddle to set up magazines between the Delaware River and the North River. As the army might be forced to move without proper logistical support, he ordered Biddle to have Furman locate the suggested depots along what would probably become the line of march, through Sussex Courthouse, Hacketstown, Pompton and Morristown, with a magazine at the Clove near the Hudson River. Washington would later modify this route because of the scarcity of good roads, as most were in such horrendous condition it would be difficult to move an army. He expanded his request to also set up smaller magazines at Trenton, Princeton and Allen Town (New Jersey). In summarizing the requirements of the army, Biddle exuded confidence that the needed items could be purchased or obtained on promises to pay.[3]

Another Deputy Quartermaster, General James Caldwell, functioning in the same region as Furman had encountered difficulties in gathering cattle. A dangerous shortage of hay had prevented fattening the cattle, and the unreliability of payment by Congress had convinced farmers to sell to a second party who could, if desired, negotiate with the army. Caldwell's search had located some quantities of hay near Bound Brook and Chatham, and he suggested depots be established at those locations. To compound his problems, he had met with insurmountable hurdles in the Quartermaster Department at Morristown, stating it "is in great confusion, & occasions both trouble & expense to me." Up to March 15, he had accumulated debts of $30,000 and more were being presented daily.[4]

By May 17, Washington's suspicions had been confirmed, as it became obvious the British planned to evacuate the city. Intelligence had verified previous rumors that all of their heavy cannon and equipment was being loaded on shipboard. Reliable information had corroborated the report that the enemy did not have sufficient shipping to accommodate the army, thousands of Loyalists with their possessions, and an arsenal of heavy weapons.

In the meantime, Wadsworth had returned to his native Connecticut to protest a regulatory act passed by the state legislature to control prices. It confounded Wadsworth to know that farmers could feed cattle at the established price, but in a rebellious mood were fattening horses to be sold. They had been urged to consider waiting for their herds to be grass fattened in late spring. An angry Wadsworth remonstrated saying the cattle were needed now, not in mid-summer. A disenchanted Commissary General knew the army could not move without logistical support.

Wadsworth was disappointed by the handicap the act had placed on the performance of his duties, advising Washington he would not have accepted the appointment as Commissary General under these restrictions. To further chafe him, Samuel Huntington claimed the employees of Wadsworth's Department were careless in purchasing provisions, and should be directed to exert greater care, as they were contributing to inflation and the instability of the Continental Currency. Wadsworth engaged in a voluminous correspondence with his chief aides to spur the efforts of their purchasing assistants. These agents were to use every method in their repertoire to entreat, emphasize patriotic duty, cajole, or, if necessary, threaten confiscation.[5]

Deputy Commissary General Colonel Ephraim Blaine had the responsibility to staff the area from Maryland to New York with purchasing assistants, paying them the acceptable rate of two per cent of disbursements. In his first effort, Blaine fortunately uncovered a large cache of salt, which would facilitate the preserving of many kinds of food. At this time in the Revolution, salted provisions were considered beneficial to the men's health in hot weather, whereas fresh meat was deemed injurious. Pleased at his good fortune, Blaine was, nevertheless, exasperated at the lack of cooperation or sympathy he encountered from farmers and authorities. He wrote Wadsworth that he had been kept "from hand to Mouth, respecting Beef Cattle," imploring the Commissary General to exhaust every area of supply to obtain fresh meat for current use in the army. He painted a dark picture of the middle states plundered of all cattle, and the only savior for the encampment was the New England states.[6]

On May 17, a vexatious John Chaloner, Deputy Commissary of Purchases, penned two letters to Wadsworth begging for succor, as he had conducted a fruitless search for fresh meat and that Washington had issued an order impossible to fulfill under present conditions. He had been directed by Washington to select suitable roads across New Jersey, with a further suggestion that he establish magazines along the route at Coryell's Ferry, Morristown, Bound Brook and Westfield, with sufficient quantities of food to sustain the army. To compound his logistical problems, he had located a supply of provisions at Head of Elk, but there were no wagons available to transport them to the magazine.[7]

As the days passed an harassed Chaloner, in desperation, wrote to Charles Stewart that he had just issued the last pound of meat and fish in camp, but luckily ninety head of cattle had just arrived. Although this small herd was a welcome expedient, it would be consumed within a day. Chaloner expressed his despondency with the indifference or inability he met with, in undertaking the buying of provisions for the army. Reflecting his indignation, he demanded that Champion guarantee

30,000 rations a day which he was to stock along the line of march. As Chaloner's frustrations piled up, his bitterness became more evident as he issued biting commands. On May 29, he advised John Huggins and John Howell that "so great is our Distress," he must insist that three brigades of teams loaded with salt provisions be sent from Maryland and stored at convenient locations for the army. On the same day, Thomas Jones informed Stewart that there were only three head of cattle in camp. He bemoaned that his latest order neglected to consider his difficulties, as he was instructed to provide the troops with biscuits and salted provisions for three days, none of which he had.[8]

Chaloner's gloom began to spread over all those engaged in purchasing foodstuff for the soldiers. On June 1, he wrote to Wadsworth that the army had not been able to move, as it had been without beef for three days. Apparently scraping the bottom of his resolve, he lamented the futility involved in trying to provide for the troops, considered his "assignment greatly prejudicial to my Interests," and wanted to resign. Others besides Chaloner were having misgivings. Moore Furman was ordered to direct every effort to collect sufficient straw for bedding on the march. He was to gather 1,000 sheaves (wheat sheaf size) for each brigade. No one was more conscious of the negative receptions encountered by members of the Commissary Department than Washington; but the welfare of his soldiers made it mandatory that he exert constant pressure on them to gather life-sustaining supplies for the army.[9]

Before the army could move out of Valley Forge, it was necessary to determine the capabilities of the support group. As mentioned, during the Revolution the combat readiness of an army depended on the efficiency of its logistical operations.

To sustain the army it was necessary to have available transportation, artisans to maintain equipment after breakdowns on bad roads and an adequate arsenal of arms. Washington and Greene, frantic to develop a chain of magazines or depots, had met with indifference, inattention and malfeasance. Discipline, training and efficient service units were needed, but in the case of the latter, seldom attained.

As the army prepared to take the field, Washington, probably out of despair, offered another possible panacea for the support system. He suggested the Board of War adopt water transport as speedier and less likely exposed to attack. The use of small boats of shallow draft would be faster and a safer way to move provisions. As a backup, he advocated the creation of supply stages at intervals of forty or fifty miles throughout the Eastern States, that could guarantee a steady supply of provisions. Expressing confidence, Washington wrote that a system of stages would be acceptable to reluctant farmers and safer from attack, although "sometimes thro' whim and sometimes thro' accident" they might be the object of British raiding parties.[10]

The army was composed of many unheralded heroes such as armorers, pioneers, artificers and those who could repair wagons, shoe horses, assist in the preparation of camp sites, and perform any service functions vital to the army. In May, concern was evident at headquarters that the Quartermaster Stores might not have sufficient tools and equipment for the artisans when the army departed from the encampment. An inventory was ordered to ascertain the type and quantities of articles available and usable. The tally disclosed a widely diversified stock off 111 items, consisting of thousands of spades and shovels, also bits and pieces of clothing including three petticoats. Also in stock were many miscellaneous articles such as tents, writing paper, knapsacks and water buckets. The findings of the inventory were apparently satisfactory for no criticisms of the Stores' supply is on record.[11]

On May 23, Washington issued preliminary plans for the command arrangement in the field. Major General Charles Lee, lately an exchanged prisoner of war, was to take charge of Greene's Division "and in Case of Action or any general Move of the Army" would become second in command of the army. The three senior Major Generals present were to direct the two wings and the second line in accordance with their seniority of service. All Regimental and Corps commanders were to immediately make certain that their men were fully equipped with "Arms and Accoutrements." Each soldier was to be supplied with forty rounds of ammunition and two flints. These instructions would be supplanted by a more detailed order of march at a later date.[12]

As the army was being readied to move, an irritating condition surfaced that had plagued it throughout the encampment. The morale of the camp was being prejudiced by an increase of unlicensed tippling houses in the vicinity. Each Brigadier was ordered to send a squad of two non-commissioned officers and eight privates to seize all liquors being dispensed near its position, and to give a receipt for those items confiscated. However, the soldiers were to warn the owners that if they returned their stock would face "unconditional seizure."[13]

Washington's anger mounted when he was informed that the sick included an excessive number of malingerers. Many officers and men had purposefully faked illness. Obviously, as this practice had to be stopped, he ordered a check of all patients to determine who would remain at Valley Forge for additional medical care. Although Washington contemplated methods to reduce the number of sick, he was fearful that the tally would reveal more than 2,000 sick in the various hospitals.[14]

Uncleanliness and sanitation problems had again cast a shadow over the camp. These conditions had made most huts unbearable and unhealthy while filth and stench overspread large areas of the encampment. To

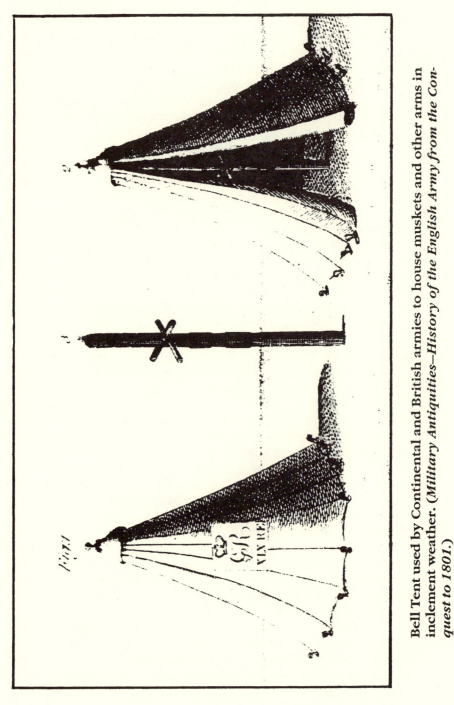

Bell Tent used by Continental and British armies to house muskets and other arms in inclement weather. (*Military Antiquities—History of the English Army from the Conquest to 1801.*)

Washington's disappointment and surprise reports reaching head-quarters divulged that entire regiments were suffering from camp fever. Prompted by this discouraging information, he took immediate measure to relieve the situation before it became epidemic.

Washington believed by improvisation a temporary adjustment could be found to make the huts habitable until the troops moved out of camp. He ordered that at least two windows be installed in each hut and to remove the "mud plastering" between the logs and afford a free circulation of fresh and healthful air. Several days later, on May 27, he stated it was essential that "every other method [be] taken to render them [huts] as airy as possible." He considered one technique beneficial that would have the "Powder of a Musquet Cartridge burnt in each hut daily to purify the air or a little tar if it can be procured." The Commissary of Military Stores was to provide blank cartridges for this purpose. Unfortunately these expedients would be too late for some regiments like the Second North Carolina, Second Rhode Island and Fourth New York, whose incidence of sickness was so high they were moved into tents immediately.[15]

As a more permanent remedy, the entire army would be unable to occupy tents until a few days before the evacuation of Valley Forge. A shortage of tents had persisted since the few remaining were stored in January. This paucity of tents had been addressed in March, but it had been disclosed that the duck cloth obtained to make these shelters, had been used instead to produce bell tents. On June 13, by Washington's order, the bell tents were finally utilized, as the Regimental Commanders were directed to see "...that the Arms be properly disposed in the Bell–Tents. The Musquets by being leaned against the Canvas covering instead of the Rack wear it out and are exposed to the Rain."[16]

On May 16, Washington believing that the fitness of the men would not improve as long as they were subject to the enervating effect of weather and close confinement in the huts and tents, ordered the army under arms at five o'clock each morning for exercise. With such a program he was confident the troops would be healthier and alert for a "sudden and rapid movement."[17]

A gratifying report informed headquarters that the number of sick who could not accompany the army was less than feared, with only about 1,000 needing further medical attention in the encampment hospitals and huts. With this knowledge, Washington made instant preparations to provide for the welfare and care of those to be left behind. Colonel Philip Van Cortlandt, of the Second New York Regiment was ordered "to tarry in Camp to superintend the sick on the Ground when the army moves...." As the recuperating soldiers became fit for duty, they were to be returned to the army under proper escort. Major James Grier, of the

Tenth Pennsylvania Regiment, was to assume direct administrative responsibility for the military hospitals at Yellow Springs and others near the campsite. Dr. Bodo Otto was ordered to remain at Yellow Springs as Medical Director of the flying and military hospitals.[18]

As the army pulled out of the Valley Forge area on June 18, they left a larger number of sick and wounded comrades than Washington desired. Although uncertain, Dr. Bodo Otto had assumed that between 1,500 and 1,700 patients would be confined to the various medical facilities at and near the encampment. On August 10, Dr. William Shippen, Director of the Medical Department, reported the sick, discharged and those who had died while under Otto's care totaled 1,294 (725 sick, 445 discharged, and 124 dead). These numbers are probably conservative, when related to those discharged or deceased between June 18 and the date covered in Shippen's report, thereby making Otto's estimate reasonably accurate. The First New Hampshire Regiment commanded by Colonel Joseph Cilley, maintained an orderly book that recorded the weekly status of soldiers fit for duty and those sick or on command. Consistently during the period of the encampment, there were more men unavailable for active duty than those fit for service. As the regiment marched out of the camp, they left at least seventy-eight comrades with an unspecified guard and eight nurses. Two months later this number had been reduced to forty-eight. A precise tally could not be made when the army evacuated the area because the many sick and wounded, who could not be moved, were widely scattered in the flying hospitals, improvised facilities in neighborhood barns and churches, and in some huts under the care of regimental surgeons. In fact, on May 29, Washington believed "upwards of 3,000 sick which we have not the conveniency to remove...." Against his inclination or desire, Washington had to permit many sick to remain confined in these makeshift accommodations, as all available horses and wagons were needed to support the army. These patients would ultimately be transferred to Yellow Springs and other better equipped and staffed hospitals.[19]

Washington's unhappiness was punctuated by a feeling of helplessness because he could only partially provide quarters for those sick and wounded who had to remain at the encampment. It was obvious the army could not be encumbered with those unfit for active duty. To assure that the army on the move was not hampered by the unfit, General Charles Lee, in command of the van, was directed to leave any sick or lame soldiers incapable of marching, at the nearest housing with a proper officer. They were to return to the army only if capable of enduring the hardships of the campaign.[20]

Washington had no alternative but to make the best provision, in the power of his resources, for those left behind. To guarantee that the sick received the best possible attention the army could offer, he directed each Brigadier to appoint a sufficient number of qualified officers to remain with the brigade sick. Volunteers were solicited among the walking wounded and camp followers to act as nurses. Many ladies of the neighborhood assisted the women nurses. The Brigade surgeons were to be temporarily supervised by Dr. Hutchinson,[21] until Surgeons from the Yellow Springs hospital reported to assume responsibility for the regimental sick. All small pox victims, or those under inoculations, were to be left with the sick. Disturbed by a shortage of medicines, Washington made it mandatory that all brigade medicine chests be taken with the army. From the meager supply of camp kettles, a quantity were sent to the hospitals. One condition that continued to be disquieting was a difference between the hospital reports and the regimental musters with names of those confined as sick. Repeated orders failed to correct these discrepancies.[22]

Regardless of his concern for the sick, Washington had to turn his attention to planning the order of march and the army's objective predicated on British movements. However, these intentions would be interrupted once again, when the incidence of sickness increased despite the measures taken to move part of the troops into tents, and some who had remained in the more habitable huts. On June 8, he ordered Greene and Duportail to "reconnoitre a new camp." Their principal goal was to find a "wholesome situation convenient for the accommodation of the men, well provided with wood and water, and at such a distance from this [Valley Forge] position..." that it could not be overrun by a sudden move by the enemy. The urgency of the move was manifest in Washington's command to bring their recommendations to headquarters that evening.[23]

The consequence of Greene and Duportail's reconnaissance was an order on June 9 that "The Army is to take a new Camp tomorrow at 8 oClock, The whole is to be in readiness, accordingly and march to the respective Ground of Encampment which will be pointed out for each division by the Quarter Mastr. Genl." Several officers and soldiers recorded the move, Lieutenant Colonel Henry Dearborn of the Third New Hampshire Regiment noted that "...the whole army mov'd out of the huts into tents to Day, about one Mile in front of our old incampment for the sake of fresh Air." Joseph Greenman agreeing with Dearborn recorded that we "...struck our tents. marcht about a mild [mile] over Schoolkills River & Piched [pitched] our tents in a field in providence town Ship." Joseph Plumb Martin, recalling the move a half-century after the war, said "...we left our winter cantonments, crossed the Schuylkill and encamped on the left bank of that river, just opposite our winter quarters." Another soldier, Joseph Clark, commented on the debilitating fever prevailing in the huts that had "in many instances proved mortal." He asserted the new camp ground was in a clear field with good air, water and shelter.[24]

The site of the temporary camp was about one mile beyond the north bank of the Schuylkill. It was a more healthy location than the old encampment at Valley Forge and afforded the army greater maneuverability when the British revealed their plans to pull out of Philadelphia.[25]

Whether Washington moved headquarters to the new location is inconclusive, inasmuch as all correspondence from June 10 to 18 was merely issued from "Head Quarters," except for a letter to his brother on June 10, from "Camp, near Valley Forge." He noted among other conditions at Valley Forge, there had been extreme fatigue and hardships during the winter resulting in many deaths, "and yet the Army is in exceedingly good spirits."[26]

On June 13, in a final gesture to the welfare of the sick remaining at camp, Washington ordered a fatigue party from each brigade be assigned for the "Purpose of cleaning the old Encampment, filling up the Pitts [vaults] and burying all kinds of Garbage and Carrion that may remain."[27]

Earlier Brigadier General William Maxwell, with the two remaining regiments of his brigade, had been ordered to New Jersey to join the other two regiments of his command under Colonel Israel Shreve. General Philemon Dickinson of the State militia was requested to support any movement by Maxwell. The principal purpose of Maxwell's brigade was to act as an observation force to garner "exact intelligence of what is passing in Philadelphia...[and] the earliest advice of any movement that may happen."[28]

Maxwell quickly met with some perplexing situations. As soon as his brigade set foot on the New Jersey side of the Delaware, it encountered a sweltering heat wave. The debilitating effects of the weather resulted in the collapse of many soldiers, thereby limiting the effectiveness of Maxwell's force. He quickly sent an urgent request to Washington for shirts of a light texture, to replace their heavy coats. To his chagrin, the Commander in Chief discovered that there was not one shirt at Valley Forge. He suggested Maxwell apply to Mease at Lancaster, another instance where relief would be too little and too late. Also, Maxwell's brigade was imperatively in need or arms and had moved to Trenton where a cache was supposed to be awaiting its arrival. To his dismay they were missing, and he inquired of Washington as to their whereabouts. The Commander in Chief discovered that Gates had preemptively ordered them back to New Windsor, New York. Washington indignantly "ordered them down [to Trenton] in the most express manner." Gates vigorously protested the arms were transferred without either his approval or knowledge. He accused Major Andrew Taylor, Deputy Quarter-master General, of unilaterally ordering their return to New York. Taylor's orders in "a P.S." had stated "It is Major Genl. Gates's positive orders." Washington wrote Gates that if Taylor used his name, he was to blame for this miscarriage of orders, but for "the good of the Service, and my duty" with the information at hand, he was "indispensably required to have the arms returned to Maxwell." Maxwell's problems continued to multiply when he disobeyed orders and planned to establish his post at Bordentown, rather than at Mt. Holly. Incensed, Washington explained, what should have been evident to Maxwell, that any of the towns along the Delaware, "flanked by deep creeks" could become a veritable cul-de-sac, and ordered him to set up his positions at a more secure location.[29]

During the last week of May, Washington was confident Clinton, Howe's successor, would march overland through New Jersey, but with the arrival of a Peace Commission from Great Britain, all plans to abandon Philadelphia had been shelved. They had requested Clinton to make no move that might show a sign of weakness, until they had presented their proposals to the Continental Congress. King George the Third, had named a Commission that consisted of William Eden, George Johnstone, Frederick Howard, the Earl of Carlisle and the Howe brothers, Sir William and Admiral Lord Richard. They were empowered to make concessions to the Americans short of Independence. To some members of the Commission it was a foregone conclusion that without recognition of America's freedom, any proposals would be rejected. Their omniscience would reflect more foresight, than their ability as negotiators.[30]

To Washington's dismay, the confusion and apparent indecision by the British would complicate his plans for the ensuing campaign. Nevertheless, he issued preliminary instructions to prepare the army for the eventual move out of Valley Forge. Orders were circulated to all detachments serving as outposts and to Smallwood at Wilmington to ready their commands, and when certain the enemy did not threaten their sector, to return to the main army. Washington declared the army when concentrated at camp, would have an effective strength of nearly 15,000.[31]

After reviewing the results of the prideful precision of Steuben's troop formations, Washington was confident the army would be prepared to move out of Valley Forge, when ordered. He had made an exhaustive study of the available maps covering the roads and terrain between the encampment and the North River, and was satisfied that Clinton would eventually follow a route closely paralleling the same roads to New York. Washington believed by taking an interior line of march, he would be in a favorable position to harass or attack a British Army stretched out for miles along the roads. If misfortune should befall the Continental Army, it could pull back into the Watchung Mountains of New Jersey.

With mature reflection, it plainly demonstrated that to accomplish his objective, the five divisions and the supporting units had to leave Valley Forge in three columns on divergent roads and crossings of the Delaware to consolidate with Maxwell in New Jersey. Under these marching arrangements, if any division encountered difficulties, it would not block the progress of those following. Also, the columns were to march out over two days, at intervals of several hours.

On May 28, Washington issued the first marching orders and the route to be taken to the North River. The first column made up of Lee, Mifflin and Stirling's Divisions was to move out as soon as verification was received of the British departure from Philadelphia. Lafayette's Division was to follow the next morning, with de Kalb leaving the following day. Every morning at four o'clock the divisions were to begin the day's advance. Washington's background as a surveyor became obvious in his precise schedule of the movement of each division, estimated to cover 143 miles to Smith's Clove in New York, with all columns to take thirteen days to cover that distance. Interestingly, he outlined the details of the line of march, where to setup nightly campsites, and the exact daily mileage to be covered. It varied with each column but never more than eighteen miles.[32]

Washington would modify these instructions on June 17. His endorsement on the face of the early order states "—this March was changed by the Enemy's March through New Jersey." The movement to the Delaware would remain as profiled, however, when the various columns merged in New Jersey, the line of march would be changed to intercept the British. Unknown to Washington, Clinton's decision to move directly toward Staten Island placed the British Army southeast of the principal road to New York, through New Brunswick and Elizabeth.[33]

Simultaneously with the preliminary order of march, Washington issued a command that itemized in detail the conduct of the van, under General Charles Lee. Lee was admonished not to permit the sick or lame to delay his march, not to permit impressment of horses, burning or destroying private property and positively not to suffer any insult or abuse to a citizen. Washington's order also covered such detail as the need to march before the heat of the day, avoid heat prostration, and make certain the troops had enough time to cook and refresh for the next morning's march. To have received such minute particularization of the duties of his command undoubtedly rankled the self-important Lee who was disdainful of the ability of all native born American officers, and especially the Commander in Chief.[34]

The plans for evacuating Valley Forge were interrupted by the receipt form Congress of their final resolutions for reorganizing the army. On

June 7, General Orders provided reform of the United States's military establishment. The regulations of the new army itemized the makeup of each battalion of Infantry, Artillery, Cavalry, Provost (including four executioners), and the Medical and Engineering Departments. Included were explicit rules to govern the responsibilities and functions of the different ranks, with the caution that "...commissioned officers be skilled in the necessary branches of mathematicks, the non-commissioned officers to write a good hand."[35]

With undisguised petulance, Lee's officiousness finally surfaced on June 15, when he informed Washington how he viewed Clinton's possible strategy. He believed it to be inconceivable that the British would march across New Jersey. Rather, if in a position to take the offensive, Clinton would conduct a number of feints to distract the Continental Army, and then quickly turn his attention and "...cast their eyes...on the lower Counties of Delaware and some of the Maryland Counties on the Eastern Shore." Unfortunately, Lee's belief that Clinton would not cross New Jersey was shared by some Americans, notably Elias Boudinot.

Obviously nettled, Washington wasted no time in replying to Lee. The same day he wrote thanking Lee: "...as I shall do any Officer over whom I have the honor to be placed for his opinion and advice, in matters of importance; especially when they proceed from the fountain of candor, and not from a captious spirit, or an itch for criticism."

Washington closed his letter with the caustic observation that the army had made every effort to remove all supplies from the Eastern Shore area, a fact that was known to British intelligence. In an attempt to soften his displeasure, he added: "I shall be always happy in a free communication of your Sentiments upon any important subject relative to the Service; and only beg that they may come directly to myself; the custom which many Officers have of speaking freely of things and reprobating measures which upon investigation may be found to be unavoidable...."[36]

Up to this exchange, he had considered Lee the most qualified General in the army, but with the General's attack on an army that had struggled valiantly for three years to gain respect, he was visibly questioning Lee's judgment.

Washington was appalled to hear that a number of generals apparently shared Lee's objection to move into New Jersey. There appeared to be no agreement among his general staff on a purpose or movement for the forthcoming campaign. he had not wavered in his belief that a movement into New Jersey was well-grounded, and presented an opportunity to attack an enemy strung out along the roads. His confidence in the Continentals assured him of a successful outcome. However, to explain his objective and bring an awareness of the validity of his project, he decided to call a Council of War. There must be unanimity of purpose in the army's leadership to ensure success.

On June 17, the Council of War was called, a procedure for which he has frequently been criticized as reflecting indecision as Commander in Chief. Attending the Council were Major Generals Greene, Lee, Arnold, Stirling, Lafayette and Steuben, and Brigadier Generals Knox, Poor, Smallwood, Wayne, Paterson, Woodford, Muhlenberg, Huntington and Duportail. Although not a member of the Council, Brigadier General John Cadwalader was asked for his thoughts. Washington outlined the reasons for the Order of March, trying to encourage unanimity among the Generals. He probably reiterated part of the advice he had imparted to Maxwell the day before. Confident of his judgment, he stated that if the enemy did not intend to: "...march thro' Jersey they have been making a deal of useless preparation, and indeed I do not see how they can carry off the great number of Horses and Carriages that they have been collecting with so much industry." After the generals expressed their opinions, Washington was astonished to hear most of the staff opposed dispatching any detachment to New Jersey prior to a British move, even though Maxwell's Brigade was already there. Another surprise was the negative reaction of Lafayette, Steuben and Knox, who favored harassing the British but avoiding a general engagement. They were joined in their convictions by Smallwood and Stirling. Duportail and Muhlenberg were somewhat equivocal, favoring annoying the enemy but not taking the offensive nor moving into New Jersey unless provoked by some unforeseen move by Clinton. Except for Greene, Wayne and Cadwalader all opposed moving out of Valley Forge until the British Army had already committed itself to march. Under such conditions the Continental Army would be placed at a disadvantage as to time and position.[37]

In explaining the necessity of inflicting a defeat on Clinton's column before he could form a junction with the New York garrison, Washington underestimated the strength of the combined British force. Nevertheless, this miscalculation did not detract from the validity of his proposed move. His intelligence had estimated that Clinton would have a combined force of nearly 15,000, while his Continentals would number about 14,000. Even with this information as to the relative strength of the two armies, his strategy to attack the numerically larger British column in New Jersey could enhance the possibility of an American victory.

Despite divergent opinions, the generals could not alter Washington's decision to pursue the British into New Jersey and look for a favorable opportunity to attack their column. About eleven o'clock on June 18, he received intelligence that confirmed his belief that Clinton would cross New Jersey. The enemy had put 3,000 troops—mostly certain Hessian units Clinton believed would desert given an opportunity—on board the transports, while the main column was making preparations to cross the

Delaware into New Jersey. Within a half hour, Lee's Division of Poor, Varnum and Huntington's Brigades were on the march to Coryell's Ferry. They were to be followed at three o'clock by the two Pennsylvania and "Late" Conway's Brigades, commanded by Wayne in the absence of Mifflin. The remainder of the army, comprising the Divisions of Lafayette, de Kalb and Stirling with Knox's Artillery Park, were to be underway by five o'clock on the morning of June 19—exactly six months after entering the encampment.[38]

Accompanying this column were the wagon brigades carrying the baggage of the Commander in Chief and each Division, the Quartermaster General, Flying Hospitals and Forage Master General. It was important that the security of these brigades be assured by placing sufficient guards on their flanks and rear. Pioneers were to move in front of the column to assist the artificers in repairing bridges, bad roads and broken carriages. The light horse was to cover the front and right flank of the column during the day, and encamp in the rear of the troops at night.[39]

As the last wagons rolled out of the encampment of six months, there were probably nostalgic recollections of the rag tag rabble that had entered the Valley Forge area on December 19, that now were departing proud, well-disciplined Continentals.[40]

Washington probably took a last look around his home and headquarters of six months with mixed emotions. He had one last chore to perform, to reimburse Mrs. Deborah Hewes for the rent of the headquarters house and its furniture. A payment of £100 Pennsylvania currency was made to Mrs. Hewes by Captain Caleb Gibbs of the Commander in Chief's guard.[41]

A bit of doggerel verse was written for his wife by Captain Edward Lounsbury of the Second New York Regiment. It seems to summarize the dedication of the Continental soldier at Valley Forge:

> Dear Polly when once that the Wars are all o'er
> I return to your Arms and will leave you no more
> Since you and my Country, are threatened with chains
> I'll fight while life has...(illegible)...your Freedom to gain.[42]

Appendix A

Search for World's Most Celebrated Encampment

Opinions on the proposed locations for a winter cantonment were received from those generals attending the Councils of War, and others on command. Those favoring Wilmington were Major Generals Nathanael Greene and Marquis de Marie Paul Joseph Roch Yves Gilbert duc Motier Lafayette, Brigadier Generals William Smallwood, Anthony Wayne, Charles Scott, Louis Lebégue Duportail (Duportail also expressed favor for the Great Valley), and John Armstrong of the Pennsylvania Militia. A number of generals considered the line between Lancaster and Reading as the most defensive against surprise. They were Major General John Sullivan, Brigadier Generals John (Baron) de Kalb, William Maxwell, Henry Knox, Enoch Poor, Peter Muhlenberg (he also recommended a line from Reading to Easton), James Mitchell Varnum, George Weedon, and William Woodford. Major General Earl of Stirling (William Alexander) and Duportail proposed hutting in the Great Valley. Another militia general, James Irvine, expressed a preference for hutting in any strong position. Brigadier General Casimir Pulaski, reverting to his previous experience of winter campaigning in Poland, vigorously opposed any winter encampment, preferring a campaign.

The differing judgments were accompanied with a wide and varying range of reasons why each location was hazardous or advantageous. Washington, displeased with the inconsistencies of the various comments, accepted full responsibility as Commander in Chief and made the selection of a site. He picked an area along the south bank of the Schuylkill River that included a location described by the distinguished English historian, Sir George Otto Trevelyan, as one that could become "...the most celebrated encampment in the world's history [Valley Forge]."

Washington's decision may have been influenced or confirmed by his interchange of views with Joseph Reed, or possibly an apparent unsolicited opinion of Lieutenant Colonel Lutterloh.

On December 1, Deputy Quartermaster General, Lieutenant Colonel Henry Emanuel Lutterloh (a former major in the Duke of Brunswick's Quartermaster General Department) presented the Commander in Chief with an interesting overview on where to quarter the army for the winter. Lutterloh wrote:

> I have been lucking [looking] out where you could forme such a Line, Sufficiently stocked with houses for that purpose & find we could form such a Line between the Two Rivers Schuylkill & Delawar, where we could effectually cover our Country, Stores, & provide the Necessary Supplyes

222

easy...place our Right Wing allongst the Schuylkill...left on the Delawar. Our Van Troops in German Town & those hights...up towards Reading all the Army could lay. Head Quarter to be at Pots Grove (Pottstown)...great Magazin to be in Reading & in the Trap (Trappe) & [in] Hickery Town (Plymouth Meeting) the Mooving Magazines & Backerys (Bakerys)...Right Whing Melitia...over Schuylkill as from Mottrom's (Matson's) ford upwards I find the Country very advantagious with hills where no Surprise could happen...Over Schuylkill must be Two bridges more one by Wolley forge (Valley Forge) & one near Potsgrove to get quik Communications.

Lutterloh's comments are the first that note the defensive characteristics along the Schuylkill north of Matson's Ford and with a reference to Valley Forge. What influence this had on Washington's decision to reconnoiter on the south side of the Schuylkill River above Swede's Ford can only be conjectured.[1]

Appendix B

Duportail and the French Engineers

Louis Lebégue Duportail landed in North Carolina in June 1777, with an entourage that included engineers, Lewis de la Radiere, Jean Baptiste Joseph, Chevalier de Laumoy, and Jean Baptiste Gouvion, a lieutenant and two sergeants. To avoid detection and being ordered to return to France, the Frenchmen had traveled under assumed names. However, they quickly resumed their aristocratic identity when presenting Benjamin Franklin's endorsement of their engineering qualifications to the Continental Congress.

Unfortunately for Duportail and his companions their appearance before Congress, at this time, could not have been more inopportune. Congress had been inundated with foreign officers who had varying military backgrounds and experience seeking preferment in the Continental Army. Congressional reaction was unfavorable to the French engineer's pretensions. They had been constantly badgered and bewildered by the recommendations and guarantees made to numerous foreign mercenaries by Franklin, Silas Deane, and other Americans in Paris.

Duportail with his tendency to be haughty and imperious did little to impress the Congressmen. They were provoked by demands for a specific rank for himself and his fellow engineers; accompanied by a vehement objection to serving under or with French officers who had been his subordinate in France, or were less qualified. Duportail was particularly nettled with the presence of Philippe Charles Trouson du Coudray who had been appointed by Congress as Inspector General of Ordnances and Military Manufactories. Although rankled by the French engineer's officious demeanor, Congress, recognizing that the Continental Army was bereft of qualified military engineers, reservedly named Duportail Colonel of Engineers.

While Duportail's asperity and waspishness would never endear him to his fellow officers, they would be quick to perceive his wisdom and experience in the field of engineering and fortifications. Nevertheless, for the moment, Duportail continued to seethe under what he considered unfair treatment of the engineering branch of the service. Threatening to return to France, he determined first to make a final appeal to Washington. Duportail importuned the Commander in Chief to present his memorial to Congress requesting the elevation of the Engineering function to equal status with a brigade of the line—concurrently he wanted to be commissioned Brigadier General of the Corps, and each of his subordinates to a Colonelcy.

Brigadier General Louis Le Bégue de Presle Duportail by Charles Willson Peale. (Independence National Historical Park Collection.)

Washington had become annoyed by the frequent badgering and jealousies of many foreign officers, but was cognizant of the needs of the Continental Army for engineering expertise. On November 3, after mature reflection and consultation with his generals, he agreed to present Duportail's petition to Congress. Nevertheless, he cautioned that body that he knew little of the French officer's abilities, except for the memorialist's self-appraisal. In an effort to mollify the indictment, Washington acknowledged that the French engineers had had little opportunity to date to exhibit their talents.

On November 17, after considering the merits of Duportail's memorial, and again noting the need for engineers, Congress created a Corps of Engineers with the status requested by Duportail and appointed him Brigadier General and Commandant. Radiere and Laumoy were given the rank of Colonel and Gouvion that of Lieutenant Colonel. Surprisingly, this decision did not annoy Washington, in fact, he was pleased as the daily observations of Duportail's military knowledge and competence as an engineer had demonstrated his value to the army.

Washington's increased faith in Duportail's ability was evident when the army reached Valley Forge where his first orders were for the Frenchmen to prepare sketches for quartering the troops and the defenses necessary for their security. During the six months at the encampment, Washington never issued written orders or instructions to Duportail. The engineer's biographer believed this demonstrated the close face-to-face coordination that existed between him and the Commander in Chief. While language differences arose, the appointment of one of Washington's aides-de-camp, Lieutenant Colonel John Laurens, as interpreter and translator bridged any misunderstandings.

Following Washington's first order Duportail and his assistants surveyed the proposed camp site and carefully detailed arrangements to quarter the troops, and outlined preliminary fortifications to defend the encampment. Duportail's astute judgment was soon manifested but he realized that his staff was hopelessly inadequate for the task that confronted it. His only recourse, with no engineers among the Americans was to visit the provisional capital at Yorktown (York) in search of engineers among the foreign officers seeking employment. The first priority was to find a cartographer. In early January 1778, a fortuitous meeting with Jean Louis Ambroise de Genton, Chevalier de Villefranche, a superbly qualified cartographic engineer, answered his needs.

Villefranche had had the misfortune of coming to America as a member of the entourage of the irascible, self-seeking, and ill-fated du Coudray. After the drowning of the latter officer in September 1777, Villefranche spent four futile months at Yorktown seeking employment. All members of du Coudray's staff soon discovered they were as unacceptable by the

American generals as their late willful commander. However, Duportail was not daunted by Villefranche's unfortunate association with the man he despised. Unhesitantly Duportail, in dire need of a cartographer, memorialized Washington with an outline on the theory of fortifications and plans for an expanded Engineer Corps. He emphasized the need for an experienced cartographic engineer and recommended Villefranche for the position. Fortunately for the frustrated Villefranche and the Engineer Corps this request was immediately granted, and he was commissioned Major of Engineers and directed to report to Washington at Valley Forge.

While pleased with the addition of Villefranche to his staff, Duportail remained concerned that the Corps was still undermanned. Providentially at Yorktown, he encountered a young French engineer, John Bernard de Murnan, who carried excellent credentials as an engineer. For many months the young Frenchman had been unable to obtain employment so when approached by Duportail, he readily agreed to serve as a volunteer until such time as Congress would grant him a commission. His anticipation would be long as Congress waited nearly one year before appointing him Major of Engineers. In January 1779, he received his commission retroactive to March 1, 1778, and pay to February 1, 1778.

At last Duportail was satisfied with his staff of four engineers and the indispensable cartographic engineer. Each engineer was given a specific assignment, with Villefranche instructed to draw all necessary position sketches and maps.[1] Maps usually referred to as Duportail's were actually the cartographic work of Villefranche. In French engineering operations the commandant's name was affixed to maps.

In early January the Engineering Corps was hampered by a shortage of manpower. Each brigade needed every able-bodied man to fell trees, gather leaves and straw—for roofs and bedding—build huts and camp hospitals. This left few men at Duportail's disposal to work on the fortifications.

Duportail and Villefranche were continually seen riding over the landscape, as the former selected locations for various types of fortifications needed for defense of the encampment, with Villefranche making sketches of his commandant's ideas. It is impossible to determine the number of these sketches as none have apparently survived the vicissitudes of time. While not of the cartographic excellence of Villefranche's later maps, two copies of the Valley Forge encampment have survived. From these rough renditions the cartographer prepared maps for presentation to Washington.

Further evidence of the expertise of Villefranche's skill as a cartographer can be seen in the excellent map he prepared in 1779 for the defense of Philadelphia and the Delaware River. In the early spring of

1779, Washington directed Duportail to reconnoiter both banks of the Delaware and prepare plans to include river fortifications for the defense of the city, with a reconstructed Fort Mifflin as the hub of the defense line. As usual, Villefranche acted as Duportail's cartographer and drafted what has recently been called "a superb exercise in cartography." This map is forty-four by sixty-seven inches with an extension at the upper right corner fourteen by eighteen inches. Two small auxiliary maps were also drawn.

Villefranche was acclaimed by several general officers during the Revolution for his outstanding professional military and cartographic ability. Washington added a postscript to these commendations by writing that it gave him: "great pleasure to give this testimony of my entire satisfaction at every part of his conduct...which...justly entitles him to the Character of a brave and deserving Officer."[2]

Appendix C

Commander in Chief's Guard

The Commander in Chief's Guard was organized at Cambridge, Massachusetts, in March 1776, as a special detachment to protect the Commander in Chief, his official family, and the "rapid accumulation of valuable papers" at headquarters. In the General Orders of March 11, Washington detailed the specifications he wanted in the recruits for the new unit:

> The General being desirous of selecting a particular number of men, as a Guard for himself, and baggage, The Colonel, or commanding Officer, of each of the established Regiments, (the Artillery and Riflemen excepted) will furnish him with four, that the number wanted may be chosen out of them. His Excellency depends upon the Colonels for good Men, such as they can recommend for their sobriety, honesty, and good behaviour; he wishes them to be from five feet, eight Inches high, to five feet, ten Inches; handsomely and well made, and as there is nothing in his eyes more desirable, than Cleanliness in a Soldier, he desires that particular attention may be made, in the choice of such men, as are neat, and spruce. They are all to be at Head Quarters to morrow precisely at twelve, at noon, when the number will be fixed upon. The General neither wants men with uniforms, or arms, nor does he desire any man be sent to him, that is not perfectly willing, and desirous of being of this guard. They should be drill'd men.[1]

About three months later a disturbing intrigue was uncovered that implicated several members of the Commander in Chief's Guard. With some British officials remaining in New York City, rumors of plots and counterplots were a common occurrence. One authority was the undeposed Loyalist Mayor of the city, David Matthews. He was accused of offering money to various soldiers in the Continental Army to desert and enlist in the British Army or to go aboard the King's ships. At the same time an unsupported rumor circulated that an attempt had been made to assassinate Washington by poisoning his food. Although there is little evidence to support either charge, several members of the Guard were accused of complicity in the plot. A soldier of the Guard, Thomas Hickey, was convicted and executed. It had been determined to make an example of Hickey before the plot became widespread. Others of the Guard taken into custody were William Greene, drummer, a fifer named Johnson, and two privates, Lynch and Barnes. While placed under arrest, the punishment, if any, of these men has become shrouded in conjecture. It has been claimed others were involved in the intrigue but they remain unnamed. Most of the soldiers associated with the conspiracy are believed to have been foreign born, with Hickey a supposed deserter from the British Army.[2]

The scheme to lure men from the army had wide ramifications and an unsettling affect on the soldiers in the Guard. As months passed, several flagrant derelictions of duty and insubordinations occurred which convinced Washington that drastic measures had to be adopted. By now he had become distrustful of the current guard unit and foreign born soldiers in particular. By April 1777, he had decided to return the present members of the Guard to their original regiments, and completely reorganize the unit with soldiers chosen from the Virginia regiments. On April 30, letters were dispatched to four colonels commanding Virginia regiments[3] in which he stated:

> I want to form a Company for my Guard. In doing this I wish to be extremely cautious; because it is more than probable, that in the Course of the Campaign, my Baggage, Papers, and other Matter of great public Import, may be committed to the Sole care of these Men. This being premised, in order to impress you with proper attention in the Choice, I have to request that you will immediately furnish me with four Men of your Regiment, And, as it is my further wish, that this Company should look well and be nearly of a Size, I desire that none of the Men may exceed in Stature 5 feet 10 Inches, nor fall Short of 5 feet 9 Inches, Sober, Young, Active and well made. When I recommend care in your Choice, I would be understood to mean Men of good Character in the Regiment, that possess the pride of appearing clean and Soldierlike. I am satisfied there can be no absolute security for the fidelity of this Class of people, but yet I think it most likely to be found in those who have Family Connections in the Country. You will therefore send me none but Natives, and Men of some property, if you have them. I must insist, that in making this Choice, you give no Intimation of my preference of Natives, as I do not want to create any invidious Distinction between them and the Foreigners.[4]

Washington's choice of native born Americans may appear to be prejudicial, and as some critics claim snobbish, when he asserted men with a vested interest were more likely to be loyal. Experience had strengthened his belief that men with property were more dependable in fighting for their country than those who had recently emigrated to America. Of course his belief did exhibit some bias against those men in the service who had come to America and were now property owners.

Washington's lack of confidence in the foreign born soldiers was largely due to desertions each time the army was confronted with extreme privations. The reports of Joseph Galloway, Superintendent General of Philadelphia (the civilian head), confirmed Washington's opinion when, during the winter a Valley Forge, nearly 1,300 Continental soldiers entered the British lines, of which about 300 were native born.

These statistics did not include galleymen from the Pennsylvania Navy or militiamen.[5]

Nevertheless, Washington's known compassion and concern for the welfare of the faithful core that comprised the Continental Army never wavered.

As the Commander in Chief's Guard entered the Valley Forge encampment, the rank and file were composed of Virginians. The command of the Guard remained with Captain Caleb Gibbs and Lieutenant Henry Philip Livingston. The unit consisted of four sergeants, four corporals, one fifer, and forty-seven privates.[6]

With the arrival of Frederick von Steuben at Valley Forge in late February, the Guard was singled out for a distinguished assignment. The Prussian officer soon manifested his ability as a drillmaster and disciplinarian. Washington's recognition of Steuben's competence, and his subsequent offer to serve as Volunteer Inspector General, became the stimulus for developing the effective fighting machine Washington wanted to open the next campaign.

On March 17, complying with Steuben's request for a model drill company, Washington's General Orders directed that: "One hundred chosen men are to be annexed to the Guard of the Commander in Chief for the purpose of forming a Corps to be instructed in the Manoeuvres necessary to be introduced in the Army and serve as a Model for the execution of them. As the General's guard is composed intirely of Virginians the one hundred draughts are to be taken from the troops of the other States."[7]

Since the Guard arrived at Valley Forge, eleven privates had been returned to their line regiments. The addition of the company of carefully selected men had increased the strength of the unit to 136 privates. Of that number 100 would always be available for Steuben's model drill detachment, while the remaining thirty-six would be on duty at headquarters. Although not specifically designated, the headquarters guard was probably Washington's trusted Virginians. To properly staff the expanded Guard, additional commissioned officers were assigned to join Gibbs and Livingston; they being First Lieutenant Benjamin Grymes, Second Lieutenant William Colfax, and Surgeon Samuel Hanson (son of John Hanson, later President of the Continental Congress under the Articles of Confederation).

No other changes occurred in the Guard until May 1, when the cavalry troops commanded by Captain George Lewis (nephew of Washington and lieutenant of the originial Guard) and Lieutenant Robert Randolph, with thirty-eight troopers, were assigned as the Guard's first mounted unit. This detachment was never officially entered on the muster roll of the Guard, therefore they were probably carried on the regimental rolls as "on command"—a term used when soldiers were on duty away from their regiment.

At this time the army was undergoing a number of changes as detailed in the Congressional plan for the army's reorganization. In January a Committee of Congress, with the acquiescence of Washington, had visited Valley Forge to conduct a study of the army. Washington submitted forty-one pages of suggested improvements for the army. These recommendations conjointly with interviews, and the Committee's personal observations at camp, would form the basis of a plan to be submitted to Congress. The assignment of Lewis' dragoons was one detail of the reorganization intended to give the Commander in Chief and the headquarters staff greater protection on the march.

The scope of this appendix is only intended to describe the beginning of the Commander in Chief's Guard through Valley Forge. For their subsequent activities other studies are available.[8]

As a reverent footnote to the Guard at Valley Forge, it is worthy to record that Nathaniel Berry, later a lieutenant, was the last survivor of the Commander in Chief's Guard. Berry was one of the 100 soldiers transferred to the Guard in March 1778. He was honorably discharged on the expiration of his enlistment on January 1, 1780. On August 20, 1850, Berry died at Pittston, Maine, aged ninety-five years.[9]

Appendix D

Congress Blunders

In January 1777, Congress resurrected a cherished project by ordering the invasion of Canada. The results of the earlier incursion, in 1775, had been disastrous. Congress, forgetting that catastrophe and ignoring the difficulties of invading Canada in the winter, ill-advisedly believed that if the expedition was successful it would bring the predominantly French Canadian province into the struggle on the side of the United States. To buttress their thinking, Congress was aware that Sir Guy Carleton's British garrison in Canada was understrength as a result of Burgoyne's surrender at Saratoga. With the severity of the weather, Carleton could not expect reinforcements from Great Britain until spring.

It has been contended that without discussing the validity of such an expedition with Washington, it represented a deliberate effort to bypass the Commander in Chief. Rather, the unfortunate resolve seems to be another example of Congress to exert civil authority in matters pertaining to the strategic use of elements of the army.

On January 23, although previously committed to the command staff for the expedition, Congress surprisingly decided to cast ballots for the general officers to command the invasion force. Militia General John Stark received eight votes, Lafayette and Conway six, with Major General Alexander McDougall and Brigadier General John Glover one vote each. Lafayette's name soon surfaced as the logical choice for the command. It was hoped his presence, as a French aristocrat, would enhance the acceptance of the American troops by the French Canadian inhabitants. Five days later, Lafayette's acceptance apparently was not certain, when Congress ordered 30,000 French livres to "Lafayette or the general officer who would command the expedition." Before accepting the command, Lafayette desired to confer with Washington and obtain his approval. Although reluctant to lose the young Frenchman, Washington advised him to assume the proffered post. Lafayette, seeking a wise and experienced field officer, asked that Baron de Kalb be named second in command. Congress then named Conway, McDougall and Stark to Lafayette's general staff, and at his request, appointed a number of French officers serving in the Continental Army. These officers were to carry the same rank they enjoyed in the French service.[1]

Arriving at the staging area near Albany, Lafayette and his generals quickly reviewed the assembled regiments and were stunned at the lack of every article needed to conduct a campaign. The badly under strength units were obviously incapable of invading Canada—with the exception of Colonel Moses Hazen's Canadian regiment. Orders were issued to Stark

Major General Marquis, Marie Joseph Paul Yves Roche Gilbert du Notier de Lafayette by Charles Willson Peale. (Independence National Historical Park Collection.)

to recruit militia units in New England. Lafayette, seized by a sense of helplessness and hopelessness, directed Hazen to assume the role of Quartermaster of the expedition, in addition to his line command.[2]

Hazen was overwhelmed by several tasks that seemed impossible to fulfill. New York and western New England were to be scoured for large quantities of forage. In addition, he was enjoined to obtain sixty days provisions and other necessities such as baggage, artillery and ammunition for an army of 3,000 men. Lafayette was cognizant that Hazen was familiar with Canadian winters directing him to furnish "all clothing and other comforts" that could be "found." After a conference Hazen and Conway recognized the futility of marching an army through the roadless wastes of snow. Conway asked the harassed Hazen to locate as many sleighs as possible to "carry the army."[3]

It soon became obvious to Hazen that orders were more easily given than fulfilled. Nevertheless, his diligence was partially rewarded when he was able to impress 500 carriages to transport the army, and between 700 and 800 sleighs to convey "Provisions, warlike Stores, Hospital Stores and Baggage to St. Johns [Canada] or Montreal." A number of owners had agreed to serve as drivers for the expedition, but more volunteers were needed. The efforts of Hazen and his assistants were little better than an exercise in motion, as it was apparent there was not a sufficiency of any supplies, especially clothing. To add to this dilemma, it was soon discovered that the under strength regiments had a number of inexperienced soldiers, some only twelve years old and others over sixty who would not be able to withstand the rigors of a winter campaign.[4]

Other generals were equally skeptical of the proposed campaign. Major Generals Nathanael Greene, Benjamin Lincoln and Brigadier General George Clinton voiced their opposition, with Lincoln writing that the "sooner all ideas of executing that Plan [the expedition to Canada] are quitted the more it will be for the interest of the United States." One veteran who had fought in the earlier Canadian disaster was Benedict Arnold. After reviewing the wretched condition of the troops and the state of Quartermaster stores, Arnold suggested to Lafayette that he recommend to Congress the advisability of cancelling the venture. Most military critics agreed that if the troops at Albany had taken the offensive, New York City would have been an easier and more important objective. The city had a reduced garrison with the bulk of the British Army in Philadelphia.[5]

The clamor against the proposed expedition was not confined to military personnel, as many members of Congress voiced similar doubts about the merits of the plan. James Duane noted it was evident that the planned project was in "Want of almost every Necessary." He added: "The Number of men was greatly deficient. They were destitute of warm

Cloathing; their pay in Arrear, and both Officers and Privates visibly averse to the Expedition." Duane detailed other deficiencies such as forage and teams. Joseph Reed said: "I know in some Instances it has been found politick to transfer the Seat of War into your Enemy's Country, but that can only be, when you are able to carry it on there, which I fear in the present Instance will not be our Case." With these criticisms infiltrating the halls of a frustrated Congress, wiser heads prevailed and on March 2, they directed the Board of War to order the suspension of the intended expedition.[6]

Until requested by the Board of War, Washington had refrained from commenting on the validity of an invasion of Canada. Still unwilling to censure the plan of a civil body, his reticence was obvious as he wrote: "In the present instance, as I neither know the extent of the Objects in view, nor the means to be employed to effect them, It is not in my power to pass any judgment upon the subject."[7]

Later to a personal friend, Brigadier General Thomas Nelson, he offered his only critique on the expedition. Unburdening himself, Washington candidly expressed his opinion: "...if they go to frittering their army into detachments, for the accomplishment of some local and less important purpose, the campaign will be wasted, and nothing decisive (on our part) attempted. It is our business to crush, if possible the army under Genl. Howe's immediate command; this once done the branches of it fall of course, and without it, the body will always afford nourishment to its members." Washington's sound judgment reflected his acumen as a strategist.[8]

While patiently waiting at Albany, Lafayette and de Kalb waited for instructions for reassignment. After eleven days Congress ordered them to report to the "grand army" at Valley Forge as soon as possible. In the meantime, a chagrined Lafayette was apprehensive that the abortive campaign would reflect negatively on his ability as an independent field commander. On March 10, Washington advised him that his concern was unwarranted as Congress had "manifest a proof of [their] good Opinion and confidence..." He continued by expressing the belief: "...that every one will applaud your prudence in renouncing a Project, in pursuing which you would vainly have attempted Physical Impossibilities." Ten days later Washington directed Lafayette "without loss of time return to camp, to resume command of a Division of the Army." Lafayette was to "communicate a similar order to Major General de Kalb." With this letter the curtain fell on the ill-fated attempt by Congress and the Board of War to direct a campaign that had been doomed at inception.[9]

Notes

Prologue

1. Douglas S. Freeman, *George Washington*, Vol. IV, p. 488.
2. *Tredyffrin Easttown History Club Quarterly*, April, 1938, Vol. I, No.3, "Isaac Wayne to Richard Peters," March 4, 1814.
3. Peter Force, comp., *American Archives*, 5th, Vol. III, p. 1181, "Major Irving to Major [Theodorick] Bland," December 12, 1776; *Pennsylvania Archives* (hereafter cited P.A.), Second Series, Vol. VI, p. 499.
4. Washington Papers, Library of Congress (hereafter cited as LC), Clement Biddle to Washington, September 16, 1777.
5. John C. Fitzpatrick, ed., *Washington-Writings* (hereafter cited as *Washington-Writings*), Vol. IX, to William Maxwell, September 17, 1777, pp. 231-32, to Anthony Wayne (2 letters), September 18, 1777, pp. 235-36.
6. E.D. Scull, ed., *John Montresor Journals*, pp. 454-55.
7. *Ibid.*, pp. 455-57.
8. General John Sullivan with the main column of Continentals was to move down Skippack and North Wales (Bethlehem Pike) Roads. Washington accompanied this column. General Nathanael Greene was to approach the village from the east moving down Limekiln Road, his left flank would be protected by a column of militia on York Road under General William Smallwood. The right flank on Manatawny (Ridge Pike) Road was a Pennsylvania militia column commanded by General John Armstrong.
9. *Pennsylvania Magazine of History and Biography* (hereafter cited as PMHB), "Diary of Lieutenant James McMichael of the Pennsylvania Line," Vol. XVI, p. 153; *Washington-Writings*, Vol. IX, to President of Congress, October 5, 1777, pp. 308-12, to Major General Israel Putnam, October 8, 1777, pp. 335-37.
10. *The Army Correspondence of John Laurens in the Years 1777-8* (hereafter cited as *John Laurens-Correspondence*), to Henry Laurens, November 26, 1777, pp. 80-88.
11. John Reed Collection, Peter Zantzinger to Anthony Wayne, December 4 and 6, 1777, Joseph Donaldson to Zantzinger, December 5, 1777.
12. Otis G. Hammond, ed., *Letters and Papers of Major-General John Sullivan, Continental Army* (hereafter cited as *Sullivan-Letters*), Vol. I, pp. 590-92.

VALLEY FORGE

Chapter I

1. *John Laurens-Correspondence*, Laurens to Henry Laurens, December 3, 1777, pp. 89-93.

2. Worthington C. Ford, *Journals of Continental Congress* (hereafter cited as *Journals-Congress*), December 15, 1777, Vol. IX, pp. 1029-31.

3. *Ibid.*, November 28, 1777, Vol. IX, p. 972, The committee members were Robert Morris, Elbridge Gerry, and Joseph Jones; *Washington-Writings*, Vol. X, pp. 144-45, f.6.

4. LC, Force MSS, Series 7E, New Hampshire Miscellaneous, Enoch Poor to Thos. Odiorne, December 17, 1777.

5. See Appendix A.

6. William B. Reed, *Life and Correspondence of Joseph Reed*, John Cadwalader to Reed, November 30, 1777, Vol. II, pp. 348-49f.

7. *Washington-Writings*, Washington to Joseph Reed, December 2, 1777, Vol. X, pp. 133-34.

8. *Sullivan-Letters*, Order of March, Dec. 1777, Vol. I, pp. 590-93; *John Laurens-Correspondence*, Laurens to Henry Laurens, December 23, 1777, pp. 94-98; *Washington-Writings*, Washington to President of Congress, December 14, 1777, Vol. X, pp. 155-58.

9. *Ibid.*; For the best detailed description of Potter's engagement see *Bulletin of the Historical Society of Montgomery County*, "The Fight on Old Gulph Road," John F. Reed, Vol. XV, Nos. 1 and 2; *PMHB*, "Memoirs of Brigadier General John Lacey," Vol. XXVI, pp. 107-110; *P.A.*, 1st Series, Potter to Thomas Wharton, Vol. VI, pp. 97-98; Frederic Kidder, *History of the First New Hampshire Regiment*, "Lieutenant Thomas Blake's Journal," Dec. 11 [12], p. 39; *PPost*, "Whitemarsh to Valley Forge," Major William H. Bean, January 1951, pp. 31-39.

10. *John Laurens-Correspondence*, Laurens to Henry Laurens, December 23, 1777, pp. 94-98; *PMHB*, "Diary of Lieutenant James McMichael," December 12, 1777, Vol. XVI, p. 157; *PMHB*, "Valley Forge, 1777-1778, Diary of Surgeon Albigence Waldo" (hereafter cited as "Diary-Waldo"), December 12, 1777, Vol. XXI, p. 305.

11. *Washington-Writings*, General Orders, December 13, 1777, Vol. X, p. 151; Regimental Orderly Book, Colonel Joseph Storer, New York Historical Society (hereafter cited as NYHS), December 13, 1777.

12. *PMHB*, "General Muhlengerg's Orderly Book," December 12, 1777, Vol. XXXV, p. 297; Orderly Book of Captain Peter Brown's Company of Philadelphia Militia Artillery, NYHS, December 9, 1777; *Washington-Writings*, General Orders, December 12, 1777, Vol. x, pp. 150-51; John W. Jackson, *Whitemarsh 1777: Impregnable Stronghold*, p. 50.

13. *Washington-Writings*, Washington to President of Congress, Sep-

tember 17 and 19, 1777, pp. 230-31, 237-39, to Anthony Wayne, September 18, 1777 (2 letters), pp. 235-36.

14. The hamlet of Swedesford has been incorporated into the boroughs of Bridgeport and Swedesburg.

15. See Appendix B.

16. *Norristown Times Herald*, December 29, 1970, article by Ed Dybicz, Correspondent.

17. *PMHB*, "Diary of Lieutenant James McMichael," December 12, 1777, Vol. XVI, p. 157; *John Laurens-Correspondence*, Laurens to Henry Laurens, December 23, 1777, pp. 94-98; *Continental Journal*, "Letter from the army," January 15, 1778.

18. *Washington-Writings*, General Orders, December 13, 1777, Vol. IX, p. 151.

19. *Ibid.*, General Orders, December 15, 1777, pp. 163-64.

20. Diary of John Miller, John Reed Papers, NYHS, December 14, 1777; Frederic Kidder, *History of the First New Hampshire Regiment*, "Lieutenant Thomas Blake's Journal," Dec. 16, p. 40; LC, Force MSS, Series E, New Hampshire Miscellaneous, Enoch Poor to Thos. Odiorne, December 17, 1777; Jared Sparks, ed., *The Writings of George Washington*, Orderly Book, near Valley Forge, December 17, 1777, Vol. VI, p. 523-24; *PPost*, "Whitemarsh to Valley Forge," Major William H. Bean, January, 1951, pp. 36-37; *Washington-Writings*, General Orders, December 17, 1777, Vol. X, pp. 167-68.

21. *Ibid.*; *Journals of Congress*, November 1, 1777, Vol. IX, pp. 854-55.

22. *Washington-Writings*, Washington to President of Congress, December 23, 1777, Vol. X, pp. 192-98.

23. Pennsylvania Archives, RG 29, Roll 13, Thomas Wharton to Elias Boudinot, December 13, 1777; HSP, Dreer Collection, Members of Old Congress, Abraham Clark to Lord Stirling, December 20, 1777.

24. *Journals of Congress*, December 15, 1777, Vol. IX, pp. 1029-31.

25. *Ibid.*, December 19, 1777, Vol. IX, p. 1036; *Colonial Records*, Vol. XI, pp. 386, 394; *P.A.*, 1st Series, Vol. VI, pp. 61, 104-105, 109, 111, Colonel John Bayard to President Wharton, December 4, 1777, Remonstrance of Council and Assembly to Congress, 1777, J.B. Smith to Vice President George Bryan, December 19, 1777; HSP, Dreer Collection, Signers of Declaration, Petition, December 31, 1777.

26. *Washington-Writings*, General Orders, December 18, 1777, Vol. X, p. 171, to General William Smallwood, December 19, 1777, pp. 171-72, to President George Reed, December 19, 1777, pp. 174-75.

27. *John Laurens-Correspondence*, Laurens to Henry Laurens, December 15, 1777, pp. 93-4; *Washington-Writings*, General Orders, December 18, 1777, Vol. X, pp. 169-71.

28. *Ibid.*, General Orders, December 20, 1777, pp. 180-81.

29. Massachusetts Historical Society, Dudley Coleman Papers, Dudley Coleman to his wife, December 13, 1777.

30. Connecticut Historical Society, Joseph Trumbull Collection, Jedediah Huntington to Joseph Trumbull, December 10, 1777.

Chapter II

1. See Appendix C.

2. *Washington-Writings*, Washington to President of Congress, October 5, 1777, Vol. IX, pp. 308-11, General Orders, October 5, 1777, pp. 311-12, to Isreal Putnam, October 8, 1777, pp. 335-37.

3. *Ibid.*, Washington to President of Congress, December 23, 1777, Vol. X, pp. 192-98.

4. *Ibid.*, General Orders, December 20, 1777, pp. 180-81.

5. *Ibid.*

6. A.E. Zucker, *General De Kalb, Lafayette's Mentor*, p. 163.

7. *Washington-Writings*, General Orders, December 22, 1777, Vol. X, p. 190; *PMHB*, "Historical Notes of Dr. Benjamin Rush, 1777." Contributed by Dr. S. Weir Mitchell, Vol. XXVII, p. 148. On January 3, 1778, Dr. Benjamin Rush visited the quarters of General John Sullivan where he espied a paper hanging on the wall titled "Names of Officers who distinguished themselves in building Ye bridge over Schuilkill [Schuylkill] 1778." Rush, who maintained a succinct day to day diary, added this paper as a footnote to his recording of that date.

His Exy Genl Washington

Major Pollard	(probably 1st Lietuenant Benjamin Pollard, 13th Massachusetts)
Major Thayer	(Major Simeon Thayer of the 2nd Rhode Island and hero of Fort Mifflin)
Capt. Chadwick	(Captain John Chadwick, 12th Massachusetts)
Lieut. Parker	(probably Lieutenant Isaac Parker, 8th Massachusetts)
Col. Chandler	(Colonel John Chandler, 8th Connecticut)
Capt. Frye	(either Captain Ebenezer Frye, 1st New Hampshire or Captain Isaac Frye, 3rd New Hampshire)

Honble Major General Sullivan

Col. Charlton	(probably Lieutenant Colonel Samuel Carlton, 12th Massachusetts)
Lieut. Mason	(probably 2nd Lieutenant David Mason [Massachusetts] 3rd Continental Artillery)

Majr Cortland	(Major Philip Van Cortland, 2nd New York)
Majr Brum	(Major Peter Bryant Bruin [Virginia] Aide-de-camp to General Sullivan)
Col. Basset	(Lieutenant Colonel Barachiah Basset, 14th Massachusetts)
Lieut [torn]	
Capt. Smith	(either Captain David Smith, 8th Connecticut; Captain George Smith, 1st Massachusetts; or 1st Lieutenant and Adjutant John Kilby Smith, 13th Massachusetts—became Captain on February 12, 1778)
Lieut. Jewet	(Lieutenant James Jewett, Baldwin's Artillery Artifice Regiment)

As is evident, most of these officers were from Sullivan's Division or other New England Brigades.

8. "Troops Marched Out of Valley Forge, June 19, 1778," PP, July, 1963. A small redoubt was discernible at the eastern tip of the island at the time of the Centennial celebration of the Continental Army abandoning Valley Forge. *The Daily Republican* of Phoenixville on June 18, 1962, quoting from the Centennial program of June 19, 1878, noted that "Entrenchments could be seen dimly in the woods, and several redoubts could be traced: one on an island in the Schuylkill." The channel on the north side of the island has silted in and no longer exists.

9. The Star Redoubt has been reconstructed on the traditional site of the original. "Historic Resource Study," Jacqueline Thibaut, Valley Forge National Historical Park, Vol. III, pp. 101-02.

10. A subaltern was any commissioned officer below the rank of captain.

11. Orderly Book (microfilm), Huntington Library, AM 660, February 15, 1778; *Washington-Writings*, General Orders, December 21, 1777, Vol. X, p. 181, March 3 and April 1, 1778, Vol. XI, pp. 18, 194-95; *Valley Forge Orderly Book of General George Weedon* (hereafter cited as *Weedon-Orderly Book*), December 25, 1777, p. 167.

12. Chevaux-de-frise, translated literally, means Friseland horses, Most of the hoppers or bins laid in the Delaware River were approximately thirty feet square. After being lowered into the river bed they were filled with from twenty to forty tons of stones. The hoppers were equipped with three massive timbers set obliquely downstream—a few had two spikes—tipped with large iron spikes. The chevaux-de-frise could rip the hull of any eighteenth century wooden ship. For further details on these river constructions, see John W. Jackson, *Pennsylvania Navy 1775-1781,* Appendix B, pp. 353-376.

13. *Ibid.*, pp. 147, 206-210; G.W. Papers, Reel 44, State Navy Board (Joseph Blewer) to Washington, October 14, 1777.

14. *Washington-Writings*, Washington to Hazelwood, October 14, 1777, General Orders, October 29 and 30, 1777, Vol. IX, pp. 369, 461, 469; *State Records of North Carolina*, Walter Clark, ed., Vol. XI, pp. 667, 676, 690, 700, 703. The rosters of the North Carolina regiments shows an average of 120 men on command, a few may have been on scouting or foraging details, but the majority were with Hazelwood.

15. For a detailed description of the defense of the Delaware River, see Jackson, *Pennsylvania Navy 1775-1781* and *Fort Mifflin, Valiant Defender of the Delaware.*

16. *Washington-Writings*, Washington to Bradford, March 18, 1778, Vol. XI, p. 105; Captain Lieutenant George Fleming to Captain Sebastian Bauman or General Henry Knox, February 13, 1778, NYHS, Sebastian Bauman Papers.

17. *Sullivan-Papers,* Sullivan to the Pennsylvania General Assembly, November 20, 1778, Vol. II, pp. 440-41.

18. The British Convention Army were members of the invasion force commanded by General John Burgoyne that surrendered to General Horatio Gates at Saratoga in October 1777.

19. *Journal of Du Roi the Elder, Lieutenant Adjutant, in the Service of the Duke of Brunswick, 1776-1778*, Translated by Charlotte S. J. Epping, p. 141.

20. Thomas Anburey, *Travels through the Interior Parts of America*, Vol. II, p. 170.

21. *Jackson-Fort Mifflin*, pp. 105-115.

22. The definitive study for the Revolutionary War is Erna Risch, *Supplying Washington's Army*, a special study for the Center of Military History, United States Army, Washington, 1981; An older study, but still useful, is *The Administration of the American Commissariat During the Revolutionary War*, Victor LeRoy Johnson, a Doctoral Dissertation, Philadelphia, 1941.

23. *Washington-Writings*, Washington to Gerry, December 25, 1777, Vol. X, pp. 200-01.

24. John C. Fitzpatrick lists Washington's undated plan as prepared on December 25, 1777, *Washington-Writings*, Vol. X, pp. 202-05. The document is in the handwriting of Washington and is endorsed by him and titled "Orders for a Move that *was* Intended against Philadelphia by Way of Surprise." Note that the plan is written to imply Washington had discarded it on Christmas day. According to several journalists heavy snow fell on December 24 and 25, a condition that would have seriously inhibited any movement by the Continental Army. Fitzpatrick is correct in dating the plan December 25 as it refers to Jameson's dragoons on duty

guarding the roads into the city. See *Washington-Writings*, Washington to Jameson, December 24, 1777, p. 199.

25. Henry Knox Papers, New England Historic Genealogical Society, Massachusetts Historical Society, Reel L111, p. 137, Knox to David Ramsay, for Ramsay's *History of the American Revolution*, 2 Vol. Trenton, 1811; *Sullivan-Letters*, Sullivan to Washington, December 26, 1777, Vol. I, pp. 602-03; *Correspondence of the American Revolution, being Letters of Eminent Men to George Washington*, Edited by Jared Sparks, Vol. II, pp. 63-4.

26. *Ibid.*

27. The Philadelphia campaign began with the sailing of the British fleet from New York carrying Sir William Howe's expeditionary force on board. On September 1, Daniel Wier, Commissary to the British Army in America, stated in a letter to John Robinson, Secretary to the Lords Commissioners in London that: "He supposes 20,000 men had been victual'd on board the transports at 2/3 allowance." Four days later at Head of Elk, Maryland, he filed a ration return showing 18,006 rank and file, exclusive of officers and 650 women and children who had received daily ration allotments during the voyage. In the British Headquarters Papers at the Public Record Office in London is a "Precis of the 1777-1778 Campaign," and a supplemental number of returns, obviously rough calculations, that are at a slight variance with Howe's official return of October 13, 1777. This latter return compiled after the battles of Brandywine, Germantown, and other engagements around Philadelphia, lists 17,752 on the regimental and battalion musters as present and fit for duty with an additional 2,612 sick and 850 wounded. To this number must be added a reinforcement division commanded by Sir Thomas Wilson of about 3,500 that reached the Delaware River shortly after the fall of Fort Mifflin. As eighteenth century muster rolls rarely removed those on command or killed in action or sick, Howe probably had at least 17,000 rank and file fit for duty exclusive of officers at the end of December. Sir Henry Clinton confirmed this number when on December 16, he wrote to his cousin the 2nd Duke of Newcastle, that as commander in New York he had "little more than 6,000 provincials (Loyalists)" while Howe had under arms in Philadelphia at least 17,000. University of Nottingham, Newcastle MSS, Clinton to Henry F. Clinton, 2nd Duke of Newcastle, December 16, 1777, NEW 2350; Public Record Office-London, British Headquarter Papers, Precis of Correspondence on Military Campaign, 1777-1778, Abstract of the State of the Forces under Sir William Howe, October 13, 1777, C.O. 5/253; HSP, Dreer Collection, Daniel Wier, Commissary to the British Army in America Correspondence [with John Robinson]; Jackson, *Pennsylvania Navy 1775-1781*, p. 272.

28. Washington apparently did not remain in the dark as to the number

of troops in Howe's command. Although written over two years later, he directed a circular to the States stating: "...in the winter of 77 at Valley Forge, within a days march of the enemy, with a little more than a third of their strength..." *Washington-Writings*, Circular to the States, October 18, 1780, Vol. XX, pp. 204-12.

29. National Library of Scotland (Edinburgh), Steuart Papers, Charles Steuart, MS5030, Sir James Murray to Charles Steuart, Esq., December 21, 1777, f168.

30. An analysis of British and Hessian journals support Baurmeister's statement that "the largeer part of the army" accompanied Howe. Montresor recorded that the army moved over the Schuylkill's two floating bridges, this would indicate that most army units crossed the Middle Bridge (modern Market Street). *Revolution in America...Confidential Letters...of Adjutant General Baurmeister*, Translated by Bernhard A. Uhlendorf (hereafter cited as *Baurmeister*), p. 145; *Major Andre's Journal*, edited by Henry Cabot Lodge (hereafter cited as *Andre's Journal*), Vol. I, p. 131; *Diary of the American War A Hessian Journal*, Captain Johann Ewald, edited by Joseph P. Tustin, p. 131; Scottish Record Office, General Register House, Edinburgh, Cunningham Thornton Papers 1776-82, Journal of Captain John Peebles, December 22-28, 1777, 21.492.4.

31. *Washington-Writings*, Washington to Potter, December 21, 1777, Vol. X, p. 182.

32. *Ibid.*, Washington to President of Congress, December 22, 1777, General Orders-After Orders, December 22, 1777, pp. 183-88, 189-92.

33. *Ibid.*, Washington to President of Congress, December 23, 1777, pp. 192-98; *PMHB*, "Memoirs of Brigadier-General John Lacey of Pennsylvania," Vol. XXVI, pp. 265-66, John Armstrong to Lacey, December 23, 1777.

34. *Washington-Writings*, Washington to Lord Stirling, December 27, 1777, General Orders, January 18, 1778, pp. 213, 312-15; Maryland Historical Society, Tench Tilghman Papers, Tilghman to General John Cadwalader, January 18, 1778; Henry Knox Papers, owned by the New England Historic Genealogical Society, deposited with the Massachusetts Historical Society, at David Library of the American Revolution, Reel L101, p. 137.

35. General Register House, Cunningham Thornton Papers, 1776-82, Journal of Captain John Peebles, December 22-28, 1777, 21.492.4; *Baurmeister*, pp. 147-49; *Andre's Journal*, Vol. I. pp. 131-34.

Chapter III

1. Continental officers entering the city under a flag of truce stated Sir William Howe referred to the Valley Forge Camp as a "Log Town."

2. *Washington-Writings*, General Orders, December 24, 1777, Vol. X, p. 200; *Weedon-Orderly Book*, p. 160. The ration at this time was usually one and a quarter pound of beef or pork, quarter pound of flour, half pint of rice and hopefully a half gill of rum.

3. *Washington-Writings*, General Orders, November 7, 1777, Vol. X, pp. 18-19; *Weedon-Orderly Book*, November 7, 1777, pp. 119-121, "Since the General left Germantown in the Middle of September last he has been without his baggage and on that account is unable to receive company in a manner he could wish; he nevertheless desires, the Generals, Field Officers, and Brigade Major of the day, to dine with him in the future, at three o'clock in the afternoon."

4. *Washington-Writings*, to Thomas Wharton, March 17, 1778, Vol. XI, pp. 267-68. Washington advised Wharton of Patrick Maguire's dismissal. He was very insolent "given to liquor" and Washington believed he took every opportunity of "defrauding me."

5. John C. Fitzpatrick, *The Spirit of the Revolution*, "General Washington's Valley Forge Expenses," pp. 88-93.

6. The aides-de-camp at the time were Lieutenant Colonels John Fitzgerald, John Laurens, Richard Kidder Meade, Alexander Hamilton, Robert Harrison, Presley Peter Thornton and Captain Tench Tilghman a volunteer aide. It is possible Lieutenant John Walker another aide was present.

7. *Washington-Writings*, General Orders, March 4, 1778, Vol. XI, p. 21.

8. *Laurens-Correspondence*, to Henry Laurens, January 1, 1778, pp. 98-101.

9. Meteorological Observations near Philadelphia January 1777-10 May 1778, [Phineas? Pemberton], American Philosophical Society (hereafter cited as APS).

10. Harold E. Selesky, *A Demographic Survey of the Continental Army that Wintered at Valley Forge, Pennsylvania, 1777-1778*, all demographic citations are taken from this excellent study.

11. Report of Joseph Galloway, Clements Library, Sackville-Germain Papers, 7:31, 46.

12. James Thacher, *Military Journal during the Revolutionary War from 1775 to 1783*, pp. 127-28; Colonel John N. Brooks to a friend, January 5, 1778, Massachusetts Historical Society, Miscellaneous Collection; Hiram Bingham, *Five Straws Gathered from Revolutionary Fields*, letters of William Weeks to Major William Weeks (father), February 16,

1778, pp. 23-25; *The Last Men of the Revolution*, Reverend E. B. Hillard, Edited by Wendell D. Garrett, p. 37.

13. Harold E. Selesky, *Demographic Survey-Valley Forge*, pp. 33-34, Tables 203-15.

14. *Washington-Writings*, General Orders, January 27, 1778, Vol. X, pp. 353-54; Huntington to Jeremiah Wadsworth, January 23, 1778, Connecticut Historical Society, Wadsworth Athenaeum Loan Collection.

15. A number of Jewish Americans were at Valley Forge, but more served with distinction as members of the various Philadelphia militia battalions. Edwin Wolf 2nd and Maxwell Whiteman, *The History of the Jews of Philadelphia from Colonial Times to the Age of Jackson*, pp. 79-97 passim; Jonathan Todd to his father, December 25, 1777, NA, RG 15, M806, roll 1561; A study by a national Park Ranger, Joseph Becton, "Black Soldiers at Valley Forge" is a fine analysis, but as Becton states additional research should be done. Becton in Appendix 1 presents Adjutant General Alexander Scammell's "Return of Negroes in the Army, 24th Aug. 1778." Scammell's Return is not definitive for Valley Forge as it included three regiments not at the encampment, and excluded four regiments and Knox's artillery that were at the camp.

16. *PMHB*, "Military Operations near Philadelphia in the Campaign of 1777-8," Vol. II, p. 294.

17. *Maine at Valley Forge*, Maine Society of the Sons of the American Revolution, Second Edition, p. 12.

18. C.A. Weslager, *The Log Cabin in America*, p. 14.

19. *Ibid.*, "Clapboards were split from a section of log, not sawn, by the use of a riving tool called a frow, a coarse knife with a wedge-shaped blade having a handle set at right angles. The blade was pounded with a wooden mallet called a frow club to split the clapboards from the log." (Should not be confused with today's longer clapboards).

20. Fraise were sharp pickets usually placed horizontally in the ramparts of fortifications to prevent an attacking force from scaling the wall.

21. *Washington-Writings*, General Orders, January 1, 1778, Vol. X, pp. 242-43.

22. *Ibid.*, to President of Congress, November 27, 1778, General Orders, December 14, 1778, Vol. XIII, pp. 350-52, 375; William Gifford to Colonel Benjamin Holme, January 12, 1779, New Jersey Historical Society.

23. Andrew Gray for Mark Bird to Colonel Jonathan Mifflin, December 22, 1777, Chicago Historical Society.

24. Jonathan Todd to Timothy Todd, January 19, 1778, RG15, M806, Roll 156. Todd was a surgeon's mate in the 7th Connecticut Regiment.

25. *Washington-Writings*, General Orders, January 9 and 13, 1778, Vol. X, pp. 283-5, 299-300.

26. *Ibid.*, General Orders, January 15, 1778, Vol. X, p. 306; Henry Woodman, *The History of Valley Forge*, p. 133.

27. 12th Virginia Continental Regiment Orderly Book, January 15, 1778, HSP; Henry Knox Papers, Knox to William Knox, May 27, 1778, Reel IV, David Library of the American Revolution (New England Historic Genealogical Society deposited in Massachusetts Historical Society).

28. The number of huts at the encampment have been variously estimated between 900 and 3,000, but it does not account for many huts or shed type structures built for service needs by the army. Also, not included were numerous surface huts constructed to quarter the reinforcements that arrived at Valley Forge in April and May. These huts were without fireplaces and most were replaced by tents as the weather moderated.

29. Jedediah Huntington to Matthew Irwin, January 20, 1778, HSP, Society Collection; *Washington-Writings*, General Orders, April 19, 25, and May 11, 1778, Vol. XI, pp. 280-1, 308-9, 375-7; *Journal of Du Roi the Elder*, December 16, 1778, p. 141.

30. Diary of Gideon Savage, member of Captain William Mills' Company of Artillery Artificers (in Colonel Jedutham Baldwin's Regiment of Artillery Artificers). Used with the permission of Stuart A. Goldman of Randolph, MA.

31. *Washington-Writings*, To John Parke Custis, February 1, 1778, Vol. X, pp. 413-14; *The Letters of Lafayette to Washington, 1777-1799*, Lafayette to Washington, February 9, 1778, pp. 24-25, Louis Gottschalk, ed.; Martha Washington to Mercy Warren, March 7, 1778, Adams-Warren Papers, Massachusetts Historical Society.

32. Diary of Joseph Clark, *Proceedings of the New Jersey Historical Society*, 1st Series, Vol. 7, December 19, 1777, p. 103; Journal of Lieutenant Thomas Blake, *History of the First New Hampshire Regiment*, Frederic Kidder, p. 40; *George Ewing, Gentleman, a Soldier at Valley Forge*, p. 25.

33. Archilaus Lewis to Jesse Partridge, February 1, 1778, Massachusetts State Archives, Government and Council Papers; Jonathan Todd to his father, Timothy Todd, December 25, 1777 and January 19, 1778, NA, RG15, M806, Roll 1151; *PMHB*, "Diary of Lieutenant James Mc-Michael...1777-1778," January 8, 1778, p. 157.

34. *Ibid.*; *George Ewing...Soldier...Valley Forge*, pp. 26, 33, 35.

35. Henry Woodman, *History of Valley Forge*, pp. 54-6; Benson J. Lossing, *Mary and Martha Washington*, pp. 170-1.

36. B.F. Stevens, *Facsimiles of Documents Relating to the American Revolution in European Archives, 1775-1783*, Vol. XXIV, Galloway to Serle, December 15, 1777, No. 2074, Galloway to Lord Dartmouth, January 20, 1778, No. 2078, March 4, 1778, No. 2090.

37. Thomas Anburey, *Travels through the Interior Parts of America*, Letter LX, December 17, 1778, Vol. II, pp. 171-2.

38. *Journal of Du Roi the Elder*, Translated by Charlotte S.J. Epping, December 16, 1778, p. 141.

39. *PMHB*, "Extracts from the Letter-Books of Lieutenant Enos Reeves," [Letter 202], September, 1781, Vol. XXI, p. 235.

40. *The Diaries of George Washington 1748-1799*, Edited by John C. Fitzpatrick, July 31, and August 19, 1787, Vol. III, pp. 230, 233.

41. This servant was probably Christopher, a young black man, who had replaced the aging but ever devoted Billy who had been by Washington's side throughout the war.

42. Henry Woodman, *The History of Valley Forge*, pp. 126-27; *The Diaries of George Washington 1748-1799*, John C. Fitzpatrick, editor, Vol. IV, p. 243.

Chapter IV

1. Supreme Executive Council, signed by Timothy Matlock, April 18, 1778, HSP, Miscellaneous Society Collection; Charles K. Bolton, *The Private Soldier Under Washington*, p. 78.

2. *Washington-Writings*, to John Cadwalader, March 20, 1778, Vol. XI, p. 117.

3. HSP, Order Book of Lieutenant John Irvin, Adjutant, 2nd Pennsylvania Regiment.

4. NA, Washington Papers, Nelson to Washington, June 30, 1778; Emory G. Evans, *Thomas Nelson of Yorktown*, p. 77.

5. Long Island Historical Society, Report of Captains Joseph Pettingill, John Wiley and Seth Drew to Baron de Kalb, December 20, 1777, Laurens Papers.

6. Greene to Samuel Chase, January 2, 1778, Greene Papers, Vol. II, pp. 242-45.

7. Burke Davis, *The Cowpens-Guilford Courthouse Campaign*, p. 101.

8. Butler to Wharton, February 12, 1778, Princeton University (also *P.A.* 1st Series, Vol. VI, pp. 252-53); Butler to Wharton, March 26, 1778, *PMHB*, Vol. XXVIII, pp. 376-77.

9. Carlton to Heath, January 28, 1778, Massachusetts State Archives, Government and Council Letters.

10. Platt to McDougall, December 29, 1777, January 24, 1778, Rosenbach Foundation.

11. Livingston to Robert B. Livingston, December 24, 1777, NYPL, RRL/Bancroft Transcripts.

12. Jones to Charles Stewart, February 18, 1778, NYSHA, Charles

Stewart Collection; Lewis to Lt. J. Partridge, February 1, 1778, Massachusetts State Archives, Government and Council Letters.

13. Cropper to his wife Peggy, March 13, 1778, Virginia Historical Society, MS/52 C8835.

14. Poor to a member of the New Hampshire Council, January 1, 1778, LC, Force MSS, Series 7E; Huntington to Governor Trumbull, February 20, 1778, Connecticut State Library, Trumbull Papers.

15. Paterson to Marshall, February 23, 1778, NJHS, MG14.

16. "Ebenezer Wild's Diary of the American Revolution," *Massachusetts Historical Society Proceedings*, Second Series, Vol. VI, p. 104.

17. Samuel Harris to his wife, March 14, 1778, Massachusetts Historical Society, Miscellaneous Collection.

18. Herbert T. Wade and Robert A. Lively, *This Glorious Cause,* Hodgkins to his wife, April 17, 1778, pp. 237-38. In an effort to capture the spirit of Hodgkin's letter it is printed verbatim, without changes in grammer, punctuation or orthography.

19. *Letters to Washington,* Jared Sparks, ed., Wharton to Washington, March 10, 1778, Vol. VII, pp. 82-83.

20. *Washington-Writings,* to Governor George Clinton, February 16, 1778, Vol. X, p. 469.

Chapter V

1. *Journals of the Continental Congress,* October 8, 1776, Vol. V, p. 855.

2. *Washington-Writings,* General Orders, July 24, 1776, Vol. V, p. 336.

3. *JCC,* September 6, 1777, Vol. VIII, p. 717.

4. *Ibid.,* November 14, 1777, Vol. IX, p. 905.

5. Edmund C. Burnett, *The Continental Congress,* p. 281; The Board of War was appointed of non-members of Congress in November 1777. Chosen were General Thomas Mifflin, Colonels Timothy Pickering and Robert H. Harrison, General Horatio Gates (as President), Joseph Trumbull and Richard Peters (as secretary). Harrison declined the appointment and Trumbull did not attend because of ill health. At best the board was lukewarm toward the Commander in Chief.

6. *Washington-Writings,* to Board of War, December 14, 1777; to Wharton, January 18, 1778, Vol. X, pp. 152-53, 317-19.

7. *JCC,* December 10 and 20, 1777, Vol. IX, pp. 1013, 1042-47.

8. *Washington-Writings,* to Board of War, February 10, 1778, Vol. X, pp. 443-44.

9. *Ibid.,* to Wharton, February 10, 1778, Vol. X, pp. 447-50.

10. *Ibid.,* to Henry, December 19 and 27, 1777, Vol. X, pp. 172-3,

208-10.

11. *Ibid.,* To Trumbull, January 24, 1778, Vol. X, pp. 344-46.

12. *Ibid.*, General Orders, January 1, 1778, to Board of War, January 2-3, 1778, Vol. X, pp. 242-43, 250-54.

13. *Ibid.*

14. *Ibid.*, to Board of War, January 2, 1778, Vol. X, pp. 250-53; NYPL, Emmet Collection, George Ross to Lieutenant Colonel Gibson, March 2, 1778.

15. *Washington-Writings*, to Putnam, February 26, 1778; to Mease, February 27, 1778, Vol. X, pp. 515-16, 523.

16. *Ibid.*, to Heath, January 9, 1778, to Putnam, January 22, 1778, to Mease, January 27, 1778, to Wharton, February 23, 1778, Vol. X, pp. 284-85, 334, 358, 501-3.

17. *Ibid.*, to Sullivan, February 25, 1778, Vol. X, pp. 516-17; to McDougall, March 27, 1778, vol. XI, p. 157; Dr. Henry S. Burrage, *Massachusetts at Valley Forge*, p. 14.

18. *Washington-Writings*, to President of Congress, April 10, 1778, Vol. XI, pp. 235-41.

19. LC, Force MSS, Series 7E, New Hampshire MSS, Poor to Meschech Weare, March 4, 1778.

20. Massachusetts State Archives, Government and Council Letters, Edward Mitchell to James Warren, Speaker Massachusetts General Court, March 2, 1778.

21. *Washington-Writings*, to Mease, April 17, 1778, Vol. XI, pp. 269-70.

22. *Ibid.*, General Orders, November 13, 17, 1775, Vol. VI, pp. 87, 96; *JCC,* November 4, 1775, Vol. III, pp. 323-24.

23. Baron de Kalb to Henry Laurens, January 7, 1778, Long Island Historical Society, Laurens Papers.

24. *Washington-Writings*, to Mease, July 18, 1777, Vol. VIII, pp. 432-33.

25. *Ibid.*, General Orders, October 8, 1777, Vol. IX, p. 341.

26. *Ibid.*, to Mease, November 12, 1777, General Orders, November 22, 1777, to Greene, November 22, 1777, Vol. X, pp. 45-46, 94-96.

27. LC, New Hampshire Council of Safety Papers, Samuel Hunt to Thomas Odiorne, January 23, 1778.

28. *Washington-Writings*, to Smallwood, January 3, 1778, General Orders, January 8 and 17, 1778, Vol. X, pp. 260-61, 276-77, 310-11, General Orders, March 6, 1778, Vol. XI, pp. 33-35.

29. *Ibid.*, General Orders, March 15, 1778, Vol. XI, pp. 84-86; *Sullivan Letters and Papers*, January 24, 1778, Vol. II, p. 17.

30. *Proceedings New Jersey Historical Society,* Vol. 50, p. 118; HSP, Society Collection, Robert L. Hooper to whom It May Concern, February

18, 1778.

31. *Washington-Writings,* General Orders, January 12, 1778, Vol. X, pp. 290-91; HSP, Society Collection, Orderly Book 12th Virginia Regiment, January 15, 1778; NYHS, 56.3, Orderly Book Captain Edward Lounsbury, Eight Company, 2nd New York Regiment, January 12, 1778; *Weedon Orderly Book,* January 12, 1778, p. 190; *Sullivan Letters and Papers,* January 24, 1777 [1778], p. 17; *The Art of Soap Making,* Marilyn Mohr, pp. 42-46, 78-80; *Colonial Craftsmen...,* Edwin Tunis, pp. 118-19; *JCC,* November 4, 1775, Vol. 3, p. 322; Erna Risch, *Supplying Washington's Army,* pp. 145, 190, 193, 245.

Chapter VI

1. *P.A.,* Jones to Wharton, December 19, 1777, 1st Series, Vol. Vi, pp. 107-8.

2. *Ibid.,* Supreme Executive Council to Delegates to Congress, December 20, 1777, Council to Deputy Wagon Masters, Circular December 22, and 26, 1777, pp. 116-17, 124, 136-37; many letters were exchanged on difficulties of renting horses and wagons, some may be found on pp. 210-12, 220-21, 252, 282-83, 289-90, 299, 320-29, 343-44, 357, 366-67, 384, 415-17, 438, 483, 513-14, 579; *Colonial Records,* Vol. XI, pp. 390, 429, 438; Tench Tilghman to Biddle, February [?], 1778, HSP, Clement Biddle Papers; Biddle to Washington, January 25, 1778, Valley Forge National Historical Park, John Reed Collection; Lutterloh to Washington, February 17, 1778, N.A. Papers of Continental Congress, Reel 199; Berks County in the Revolution, Vol. I, pp. 176-79.

3. *Colonial Records,* Council to Jefferies, March 9, 1777, Vol. XI, p. 349.

4. Colonel Henry Emanuel Lutterloh had been a major in the Quartermaster Department of the army of Brunswick. Washington considered his experience a valuable asset and he was appointed a deputy on June 14, 1777. At the beginning of the Valley Forge encampment he was one of the few competent members of an otherwise chaotic Quartermaster Department.

5. *Colonial Records,* Council to Lutterloh, March 10, 1777, December 24, 1777, Vol. XI, pp. 352-53, 390.

6. *P.A.,* Hamilton to Lutterloh, Lutterloh to Matlack, February 20, 1778, Vol. VI, p. 283.

7. *Ibid.,* Blaine to Wharton, February 12, 1778, p. 252.

8. Gloucester County Historical Society, John Ladd Howell Correspondence.

9. Connecticut Historical Society, Jeremiah Wadsworth Papers, Lutter-

loh to Deputy Quartermaster Generals in New England; *Colonial Records,* February 26, 1778, p. 429; *New Jersey in the Revolution, Newspaper Extracts,* April 28, 1778, p. 199.

10. *Washington-Writings,* to Lutterloh, December 20, 1777, Vol. X, p. 179.

11. NA, Tench Tilghman to Washington, February 19, 1778, Reel 47; Livingston to Washington, January 12, 1778, Reel 46.

12. *Ibid.; Washington-Writings,* to Jameson, April 4, 1778, Vol. XI, p. 213.

13. *P.A.,* 1st Series, Vol. VI, Blaine to Wharton, February 12, 1778, Chaloner to Young (Wagon Master General for Pennsylvania) March 2, 1778, Flower to Council, April 28, 1778, pp. 252, 320, 450.

14. Erna Risch, *Supplying Washington's Army,* p. 220.

15. LC, James Lovell to [Wharton], January 5, 1778, E.C. Burnett Collection, original in Howard Library. In mid-February a "Gang of Villians" and "a number of considerable persons [of]...Estates chiefly County people...some were apprehended in the vilanous practice of purchasing Horses for the use of Genl. Howe's Army." This conduct of civilians occurred in Lancaster County. HSP, Gratz Collection, American officers in the Revolution, Lieutenant Adam Hubley to [Wharton or Washington], February 9, 1778, George Gibson to same February 10, 1778.

16. NA, Greene to Washington, February 15 and 17, 1778, Washington Papers, Reel 47; same in *Greene Papers,* Vol. II, pp. 285, 289-90.

17. *Washington-Writings,* General Orders, April 22, 1778, to Governor Thomas Johnson, March 21, 1778, pp. 123-24, 298-99.

18. *Ibid.,* to Putnam, February 6, 1778, Vol. X, p. 423.

19. *Ibid.,* to Trumbull, February 6, 1778, Vol. X, pp. 423-24.

20. Deputy Purchasing Commissary for New Jersey, Pennsylvania and Maryland.

21. Deputy Commissary General of Purchases.

22. *Washington-Writings,* to Champion, February 7, 1778, Vol. X, pp. 475-77.

23. Commissary General of Purchases.

24. *Washington-Writings,* to Buchanan, February 7, 1778, Vol. X, p. 427.

25. *Ibid.,* to Champion, March 9, 1778, Vol. XI, pp. 54-55.

26. *Ibid.,* to Greene, February 12, 1778, Vol. X, pp. 454-55.

27. *Ibid.,* to Lee, February 16, 21, and 25, 1778, Vol., X, pp. 462-68, 491-92, 513-14.

28. *Ibid.,* to Greene, February 12, 1778, Vol. X, pp. 454-55; Lee to Wayne, February 12, 1778, *Greene's Writings,* Vol. 2, pp. 282-83f2.

29. *Ibid.,* to Washington, February 20, 1778, Vol. 2, p. 292.

30. *Pennsylvania Ledger*, February 25, 1778; Archibald Robertson, *His Diaries and Sketches in America 1762-1780*, p. 163; Scottish Record Office, Cunningham of Thornton Papers, Journal of Captain John Peebles, February 24-25, March 2, 1778, 21.492.5; Wayne to Washington, NA, Washington Papers, Reel 47, February 23, 25, and 26, March 14, 1778; Ibid., Barry to Washington, February 26, 1778.

31. *New Jersey Privy Council Minutes,* Vol. I, February 23, 1778, p. 63.

32. Authorities which include details of Wayne's expedition include: NA, Washington Papers, Reel 47, Wayne to Washington, February 23, 25 (2 letters), 26, March 5, 14, 1778, Ellis to Wayne, February 1778, Livingston to Ellis, January 8, 1778, Reel 46; Wayne to Captain Thos. Woodbridge, Connecticut Historical Society, Woodbridge Papers; Charles J. Stille, *Major General Wayne,* Wayne to Washington, March 4, 1778, pp. 131-33; William and Ruth Timmins, *The Great "Cow Chase" 1776-1976,* passim; Frank H. Stewart, *Foraging for Valley Forge, General Anthony Wayne,* passim; Jackson, *British Army in Philadelphia,* pp. 80-81, 181.

33. Blaine to Chaloner & White, HSP, Chaloner-White MSS, February 22, 1778; Blaine to Stewart, February 18, 1778, NYSHA, Stewart Collection. Blaine's letters prior to these dates were written at the main encampment. However, the Commissary is known to have had at least a magazine at Pawling's prior to these dates; Thomas Jones, Deputy Commissary of Issues, noted on February 15, that at least 242 barrels of flour was stored at that location. Jones to Charles Stewart, February 15, 1778, NYSHA, Stewart Collection.

34. Plucks were the organs such as heart, liver and lungs, etc. used as food, but usually ignored by the army butchers.

35. *Washington-Writings,* General Orders, January 13, 1778, Vol. X, pp. 297-300.

36. *JCC*, May 3, 1777, Vol VII, pp. 323-24. As pointed out by Dr. H.J. Eckenrode, most eighteenth century families in the winter "lived on meat and bread" without fresh fruit or vegetables and no method of canning or preserving. While he stated this diet was normal in Virginia, it applied to most Americans and was therefore acceptable—when available—to the soldiers at Valley Forge. H.J. Eckenrode, *The Randolphs The Story of a Virginia Family,* p. 68.

37. *JCC,* July 23, 1777, Vol. VIII, pp. 574-75.

38. *Ibid.*, November 24, 1777, Vol. IX, p. 960.

39. *Ibid.*, January 14, 15, 1778, Vol. IX pp. 48-53.

40. *Ibid.*, February 27, 1778, Vol. X, pp. 206-07, Ludwick was to receive fifty dollars per month and three rations a day; the sub-directors forty dollars per month and two rations a day; the foremen thirty dollars

a month and one ration; while the journeymen bakers were to receive twenty-four dollars a month and one ration; Papers of the Continental Congress, No. 147, folio 133; *Pennsylvania Packet,* March 2, 1778.

41. *PMHB,* "Christopher Ludwick Patriotic Gingerbread Baker," Wm. W. Condit, Vol. LXXXI, p. 381.

42. *Bulletin of Historical Society of Montgomery County,* "An Account of the Life and Character of Christopher Ludwick," Benjamin Rush, J.F. Reed, editor, Spring, 1980, pp. 149-64.

43. *Ibid.*

44. *PP.,* "Aspects of Wood in Valley Forge Encampment," E. Clyde Pyle, August 1965.

45. *Letters of the Delegates,* Committee at Camp to Henry Laurens, February [12?], 1778, Vol. IX pp. 82-85.

46. *Ibid.*

47. *JCC,* April 14, 1777, Vol. VII, pp. 266-67; *Washington-Writings,* to President of Congress and General Orders, December 22, 1777, pp. 183-84, 192.

48. *JCC,* April 14, 1777, Vol. VII, pp. 266-67; Tyler to Jackson, March 4, 1778, American Philosophical Society (also David Library of the Revolution), Feinstone Collection.

49. LC, Washington Papers, Scammel to Laurens, February 25, 1778, Reel 47.

50. Samuel Gray to Charles Stewart, February 24, 1778, NYSHA, Stewart Collection.

51. John F. Reed, "Clement Biddle at Moore Hall," *Bulletin of the Historical Society of Montgomery County,* Vol. XXII, No. 3, pp. 251-52.

52. *PA.,* 1st Series, Vol. VI, pp. 240-41; *JCC,* Resolution of Congress, February 17, 1778, Vol. X (also in *PA.* 1st Series, Vol. VI, p. 272).

53. *Washington-Writings,* to President of Congress, December 15, 1777 and January 5, 1778; to Buchanan, December 28, 1777, Vol. X, pp. 159, 217, and 267.

54. *Ibid.*, to Trumbull, February 6, 1778, to George Clinton, February 16, to Thomas Johnson, February 16, Henry Champion, February 17, to Patrick Henry, February 19, Vol. X, pp. 423-24, 469, 471-74, 483-85; Blaine to Stewart, December 26, 1777, NYSHA, Stewart Collection.

55. Chaloner to H. Champion, March 17, 1778, Connecticut Historical Society; William Shannon to Henry Hollingsworth, March 15, 1778, American Philosophical Society, Feinstone Collection.

56. *JCC,* March 13 and April 9, 1778, Vol. X, pp. 248-49, 327.

57. HSP, Resolution of Congress, April 17, 1778, Society Collection; Howell to Chaloner, February 26, 1778, Morristown National Historical Park, Smith Collection.

58. *Washington-Writings,* to Wharton, April 17, 1778, Vol. XI, pp.

267-68.

59. Colonel William Malcolm's Additional Continental Regiment Orderly Book, April 26, 1778, NYHS.

60. Howell to Governor George Johnson, March 31, 1778, Glassboro (New Jersey) College, Stewart MSS., 358.8.

61. NYPL, Letters of Charles Blagden, April 20, 1778; PP, 1946, p. 63; Jackson, *British Army in Philadelphia*, pp. 229-30.

62. H.E. Wildes, *Valley Forge*, p. 179; *Washington-Writings*, General Orders, March 19, 1778, Vol. XI, p. 107.

63. *Ibid.*, General Orders, May 14, 1778, Vol. XI, p. 387; *Elijah Fisher's Journal...War of Independence.*

64. Lieutenant Colonel Issac Sherman, 2nd Connecticut Regiment Orderly Book, March 22, 1778, Connecticut Historical Society; William Harris to ?, Washington Papers, Morristown National Historical Park.

65. *Washington-Writings*, General Orders, January 20, 1778, Vol. X, p. 321.

66. *Ibid.*, General Orders, February 8, 1778, Vol. X, pp. 436-37.

67. *Ibid.*, General Orders, April 17, 1778, Vol. XI, p. 271.

68. Jackson, *Whitemarsh 1777*, pp. 24-25.

69. *Washington-Writings*, General Orders, January 26, 1778, Vol. X, pp. 350-51, Prices were set at: "Peach brandy by the quart at 7/6; by the Pint 4/ , by the Gill 1/3. Whiskey and Apple brandy at 6/ pr. quart, 3/6 pr. pint and 1/ by the gill. Cyder at 1/3 by the quart; Strong beer 2/6 by the quart. Common beer 1/ by the quart. Vinegar 2/6 by the quart."

70. *Ibid.*, General Orders, February 19, 1778, Vol. X, p. 481.

71. *Ibid.*, General Orders, March 22, 1778, Vol. XI, p. 132.

72. *Ibid.*, General Orders, March 28, 1778, Vol. XI, p. 162; Other prices set were "West-India rum or Spirit at 15/ ; Continental rum 10/ ; Gin 9/ ; French brandy 19/ , and Cyder royal 2/ pr quart and in larger or smaller quantities at the same rates." These prices except for Cyder Royal are for gallons.

73. *Ibid.*, General Orders, April 16, 1778, Vol. XI, pp. 264-65; The prices are similar to those issued on March 28 with some additions: "Whiskey, Peach Brandy, Apple Brandy, Cordials of all kinds and any other home-made spirits at 15/ pr. gallon, pr. quart 4/ , pr pint 2/ , pr. half pint 1/3. West India spirit pr. quart full proof, 15/ , a bowl of toddy containing a half pint of spirit 7/6;...."

Chapter VII

1. National Archives, RG 93, 138 rolls including those rolls of units at Valley Forge; Charles H. Lesser, Ed., *The Sinews of Independence*, pp.

54-57, analysis of rolls of December 31, 1777.

2. *Washington-Writings*, General Orders, January 25, 1778, Vol. X, pp. 347-48.

3. *Ibid.*, General Orders, December 26, 1777, Vol. X, pp. 206-07.

4. Charles H. Lesser, ed., *The Sinews of Independence*, pp. 54-69; *Washington-Writings*, General Orders, December 22, 1777, Vol. X, pp. 189-90, Washington to Heath, April 8, 1778, Vol. XI, pp. 226-27.

5. *Ibid.*, General Orders, December 22, 1777, Vol. X, pp. 188-90.

6. *Ibid.*, to Wayne, December 23, 1777, to Glover, February 18, 1778, Vol. X, pp. 226-27, 477-78, to Varnum, April 9, 1778, Vol. XI, pp. 229-30.

7. *Ibid.*, to Sullivan, February 14, 1778, Vol. X, pp. 160-61.

8. *Ibid.*, General Orders, March 15, 1778, Vol. XI, pp. 84-5.

9. *Laurens Correspondence*, to Henry Laurens, March 9, 1778, pp. 135-36; *PMHB*, "General Duportail at Valley Forge," Elizabeth S. Kite, Vol. LVI, pp. 343-44.

10. *Washington-Writings*, General Orders, January 15, 1778, Vol. X, p. 306; *PMHB*, "Orderly Book of General Edward Hand," Vol. XLI, p. 260.

11. Paul K. Walker, *Engineers of Independence*, pp. 32-33.

12. *Ibid.*, p. 39, "the sappers and miners main task was to construct field work as directed by the engineers, but when stationed at the head of the army on the march they were to perform the duties of pioneers, clearing roads of obstructions and making repairs."

13. Duportail to Washington, January 20, 1778, Boston Public Library; *Brigadier General Louis Le Bégue Duportail*, Elizabeth S. Kite, pp. 47-50; *Records of the American Catholic Historical Society*, "General Washington and the Engineers, Duportail and Companions," Elizabeth S. Kite, Vol. XLIII, pp. 110-13; Paul K. Walker, *Engineers of Independence*, pp. 34-36.

14. *Washington-Writings*, to The Committee of Congress with the Army, January 29, 1778, Vol. X, p. 399, General Orders, February 8, 1778, Vol. X, p. 433.

15. Paul K. Walker, *Engineers of Independence*, p. 36.

16. *Laurens Correspondence*, to Henry Laurens, January 1, 1778, pp. 98-101.

17. *Washington-Writings*, to President of Congress, December 22, 1777, to Thomas Wharton, Jr., January 1, 1778, Vol. X, pp. 183-87, 246-47; HSP, Dreer Collection, Soldiers of the Revolution, Erskine to Greene, January 12, 1778.

18. *Washington-Writings*, to Smallwood, December 29, 1777, pp. 218-20.

19. An abatis was a barrier of felled trees with the branches sharpened and faced outward toward an advancing enemy. Fraise were pointed stakes or pickets, pointing outward in an horizontal position from the

ramparts or walls of an earthen redoubt or fort. Sometimes fraise or pickets were pounded into the ground fronting an earthwork, with their points at a slightly oblique angle. Fascines were bundles of long sticks used to reinforce the building of earthworks. In building breastworks or redoubts, fascines were anchored and held in place by wooden frames called chandeliers. Gabions were basket type cylinders made of branches and filled with earth.

20. Sir George Otto Trevelyan, *The American Revolution,* Part III, f2, pp. 290-91.

21. Duportail to Stirling, April 7, 1778, New York Public Library, Emmet Collection.

22. *Washington-Writings,* General Orders, April 2, 1778, Vol. XI, pp. 199-200.

23. Orderly Book, 12th Virginia Regiment, January 13, 1778, HSP, Miscellaneous Collection.

24. *Weedon-Orderly Book,* Division Orders, January 20, 1778, pp. 201-02.

25. Orderly Book, January 27, 1778. This orderly book is believed to be that of General Enoch Poor. Huntington Library, HM 634.

26. *Proceedings of the New Jersey Historical Society,* Gifford to Holmes, January 24, 1778, 1st Series, Vol. 7, p. 104.

27. Rosenbach Foundation, Richard Platt to McDougall, January 24, 1778; Frederic Kidder, *History of the First New Hampshire Regiment,* "Journal Lieutenant Thomas Blake,: p. 40.

28. *PMHB,* "Dr. Physick and His House," [George B. Roberts], Vol. XCII, p. 67.

29. Henry Woodman, *The History of Valley Forge,* p. 53; Thomas Anburey, *Travels Through the Interior Parts of America, 1776-1781,* Vol. II, pp. 170-71.

30. Gates Papers, Conway to Gates, November 11, 1777 and January 4, 1778; *Journals of Continental Congress,* Worthington C. Ford, ed., Vol. 9, p. 1026; Robert K. Wright, Jr., *The Continental Army,* pp. 122-23.

31. Rosenbach Foundation, Platt to McDougall, December 29, 1777, January 24, 1778; Connecticut Historical Society, Huntington Papers, Huntington to Jabez Huntington, December 29, 1777.

32. Conway to Washington, Washington Papers, December 29, 1777; *Washington-Writings,* Vol. X, pp. 226-27f.

33. *Ibid.*

34. *Ibid.*

35. *Weedon-Orderly Book,* January 9, 1778, p. 188.

36. *Letters of the Delegates to Congress* [hereafter cited as *Letters-Delegates*], Reed to Thomas Wharton, February 1, 1778, Vol. IX, pp. 4-6; *Washington-Writings,* to Committee of Congress, January 29, 1778, Vol.

X, p. 362f.

37. *Letters-Delegates*, Gerry to Washington, January 13, 1778, Vol. VIII, pp. 575-77.

38. *Ibid.*, Committee to Henry Laurens, February 6, 1778, to George Clinton, February 17, 1778, Joseph Reed to John Bayard, March 8?, 1778, Committee to Livingston, February 13, 1778, Vol. IX, pp. 36-38, 112-13, 241-43.

39. New York Public Library, Ward to Adams, January 26, 1778, Miscellaneous Manuscripts.

40. Ward, despite his feelings about the regular army, served throughout the war and never wavered in his loyalty to the rights of Americans. When the war began he was aide-de-camp to General Artemus Ward. After serving several years as Commissary General of Musters, he was named Commissary General of Prisoners in 1780, and continued in that station until the end of the war. New York Public Library, Miscellaneous Manuscripts, Ward to Adams, January 26, 1778.

41. *Washington-Writings,* to Committee, January 29, 1778, Vol. X, pp. 362-404, 403f. The report submitted to the Committee, apparently after prior consultation with the General Staff and Committee, was endorsed by Francis Dana. The original of thirty-eight pages is in the Washington Papers.

42. Edmund Burnett, *The Continental Congress,* pp. 298-316 passim; *Letters-Delegates*, Committee to Washington, February 11, 1778, Vol. IX, pp. 75-77, (Papers of the Continental Congress, Roll 40).

43. *Ibid.*, Reed to Jonathan Bayard Smith, February 5, 1778, Vol. IX, pp. 57-61, George Frost to Josiah Bartlett, January 31, 1778, Vol. VIII, pp. 695-96.

44. *Ibid.*, Thomas Burke to Richard Caswell, April 9, 1778, James Lovell to John Adams, May 15, 1778, Vol. IX, pp. 394-95, 675-76.

45. *Washington-Writings,* to the Congressional Committee, March 1, 6, 19, 1778, Vol. XI, pp. 1-2, 31, 111, to William Livingston, February 14, 1778, Vol. X, pp. 459-60.

46. *Ibid.*; *Letters-Delegates*, Joseph Reed to Jonathan Bayard Smith, February 19, 1778, Reed to John Bayard, March 8?, 1778, Abraham Clark to Wadsworth, March 29, 1778, James Lovell to Joseph Trumbull, April 13, 1778, Vol. IX, pp. 141-43, 241-43, 349-50, 407.

Chapter VIII

1. It is claimed when Steuben received the title of Baron, it is believed to have been conferred on him by the Prince Hozenzollern-Hechinger.

2. N.A. Papers of the Continental Congress, Deane to Morris, Roll 181;

John McAuley Palmer, *General Von Steuben,* pp. 63-4.

3. *Ibid.,* p. 115; *Washington-Writings,* to President of Congress, February 27, 1778, Vol. X, pp. 518-19.

4. *John Laurens Correspondence,* to Henry Laurens, February 28, 1778, pp. 131-33. Steuben could neither speak nor write English, but was conversant with the French language. To bridge the communication gap, Washington appointed three aides-de-camp to translate and transcribe for the Prussian. John Laurens, Alexander Hamilton and Tench Tilghman were all fluent in French, with Laurens assigned as principal aide.

5. *Ibid.,* March 9, 1778, pp. 134-41.

6. *Washington-Writings,* General Orders, March 13, 1778, Vol. XI, pp. 74-6.

7. *Ibid.,* General Orders, March 13 and May 4, 1778, Vol. XI, pp. 74-6, 346-47.

8. *Ibid.,* General Orders, April 8 and 9, 1778, Vol. XI, pp. 228-31.

9. *Ibid.,* General Orders, March 17 and 19, 1778, Vol. XI, pp. 98, 108.

10. *Ibid.*

11. *Ibid.,* General Orders, March 22, 28, and 29, 1778, Vol. XI, pp. 132, 162-63, 173-75. The officers accepting the post of Sub-Inspector were Lieutenant Colonels William Davies, 5th Virginia; John Brooks, 8th Massachusetts and Francis Barber, 3rd New Jersey. Jean Baptiste Ternant was assigned as a volunteer, but soon became a Deputy Quartermaster General and by September 1778 Lieutenant Colonel and Inspector of the Continental Army. One day later the Brigade Inspectors were announced including Colonel Benjamin Tupper, 11th Massachusetts; Lieutenant Colonel Ebenezer Sprout, 4th Massachusetts; and Majors Gustavus B. Wallace, 15th Virginia; Samuel J. Cabbel, 14th Virginia; William Hull, 8th Massachusetts; Nicholas Fish, 2nd New York; Joseph Bloomfield, 3rd New Jersey; Michael Ryan, 10th Pennsylvania; John Huling, 3rd Pennsylvania. Captains named were Royal Smith, Stanton's Rhode Island State, (Varnum); Thomas Converse, 3rd Connecticut; John Ingles, 2nd North Carolina; John McGovern, 4th Pennsylvania. Captain Benjamin Walker apparently acted as a volunteer to Steuben, and later became his aide-de-camp and lifelong friend. Steuben is reported to have said that Walker's offer was like an "angel from heaven."

12. *Ibid.,* General Orders, April 19, 1778, Vol. XI, pp. 250-51; The assignments for Ternant were the Woodford, Scott and McIntosh brigades; the 1st and 2nd Pennsylvania regiments and Glover and Poor's brigades were Brook's responsibility; Davies had the brigades of Learned, Paterson, Weedon and Muhlenberg; Barber those of Maxwell, late Conway, Huntington and Varnum.

13. *Ibid.,* General Orders, March 28, 1778, Vol. XI, pp. 162-63; Steuben to H. Laurens, March 12, 1778, Laurens Papers, Long Island Historical

Society.

14. *Washington-Writings,* General Orders, May 9, 1778, pp. 366-67; Steuben to H. Laurens, May 15, 1778, Laurens Papers, Long Island Historical Society.

15. *Ibid.*, Steuben to Laurens, April 2, 1778; Steuben to Gates, March 21, 1778, Gates Papers, New York Historical Society.

16. Orderly Books of Richard C. Anderson, Virginia State Library; Orderly Book of Nathaniel Webb, Lloyd W. Smith Collection, Morristown National Historical Park; *A Salute to Courage, The American Revolution as Seen Through Wartime Writings of Officers of the Continental Army and Navy,* Dennis P. Ryan, ed., pp. 79-83.

17. The Military Instructions of Baron Steuben to Washington, given at Valley Forge for the Re-organization of the Revolutionary Army. The three papers were "The Distributions of the Principal Departments of the Prussian Army, together with the Duties of the Staff Officers at the Head of each Department," second "A Scheme of a Body of Light Troops, divided in Two Legions," and directly pertinent to Valley Forge, "A Few Observations made on my reconnoitering the Camp, march ye 5th, 1778," Chicago Historical Society; The French version of the third paper is in the Manuscript Collection, American Antiquarian Society.

18. *Ibid.*

19. Knox to his brother, May 27, 1778, Knox Papers, Reel IV, Massachusetts Historical Society; *Washington-Writings,* General Orders, April 2, 1778, Vol. XI, pp. 199-200.

20. Duportail to Stirling, April 7, 1778, New York Public Library, Emmett Collection.

21. J. Laurens to Pettit, April 14, 1778, HSP, Dreer Collection, Soldiers of the Revolution.

22. *Ibid.*, Laurens to Stirling, April 15, 1778, Stirling to Pettit, April 16, 1778; Caleb North to [Stirling], May 2, 1778, LC, Mrs. Archibald Crossley Autograph Collection.

23. *Washington-Writings,* General Orders, April 2 and 3, 1778, Vol. XI, pp. 199-202.

24. Duportail to Stirling, April 13, 1778, Washington Papers, Morristown National Historical Park; "General Washington and the French Engineers Duportail and Companions," *Records of the American Catholic Historical Society,* Elizabeth S. Kite, Duportail to Washington, April 13, 1778, pp. 116-17.

25. *Washington-Writings,* to Stirling, May 11, 1778, Vol. XI, p. 374.

26. Howe to Germain, April 19, 1778, Clements Library, Germain Papers.

Chapter IX

1. Frederic Kidder, *History of the First New Hampshire Regiment in the War of the Revolution*, "Journal of Lieutenant Thomas Blake," p. 40.
2. *PMHB*, "Delaware Memorial at Valley Forge," Vol. XXXIX, p. 75; *Washington-Writings*, to Smallwood, December 19, 1777, Vol. X, pp. 171-72.
3. *Ibid.*, to Read, December 19, 1777, pp. 174-75.
4. Morris A. Barr and Leta Bender, *Immortalizing the Sentry Tree of George Washington*, pp. 13-15, 19. Barr and Bender list a number of residents who saw the sentry trees, which, with a few personal interviews by the author, confirm the trees' locations mentioned by Mr. Burns; *Tredyffrin Easttown History Club Quarterly*, "New Light on the Encampment of the Continental Army at Valley Forge," Franklin L. Burns, July 1939, pp. 51-71.
5. *Ibid.*; *PP*, "The Stone Chimney Picket," S. Paul Teamer, October 1939, pp. 104-06; *PP*, "Old Stone Chimney Picket Site Vital Outpost for Valley Forge," S. Paul Teamer, April, 1946, pp. 34-5.
6. *Ibid.*, Submitted by Ronald E. Heaton, July, 1961, p. 41.
7. Jackson, *Pennsylvania Navy*, p. 285; William Bell Clark, *Gallant John Barry*, pp. 142-44.
8. John Almon and John Debret, *Parliamentary Register or History of the Proceedings and Debates of the House of Commons*, Howe to Germain, April 19, 1778, Vol. XI, pp. 464-65; Clements Library, Howe's Orderly Book, January 16, 1778; Scottish Record Office, Cunningham Thornton Papers, Journal of Captain John Peebles, February 4, 1778, 21.492.4&5.; *PMHB*, "Extracts from the Journal of Elizabeth Drinker," Vol. XIV, p. 303.
9. *Washington-Writings*, to President of Congress, January 2, 1778, to Clark, January 24, 1778, Vol. X, pp. 250, 346-47; John Bakeless, *Turncoats, Traitors and Heroes*, pp. 173-215, passim.
10. Occasionally John Craig has been identified as Major Charles Craig, who was also engaged in the intelligence service.
11. Over 200 merchants with an inventory of various commodities had entered the city from New York.
12. *Washington-Writings*, to Clark, December 16, 1777, Vol. X, p. 164; NYHS, Scammel to McLane, May 20, 1778, McLane Papers.
13. "Letters from Major John Clark to George Washington," *Historical Society of Pennsylvania Bulletin*, No. 1; *PMHB*, "The Diary of Robert Morton," Vol. I, No. 1, pp. 19-20; NYHS, "A Letter brought to me by a Spy sent into the City of Philadelphia," by order of General Washington, (unsigned); N.A., Washington Papers, Reel 45; John Bakeless, *Turncoats, Traitors and Heroes*, pp. 173-215, passim.

14. NYHS, Lacey to Washington, April 29, 1778, Lacey Papers.

15. *Ibid.*, Lacey to Council, March 4, 1778, Lacey Papers; Huntington Library, Lacey to Washington, February 20, 1778, Lacey Papers; *Washington-Writings*, General Orders, March 25, and April 18, 1778, Vol. XI, pp. 143, 274.

16. NYHS, McLane Papers.

17. HSP, Lacey to Washington, January 26, 1778, Dreer Collection; Huntington Library, Lacey to Washington, February 20, 1778, Lacey Papers; NYPL, Benjamin Ford to Daniel Morgan, May 25, 1778, Myers MSS. 853.

18. Clements Library, Howe's Orderly Book, December 30, 1777, January 7 and 10, 1778.

19. Extract from a letter of Matilda Myers Law, Wilbur, Nebraska, July 9, 1891; Papers of the Von Myer Family, copied by H.B. Irey, West Chester, Pennsylvania. For this data the author is indebted to the late Mrs. Robert E. Frith.

20. *Washington-Writings*, to Chambers, February 27, 1778, Vol. X, pp. 522-23.

21. Frank H. Stewart, *Salem County in the Revolution*, passim; Jackson, *British Army in Philadelphia*, pp. 181-83, 327-28f10 (for other authorities).

22. *Ibid.*, pp. 223-25, 327f7, 8 and 9 (for other authorities and depositions of witnesses); *Bulletin of the Historical Society of Montgomery County*, "General Lacey's Campaign in 1778," Charles Harper Smith, Vol. II, No. 4, pp. 286-293.

23. Jackson, *British Army in Philadelphia*, pp. 225-26, 327f10; *Pennsylvania Navy*, pp. 295-98, 46f28 (for other authorities).

24. *Washington-Writings*, General Orders, January 20, 1778, Vol. X, p. 321; *New Jersey Gazette*, January 28, 1778; *Tredyffrin Easttown History Club Quarterly*, "New Light on the Encampment of the Continental Army at Valley Forge," Franklin L. Burns, July, 1939.

25. *Washington-Writings*, to Lafayette, May 18, 1778, Vol. XI, pp. 418-19.

26. Local tradition says the obese Grant stopped for refreshments at the Broad Axe Tavern. This appears to be improbable as the column passed this point between 4:00 and 5:00 A.M.

27. C. Stedman, *The History of...the American War*, Vol. 2, pp. 420-23; *Montressor Journals*, Ed. G.D. Scull, pp. 492-93; J. Simcoe, *Military Journal*, pp. 60-61; *PMHB*, "Letters of Major Baurmeister during the Philadelphia Campaign 1777-1778," Edited by B.A. Uhlendorf and Edna Vosper, Vol. LX, pp. 176-78; W.H. Wilkins, *Some British Soldiers in America*, W. Hale to his parents, June 15, 1778, pp. 252-57; Scottish Record Office, Cunningham of Thornton Papers, Journal of Captain John

Peebles, May 20, 1778, 21,492.5; HSP, Journal of Sergeant Thomas Sullivan, May 19-20; Massachusetts Historical Society, Dudley Coleman to his wife, May 22, 1778, Coleman Papers; *Pennsylvania Packet,* June 3, 1778; *Pennsylvania History*, "The Comic Opera that made a General," Wm. J. Wilcox, Vol. 13, pp. 265-73; *Sketches of the Montgomery County Historical Society,* "Lafayette at Barren Hill," Irvin C. Williams, Vol. 2, pp. 291-305; *Ibid.*, "Lafayette's Retreat from Barren Hill," Levi Streeper, Vol. 2, pp. 268-81; *PP,* "Lafayette's Escape from the British at Barren Hill in the Spring of 1778," James K. Helms, 1945, pp. 9-13; Jackson, *British Army in Philadelphia*, pp. 226-29, 328f11-15 for description of some British units engaged and other authorities.

28. Frederick Wagner, *Submarine Fighter of the American Revolution,* pp. 84-89; *New Jersey Gazette,* January 21, 1778; *Pennsylvania Ledger,* February 11, 1778; Jackson, *British Army in Philadelphia*, p. 179; Jackson, *Pennsylvania Navy,* pp. 288-89.

Chapter X

1. *Weedon Orderly Book*, December 26, 1777, pp. 169-70.
2. *Washington-Writings,* Circular to the States, December 29, 1777, Vol. X, pp. 223-24.
3. *Ibid.*, to Livingston, December 31, 1777, Vol. X, pp. 231-34.
4. *Ibid.*, General Orders, January 2, 1778, Vol. X, p. 248.
5. HSP, Papers of Jonathan Potts, Craik to Potts, May 15, 1778; Mary C. Gillett, *The Army Medical Department 1775-1818,* p. 87.
6. *Washington-Writings,* General Orders, January 6, 1778, Vol. X, p. 272.
7. *Ibid.*, January 9, 1778, Vol. X, p. 284.
8. HSP, Peters to Morris, February 3, 1778, Dreer Collection.
9. *Washington-Writings*, to Rush, January 12, 1778, Vol. X, pp. 296-97.
10. *Ibid.*, to The Committee of Congress with the Army, [January 29, 1778], Vol. X, pp. 362-403.
11. *JCC.*, February 6, 1778, Vol. 5, pp. 128-131.
12. *Weedon Orderly Book,* February 26, 1778, pp. 242-43; Orderly Book, Lieutenant Colonel Isaac Sherman, 2nd Connecticut Regiment, March 14, 1778, Connecticut Historical Society.
13. HSP, 12th Virginia Regiment Orderly Book, January 24, 1778, Miscellaneous Collection.
14. *PMHB,* "Valley Forge, 1777-1778, Diary of Surgeon Albigence Waldo of the Connecticut Line," December 21 and 25, 1778, Vol. XXI, pp. 309, 312.
15. James C. Gibson, *Dr. Bodo Otto and the Medical Background of*

the American Revolution, pp. 149-50; *PP.*, "Medicine at Valley Forge," William C. Middleton, July 1962, p. 19 (Paper given at the University of Wisconsin).

16. Report of Alexander Scammel, April 3, 1778, Morristown National Historical Park, Washington Papers; NA, Shippen to Washington, [April, 1778], Papers of Continental Congress, Reel 102; *West Chester Local News,* December 18, 1893, lists many houses, barns and churches that served as hospitals that are not found in official correspondence; *PP,* "Physicians, Surgeons and Mates with Washington at Valley Forge," Charles W. Heathcote, January, 1948, pp. 20-24; *Ibid.,* "Medical Men Deserve Tribute for Care of Washington's Men at Valley Forge," Edward W. Hocker, January 1947, pp. 7-15; George Thomas to Richard Thomas, June 14, 1778, Chester County Historical Society.

17. *Washington-Writings,* General Orders, January 21, 1778, Vol. X, p. 333; *Weedon Orderly Book,* January 21, 1778, p. 204; Bradford to Colonel Richard Varick, April 16, 1778, Massachusetts Historical Society, Miscellaneous Collection.

18. *Washington-Writings,* General Orders, January 20, 1778, Vol. X, p. 199; HSP, 12th Virginia Regiment Orderly Book, January 18, 1778, Miscellaneous Collection.

19. *Washington-Writings*, to Thomas Nelson, February 8, 1778, Vol. X, pp. 431-33.

20. LC, Poor to New Hampshire Council, April 15, 1778, Force MSS. Series 7E, New Hampshire Council Papers; Hiram Bingham, *Five Straws Gathered from Revolutionary Fields,* April 30, 1778, p. 26; *West Chester Local News,* December 12, 1893; *The Valley Forge Centennial,* January 24, 1778; Orderly Book, Lieutenant Colonel Isaac Sherman, March 17, 1778, Connecticut Historical Society.

21. *Ibid.*

22. Tartar Emetic is "a poisonous salt with a sweet metallic taste." Jalap is "a purgative drug obtained from convolvulaceous plants (morning glory family)."

23. "Manuscript Report on Smallpox Inoculation on the Continental Troops," Albigence Waldo, Surgeon, Duke University Center Library, Trent Collection. This study has been printed verbatim, and in part in several major medical studies; LC, Dr. Tenney to Dr. Peter Turner, March 22, 1778, Dr. Peter Turner Papers; Chaloner to James White (Assistant Commissary of Purchases), January 26, 1778, HSP, Chaloner & White MSS, Box 6.

24. Louis C. Duncan, *Medical Men in the American Revolution, 1775-1783,* pp. 9, 13, 234, 240-44; Mary C. Gilbert, *The Army Medical Department, 1775-1818,* p. 83; *Weedon Orderly Book,* April 29, 1778, p. 299.

25. *PMHB,* "Extracts from the Journal of Rev. James Sproat, Hospital Chaplain of the Middle Department, 1778," Vol. XXVII, pp. 441-45, passim.

26. *PP,* "Revolutionary War Hospitals in the Pennsylvania Campaign 1777-78," Dr. Douglas McFarlan, Jan. 1958, p. 29.

27. *Washington-Writings,* General Orders, April 14 and May 4, Vol. XI, pp. 260, 346.

28. *Ibid.,* to MacIntosh, April 4, 1778, Vol. XI, pp. 206-08; *PMHB,* "Extracts...Journal...Rev. James Sproat," April 18, 1778, Vol. XXVII, p. 442.

29. *Washington-Writings,* to the Officers Commanding at the Several Hospitals, April 4, 1778, Vol. XI, p. 209.

30. *Ibid.,* General Orders, April 14, 19, 28, May 3, 1778, Vol. XI, pp. 260, 280, 317, 346, 356. Apparently a staggered rotation of divisions was adopted for filling medicine chests, probably due to temporary shortages at the Apothecary General's Office.

31. *Ibid.,* General Orders, May 14, 1778, Vol. XI, p. 387.

32. *PP,* "Valley Meeting Friends cared for Washington's Men," Henry R. Frorer, October 1946, pp. 13-15; *Bulletin of Historical Society of Montgomery County,* "Valley Friends Meeting House," Mrs. Ivins C. Walker, Vol. II, No. 3, October 1940, pp. 214-19.

33. *Ibid.,* "Burial Places of the Soldiers at Valley Forge," William M. Stephens, Vol. III, No. 2, pp. 154-56; *West Chester Local News,* May 20, 1896; NA, Plunket Fleeson for 13th Virginia Regiment, RG93, M247, Roll 52:564.

34. *Weedon Orderly Book,* April 12, 1778, pp. 287-88.

35. Report of Louis J. Venuto, Supervisory Park Historian (Valley Forge National Historical Park), August 31, 1983.

Chapter XI

1. *Washington-Writings,* General Orders, April 4, 1778, Vol. XI, p. 224.

2. *JCC,* July 7, September 11, 1777, Vol. VIII, pp. 536, 733-35.

3. NA, Wayne to President of Congress, May 11, 1778, Continental Congress Papers, Roll 179, Scott to Congress, June 8, 1778, RG93, M247, Roll 102:267, Petition of Colonels of Late Conway's brigade May 28, 1778, RG93, M247, Roll 101:231, Colonel Francis J. Johnston to Congress, May 12, 1778, RG93, M247, Roll 97:75; Several studies were published in the *Picket Post* showing the development of the chaplaincy in the Continental Army. Two that are more pertinent are "Army Chaplains at Valley Forge Recognized for Their Leadership and Sacrifices at Winter Camp"

Dr. Charles W. Heathcote, April 1947, pp. 6-13, "Organization and Development of the American Chaplaincy during the Revolutionary War" Howard L. Applegate, May, 1960, pp. 19-21, 37-41.

4. *Washington-Writings,* General Instructions for Colonels and Commanding Officers of Regiments in the Continental Service, [1777], Vol. X, p. 242.

5. NYHS, Orderly Book of Colonel William Malcolm's Additional Continental Regiment, May 2, 1778; HSP, Orderly Book of the German Battalion of Continentals, May 2, 1778.

6. Connecticut Historical Society, Lieutenant Colonel Isaac Sherman Orderly Book, 2nd Connecticut Regiment, March 14, 1778.

7. *Ibid.,* Chapman to Major Theodore Woodbridge, March 7, 1778.

8. HSP, Dreer Collection, Wier Robinson Correspondence, Ration return September 5, 1777; Walter H. Blumenthal, *Women Camp Followers of the American Revolution,* p. 44; M. Antonia Lynch, *The Old District of Southwark in the County of Philadelphia,* p. 114.

9. *PP,* "Lost Women of History," Virginia L. Atkinson, Summer 1976, pp. 13-17.

10. Reverend E. B. Hillard, editor Wendell D. Garrett, *The Last Men of the Revolution*; John J. Stoudt, *Ordeal at Valley Forge,* p. 237 (quoting from John Laurens); *Washington Writings*, General Orders, May 14, 1778, Vol. XI, p. 387; Walter H. Blumenthal, *Women Camp Followers of the American Revolution*, p. 62; Elswyth Thane, *Washington's Lady*, p. 187.

11. *Ibid.,* p. 70; *Philadelphia Item* (Glen Rock), May 27, 1898.

12. John J. Stoudt, *Ordeal at Valley Forge,* pp. 70, 259; Harry E. Wildes, *Valley Forge,* p. 233 (Taken from the Church Book of the First Baptist Church, Philadelphia, Reverend William Rogers, pastor).

13. *Washington-Writings,* General Orders, February 4, 1778, Vol. X, p. 421; *Weedon Orderly Book,* February 4, 1778, p. 221.

14. *Ibid.,* January 29, 1778, p. 215.

15. Anne Hollingsworth Wharton, *Martha Washington,* pp. 122-23, (quotation from Benson J. Lossing, *Life of Mary and Martha Washington*); The information about Mrs. Bowers was furnished by a DAR historian, Mrs. Margaret B. Harvey.

16. *PMHB,* "Extracts from the Journal of Mrs. Henry Drinker, of Philadelphia, from September 25, 1777 to July 4, 1778," (entry of April 6), Vol. XIII, No. 3, pp. 304-05.

17. *Letters of the Delegates,* Paul Smith, editor, Committee at Camp to Henry Laurens, February 20, 1778, Vol. IX, pp. 143-45.

18. Report on Smallpox Inoculation of the Continental Troops [at Valley Forge], Albigence Waldo (early spring of 1778), Duke University Medical Center Library.

19. *Letters of the Delegates*, Paul Smith, editor, James Duane to George Clinton, March 13, 1778, Vol. IX, pp. 287-291, Philip Schuyler, James Duane and Volkert Pieterse Douw were Commissioners of Indian Affairs for the Northern Department; *A French Volunteer of the War of Independence—the Chevalier de Pontigaud*, Robert B. Douglas, translator and editor, pp. 48-49.

20. *JCC*, March 6 and 7, 1778, Vol. X, pp. 220-21, 228-29; *Washington-Writings*, to Commissioners of Indian Affairs, March 13, 1778, Vol. XI, pp. 76-77.

21. *Ibid.*, to President of Congress, May 3, 1778, Vol. XI, pp. 343-44.

22. Louis de Tousard was a volunteer without rank. Following the Battle of Rhode Island, he was cited for gallantry in action. He was wounded and lost an arm in this engagement. For his heroism he was appointed a Lieutenant Colonel in the Continental Army. In 1797, Tousard was assigned to complete the reconstruction of Fort Mifflin.

23. *Washington-Writings*, to Schuyler, May 15, 1778, Vol. XI, pp. 389-91; Tousard to Lieutenant Colonel Marinus Willet, May 16, 1778, NYPL, Emmet Collection; Major George Fleming to Captain Sebastian Bauman, May 14, 1778; NYHS, Sebastian Bauman Papers; Fleming stated that the number of Indians was 50, however, this was an arbitrary round figure used by many since the Revolution.

24. *Chevalier de Pontigaud*, edited by Robert B. Douglas, pp. 49-50; Carlos E. Godfrey, *The Commander-in-Chiefs Guard*, "Elijah Fisher Diary," May 15, 1778, p. 276.

25. *PMHB*, Notes and Documents, "Autobiography of Peter Stephen du Ponceau," pp. 218-19. Peter du Ponceau was a member of Steuben's entourage on its way from Portsmouth, New Hampshire, to Valley Forge. He became an American citizen and settled in Philadelphia, where he was a distinguished lawyer, a learned scholar of the arts and sciences, and an eminent philologist.

26. *Washington-Writings*, to President of Congress, June 21, 1778, Vol. XII, pp. 98-99.

27. *The Keystone*, July 24, 1874, Vol. 8, April 10, 1880, Vol. 13; *Old Masonic Lodges of Pennsylvania*, Julius F. Sachse, Vol. I, pp. 213-17, Vol. II, pp. 38-9; *The Short Talk Bulletin*, "Freemasonary and Freemasons at Valley Forge" Ronald E. Heaton, Vol. XLVII, No. 7, pp. 3-7; *Freemasonry in the American Revolution*, Sidney Morse, pp. 102-05; PP, "Free Masonry during the Revolution," April 1953, pp. 35-6; Masonic Data About Valley Forge, Valley Forge Park Commission Minute Book, 1930-32, p. 260; *Washington and His Masonic Compeers*, Sidney Hayden, p. 48; *Historical Sketches of the Montgomery Historical Society*, "Montgomery County in the Campaign of 1777-78," W.H. Richardson, Vol. 7, 1935; "Information pertaining to Early Freemasonry in the Western Hemi-

sphere, Including the Warrant and Constitution Dates of the Subordinate Lodges under the Provincial and Present Grand Lodge of Free and Accepted Masons of Pennsylvania," typescript, Grand Lodge of Pennsylvania Library.

28. John C. Fitzpatrick, *The Spirit of the Revolution*, "The Bands of the Continental Army," pp. 158-78 passim.

29. Robert K. Wright, Jr., *The Continental Army*, p. 38; Paterson to Marshall, February 23, 1778, NJHS, MG14.

30. *Washington-Writings*, General Orders, May 9, 1778, Vol. XI, p. 366.

31. Bloomfield, Curtis and Kersey were in the 3rd New Jersey Regiment, with Weyman in the 4th. Ewing indicates Parker's but was in the 4th under Colonel Ephraim Martin. This was probably Major Samuel F. Parker of the New Jersey Militia.

32. *George Ewing Gentleman, a Soldier at Valley Forge*, pp. 38-39.

33. *PMHB*, "Selections from the Wallace Papers," Wallace to Rachel, May 14, 1778, Vol. XL, pp. 342-43; *Ibid.*, "John Leacock and the Fall of British Tyranny," Francis J. Dallet, Jr., Vol. LXXVIII, pp. 468-69; Thomas C. Pollack, *The Philadelphia Theatre in the Eighteenth Century*, pp. 36-8; *William and Mary Quarterly*, "Addison's Cato in the Colonies," Vol. 23, pp. 431-49, passim; H. Trevor Colbourn, *The Lamp of Experience*, p. 153.

34. HSP, Wallace Papers-William Bradford Papers, Wallace to Rachel, May 20, 1778.

35. *Washington-Writings*, General Orders, January 8, February 18 and 25, 1778, Vol. X, pp. 276, 475, 510-11.

36. *George Ewing Gentleman, a Soldier at Valley Forge*, pp. 26, 33, 35, 37, 47.

37. *Ibid.*, p. 35; *PP*, "Sporting Life at Valley Forge," John F. Reed, July, 1963, pp. 33-35; Georgia Historical Society, Report of Thomas Clark, May 2, 1778, Lachlan McIntosh Collection.

38. *George Ewing Gentleman, a Soldier at Valley Forge*, p. 37.

39. *Ibid.*, pp. 39-40.

40. *Ibid.*, p. 47.

41. *Ibid.*, pp. 44-6.

42. *PMHB*, "Notes and Documents, The Autobiography of Peter Stephen du Ponceau," Vol. LXIII, p. 208.

43. *Ibid.*, p. 457.

44. *Ibid*, p. 210.

45. Alexander Graydon, *Memoirs of His Own Time with Reminiscences of the Men and Events of the Revolution*, pp. 313-14.

46. *Tredyffrin Easttown History Club*, "New Light on the Encampment of the Continental Army at Valley Forge" Franklin L. Burns, July,

1939, pp. 56-7.

47. *JCC*, November 1 and 18, 1776, Vol. VI, pp. 917, 959-61.

48. *Ibid.*, March 22, 1777, Vol. VII, p. 192.

49. *Ibid.*, November 18, 1776, Vol. VI, pp. 959-61; "Broadside, United States Lottery Scheme..." Philadelphia, [1776].

Resolved, The scheme of the lottery be as follows, viz. That it consist of 100,000 tickets, each ticket to be divided into four billets, and to be drawn in four classes.

First class, at 10 dollars each billet,	-	-		1,000,000
Deduction, at 15 per cent.	-		-	150,000
				850,000

Prizes.	1 of 10,000	-	-	10,000	
	2 of 5,000	-	-	10,000	
	30 of 1,000	-	-	30,000	
	400 of 500	-	-	200,000	
	20,000 of 20	-	-	400,000	
Carried to the fourth class		-		200,000	850,000

Second class, 100,000 billets at 20 dollars each,			2,000,000
Deduction, at 15 per cent.			300,000
			1,700,000

Prizes.	1 of 20,000	-	-	20,000	
	2 of 10,000	-	-	20,000	
	10 of 5,000	-	-	50,000	
	100 of 1,000	-	-	100,000	
	820 of 500	-	-	410,000	
	20,000 of 30	-	-	600,000	
Carried to the fourth class		-		500,000	1,700,000

Third class, 100,000 billets at 30 dollars each,			3,000,000
Deductions at 15 per cent 450,000			
			2,550,000

Prizes.	1 of 30,000	-	-	30,000	
	1 of 20,000	-	-	20,000	
	2 of 15,000	-	-	30,000	
	2 of 10,000	-	-	20,000	
	10 of 5,000	-	-	50,000	
	200 of 1,000	-	-	200,000	
	1,000 of 500	-	-	500,000	
	20,000 of 40	-	-	800,000	
Carried to the fourth class		-		900,000	2,550,000

Fourth class, 100,000 billets at 40 dollars each,				4,000,000
Deductions at 15 per cent.				600,000
				3,400,000
Brought from the first class,				200,000
from the second class,				500,000
from the third class,				900,000
			Total,	5,000,000

Prizes					
	1 of 50,000	-	-	50,000	
	2 of 25,000	-	-	50,000	
	2 of 10,000	-	-	20,000	
	10 of 5,000	-	-	50,000	
	100 of 1,000	-	-	100,000	
	200 of 500	-	-	100,000	
	1,000 of 300	-	-	300,000	
	15,000 of 200	-	-	3,000,000	
	26,000 of 50	-	-	1,300,000	
					5,000,000

The lottery being intended to raise a sum of money on loan, bearing an annual interest of four per cent, which, with the sums arising from the deduction, is to be applied for carrying on the present most just and necessary war, in defence of the lives, liberties and property of the inhabitants of these United States: Resolved, That the fortunate adventurers in the 1st class, who draw more than 20 dollars, and so in the 2d and 3d classes, who draw more than 30 or 40 dollars, shall, at their option, receive a treasure bank note for the prize or prizes drawn, payable at the end of five years, and an annual interest on the same, at the rate of four per cent., or the pre-emption of such billets in the next succeeding class, as shall not be renewed within the time hereinafter limited. Every adventurer in the 1st class shall have a right to go through the subsequent classes, but shall not be obliged to do it. The drawers of 20, 30 and 40 dollars in the 1st, 2d and 3d classes, who do not apply for their money within six weeks after the drawing ends, shall be deemed adventurers in the next succeeding class, and have their billets renewed without any further trouble. If any others shall neglect or decline taking out and paying the price of their billets, for a subsequent class, within six weeks after the drawing ends, their billets shall be sold to the fortunate adventurers in the preceeding class, or to such as shall apply for the same. The fortunate adventurers in the last class, who draw 50 dollars, shall, upon application to the commissioners of the loan offices in the respective states, where the drawers reside, receive their money, without any deduction, and all who draw above that sum, shall receive in like manner, without deduction, for the sums drawn, bank treasury notes payable at the end of five years after the drawing, at the loan office of the state in which the drawers reside. The interest to commence from the last day of drawing, and to be paid annually at the said respective loan offices: That, for carrying into execution the said lottery, there shall be seven managers, who shall give bond, and be on oath, for the faithful discharge of their duty: That the money, as fast as received by the managers for billets, be lodged in the continental treasury: That the drawing of the first class begin at Philadelphia on the 1st of March, 1777, or sooner, if sooner full.

50. *Ibid.*, May 14, 1777, Vol. VII, pp. 353-54, Vol. X, January 1, 1778, p. 75, Vol. XIII, April 12, 1779, p. 441. To encourage winners to accept treasury notes in lieu of cash, interest rates were increased to six per cent in April, 1779. A blank treasury bank note "drawn in the first class...[was] in the following form."

Number.   Dollars.   Number.
Dollars.   The United States of America acknowledge themselves to be indebted to   in   dollars, being for a prize of that value, drawn in the United States' lottery, which they promise to pay to the said   or bearer, on the   day of   with interest annually, at the rate of four per cent, agreeable to a resolution of the United States, passed the eighteenth day of November, 1776. Countersigned.

51. *Washington-Writings,* General Orders, March 9 and April 27, 1778, Vol. XI, pp. 52, 313; HSP, Orderly Book of the German Battalions of Continentals, April 27, 1778; *JCC,* April 1, April 4, 1777, Vol. VII, p. 214; October 6, 1777, Vol. IX, p. 775.

52. *Ibid.*, November 27, 1776, Vol. VI, p. 986; September 19, October 28, 1778, Vol. XII, pp. 930, 1074, 1172.

53. *Ibid.*, December 18, 1778, Vol. XII, p. 1230.

54. *A List of the Fortunate Numbers in the First Class of the United States Lottery*, p. 55, Philadelphia [June 3,] 1778.

55. NYSHA, Chaloner to Stewart, May 1778, Stewart Collection; LC, Blaine Accounts, Peter Force Collection, Reel 97, Series 8 D; *Washington-Writings*, to Mitchell, February 17, 1779, Vol. XIV, pp. 127-29, 29f7, to Edmund Randolph, July 10, 1784, Vol. XXVII, pp. 442-43.

56. *JCC*, March 12, 1777, Vol. VII, p. 172, July 29, 1777, Vol. VIII, p. 588, February 13, 1778, Vol. X, p. 161.

57. HSP, Orderly Book...German Battalion of Continentals, April 23, 27, 1778.

58. *Washington-Writings*, General Orders, and to President of Congress, April 23, 1778, Vol. XI, pp. 299-302.

59. *Ibid.*, to McKean, April 1, 1778, Vol. XI, p. 196; *Pennsylvania Ledger*, February 21, 1778; *Pennsylvania Evening Post*, July 6, 1778; *New Jersey Gazette*, February 4 and 18, 1778; Kenneth Scott, *Counterfeiting in Colonial America*, pp. 253-63, passim; HSP, Greer Collection,

Letters of the American Revolution, Elias Boudinot to Elisha Boudinot, March 6, 1778.

60. *Washington-Writings*, to Lee, February 15, 1778, Vol. X, pp. 464-66, 465f, to President of Congress, April 18, 1778, Vol. XI, pp. 275-76; *Letters of Richard Henry Lee* to Washington, January 2, and May 6, 1778, Vol. I, pp. 371, 398-401; *Letters of the Delegates*, Paul Smith, editor, Henry Laurens to John Laurens, January 14, 1778, Vol. VIII, pp. 591-92; Worthington C. Ford, *The Spurious Letters Attributed to Washington*, passim.

Chapter XII

1. *Washington-Writings*, to Banister, April 21, 1778, Vol. XI, pp. 284-93.

2. *Ibid.*, to Smallwood, April 30, to President of Congress, May 1 and 4, 1778, Vol. XI, pp. 323-24, 331-33, 348.

3. *John Laurens Correspondence*, Laurens to Henry Laurens, May 7, 1778, pp. 168-71.

4. *Washington-Writings*, General Orders, After Orders, May 5, 1778, Vol. XI, pp. 353-56.

5. *Pennsylvania Packet*, May 13, 1778; *Diary of the American Revolution*, "Extract from the Letter of a Soldier at Valley Forge," Frank Moore, ed., Vol. II, pp. 49-50.

6. *Ibid.*, p. 51; *Citizen Soldier: The Revolutionary War Journal of Joseph Bloomfield*, Mark E. Lender and James K. Martin, eds., pp. 133-34.

7. *Ewing-Gentleman and Soldier*, pp. 48-51.

8. *Bloomfield-Journal*, p. 134.

9. *Diary of the American Revolution*, Frank Moore, ed., Vol. II, pp. 51-52.

10. *Bloomfield-Journal*, p. 134; *Proceedings of the New Jersey Historical Society*, 1st Series, Vol. 7, "Diary of Joseph Clark," p. 105; *Washington-Writings*, General Orders, June 7, 1778, Vol. XII, pp. 29-35.

11. *Ibid.*, to President of Congress, May 1, 1778, Vol. XI, pp. 331-32.

12. *Ibid.*, General Orders, May 7, 1778, Vol. XI, pp. 360-63.

Oath of Allegiance for Line Officers:

I   do acknowledge the United States of America to be Free, Independent and Sovereign States and declare that the People thereof owe no Allegiance or Obedience to George the Third, King of Great Britain and I renounce refuse and abjure any Allegiance or Obedience to him, and I do swear (or affirm) that I will to the utmost of my Power support, maintain and defend the said United States against the said King George the third, his heirs and Successors and his and their Abettors, Assistants and Adherents and will serve the said United States in the office of which I now hold with Fidelity according to the best of my skill and understanding. Sworn before me at this day of A.D.

Oath of Allegiance for Service Function Officers:
I   do swear (or affirm) that I will faithfully truly and impartially execute the Office of to which I am appointed and render a true Account when thereunto required of all publick Monies by me received or expended and of all stores or other effects to me intrusted which belong to The United States and will in all respects discharge the Trust reposed in me with Justice and Integrity according to the best of my skill and understanding.
13. *Ibid.*
14. *Ibid.*, General Orders, May 11, 1778, Vol. XI, p. 375.
15. *Ibid.*, to Lafayette, May 17, 1778, Vol. XI, pp. 410-11f78.

Chapter XIII

1. *Washington-Writings*, to President of Congress, October 5, to Israel Putnam, October 8, 1777, Vol. IX, pp. 308-11, 335-37.
2. *Ibid.*, to Gates, October 30, 1777, Vol. IX, p. 465.
3. *Letters of Benjamin Rush, 1761-1813*, L.H. Butterfield, ed., Vol. II, pp. 1197-1200.
4. *Ibid.*, Vol. I, pp. 182-3; HSP, Unsigned (Rush) to Patrick Henry, January 12, 1778, Dreer Collection, Henry-Washington Papers.
5. *Benjamin Rush*, Nathan Goodman, pp. 113-14.
6. *Ibid.*, p. 117.
7. *Letters of Benjamin Rush*, 1761-1813, L.H. Butterfield, ed., Vol. II, p. 1207.
8. *Washington and His Aides-de-Camp*, Emily S. Whitely, p. 211; *Supplying Washington's Army*, Erna Risch, pp. 15, 39.
9. *Army Correspondence of John Laurens*, to his father, January 3, 1778, pp. 101-04; *PMHB*, "Military Papers of General John Cadwalader," Vol. XXXII, pp. 167-70.
10. *Washington-Writings*, Order of March and Route of the Army from Valley Forge, [June 17, 1778], to Wayne, June 18, 1778, Vol. XII, pp. 74, 86-7.
11. *Ibid.*, to Gouverneur Morris, June 18, 1778, Vol. XII, pp. 413-14. Italics are those of Washington.
12. *Ibid.*, to Conway, [November 9, 1777], Vol. X, p. 29.
13. *Washington-Writings*, Jared Sparks, ed., Conway to Washington, November 16, 1777, Vol. V, p. 483.
14. *Letters of the Delegates*, Ellery to Whipple, December 21, 1777, Vol. VIII, pp. 453-57; Gerry to Knox, February 7, 1778, *Ads Autographs,* [auction], Webster, N. Y., N.D.

15. Huntington Library, Taylor to Woodford, April 12, 1778, HM8139; *PMHB*, Correspondence of John Cadwalader, Tilghman to Cadwalader, January 1778, Vol. XXXII, pp. 167-70.

16. Washington Papers, Morristown National Historical Park, Hopkinson and Wharton to Washington, December 30, 1777, John Fitzgerald to Washington, March 17, 1778; *Letters of the Delegates*, H. Laurens to J. Laurens, May 11, 1778, Vol. IX, pp. 645-47.

17. *Washington-Writings*, Fitzpatrick, ed., to President of Congress, January 2, 1778, Vol. X, pp. 249-50.

18. *Washington-Writings*, Sparks, ed., Gates to Washington, December 8, 1777, Vol. V, pp. 484, This letter and other correspondence of Gates is in the NYHS, Gates Papers.

19. *Washington-Writings,* Fitzpatrick, ed., to Gates, January 4, 1778, Vol. X, pp. 263-65.

20. NYHS, Gates to Washington, January 23, 1778, Gates Papers.

21. *Washington-Writings*, to Gates, February 9, 1778, Vol. X, pp. 437-41.

22. *Washington-Writings*, Sparks, ed., Gates to Washington, February 19, 1778, Vol. V, pp. 511-12.

23. *Washington-Writings*, Fitzpatrick, ed., to Gates, February 18, 1778, Vol. X, pp. 499-80.

24. *Ibid.*, to Gates, February 24, 1778, Vol. X, pp. 508-9.

25. *Tench Tilghman*, L.G. Shreve, p. 120.

26. *Washington-Writings*, Sparks, ed., Lafayette to Washington, December 30, 1777, Conway to Washington, July 23, 1778, Vol. V, pp. 488-90, 517.

Chapter XIV

1. *Washington-Writings*, to Greene, March 31, 1778, Vol. XI, p. 177.

2. *Ibid.*, to Wharton, Johnson and McDougall, May 11, 1778, Vol. XI, pp. 369-73.

3. Connecticut Historical Society, Richard Peters to Wadsworth, April 17, 1778, Wadsworth Papers; New Jersey Bureau of Archives and History, Biddle to Furman, April 25, 1778, Revolutionary Documents.

4. *Ibid.*, Caldwell to Biddle, May 1, 1778.

5. Connecticut Historical Society, Samuel Huntington to Wadsworth, June 4, 1778, Wadsworth to Washington, June 4, 1778, to Chaloner, June 5, 1778, to Champion, June 8 and 9, 1778, to Citizens of Several Towns, June 11, 1778, Blaine to Wadsworth, June 9, 1778, Wadsworth to Henry Laurens, May 27, 1778, Wadsworth Papers.

6. NYSHA, Blaine to Charles Stewart, May 2, 1778, Stewart Collection;

Maryland Hall of Records, Blaine to Maryland Government, May 7, 1778, Md HR 4587-11; Connecticut Historical Society, Blaine to Wadsworth, May 10, 1778, Wadsworth Papers.

7. *Ibid.*, Chaloner to Wadsworth, May 17, 1778; NA RG93, M247, Chaloner to Wadsworth, May 17, 1778; Morristown National Historical Park, John L. Howell to Colonel Francis Wade, May 19, 1778, Lloyd W. Smith Collection; *Washington-Writings*, to Blaine, May 17, 1778, Vol. XI, p. 408.

8. Glassboro State College, Chaloner to Huggins, May 29, 1778, Frank Stewart Manuscripts; NYSHA, Chaloner to Charles Stewart, May 23 and 29, 1778, Stewart Papers.

9. Connecticut Historical Society, Chaloner to Stewart, June 1, 1778, Stewart Papers; New Jersey Bureau of Archives and History, Charles Pettit to Furman, May 29, 1778, Record Group.

10. *Washington-Writings*, to Board of War, May 16, 1778, Vol. XI, pp. 395-97.

11. HSP, May, 1778, Weiss Manuscripts; *PMHB*, "Notes and Queries," Inventory of Quartermaster Stores, May, 1778, prepared by Colonel Thomas Craig, Esq. [First Pennsylvania], Vol. XXXVI, pp. 508-9.

12. *Washington-Writings*, General Orders, May 23, 1778, Vol. XI, pp. 441-42.

13. *Ibid.*, May 26, 1778, pp. 454-55.

14. Huntington Library, Orderly Book, HM719; NYHS, Colonel William Malcolm's Additional Continental Orderly Book, May 31, 1778.

15. *Washington-Writings*, General Orders, May 14 and 27, 1778, Vol. XI, pp. 387, 463.

16. *Ibid.*, General Orders, June 13, 1778, Vol. XII, P. 53; NJHS, J. Mitchell to James Abeel, May 17, 1778, Abeel Correspondence, MG110, James Cox to Abeel, June 8, 1778, Cox Correspondence; NA, RG 93, M247, Roll 199, Committee of Congress at Camp to Major Chase, March 16, 1778 (Chase is not listed in Heitman); Ibid., RG15, M804, Reel 2523, Charles Pettit to Jacob Weiss, (May ?), Weiss Papers.

17. *Washington-Writings*, General Orders, May 16, 1778, Vol. XI, p. 399.

18. *Ibid.*, June 1, 1778, Vol. XII, p. 4.

19. *Ibid.*, to Gouverneur Morris, May 29, 1778, Vol. XI, pp. 482-85; New Hampshire Historical Society, 1st New Hampshire Regiment of Foot Orderly Book, HSP, Miscellaneous Collection, Orderly Book, May 31, 1778; Mary C. Gillett, *The Army Medical Department, 1775-1818*, pp. 92, 109; James E. Gibson, *Dr. Bodo Otto*, pp. 174, 179, Gibson reports in detail Shippen's report taken from the Collection of Revolutionary War Papers at the Library of Congress.

20. Huntington Library, Orderly Book, June 9, 1778, HM719;

Washington-Writings, to Charles Lee, May 30, 1778, Vol. XI, p. 489.

21. There were two Dr. Hutchinsons serving as Surgeons Mates; Ebenezer Hutchinson of the Fifth New York Regiment and James Hutchinson of the Hospital Department. However, it appears that the Dr. Hutchinson named by Washington was Ebenezer Hutchinson. Heitman records the appointment of James Hutchinson in July 1778.

22. *Washington-Writings*, General Orders, May 26, 30, 31, Vol. XI, pp. 454-55, 487-88, 497.

23. *Ibid.*, to Greene, June 8, 1778, Vol. XII, pp. 35-6.

24. *Ibid.*, General Orders, June 9, 1778, Vol. XII, p. 40; *Journal of Henry Dearborn*, Lloyd A. Brown and Howard H. Peckman eds., June 10, 1778, p. 123; Proceedings of the New Jersey Historical Society, "Diary of Joseph Clark," 1st Series, Vol. 7, p. 105; *History of the First New Hampshire Regiment of Foot in the War of the Revolution*, "Journal of Lieutenant Thomas Blake," Frederic Kidder, p. 41; *The Commander in Chief's Guard*, "Elijah Fisher Diary," Carlos E. Godfrey, June 11, 1778, p. 279; *Diary of a Common Soldier in the American Revolution, 1775-1783*, "Journal Jeremiah Greenman," Robert C. Bray and Paul E. Bushnell, eds., p. 120; *A Narrative of Some of the Adventures, Dangers and Sufferings of a Revolutionary Soldier.* (Joseph Plumb Martin), George F. Scheer, ed., p. 122.

25. For the problems confronting the pullout of the British and Loyalists in Philadelphia see Jackson, *British Army in Philadelphia, 1777-1778*, pp. 251-64, passim.

26. *Washington-Writings*, to John Augustine Washington, June 10, 1778, Vol. XII, pp. 41-3.

27. *Washington-Writings*, General Orders, June 13, 1778, Vol. XII, p. 53.

28. *Ibid.*, to Maxwell, May 25, 1778, Vol. XI, pp. 448-49.

29. *Ibid.*, to Maxwell, May 27 and 29, 1778, Vol. XI, pp. 462, 478-79, to Gates, June 5, 1778, Vol. XII, pp. 18-9.

30. Jackson, *With the British Army in Philadelphia*, pp. 221, 261.

31. Charles H. Lesser, ed., *The Sinews of Independence*, May 30, 1778, pp. 68-70, A study of the musters of all brigades and detached units on May 30, listed total effectives of 15, 061—with a grand total including sick, on command or extra service and furlough of 24,015. *Washington-Writings*, to Stephen Moylan, May 24, 1778, to Gates, May 25, 1778, to Smallwood, May 17 and June 1, 1778, Vol. XI, pp. 446-47, Vol. XII, p. 2.

32. *Ibid.*, Arrangement of Army and Routes of March to the North River, May 28, 1778, Vol. XI, pp. 465-67.

33. *Ibid.*, Vol. XI, p. 465, f93, Order of March Route of the Army from Valley Forge, [June 17, 1778], Vol. XII, pp. 74-5.

34. *Ibid.*, Instructions to Major General Charles Lee, May 30, 1778, Vol.

XI, pp. 489-90.

35. *Ibid.*, General Orders, June 7, 1778, Vol. XII, pp. 29-35.

36. *Ibid.*, to Lee, June 15, 1778, Vol. XII, pp. 60-3 f60.

37. *Ibid.*, to Maxwell, June 16, 1778, Council of War, June 17, 1778, Vol. XII, pp. 70, 75-8.

38. *Ibid.*

39. *Ibid.*, to President of Congress, General Orders and Wayne, June 18, 1778, Vol. XII, pp. 82-3, 86-7, 91-2.

40. Huntington Library, Orders to March from Valley Forge, June, 1778, after Genl. Lee's & Genl. Mifflin's had March'd, HM519; *Washington-Writings*, Order of March from Valley Forge, [June 18, 1778], Vol. XII, pp. 90-91.

41. HSP, Record Book of the Hewes Family and Receipt of Deborah Hewes, June 18, 1778, Society Collection.

42. NYHS, Orderly Book, Captain Edward Lounsbury's Eight Company, Second New York Regiment, March 20, 1778.

Appendix A

1. *Defences of Philadelphia in 1777*, Worthington Chauncey Ford, ed., pp. 101, 175-197, 207-296; Washington Papers, Library of Congress (microfilm), Reel 46, Summary of the Opinions of the various members of the Councils of War, filed under date of December 3, 1777; *PMHB*, "Prelude to Valley Forge," Vol. LXXXII, pp. 466-471; *Picket Post*, "Valley Forge or Reading debated as Winter Quarters for the Army," J. Bennett Nolan, January, 1948, pp. 14-18; Maryland Hall of Records, Gist Family papers (also in Library Congress, Miscellaneous Division, M G Papers, Peter Force Transcripts), M. Gist to John McClure, December 16, 1777.

Appendix B

1. Position sketches were prepared in the field, often on horseback, with the simplest of materials. They probably consisted of a small board to serve as a drawing board, a pencil, rule, compass, and scale. Later these sketches would be refined by the cartographic skill of Villefranche.

2. *Washington-Writings*, Washington to Villefranche, July 22, 1783, Vol. XXVII, p. 159; Elizabeth S. Kite, *Brigadier-General Louis Lebéque Duportail*, 1777-1783, pp. 1-54 Passim; Kite, *PMHB*, "General Duportail at Valley Forge," Vol. LVI, pp. 347-54; Kite, *Records of the American Catholic Historical Society*, "General Washington and the French Engineer Duportail and Companions," Vol. II, pp. 97-116; Hubertis M.

VALLEY FORGE

Cummings, *PMHB*, "The Villefranche Map for the Defense of the Delaware," Vol. LXXXIV, pp. 424-34; John W. Jackson, *Whitemarsh 1777: Impregnable Stronghold*, pp. 14-16; Jackson, *Fort Mifflin, Defender of the Delaware*, pp. 108-09; Brigadier General Norman Randolph, *PPost*, "Duportail Map was Exceedingly Accurate Position Sketch," March, 1949, pp. 9, 11.

Appendix C

1. *Washington-Writings*, General Orders, March 11, 1776, Vol. IV, pp. 387-88.

2. Douglas Southall Freeman, *George Washington*, Vol. IV, pp. 115-21; James Thomas Flexner, *George Washington in the American Revolution (1775-1783)*, [Vol. II], pp. 91-92.

3. The letters were sent to Colonels Alexander Spotswood, of the Second; Alexander McClanahan, of the Seventh; Abraham Bowman, of the Eighth; and Daniel Morgan, of the Eleventh Virginia Regiments.

4. *Washington-Writings*, Washington to Colonel Alexander Spotswood, April 30, 1777, Vol. VII, pp. 494-95, (See note 3 for others who received the same letter).

5. Clements Library, Sackville-Germain Papers, 7:31,46; *Pennsylvania Evening Post*, January 31 and February 24, 1778; *Pennsylvania Ledger*, February 28, 1778; John W. Jackson, *With the British Army in Philadelphia*, p. 178.

6. *Washington-Writings*, General Orders, March 17, 1778, Vol. XI, p. 98.

7. *Ibid.*

8. The best study of the Guard is Carlos E. Godfrey, *The Commander in Chief's Guard*; also see Captain Louis H. Schmidt, "George Washington's Bodyguards were Wisely Selected and Loyal" PPost, January, 1946, pp. 18-25.

9. *PPost*, October, 1947, p. 17.

Appendix D

1. *JCC*, Worthington C. Ford, ed., January 23, 28, February 2, 1778, Vol. X, pp. 87, 96, 107.

2. Papers of the Continental Congress, NA, Roll 183, Stark to Lafayette, February 2, 1778, Lafayette to Hazen, February 18, 1778.

3. *Ibid.*, Conway to Hazen, February 18, 1778.

4. *Ibid.*, General Return of Lafayette's Command, February, 1778,

Hazen to Lafayette, February 18, 1778, Conway to Gates, February 19, 1778.

5. *Ibid.*, Arnold to Lafayette, February 16, 1778, Lincoln to Conway, February 16, 1778, Clinton to Conway, February 17, 1778; New York State Library, Arnold to G. Morris, February 3, 1778; *N. Greene Papers*, Greene to Nicholas Cook, February 5, 1778, Vol. II, p. 274.

6. *Letters-Delegates*, Reed to Jonathan Bayard Smith, February 8, 1778, Duane to George Clinton, March 13, 1778, Vol. IX, pp. 57-61, 287.

7. *Washington-Writings*, to Board of War, January 27, 1778, Vol. X, pp. 355-57.

8. *Ibid.*, to Nelson, February 8, 1778, Vol. X, pp. 431-32.

9. *Ibid.*, to Lafayette, March 10 and 20, 1778, Vol. XI, pp. 59-60, 113-14; *JCC*, March 2 and 3, 1778, Vol. X, pp. 217, 253.

Bibliography

Manuscripts

England

Public Records Office (London)
  British Headquarters Papers; Military Correspondence 1777-78.
    C.O. 5/93-95.
  Precis of Correspondence on Military Campaign, 1777-78.
    C.O. 5/253.

Royal Artillery Library, Old Royal Military Academy (Woolwich)
  General Orders, Sept. 1777-Feb. 1778. MS.58.
  Brigade Orders, Royal Artillery, 28 Sept. 1777-21 Feb. 1778. MS.57.

War Office (London)
  Correspondence of Generals Howe and Clinton with the Secretary
    of War, 1776-80. W.O. 1/10.

Liverpool City Libraries.
  Parker Family Papers.

Scotland

Scottish Record Office, General Register house (Edinburgh)
  Cunningham of Thornton Papers, 1776-82. Journal of Captain John
    Peebles, 1776-82. 21.492.4-6 (1777-78).

National Library of Scotland (Edinburgh)
  Steuart Papers. Chas. Steuart. MS5030, ff. 168-169v, 191.

United States

Historical Society of Pennsylvania
  Miscellaneous Society Collection:
    12th Virginia Continental Regiment Orderly Book.
    Order Book, John Irwin.
  William Bradford Papers.
  Wallace Papers.
  Chaloner-White Manuscripts.

Dreer Collection:
    Daniel Wier, Commissary of the British Army in America,
        Correspondence [with John Robinson].
    General John Lacey papers.
    Lacey Memoirs.
    General Orders issued by Lacey, 1778, 1780, 1781.
    Letters of Soldiers, Surgeons, and Chaplains of the American
        Revolution.
    Letters of the American Revolution.
    Members of the Old Congress.
    Henry-Washington Correspondence.
    Generals of the American Revolution.
  Papers of John Potts.
Weiss Manuscripts.
    Sergeant Thomas Sullivan Journal, 1775-78.
    Etting Collection:
        Generals of the Revolution.
        Revolutionary Papers.

National Archives (Washington)
    Papers of George Washington (microfilm).
    Papers of the Continental Congress (microfilm).
    War Department Collection of Revolutionary War Records
        (manuscript and microfilm).
    RG 15 and RG 93 Collections.

Library of Congress
    Washington Papers.
    Force Manuscripts:
        Samuel Gray Papers.
        New Hampshire Manuscripts.
        Massachusetts Letters.
    Mrs. Archibald Crossley Autograph Collection.
    Continental Congress Collection.
    Henry Laurens Family Papers.
    Lafayette Papers.
    Hamilton-McLane Papers.
    Miscellaneous Papers.

Connecticut Historical Society
    Joseph Trumbull Collection.
    American Revolutionary Journals and Orderly Books.
    American Revolution Miscellaneous Letters & Documents.

VALLEY FORGE

Woodbridge Papers.
Wadsworth Anthenaeum Loan Collection.
Jeremiah Wadsworth Papers.
Jedediah Huntington Letters.

American Philosophical Society
Sol Feinstone Collection.
Meteorological Observations near Philadelphia January 1777
to May 1778 (Phineas Pemberton).
Broadside of United States Lottery Scheme [1776].

Massachusetts Historical Society
Henry Knox Papers (on loan from New England Genealogical
Society).
Adams-Warren Papers.
Dudley Coleman Papers.
Miscellaneous Collection.

Maryland Hall of Records
Gist Family Papers.

New York Historical Society
Alexander McDougall Papers.
Collection of Regimental and Company Orderly Books.
Joseph Reed Papers (including John Miller Diary).
John Lamb Papers.
Allan McLane Papers.
Gates Papers.
Lacey Papers.

Rhode Island Historical Society
Orderly Book, Colonel Christopher Greene.

Valley Forge National Historical Park.
John Reed Collection.
Valley Forge Park Commission Minute Books.
Archives-copies of many quoted sources.

Huntington Library (San Marino)
Collection of Orderly Books.
Miscellaneous Collection.
Lacey Papers.

Gloucester County (New Jersey) Historical Society
John Ladd Howell Correspondence.
Account Book of John Ladd Howell.

Glassboro (New Jersey) State College
Frank H. Stewart Manuscripts.

Stuart A. Goldman
Diary of Gideon Savage.

Morristown National Historical Park
Lloyd W. Smith Collection.

Massachusetts State Archives
Government & Council Papers.

New York State Historical Association
Charles Stewart Collection.

David Library of the American Revolution
Extensive collection of microfilm Letters and Orderly Books
of the Revolution.
Sol Feinstone Collection.

Maryland Historical Society
Tench Tilghman Papers.

Princeton University
Ephraim Blaine Letters.
Elias Boudinot Collection.

New Jersey Historical Society
Jacob Platt Orderly Book.
Revolutionary Documents.

Connecticut State Library
Pierson & Sargent Family Papers.
Trumbull Papers.

University of Michigan, Clements Library
Orderly Book of Sir William Howe, 27 January 1776-1 May 1778.
Sackville-Germain Papers.
Sir Henry Clinton Papers.

VALLEY FORGE

Duke University Medical Center Library
  Trent Collection (Albigence Waldo).

New York Public Library
  Bancroft Collection:
    American Revolution, Military and Political (miscellaneous
      Letters).
    Letters of Charles Blagden.
    British Headquarters Papers in America (typescript).
  Emmet Collection.

New Hampshire Historical Society
  1st New Hampshire Orderly Book.

Long Island Historical Society
  Laurens Papers.

New Jersey Historical Society
  Abeel Collection.

Miscellaneous Collections at:
  Chicago Historical Society.
  Rosenbach Foundation.
  Virginia Historical Society.
  New York Bureau of Archives and History.

Colonial Williamsburg Research Department
  Parker Family Papers (microfilm) used with permission of
    Liverpool City Libraries.
  Simcoe Papers.

Masonic Temple Archives, Philadelphia
  Minutes Royal Arch Lodge, No. 3, 1767-1788.

Newspapers

Continental Journal (Boston)
Daily Republican (Phoenixville)
The Freeman's Journal or *New Hampshire Gazette* (Portsmouth)
The Keystone (Philadelphia every Saturday-Masonic Publishing
    Company)
Massachusetts Independent Chronicle

New Jersey Gazette (Burlington)
New York Tribune
Norristown Times Herald
North Carolina Gazette (New Bern)
Pennsylvania Gazette
Pennsylvania Ledger or *Philadelphia Market Day Advertiser*
Pennsylvania Packet
Philadelphia Public Ledger
Providence Gazette and County Journal
Royal Gazette (New York)
Village Record or *Chester and Delaware Federalist*
West Chester (Penna.) *Local News*

Bibliographical Works and Primary Printed Sources

Almon, John and Debrett, John, eds. *The Parliamentary Register*, or *History of the Proceedings and Debates of the House of Commons.* 62 vols. (especially vols. 11 and 12). London, 1775-1796.

Brigham, Clarence S., ed. *History and Bibliography of American Newspapers, 1690-1820.* 2 vols. Worcester, MA, 1947-61.

Burnett, Edmund C., ed. *Letters of Members of the Continental Congress.* 7 vols. Washington, 1921-34.

Clark, Walter, ed. *State Records of North Carolina.* Vol. XI, Winston Salem, NC, 1895-6.

Force, Peter. *American Archives: Fifth Series, Containing A Documentary History of the United States of America.* 3 vols. Washington, 1837-1852.

Ford, Worthington C. *Journals of the Continental Congress.* 39 vols. Washington, 1904-33.

Heitman, Francis B. *Historical Register of Officers of the Continental Army during the War of the Revolution.* with addenda Robert H. Kelby, Revised and Enlarged Edition, Baltimore, 1973.

Matthews, William, Compiler. *American Diaries: An Annotated Bibliography of Published American Diaries and Journals, 1492-1844.* Vol. I, Detroit (1983).

—. *American Diaries in Manuscript*, 1580-1954. Athens, GA (1974).

VALLEY FORGE

Pennsylvania Archives. First Series, 12 vols. Harrisburg, 1853.

Colonial Records of Pennsylvania. 16 vols. Harrisburg, 1838-53.

Saffell, W.T.R. *Records of the Revolutionary War*. New York, 1858.

Smith, Paul H., ed. *Letters of the Delegates to Congress, 1774-1789*. 12 vols. (to date). Washington, 1976-1985.

Sparks, Jared, ed. *Correspondence of the American Revolution being Letters of Eminent Men to George Washington*. 4 vols. Boston, 1853.

—. *The Diplomatic Correspondence of the American Revolution*. 6 vols. Washington, 1857.

Stevens, B.F., Compiler. *Facsimiles of Manuscripts in European Archives Relating to America, 1775-1783*. 25 vols. London 1889-98.

Stryker, William S. and Lee, Francis B., eds. *Documents Relating to the Revolutionary History of the State of New Jersey*. Vol. 182. Trenton, 1901-03.

Unrau, Harlan D. *Administrative History: Valley Forge National Historical Park Pennsylvania*. Denver (1985).

Unpublished Theses and Typescripts

Becton, Joseph. Black Soldiers at Valley Forge. (Valley Forge) 1985. (typescript).

Egloff, B.J., Packard, V., Ramsay, J. deM. The Excavation of Four Hut Sites at the Outer Defensive Line at Valley Forge, 1972. (typescript).

Field Structure Report, Valley Forge, 1981.

Parrington, Michael. Revolutionary Archaeology at Valley Forge, Pennsylvania (1980).

Report on the Excavation of Part of the Virginia Brigade. 1972-73.

Dixon, Martha W. Divided Authority: The American Management of Prisoners in the Revolutionary War, 1775-1783. University of Utah 1977. Doctoral Dissertation.

Grand Lodge (Masonic) of Pennsylvania Library. Information Pertaining to Early Freemasonry in the Western Hemisphere. (typescript).

Published Letters, Diaries, and Journals

Adams Family Correspondence. L.H. Butterfield, ed. 2 vols. Cambridge, MA. 1963.

Papers of John Adams. Robert J. Taylor, ed. Vols. V and VI, Cambridge, MA. 1977-83.

Anburey, Thomas. *Travels through the Interior Parts of America*, 2 vols. Boston, 1923.

Anderson, Enoch. *Personal Recollections of Captain Enoch Anderson: Delaware Regiment...Revolutionary War.* Notes Henry H. Bellas. Wilmington, DE, 1896.

Andre, John. *Major Andre's Journal*, Henry Cabot Lodge, ed. 2 vols. Boston, 1903.

Armstrong, John. *PMHB*, "Letters of General John Armstrong to Thomas Wharton, President of Pennsylvania, 1777." Vol. XXXVIII, 1914.

Baurmeister, Major. *Revolution in America Confidential Letters and Journals 1776-1784 of Adjutant General Major Baurmeister of the Hessian Force.* Translated by Bernhard A. Uhlendorf, New Brunswick, NJ, 1957.

Bicker, Col. Henry. *PMHB*, "Orderly Book of the Second Pennsylvania Continental Line." Vols. XXXV and XXXVI, 1911-12.

Biddle, Clement. *PMHB*, "Selections from the Correspondence of Colonel Clement Biddle." Vol. XLII, 1918.

Blake, Thomas. *History of the First New Hampshire Regiment*, "Lieutenant Thomas Blake's Journal," Frederic Kidder, Albany, 1868.

Bloomfield, Joseph. *Citizen Soldier: The Revolutionary War Journal of Joseph Bloomfield.* Mark E. Lender and James K. Martin, eds. Newark, 1982.

Boudinot, Elias, *Journal or Historical Recollections of American Events during The American Revolution.* Philadelphia, 1894.

—. *PMHB*, "Letter of Elias Boudinot." Vol. X, 1886.

—. *The Life, Public Services, Addresses, and Letters of Elias Boudinot.* J.J. Boudinot ed., 2 vols. New York, 1971.

Butler, Richard. *PMHB*, "Letter of Colonel Richard Butler of the Pennsylvania Line." Vol. XXVIII, 1904.

Cadwalader, John. *PMHB*, "Selections from the Military Papers of General John Cadwalader." Vol. XXXII, 1908.

Chaloner, John. *PMHB*, "Valley Forge—papers of John Chaloner." Vol. XXXVIII, 1914.

Chastellux, Marquis de. *Travels in North America in the years 1780, 1781 and 1782*. Revised translation, Howard C. Rice, Jr., 2 vols., Chapel Hill (1963).

Clark, John, Jr. *Bulletin of the Historical Society of Pennsylvania.* "Letters from Major John Clark, Jr. to General Washington during the Occupation of Philadelphia by the British Army." Vol. 1, (1845-47).

—. *PMHB*, "Memoir of Major John Clark of York County, Pennsylvania." E.W. Spangler, Vol. XX (1896).

Clark, Joseph. *Proceedings of the New Jersey Historical Society.* "Diary of Joseph Clark." 1st Series, Vol. 7, 1855.

Dann, John C. *The Revolution Remembered, Eyewitness Accounts of the War for Independence*. John C. Dann, ed. Chicago (1980).

David, Ebenezer. *A Rhode Island Chaplain in the Revolution, Letters of Ebenezer David to Nicholas Brown, 1775-1778*. Jeanette D. Black and William G. Roelker, eds. Port Washington, NY (1972).

Dearborn, Henry. *Revolutionary War Journals of Henry Dearborn 1775-1783*. Lloyd A. Brown and Howard H. Peckham, eds., biographical sketch Dunlap Smith, Chicago, 1939.

Drinker, Mrs. Henry. *PMHB*, "Extracts from the Journal of Mrs. Henry Drinker of Philadelphia, from September 25, 1777 to July 4, 1778." Vol. XIV, 1890.

Duponceau, Peter S. *PMHB*, "Autobiographical Letters of Peters S. Duponceau." Vol. XL, (1916).

—. *PMHB*, "The Autobiography of Peter Stephen Du Ponceau." James C. Whitehead, ed., Vol. LXIII, 1939.

Du Roi the Elder. *Journal of Du Roi the Elder: Lieutenant and Adjutant, in the Service of the Duke of Brunswick, 1776-1778*. Translated by S.J. Epping. New York, 1911.

Ewald, Johann. *Diary of the America War—a Hessian Journal.* Captain Johann Ewald. Translated and edited by Joseph P. Tustin, New Haven, 1979.

Ewing, George. *George Ewing Gentleman, a Soldier of Valley Forge.* Yonkers, NY, 1928.

Fisher, Elijah. *Elijah Fisher's Journal while in the War for Independence, and continued Two Years After He Came to Maine, 1775-1784.* Augusta, ME, 1880.

Ford, Worthington C. *Defenses of Philadelphia in 1777.* Collected and edited by Worthington C. Ford. Brooklyn, NY, 1897.

Graydon, Alexander. *Memoirs of His Own Time with Reminiscences of the Men and Events of the Revolution.* Alexander Graydon, Philadelphia, 1846.

Greene, Nathanael. *The Papers of General Nathanael Greene.* Richard K. Showman, ed. 4 vols. Chapel Hill, 1976-86.

Greenman, Jeremiah. *Diary of a Common Soldier in the American Revolution, 1775-1783* (Jeremiah Greenman). Robert C. Bray and Paul E. Bushnell, eds. DeKalb, IL, 1978.

Hamilton, Alexander. *The Papers of Alexander Hamilton.* Harold C. Syrett, ed. 26 vols. New York, 1961-79.

Hand, Edward. *PMHB*, "Orderly Book of General Edward Hand, Valley Forge." Vol. XLI, 1917.

Heinrichs, Johann. *PMHB*, "Extracts from the Letter-Book of Captain Johann Heinrichs of the Hessian Jager Corps, 1778-1780." Vol. XXII, 1898.

Henry, William. *PMHB*, "Letters to William Henry of Lancaster, Pennsylvania, 1777-1783," Vol. XXII, 1898.

Hillegas, Michael. *PMHB*, "Selected Letters of Michael Hillegas Treasurer of the United States." Vol. XXIX, 1905.

"Instructions to Commissary Agents, 1778." *Proceedings of the New Jersey Historical Society.* Vol. XIII, 1894-95.

Irvine, William. *PMHB*, "Selections from the Military Papers of Brig. Gen. William Irvine." Vol. XL, 1916.

Kirkland, Frederic R. *Letters on the American Revolution in the*

VALLEY FORGE

Library at "Karolfred." Frederic R. Kirkland, ed., 2 vols., Philadelphia, 1941 and 1952.

Kirkwood, Robert. *The Journal and Order Book of Captain Robert Kirkwood of the Delaware Regiment of the Continental Line.* Joseph B. Turner, ed. Port Washington, NY (1970), second edition.

Lacey, John. *PMHB*, "Memoirs of Brigadier-General John Lacey." Vols. XXV and XXVI, 1901-02.

Lafayette, Marquis. *The Letters of Lafayette to Washington 1777-1779.* Louis Gottschalk, ed. and revised, Philadelphia, 1976.

—. *Lafayette in the Age of the American Revolution, Selected Letters and Papers, 1776-1790.* Stanley J. Idzerda, ed., 5 vols., Ithaca, 1978-1983.

Laurens, Henry. *The Papers of Henry Laurens.* David R. Chestinett and C. James Taylor, eds., Vol. 12, Columbia, SC, 1990.

Laurens, John. *The Army Correspondence of Colonel John Laurens in the years 1777-8.* With memoir, Wm. G. Simms, New York, 1867.

Lee, Charles. *The Lee Papers.* Collection New York Historical Society for Years 1871-74. New York, 1872-75, Vols. 4 through 7.

Lee, Henry. *Memoirs of the War in the Southern Department of the United States.* Henry Lee, New York, 1870.

Lee, Richard Henry. *The Letters of Richard Henry Lee.* James C. Ballagh, ed., 2 vols. New York, 1914.

McMichael, James. *PMHB*, "Diary of Lieutenant James McMichael of the Pennsylvania Line, 1776-1778." Contributed by Col. William P. McMichael, Vol. XVI, 1892.

Marshall, John. *The Papers of John Marshall.* Herbert A. Johnson, ed., 3 vols., Chapel Hill (1974-79).

Martin, Joseph Plumb. *A Narrative of Some of the Adventures, Dangers and Sufferings of a Revolutionary Soldier.* George F. Scheer, ed., Boston (1962).

Massey, Samuel. *Bulletin of the Historical Society of Montgomery County.* "The Journal of Captain Samuel Massey," John F. Reed, ed., Vol. XX, No. 3, 1976.

Montresor, John. *The Montresor Journals.* G.D. Scull, ed., New York

Historical Society for 1881. New York, 1882.

Moore, Frank. *Diary of the American Revolution.* Frank Moore, ed. 2 vols., New York, 1860.

Moylan, Stephen. *PMHB,* "Selections from the Correspondence of Col. Stephen Moylan of the Continental Cavalry." Vol. XXXVII, 1913.

Munchhausen, Frederich von. *At General Howe's Side 1776-1778, Diary of Captain Frederich Ernest von Munchhausen.* Ernest Kipping, translator, Samuel Smith, annotator, Monmouth Beach, NJ, 1974.

Muhlenberg, Henry Melchior. *Notebook of a Colonial Clergyman* (Condensed from the Journals of Henry Melchior Muhlenberg), Theodore C. Tappett & John W. Doberstein, eds., Philadelphia, 1959.

Muhlenberg, John Peter. *PMHB,* "Orderly Book of Gen. John Peter Muhlenberg, March 26-December 20, 1777." Vols. XXXIII, XXXIV and XXXV, 1909-11.

Paine, Thomas. *PMHB,* "Military Operations Near Philadelphia in the Campaign of 1777-8—Letter from Thomas Paine to Dr. Franklin," Vol. II (1878).

Pontigaud, Chevalier de. *A French Volunteer of the War of Independence The Chevalier de Pontigaud.* Robert B. Douglas, ed., New York, 1897.

Rankin, Hugh F. *Narratives of the American Revolution.* Hugh F. Rankin, ed., Lakeside Classics No. 74.

Reeves, Enos. *PMHB,* "Extracts from the Letter-Books of Lieutenant Enos Reeves, of the Pennsylvania Line." Contributed by John B. Reeves, Charleston, SC, Vols. XX and XXI, 1896-97.

Rush, Benjamin. *PMHB,* "Historical Notes of Dr. Benjamin Rush, 1777." Contributed by S. Weir Mitchell. Vol. XXVII, 1903.

—. *The Autobiography of Benjamin Rush.* George W. Conner, ed. Princeton, 1948.

—. *Letters of Benjamin Rush 1761-1813.* L.H. Butterfield, ed., 2 vols., Princeton, 1951.

Ryan, Dennis P. *A Salute to Courage, The American Revolution as*

VALLEY FORGE

Seen Through Wartime Writings of Officers of the Continental Army and Navy. Dennis P. Ryan, ed., New York, 1979.

Simcoe, J.G. *A History of the Operations of a Partisan Corps, called the Queen's Rangers.* Lieutenant Colonel J.G. Simcoe. New York, 1844.

Sproat, James. *PMHB,* "Extracts from the Journal of Rev. James Sproat, Hospital Chaplain of the Middle Department." John W. Jordan. Vol. XXVII, 1903.

Sullivan, John. *Letters and Papers of Major-General John Sullivan Continental Army.* Otis G. Hammond, ed., 3 vols. Concord, NH, 1930-39.

Thatcher, James. *Military Journal, during the American Revolutionary War From 1775 to 1783.* James Thatcher, M.D. Hartford, 1854.

Thomas, George C. *PP,* "From a Valley Forge Orderly Book." (George C. Thomas), January 1969.

Tilghman, Tench. *Memoir of Lieut. Col. Tench Tilghman.* Albany, 1876.

Wade, Herbert T. and Lively, Robert A. *This Glorious cause...The Adventures of Two Company Officers in Washington's Army.* Herbert T. Wade and Robert A. Lively, Princeton, 1958.

Waldo, Albigence. *PMHB,* "Valley Forge, 1777-1778, Diary of Surgeon Albigence Waldo, of the Connecticut Line." Vol. XXI, 1897.

Wallace, William. *PMHB,* "Selections from the Wallace Papers." Vol. XL, 1916.

Warren & Gerry. *A Study in Dissent: The Warren-Gerry Correspondence, 1776-1792.* C. Harvey Gardiner, ed., Carbondale, IL, (1968).

Washington, George. *The Diaries of George Washington, 1748-1799. John Fitzpatrick,* ed., 4 vols., Boston, 1925.

—. *Orderly Book of General George Washington, Commander in Chief of the American Armies Kept at Valley Forge, 18 May-11 June 1778.* Boston, 1898.

—. *Revolutionary Orders of General Washington, Issued During the Years 1778, 80, 81, & 82.* Henry Whitney, ed., New York, 1844.

—. *The Writings of George Washington.* John C. Fitzpatrick, ed., 39 vols., Washington, (1931-44).

—. *The Writings of George Washington.* Jared Sparks, ed., 12 vols., New York (1837).

Wayne, Anthony. *PMHB,* "Letter of General Anthony Wayne." Vol. XI, 1887.

Wayne, Isaac. *Tredyffrin-Easttown History Club,* "Letter Isaac Wayne to Richard Peters." Vol. 1, No. 3, April 1938.

Weedon, George. *Valley Forge Orderly Book of General George Weedon of the Continental Army...1777-8.* New York, 1902.

Weeks, William. *Five Straws Gathered from Revolutionary Fields.* (letters of William Weeks) Hiram Bingham, Jr. Cambridge, MA, 1901.

Weiss, Jacob. *The Letter Book of Jacob Weiss.* Melville J. Boyer, ed. (from Vol. 21 *Proceedings of the Lehigh County [PA] Historical Society*). Allentown, PA, 1956.

Wild, Ebenezer. *Massachusetts Historical Society Proceedings.* Second Series. "Ebenezer Wild Diary in the American Revolution." Vol. VI, October 1890.

Wilkins, W.H. *Some British Soldiers in America.* W.H. Wilkins, ed. (letters of Lieutenant Hale). London, 1914.

Wilkinson, James. *Memoirs of My Own Times.* General James Wilkinson, 3 vols., Philadelphia, 1816.

Willard, Margaret W. *Letters on the American Revolution.* Margaret W. Willard, ed., Port Washington, NY (1968).

Wister, Sally. *Sally Wister's Journal.* Albert Cook Meyers, ed., Philadelphia (1902).

Publications and Periodicals of Learned Societies

Applegate, Howard L. "The Pennsylvania Military Medical Department of the American Revolution." *PP,* November, 1960.

—. "The Provincial Medical Departments During the American Revolutionary War." *PP,* July, 1963.

Atkinson, Paul G., Jr. "The System of Military Discipline and Justice in the Continental Army: August 1777-June 1778." *PP,* Winter 1972-73.

VALLEY FORGE

Bailey, Olive & Worth. "Washington's Wartime Holidays and Christmas at Valley Forge." *PP*, April, 1946.

Baker, William S. "The Camp by the Old Gulph Mill." *PMHB*, Vol. XVII, 1893.

Bean, William H. "Whitemarsh to Valley Forge." *PP*, January, 1951.

Beck, Herbert H. "The Military Hospital at Lititz, 1777-78." *Papers of the Lancaster Historical Society*. Vol. XXIII, No. 1, 1919.

Brenneman, Gloria E. "The Conway Cabal: Myth or Realty." *Pennsylvania History*. Vol. XL, (Gettysburg, PA, 1973).

Buck, William J. "A British Capture." *Historical Sketches of the Historical Society of Montgomery County* (hereafter cited as *HSMC*), Vol. I.

Burk, Rev. W. Herbert. "Valley Forge: Its Past, Present and Future." *HSMC*, Vol. IV, 1910.

Burns, Franklin L. "A New Light on the Encampment of the Continental Army at Valley Forge." *Tredyffrin-Easttown History Club Quarterly*. Vol. II, No. 3, July, 1939.

—. "Local Historian Reminiscent of Valley Forge Sixty Years Ago." *PP*, October, 1944.

—. "The Stone Chimney Picket Post." *PP*, April, 1944.

Carson, Hampton L. "Washington at Valley Forge." *PMHB*, Vol. XLIII, 1919.

Condit, William W. "Christopher Ludwick Patriotic Gingerbread Baker." *PMHB*, Vol. LXXXI, 1957.

Corey, Albert B. "Steuben: Indispensable to the Achievement of American Independence." *PP*, February, 1963.

Cummings, Hubertis M. "The Villefranche Map for the Defense of the Delaware." *PMHB*, Vol. LXXXIV, 1960.

Dallet, Francis J., Jr. "John Leacock and The Fall of British Tyranny." *PMHB*, Vol. LXXVIII, 1954.

Einhorn, Nathan R. "The Reception of the British Peace Offer of 1778." *Pennsylvania History*, Vol. 16, 1949.

Fortenbaugh, Robert. "York as the Continental Capital." *Pennsylvania*

History, Vol. XX, 1953.

Francis, Rev. J.G. "Providence's Part in Provisioning the Camp at Valley Forge." *HSMC*, Vol. I, No. 6, April 1939.

Frorer, Henry R. "Valley Meetings Served Friends and Cared for Washington's Men." *PP*, October, 1944.

Gibson, James E. "The Role of Disease in the 70,000 Casualties in the American Revolutionary War." *Transactions and Studies College of Physicians*, Vol. 17, No. 3, Fourth Series, Philadelphia, n.d.

Hart, Charles H. "Colonel Robert Lettis Hooper." *PMHB*, Vol. XXXVI, 1912.

Heathcote, Charles W. "Army Chaplains at Valley Forge." *PP*, April, 1949.

—. "The Conway Intrigue." *PP*, July, 1952.

—. "General George Weedon and His Valley Forge Orderly Book." *PP*, April 1955.

—. "General Steuben's Services for American Independence." *PP*, April 1952.

—. "Physicians, Surgeons and Mates with Washington at Valley Forge." *PP*, January, 1948.

—. "Washington and His Soldiers at Valley Forge." *PP*, October, 1951.

—. "Washington, Lafayette, Valley Forge and Barren Hill." *PP*, October, 1949.

—. "Washington, the Governors and Valley Forge." *PP*, January, 1951.

Heaton, Ronald E. "South Carolina and Georgia Troops at Valley Forge," *PP*, April , 1965.

Helms, James K. "Lafayette's Escape from the British at Barren Hill," *PP*, 1945.

Heydinger, Earl J. "The Schuylkill, Lifeline to Valley Forge." *HSMC*, Vol. IX, No. 3, October, 1954.

Hocker, Edward W. "Desperate Fight Against Famine and Rank Stupidity and Cupidity by Commissary at Valley Forge." *PP*, July, 1947.

VALLEY FORGE

—. "Medical Men Deserve Tribute for Care of Washington's Men at Valley Forge Encampment." *PP*, January, 1947.

—. "Spies, Hangings and other Crimes during Winter at Valley Forge." *PP*, April, 1948.

Jenkins, Howard M. "The Old Iron Forge—Valley Forge." *PMHB*, Vol. XVII, 1893.

Jones, Gilbert S. "Joy Reigned at Valley Forge and York Over News of French Alliance." *PP*, October, 1944.

—. "Prayer of Valley Forge May Be Legend or Tradition or a Fact Yet It Remains Symbol of Faith." *PP*, April, 1945.

—. "Pulaski Campaigned Valley Forge Area; Opposed Going into Winter Camp Here." *PP*, January, 1948.

Jordan, John W. "Bethlehem During the Revolution." *PMHB*, Vol. XII, (1888).

—. "Continental Hospital Returns 1777-1780." *PMHB*, Vol. XXIII, 1899.

—. "The Military Hospitals at Bethlehem and Lititz During the Revolution." *PMHB*, Vol. XX, 1896.

—. "Orders of March of the Pennsylvania Line from Valley Forge, June 18, 1778." *PMHB*, Vol. XXXIX, 1915.

Kite, Elizabeth S. "General Duportail at Valley Forge." *PMHB*, Vol. LVI, 1932.

—. "How French Viewed Alliance; Washington Believed Its Value." *PP*, April, 1953.

—. "New Light on the Franco-American Alliance; Its Relation to American Independence." *PP*, April, 1949.

—. "General Washington and The French Engineers Duportail and Companions." *Records American Catholic Historical Society,* Vol. XLIII and XLIV, (Philadelphia), 1932-33.

Lefler, Dr. Hugh. "North Carolinians at Valley Forge." *PP*, July, 1964.

Lewis, John F. "Casimir Pulaski." *PMHB*, Vol. LV, 1931.

Litto, Frederic M. "Addison's Cato in the Colonies." *William & Mary Quarterly*, Vol. XXIII, 1966.

Lynch, M. Antonia. *The Old District of Southwark In the County of Philadelphia.* City History Society, Philadelphia, 1909.

MacFarlan, Douglas, M.D. "Medicine in the Colonial Period and Especial Reference to Valley Forge." *PP*, July, 1965.

—. "Revolutionary War Hospitals in the Pennsylvania Campaign 1777-78." *PP*, January, 1958.

—. "Signal Trees, Pickets and Outposts at the Valley Forge Encampment 1777-78." *PP*, October, 1963.

—. "Washington's Movements Around Philadelphia, 1777-78." *HSMC*, Vol. IV, No. 1, October, 1943.

Markland, John. "Revolutionary Services of Captain John Markland." *PMHB*, Vol. IX, 1885.

Markley, Andrew W. "The Cause of the Supply Problems Encountered by the Continental Army at Valley Forge." *Valley Forge Journal* (hereafter cited as *VFJ*), Vol. II, No. 1, 1984.

Middleton, William S. "Medicine at Valley Forge." *PP*, (taken from *Annals of Medical History,* November, 1941). July & October, 1962.

Nolan, J. Bennett. "Valley Forge or Reading Debated as Winter Quarters for the Army." *PP*, January, 1948.

Pennypacker, Samuel W. "Anthony Wayne." *PMHB,* Vol. XXXII, 1908.

Powers, Fred P. "On the Trail of Washington." *HSMC,* Vol. VII, 1925.

Pyle, E. Clyde. "Aspects of Wood in Valley Forge Encampment." *PP*, August, 1965.

Randolph, Brigadier General Norman. "Duportail Map was Exceedingly Accurate position Sketch." *PP*, March, 1949.

—. "Lost Redoubt is Found at Valley Forge." *PP*, 1949.

Reed, John F. "Clement Biddle at Moore Hall." *HSMC,* Vol. XXII, No. 3, 1980.

—. "Campaign of 1777." *HSMC,* Vol. XXI, No. 1, 1977, No. 2, Spring, 1978.

—. "Clothing an Army." *VFJ*, Vol. III, No. 1, June, 1986.

—. "Date Line Valley Forge." *PP*, November, 1960.

VALLEY FORGE

—. "The Fight on Old Gulph Road." *HSMC*, Vol. XV, Nos. 1 and 2, Spring, 1966.

—. "Indians at Valley Forge." *VFJ*, Vol. III, No. 1, June, 1986.

—. "Lesser Problems at Valley Forge." *VFJ*, Vol. III, No. 1, June, 1986.

—. "Sporting Blood at Valley Forge." *PP*, July, 1963.

—. "Spy System 1777." *PP*, Winter, 1976.

Reed, Dr. W.H. "Sullivan Bridge Marker." *HSMC*, Vol. IV, 1910.

Richardson, W.H. "Montgomery County in the Campaign of 1777-78." *HSMC*, Vol. 7, 1935.

Roark, Carol S. "Historic Yellow Springs." *PP*, Summer, 1975.

Roshong, Margaret D. "Mrs. Washington at Valley Forge." *PP*, April, 1955.

Ross, Howard D. "Sir Henry Clinton's Map of Valley Forge and Vicinity." *PP*, April, 1949.

—. "Valley Forge and the Memorable Winter Encampment of 1777-78." *PP*, March, 1949.

Rossman, Kenneth R. "Thomas Mifflin-Revolutionary Patriot." **Pennsylvania History**, Vol. XV, 1948.

Rush, Benjamin. "An Account of the Life and Character of Christopher Ludwick." John F. Reed, ed. *HSMC*, Vol. XXII, No. 2, Spring, 1980.

Schultz, George W. "The Fords of the Schuylkill." *PP*, April, 1954.

Schmidt, Captain Lewis H. "George Washington's Bodyguards were Wisely Selected and Loyal." *PP*, January, 1946.

Seiple, Lenora D. "Washington Hall in Chester Springs." *PP*, January, 1949.

Sellers, Horace W. "Engravings by Charles Wilson Peale, Limner." *PMHB*, Vol. LVII, 1933.

Sheas, Jerome J. "The Forges at Valley Forge." *PP*, July, 1944.

Shrawder, Joseph. "Freemasonry During the Revolution." *PP*, April, 1953.

Smith, Charles H. "General Lacey's Campaign in 1778." *HSMC*, Vol. II, No. 4, April, 1941.

Smith, Helen B. "Surgeon Jonathan Potts Planned Inoculation at Valley Forge." *PP*, April, 1947.

Smyth, Samuel G. "The Gulph Mills in the Annals of the Revolution." *HSMC*, Vol. III, 1905.

—. "Valley Forge—A Retrospect." *HSMC*, Vol. VII, 1925.

—. "The Valley Forge Reservation." *HSMC*, Vol. V. 1915.

Stephens, William M. "Burial Places of the Soldiers at Valley Forge." *HSMC*, Vol. III, 1942.

Stoudt, John B. "The Feu de Joye." *PP*, April, 1967.

Streeper, Levi. "Lafayette's Retreat from Barren Hill." *HSMC*, Vol. II, 1941.

Taxis, Alfred. L. Jr. "Christmas at Valley Forge, 1777: A Day of Remembrance." *HSMC*, VOl. XXI, No. 4, Spring, 1979.

Teamer, S. Paul. "The Stone Chimney Picket." *Tredyffrin-Easttown History Club*, Vol. II, No. 4, October, 1939.

Walker, Mrs. Ivins C. "Valley Friends Meeting House." *HSMC*, Vol. II, No. 3, October, 1940.

Weigley, Russell F. "Valley Forge and the Strategy of an Army in Being." *VFJ*, Vol. II, No. 2, December, 1984.

Wilcox, William J. "The Comic Opera Battle that Made a General." *Pennsylvania History*, Vol. XIII, 1946.

Wildes, Harry E. "The Meaning of Valley Forge." *HSMC*, Vol. IV, No. 3, 1944.

Wilkins, Major Fred J. "Steuben Screamed but Things Happened and an Army was Born at Valley Forge." *PP*, January, 1948.

William, Irwin C. "Lafayette at Barren Hill." *HSMC*, Vol. II, 1941.

Zlatich, Marko. "Uniforming the 1st Regiment of Continental Light Dragoons, 1776-1779." *Military Collector & Historian*, Vol. XX, No. 2, Summer, 1968.

Secondary Sources: Books and Pamphlets

_____. *A List of the Fortunate Numbers in the First Class of the United States Lottery. Philadelphia,* June 3, 1778.

Addis, Mahlon. *200 Years of Ancient York Masonry in the Western World.* Philadelphia, n.d.

Alden, John R. *A History of the American Revolution.* New York, 1969.

Bakeless, John. *Turncoats, Traitors and Heroes.* Philadelphia (1959).

Baker, William S. *Itinerary of General Washington, June 15, 1775 to December 23, 1783.* Lamberville, NJ (1970) second edition.

Barr, Morris A. & Berden, Leta S. *The Sentry Tree of George Washington.* Friend, NE, 1958.

Bell, Whitfield J., Jr. *John Morgan, Continental Doctor.* Philadelphia (1965).

Bill, Alfred H. *Valley Forge, The Making of an Army.* New York (1952).

Billias, George A. *General John Glover and His Marblehead Mariners.* New York (1960).

—. *George Washington's Generals.* New York, 1964.

Bining, Arthur C. *Pennsylvania Iron Manufacture in the Eighteenth Century.* Harrisburg, 1973, second edition.

Blumenthal, Walter H. *Women Camp Followers of the American Revolution.* New York, 1974.

Bolton, Charles K. *The Private Soldier Under Washington.* New York, 1902.

Booth, Sally S. *The Women of '76.* New York, 1973.

Bowman, Allen. *The Morale of the American Revolutionary Army.* Port Washington, NY (1964).

Boyd, George A. *Elias Boudinot, Patriot and Statesman 1740-1821.* Princeton, 1952.

Brooks, Noah. *Henry Knox.* New York, 1900.

Burnett, Edmund C. *The Continental Congress*. New York, 1941.

Busch, Noel F. *Winter Quarters, George Washington and the Continental Army at Valley Forge*. New York (1974).

Callahan, North. *Henry Knox*. South Brunswick (NJ) (1958).

Carp, E. Wayne. *To Starve the Army at Pleasure*. Chapel Hill (1984).

Chidsey, Donald B. *Valley Forge*. New York (1959).

Clarfield, Gerard H. *Timothy Pickering and the American Republic*. (Pittsburgh, 1980).

Clarke, James F. *Revolutionary Services and Civil Life of General William Hull*. New York, 1848.

Colbourn, H. Trevor. *The Lamp of Experience*. Williamsburg and Chapel Hill (1965).

Coleman, John M. *Thomas McKean-Forgotten Leader of the Revolution*. Rockaway, NJ (1975).

Commanger, Henry S. and Morris, Richard B. *The Spirit of Seventy-Six: The Story of the American Revolution as told by Participants*. Indianapolis (1958).

Corner, Betsy C. *William Shippen, Jr. Pioneer in American-Medical Education*. Philadelphia, 1951.

Cornau, Rudolph. *The Army of the American Revolution and its Organizer*. New York (1923).

Doyle, Joseph B. Frederick *William von Steuben and the American Revolution*. Steubenville, OH, 1913.

Duncan, Lewis C. *Medical Men in the American Revolution*. Carlisle Barracks, PA, 1931.

Egleston, Thomas. *The Life of John Paterson, Major General in the Revolutionary Army*. New York, 1898, second edition.

Egly, T.W., Jr. *History of the First New York Regiment 1775-1783*. (Hampton, NH, 1981).

Ellet, Elizabeth F. *The Women of the American Revolution*. 2 vols., New York, 1848.

Engle, Paul. *Women in the American Revolution*. Chicago (1976).

VALLEY FORGE

Evans, Emory G. *Thomas Nelson of Yorktown.* Williamsburg (1975).

Faris, John T. *Old Roads out of Philadelphia.* Philadelphia, 1917.

Fisher, Sydney G. *The Struggle for American Independence.* 2 vols., Philadelphia, 1908.

Fiske, John. *The American Revolution.* 2 vols., Boston (1896).

Fitzgerald, John C. *George Washington Himself.* Indianapolis (1933).

—. *The Spirit of the Revolution.* Boston, 1924.

Flexner, James T. *George Washington.* 4 vols., Boston, 1965-72.

—. *The Traitor and the Spy.* New York (1953).

Flood, Charles B. *Rise and Fight Again.* New York (1976).

Ford, Worthington C. T*he Spurious Letters Attributed to Washington.* Brooklyn, 1889.

_____. *Forges and Furnaces in the Province of Pennsylvania.* Pennsylvania Society of Colonial Dames of America, Philadelphia, 1914.

Fowler, William M.J. *William Ellery: A Rhode Island Politico and Lord of Admiralty.* Metuchen, NJ, 1973.

Freeman, Douglas S. *George Washington.* 7 vols., New York, 1948-57.

Garrison, Webb. *Sidelights on the American Revolution.* Nashville (1974).

Gelb, Norman. *Less Than Glory.* New York (1984).

Gibson, James E. *Dr. Bodo Otto and the Medical Background of the American Revolution.* Springfield, IL (1937).

Gillett, Mary C. *The Army Medical Department 1775-1818.* Washington (1981).

Godfrey, Carlos E. *The Commander-in-Chief's Guard.* Washington, 1904.

Goodman, Nathan G. *Benjamin Rush, Physician and Citizen 1746-1813.* Philadelphia, 1934.

Greene, George W. *The Life of Nathanael Greene.* 3 vols., New York, 1871.

Griffin, Martin I. J. *Catholics and the American Revolution.* 3 vols., Philadelphia, 1911.

—. *General Stephen Moylan.* Philadelphia, 1909.

Hall, Charles S. *Benjamin Tallmadge.* New York, 1943.

Hatch, Louis C. *The Administration of the American Revolutionary Army.* New York, 1904.

Hawke, David F. *Paine.* New York (1974).

—. *Benjamin Rush, Revolutionary Gadfly.* Indianapolis (1971).

Hay, Thomas R. & Werner, M.R. *The Admirable Trumpeter, Biography of General James Wilkinson.* Garden City, NY, 1941.

Hayden, Sidney. *Washington and His Masonic Compeers.* New York, 1866.

Heston, Ronald E. *Valley Forge, Yesterday and Today.* Norristown, PA, 1960.

Higginbotham, Don. *Daniel Morgan, Revolutionary Rifleman.* Chapel Hill (1961).

—. *The War of American Independence.* New York (1971).

Hillard, Rev. E.B. *The Last Men of the Revolution.* Wendell D. Garrett, ed. (Barre, MA, 1968).

Hocker, Edward W. T*he Fighting Parson (Muhlenberg) and the American Revolution.* Philadelphia, 1936.

Ives, Mabel L. *Washington's Headquarters.* Upper Montclair, NJ (1932).

Jackson, John W. *The Pennsylvania Navy 1775-1781.* New Brunswick. (1974).

—. *Whitemarsh 1777: Impregnable Stronghold.* Fort Washington, PA, 1984.

—. *With the British Army in Philadelphia.* San Rafael, CA (1979).

Jacobs, James R. *The Beginning of the U.S. Army 1783-1812.* Princeton, 1947.

Johnson, Victor L. *The Administration of the American Commis-*

sariat During the Revolutionary War. Philadelphia, 1941.

Jones, Gilbert S. *Valley Forge Park.* Valley Forge, 1947.

Kapp, Frederich. *The Life of Frederick William von Steuben.* New York, 1859.

Kite, Elizabeth S. *Brigadier-General Louis LeBéque Duportail, 1777-1783.* Baltimore, 1933.

Knollenberg, Bernhard. *Washington and the Revolution, A Reappraisal.* New York, 1941.

Leffert, Charles M. *Uniforms of the American, British, French, and German Armies in the War of the American Revolution.* New York, 1926.

Lesser, Charles H. *The Sinews of Independence, Monthly Strength Reports of the Continental Army.* Chicago (1976).

Loescher, Burt G. *Washington's Eyes: The Continental Light Dragoons.* (Fort Collins, CO, 1977).

Lossing, Benson J. *Mary and Martha Washington.* New York (1886).

—. *Pictorial Field-Book of the Revolution.* 2 vols., New York, 1859.

Lowell, Edward J. T*he Hessians and the Other German Auxiliaries of Great Britain in the Revolutionary War.* Williamstown, MA, 1970.

MacDougall, William L. *American Revolutionary—A Biography of General Alexander MacDougall.* Westport, CT (1977).

MacNeill, Henry T. & MacNeill, Aimee J. *Valley Forge Landmarks.* Whitford, PA, 1958.

_____. *Maine at Valley Forge.* Maine Society of the SAR, Maine Historical Society and Maine State Library. Augusta, ME, 1910, second edition.

Manning, Clarence A. *Soldier of Liberty, Casimir Pulaski.* New York (1945).

Marshall, John. *The Life of George Washington.* 5 vols., Fredericksburg, VA, 1926, Citizens Guild Edition.

Mayer, Henry. *A Son of Thunder. Patrick Henry and the American Republic.* New York, 1986.

Meier, Louis A. *Early Pennsylvania Medicine.* (Boyertown, PA, 1976).

Miller, John C. *Triumph of Freedom 1775-1783.* Boston, 1948.

Montross, Lynn. *Rag, Tag and Bobtail, The Story of the Continental Army 1775-1783.* New York (1952).

Morse, Sidney. *Freemasonry in the American Revolution.* Washington, n.d.

Moulton, Augustus F. *Maine Historical Sketches.* Lewistown, ME, 1929.

Muhlenberg, Henry A. *The Life of Major-General Peter Muhlenberg.* Philadelphia, 1849.

Muir, Dorothy T. *General Washington's Headquarters, 1775-1783.* Troy, AL (1977).

Nelson, Paul D. *General Horatio Gates.* Baton Rouge (1976).

Nolan, J. Bennett. *George Washington and the Town of Reading in Pennsylvania.* Reading, 1931.

—. *The Schuylkill.* New Brunswick (1957).

Palmer, John McA. *General Von Steuben.* New Haven, 1937.

Patterson, Samuel W. *Horatio Gates.* New York, 1941.

Peckham, Howard H. T*he Toll of Independence, Engagements & Battle Casualties of the American Revolution.* Chicago (1974).

—. *The War of Independence: A Military History.* (Chicago, 1958).

Pennypacker, Samuel W. *Pennsylvanians in American History.* "High Water Mark of the British Invasion (Phoenixville, PA)." Philadelphia, 1910.

Pinkowski, Edward. *Washington's Officers Slept Here.* Philadelphia, 1953.

Platt, John D.R. *Jeremiah Wadsworth, Federalist Entrepreneur.* New York, 1982.

Pollack, Thomas C. *The Philadelphia Theatre in the Eighteenth Century.* Philadelphia, 1933.

Potts, Louis W. *Arthur Lee: A Virtuous Revolutionary.* Baton Rouge (1981).

Rankin, Hugh F. *The American Revolution.* New York (1964).

—. *The North Carolina Continentals.* Chapel Hill (1971).

Reed, John F. *Campaign to Valley Forge July 1777-December 19, 1777.* Philadelphia (1965).

—. *Valley Forge Crucible of Victory.* Monmouth Beach, NJ, 1969.

Reed, William B. *Life and Correspondence of Joseph Reed.* 2 vols., Philadelphia, 1847.

Risch, Erna. *Supplying Washington's Army.* Washington, 1981.

Rossie, Jonathan G. *The Politics of Command in the American Revolution.* Syracuse, 1975.

Rossman, Kenneth R. *Thomas Mifflin and the Politics of the American Revolution.* (Chapel Hill, 1952).

Rosswurm, Steven. *Arms and Independence, The Military Character of the American Revolution.* "The Philadelphia Militia, 1775-1783: Active Duty and Active Radicalism." Ronald Hoffman & Peter J. Albert, eds., Charlottesville (VA, 1984).

Royster, Charles. *A Revolutionary People at War.* Williamsburg (1979).

Sachse, Julius F. *Old Masonic Lodges of Pennsylvania "Moderns and Ancients" 1730-1800.* 2 vols., Philadelphia, 1912-13.

Scharf, J. Thomas & Westcott, Thompson. *History of Philadelphia 1609-1884.* 3 vols., Philadelphia, 1884.

Scheer, George F. & Rankin, Hugh F. *Rebels and Redcoats.* New York, 1959.

Scott, Kenneth. *Counterfeiting in Colonial America.* New York, 1957.

Shreve, L.G. *Tench Tilghman.* Centreville, MD (1982).

Shreve, Royal O. *The Finished Scoundrel.* Indianapolis (1933).

Stager, H.J. *History of the Centennial and Memorial Association of Valley Forge.* n.p., June 19, 1911.

Stedman, Charles. *The History of the Origin, Progress and Termination of the American War.* 2 vols., London, 1794.

Stewart, Frank H. *Foraging for Valley Forge by General Anthony Wayne in Salem and Gloucester Counties.* Woodbury, NJ, 1929.

—. *Salem County in the Revolution.* Salem, NJ, 1932.

Stille, Charles J. *Major-General Anthony Wayne and the Pennsylvania Line in the Continental Army.* Philadelphia, 1893.

Stoudt, John J. *Ordeal at Valley Forge.* Philadelphia (1963).

Stryker, William S. *The Battle of Monmouth.* Port Washington, NY (1970).

Swiggett, Howard. *The Extraordinary Mr. Morris.* Garden City, NY, 1952.

Taylor, Frank H. *Valley Forge, A Chronicle of American Heroism.* Valley Forge, 1922.

Thane, Elswyth. *The Fighting Quaker: Nathanael Greene.* New York, 1972.

—. *Washington's Lady.* New York, 1960.

Thayer, Theodore. *Nathanael Greene, Strategist of the American Revolution.* New York, 1960.

Timmins, William and Ruth. *The Great "Cow Chase" 1776-1976.* n.p. (1977).

Trevelyan, Sir George, Bart. *The American Revolution.* 4 vols., New York, 1899-1907, second edition.

Trussell, John B.B., Jr. *Birthplace of an Army: A Study of the Valley Forge Encampment.* Harrisburg, 1979.

—. *Epic on the Schuylkill: The Valley Forge Encampment.* Harrisburg, 1986.

Tucker, Glenn. *Mad Anthony Wayne and the New Nation.* Harrisburg, 1973.

Valentine, Alan. *Lord Stirling.* New York, 1969.

_____. "Valley Forge Park" *HSMC*, Vol. XXI, No. 3, Norristown, PA, 1978.

_____. *Report of the Valley Forge Park Commission 1908.* Philadelphia, (1908).

—. *Report of the Valley Forge Park Commission 1910*. Philadelphia, (1910).

Wagner, Frederich. *Submarine Fighter of the American Revolution, The Story of David Bushnell*. New York, 1963.

Walker, Paul K. *Engineers of Independence: A Documentary History of the Army Engineers in the American Revolution, 1775-1783*. *Washington, n.d.*

Wallace, David D. *The Life of Henry Laurens: With a Sketch of the Life of Lieutenant-Colonel John Laurens*. New York, 1915.

Wallace, Paul A.W. *The Muhlenbergs of Pennsylvania*. Philadelphia, 1950.

Wallace, Willard M. *Appeal to Arms*. New York (1951).

Ward, Christopher L. *The Delaware Continentals 1776-1783*. Wilmington, 1941.

—. *The War of the Revolution*. 2 vols., New York, 1952.

Ward, Harry M. *Duty, Honor or Country General George Weedon and the American Revolution*. Philadelphia, 1979.

Weslager, C.A. *The Log Cabin in America*. New Brunswick (1969).

Wharton, Anne H. *Martha Washington*. New York, 1897.

Whiteley, Emily S. *Washington and His Aides-de-Camp*. New York, 1956.

Wildes, Harry E. *Anthony Wayne*. New York (1941).

—. *Valley Forge*. New York, 1938.

Williams, (Catherine R.). *Biography of Revolutionary Heroes; containing the Life of Brigadier Gen. William Barton and also, of Captain Stephen Olney*. Providence, 1839.

Woodman, Henry. *The History of Valley Forge*. Oaks, PA, 1922.

Wright, Col. John W. *Some Notes on the Continental Army*. New York, 1963.

Wright Robert K., Jr. *Arms and Independence, The Military Character of the American Revolution*. "Nor Is Their Standing Army to be Despised: The Emergence of the Continental Army as a Military Institution." Ronald Hoffman & Peter J. Albert, Charlottesville, VA (1984).

—. *The Continental Army.* Washington, 1983.

Zucker, A.C. *General De Kalb, Lafayette's Mentor.* Chapel Hill (1966).

Index

a cet endroit l'arivière forme une coude insensible qui porte son cours a l'est sud... *A*

tout cet partie du retranchement se porte jusqu'à en avant

B & *F*

328

The Duportail map of the Valley Forge encampment, courtesy of the Historical Society of Pennsylvania.

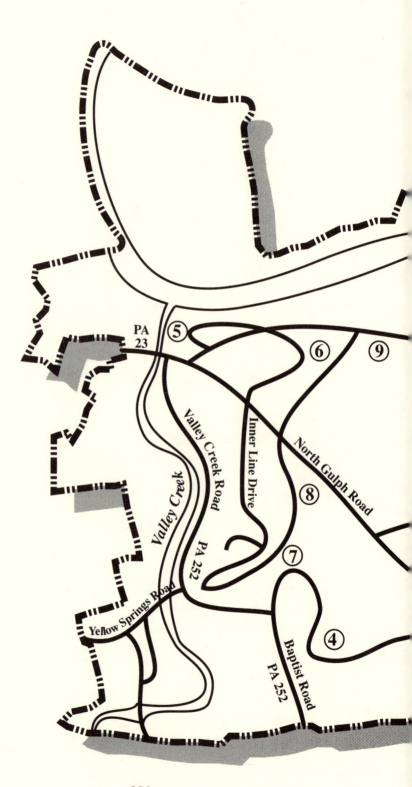

VALLEY FORGE NATIONAL HISTORICAL PARK

Map of Valley Forge National Historical Park adapted by Ryan C. Stouch from "Valley Forge: Official Map and Guide," courtesy of National Park Service.

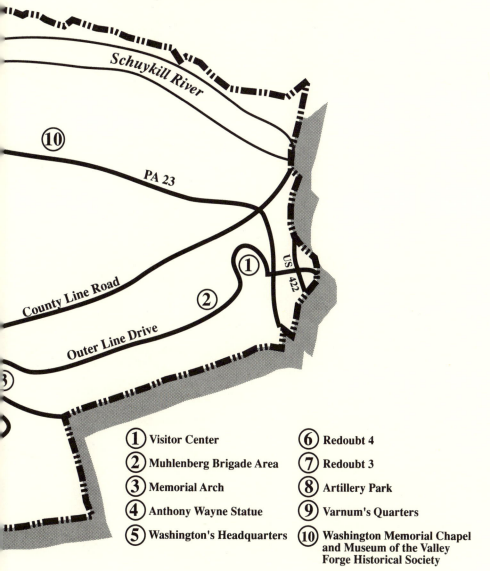

① Visitor Center

② Muhlenberg Brigade Area

③ Memorial Arch

④ Anthony Wayne Statue

⑤ Washington's Headquarters

⑥ Redoubt 4

⑦ Redoubt 3

⑧ Artillery Park

⑨ Varnum's Quarters

⑩ Washington Memorial Chapel and Museum of the Valley Forge Historical Society